Twilight of the Titans

D0887685

A VOLUME IN THE SERIES

Cornell Studies in Security Affairs

Edited by Robert J. Art, Robert Jervis, and Stephen M. Walt

A list of titles in this series is available at cornellpress.cornell.edu.

Twilight of the Titans

Great Power Decline and Retrenchment

PAUL K. MACDONALD
AND JOSEPH M. PARENT

Cornell University Press

Ithaca and London

Cornell University Press gratefully acknowledges receipt of a grant from the Institute for Scholarship in the Liberal Arts, College of Arts and Letters, University of Notre Dame, which aided in the publication of this book.

Copyright © 2018 by Cornell University

All rights reserved. Except for brief quotations in a review, this book, or parts thereof, must not be reproduced in any form without permission in writing from the publisher. For information, address Cornell University Press, Sage House, 512 East State Street, Ithaca, New York 14850.

First published 2018 by Cornell University Press

Library of Congress Cataloging-in-Publication Data

Names: MacDonald, Paul K., author. | Parent, Joseph M., author.
Title: Twilight of the titans : great power decline and retrenchment / Paul K. MacDonald and Joseph M. Parent.
Description: Ithaca : Cornell University Press, 2018. | Series: Cornell studies in security affairs | Includes bibliographical references and index.
Identifiers: LCCN 2017034805 (print) | LCCN 2017036520 (ebook) | ISBN 9781501717109 (pdf) | ISBN 9781501717116 (ret) | ISBN 9781501717093 | ISBN 9781501717093 (cloth)
Subjects: LCSH: Great powers. | Hegemony. | Regression (Civilization) | International relations.
Classification: LCC JZ1312 (ebook) | LCC JZ1312 .M34 2018 (print) | DDC 327.1/1409034—dc23
LC record available at https://lccn.loc.gov/2017034805

Cornell University Press strives to use environmentally responsible suppliers and materials to the fullest extent possible in the publishing of its books. Such materials include vegetable-based, low-VOC inks and acid-free papers that are recycled, totally chlorine-free, or partly composed of nonwood fibers. For further information, visit our website at cornellpress.cornell.edu.

To Sophie, Stella, and Nico, the rising powers in our lives

The *danger* that lies in great people and periods of greatness is extraordinary; every kind of exhaustion, and sterility, follow in their footsteps.

—Friedrich Nietzsche

The weary titan staggers under the too vast orb of its fate. We have borne the burden for many years. We think it is time our children should assist us to support it, and whenever you make the request to us, be very sure that we shall hasten gladly to call you to our Councils.

—Joseph Chamberlain

Contents

Illustrations

Figures

Tables

Acknowledgments

This book explores how states evolve to stay competitive at the highest level and argues that one way they do this is by minimizing reliance on others, or simply through self-help. We believe that this is true in international politics but know that it is false in academia. Many groups and individuals forced us beyond our ignorance and indolence and made the work materially better. At the top of the list belong our eternal advisors, Bob Jervis and Jack Snyder, who inspired us to do this kind of work and helped whip this project into shape. We also owe massive gratitude to those who participated in a workshop to discuss the book: Bill Wohlforth, David Edelstein, Sarah Kreps, and Todd Sechser. They pushed us to make the book shorter, clearer, and, above all, stronger.

Numerous others provided insights at various stages of the project: Marcia Beck, Mike Beckley, Jeff Colgan, Etienne de Durand, Jeff Engel, Charlie Glaser, Stacie Goddard, Laura Gomez-Mera, Brendan Green, Kyle Haynes, Roger Kanet, Ron Krebs, Chris Layne, Jack Levy, James McAllister, Evan Montgomery, Jon Monten, Jim Morrow, Shany Mor, Santiago Olivella, George Pedden, Robert Powell, Josh Shifrinson, Brock Tessman, Bill Thompson, Steve Ward, Alex Weisiger, and Brandon Yoder. Additional thanks to participants in seminars at Cambridge University, Cornell University, George Washington University, Southern Methodist University, Texas A&M University, the University of Georgia, the University of Miami, the University of Notre Dame, and Wellesley College. There is no forgetting the superlative research assistance of Joe Karas, Erin Pelletier, and Sasha Zheng. Everyone did their best to save us from errors, so remaining mistakes belong only to the refractory authors.

We are grateful for funding from the University of Miami Provost Research Award and Wellesley College Faculty Research Award. Additional support was provided in the final stages by the Italian Fulbright Commission, Libera Università Internazionale degli Studi Sociali Guido Carli, and the Institute for Scholarship in the Liberal Arts, College of Arts and Letters, University of Notre Dame, which aided in the publication of this book. The project was greatly facilitated by the staff at Cornell University Press, and our warm thanks to Roger Haydon, Steve Walt, Bob Art, and an outside reviewer, who must go nameless. This book contains portions of our article "Graceful Decline? The Surprising Success of Great Power Retrenchment," published in *International Security* 35, no. 4 (Spring 2011), which are reproduced courtesy of the MIT Press.

We could not have written this book without our friends and families, who may not have always understood what we were doing but understood the necessity of doing it right. Paul thanks his wife, Stacie Goddard, his mother, Betty MacDonald, his brother, Brian MacDonald, Chrystal Williams, Dave Morley, Jennifer and Andreas Papapavlou, Ramin and Polina Mahnad, Nikhil Narayan, Ngoni and Julia Munemo, Don Elmore and Julie Prentice, and Alex Montgomery for their love and support. Joe would like to thank his friends and family, Buck and Huddie, P. Rogers Nelson, Abigail Becker, Carolina Sandoval Garcia, and Maria del Pilar, infinitely.

The dedication belongs to our children: Sophie MacDonald, Stella MacDonald, and Nico Parent. While they bear some responsibility for the decline in our sleep, they fill our lives with new joys and welcome challenges and have taught us a thing or two about retrenchment. We look forward to viewing the world through their eyes and hope they see farther than their fathers.

Twilight of the Titans

Introduction

> The real cause, however, I consider to be the one which was formally most kept out of sight. The growth of the power of Athens, and the alarm which this inspired in Sparta, made war inevitable.
>
> —Thucydides

> Such extraordinary efforts of power and courage will always command the attention of posterity; but the events by which the fate of nations is not materially changed will leave a faint impression on the page of history.
>
> —Edward Gibbon

How do great powers respond to relative decline? Since Thucydides, the consensus is that great power transitions are particularly perilous.[1] Intoxicated by their newfound capability, rising powers work to undermine and overturn the existing order. Nationalist politicians rail against past humiliations and hunger for future glories. Rising states feel they are claiming their birthrights while declining states feel they are being stripped of theirs. Frightened by their loss of influence—and the looming specter of worse to come—declining powers threaten force to sustain the status quo. Diplomacy breaks down because neither side trusts that agreements will be honored. Alliances cease to deter as weak states flock to aggressors. Domestic dysfunction compounds matters as parties polarize, special interests dig in, and foreign policy whipsaws or stalemates. The results are disastrous: vicious infighting, gridlocked politics, pointless diplomacy, escalating crises, desperate decisions, and, ultimately, war. In politics as in nature, eclipses are spectacularly dark times.

If the underlying problem during relative decline is that states try to maintain or expand their ambitions with dwindling resources, the solution could be curtailing ends to match the available means. But the conventional wisdom is that retrenchment creates more problems than it cures. Overseas, retrenchment smacks of weakness, which sows anxiety in allies and avarice in adversaries. Disengagement destabilizes regions, creating cracks that split the international order. Domestically, alarmed lobbyists will mobilize to defend parochial benefits, while hardliners will equate retreat with defeat and brand advocates of retrenchment as naive appeasers. Rather than renewing investment at home, policymakers will increase military spending to keep up.[2] Bluff and bluster will trump diplomacy, provocation will substitute for deterrence, and preventive war now appears preferable to inexorable defeat later.

In this book, we argue that the conventional wisdom is wrong. Specifically, we make three main arguments. First, relative decline causes prompt, proportionate retrenchment because states seek strategic solvency. The international system is a competitive place, and great powers did not get to the top by being imprudent, irrational, or irresponsible. When their fortunes ebb, states tend to retain the virtues that made them great. In the face of decline, great powers have a good sense of their relative capability and tend not to give away more than they must. Expanding or maintaining grand strategic ambitions during decline incurs unsustainable burdens and incites unwinnable fights, so the faster states fall, the more they retrench. Great powers may choose to retrench in other circumstances as well, but they have an overriding incentive to do so when confronted by relative decline.

Second, the depth of relative decline shapes not only how much a state retrenches, but also which policies it adopts. The world is complex and cutthroat; leaders cannot glibly pull a policy off the shelf and expect desired outcomes. Because international politics is a self-help system, great powers prefer policies that rely less on the actions of allies and adversaries. For lack of a better term, we refer to these as domestic policies, which include reducing spending, restructuring forces, and reforming institutions—all to reallocate resources for more efficient uses. But international policies may also help, and they include redeploying forces, defusing flashpoints, and redistributing burdens—all to avoid costly conflicts and reinforce core strongpoints. The faster and deeper states fall, the more they are willing to rely on others to cushion their fall. Retrenchment is not a weapon but an arsenal that can be used in different amounts and combinations depending on conditions and the enemies faced.

Third, after depth, structural conditions are the most important factors shaping how great powers respond to relative decline. Four conditions catalyze the incentives for declining states to retrench. One is the declining state's rank. States in the top rungs of the great power hierarchy have more resources and margin for error than those lower down, so there is less urgency for them to retrench. Another is the availability of allies. Where states can shift burdens to capable regional powers with similar preferences, retrenchment is less risky and difficult. Yet another is the interdependence of commitments. When states perceive commitments in one place as tightly linked to commitments elsewhere, pulling back becomes harder and less likely. The last catalyst is the calculus of conquest. If aggression pays, then retrenchment does not, and great powers will be loath to do it. The world is not just complex and cutthroat, it is also dynamic. No set of conditions is everlasting, and leaders must change with the times.

Empirically, this work aims to add value by being the first to study systematically all modern shifts in the great power pecking order. We find sixteen cases of relative decline since 1870, when reliable data for the great powers become available, and compare them to their non-declining counterparts across a variety of measures. To preview the findings, retrenchment is by far the most common response to relative decline, and declining powers behave differently from non-declining powers. States in decline are more likely to cut the size of their military forces and budgets and in extreme cases are more likely to form alliances. This does not, however, make them ripe for exploitation; declining states perform comparatively well in militarized disputes. Our headline finding, however, is that states that retrench recover their prior rank with some regularity, but those that fail to retrench never do. These results challenge theories of grand strategy and war, offer guidance to policymakers, and indicate overlooked paths to peace.

Why the Question Matters

The claim that relative decline is dangerous has become a fundamental truth in international relations, one with wide-ranging implications. First and foremost, this assumption informs most of our theories of war and peace. Hegemonic stability theorists contend that relative decline undermines the ability of systemic leaders to uphold international order.[3] Power transition theorists warn that relative decline generates opportunities for revisionist challenges to the status quo.[4] Critics of the balance of power note that sudden shifts in power can upset the delicate equilibrium necessary to preserve peace.[5] Rationalist theories contend that differential growth can generate insoluble commitment problems, which are one of the main causes of war.[6] For each of the approaches, relative decline is the central factor that explains why stable and peaceful relations devolve into instability and conflict.

The idea that relative decline is dangerous also has significant policy implications. Leaders' beliefs about the importance of prestige, the need for credibility, and the dangers of appeasement are based on notions that even the mere perception of decline can spell doom for a great power.[7] Historically, fears of falling dominos and emboldened adversaries have been root causes of geopolitical overstretch and failed strategic adjustment.[8] Contemporary arguments in favor of U.S. engagement abroad rest on the claim that any retreat of American influence would upset the stability of the international system.[9] Robert Kagan prophesies that a "reduction in defense spending . . . would unnerve American allies and undercut efforts to gain greater cooperation. There is already a sense around the world, fed by irresponsible pundits here at home, that the United States is in terminal decline."[10] Robert Kaplan likewise predicts, "Lessening our engagement with the world would have devastating consequences for humanity. The disruptions we witness today are but a taste of what is to come should our country flinch from its international responsibilities."[11]

Policymakers provide strikingly similar assessments. "We have learned the hard way when America is absent, especially from unstable places, there are consequences," the former secretary of state Hillary Clinton has testified. "Extremism takes root, aggressors seek to fill the vacuum, and security everywhere is threatened, including here at home."[12] In 2012, then–secretary of defense Leon Panetta echoed, "If we turn away from critical regions of the world, we risk undoing the significant gains [our military personnel] have fought for. That would make all of us less safe in the long term. This is not a time for retrenchment."[13] In his confirmation hearings for secretary of state, Rex Tillerson made basically the same point: "In recent decades, we have cast American leadership into doubt. In some instances, we have withdrawn from the world. . . . Meanwhile, our adversaries have been emboldened to take advantage of this absence of American leadership."[14] It has become a mantra in policy circles that U.S. leadership is essential to global peace and prosperity. Talk of decline is defeatist, and the country must maintain its commitments and credibility come what may.

Assumptions about the dangers of relative decline cast a similar shadow over debates about China's rise. Graham Allison contends that "based on the current trajectory, war between the United States and China in the decades ahead is not just possible, but much more likely. . . . When a rising power is threatening to displace a ruling power, standard crises that would otherwise be contained . . . can initiate a cascade of reactions."[15] Aaron Friedberg observes, "Throughout history, relations between dominant and rising states have been uneasy—and often violent . . . the fact that the U.S.-China relationship is competitive, then, is simply no surprise."[16] "We're going to war in the South China Sea in five to ten years," future White House strategist Steve Bannon bluntly declared in a March 2016 radio broadcast. "There's no doubt about that."[17] It is precisely because shifts in power are so dangerous that many conclude the United States has no choice but to confront a rising China before it is too late.

In sum, the claim that relative decline is dangerous is a deeply important one. It shapes our theoretical understandings of the causes of war and peace. It influences assessments about the importance of continued American engagement abroad and the risks of retrenchment. It fuels concerns about how the rise of new powers might undermine the current liberal international order. If great powers respond to decline with domestic dysfunction and aggression abroad, then the twenty-first century stands to be a period of profound geopolitical turbulence. Yet if great powers can manage power shifts peacefully, this pessimism may be misplaced.

Defining Decline and Retrenchment

This book is about grand strategic responses to relative decline. The protagonists of the story are great powers, though domestic groups, decision makers, and weaker states play supporting roles. Great powers are the heavyweights in international politics; they are the class of states possessing the largest combination of military and economic resources.[18] Militarily, that means they have bigger armies, spend more on defense, and use the most advanced technology. Economically, that means they produce more economic output, participate more in the world economy, and have more complex economic systems. While small states and mid-range powers may fret about the global distribution of power, they more often concentrate on local matters and have less capacity to respond in either case. We focus on great powers because they are the most influential actors, and because they are the centerpieces of the literature.[19]

The prime cause acting on these protagonists is decline. There are many different ways to conceptualize decline, but in what follows we focus on periods of what we call "acute relative decline" (or, for brevity, simply "decline").[20] These are moments characterized by two traits. First, a great power suffers a decline in relative power that decreases its ordinal rank among the great powers. Second, this decrease in relative power is sustained for at least five years. When the rank order of great powers changes—for instance, when numbers one and two switch places—and the switch is not temporary, this is what we mean by decline. Later, we discuss how different kinds of decline may impact great power responses, but we do not usually differentiate cases based on their sources of decline. Some declines take place when a dominant state falls in absolute terms and rapidly loses its rank. Other declines are the product of a rising state outperforming its peers in relative terms before slowly overtaking them. Despite their different origins, each of these cases results in an ordinal transition, and we treat both as cases of decline.

In defining decline this way, we assume that great powers are primarily concerned about relative, rather than absolute, power.[21] Because states reside in a competitive self-help system in which they alone are responsible for providing security from external threats, they are particularly concerned about where they rank in the hierarchy of great powers. It is not a state's own trajectory that matters but how this trajectory changes its position relative to others. Absolute declines are alarming precisely because they allow rival states to overtake you rapidly. Absolute gains are cold comfort if potential competitors are steadily outpacing you. A corollary of this point is that we do not assume hegemonic transitions are substantially different from other changes in the great power ranks. Hegemonic transitions may be special, of course, but that is something that should be shown, not asserted. Great powers should be particularly alarmed any time they fall relative to their peers.

We also assume that states focus on long-term trends, especially those that threaten their current positions. Indicators of national power can fluctuate rapidly, and some shifts are short-lived and not indicative of broader trends. But shifts in power that result in an ordinal transition are different: they are easier to identify, more salient to policymakers, and pose greater threats to a state's security.[22] Next, we assume that material factors have a more substantial and predictable impact on national power than other factors. Surely nonmaterial factors like national character, political unity, status, or legitimacy shape the ability of states to exercise influence.[23] Yet it is the material resources accessible to a state, such as its taxable economic surplus or population available for military service, that form the foundation of national power. National disunity can undoubtedly prevent abundance from being exploited, but no amount of ideological harmony can make up for resource scarcity. We assume some leaders may put their faith in intangible components of power, but most will have perceptions that track closely with objective measures. A related benefit of focusing on the material elements of national power is that they can be compared systematically across cases.

What we are trying to explain is how decline affects grand strategy. We define grand strategy as the purposeful use of military, diplomatic, and economic resources by a state to seek security from external threats.[24] By security, we mean the capacity of a state to preserve its autonomy.[25] Grand strategy is distinct from military strategy in that it considers how all the instruments of statecraft combine to enhance the security of a state during war or peacetime.[26] Naturally, states often have grand strategies that are incomplete, contradictory, or misguided. What matters most is that there is a minimal consensus within the official mind about how a state should advance its interests abroad.[27]

Scholars have offered numerous ways to categorize grand strategies.[28] These distinctions are undoubtedly important in different contexts, but for

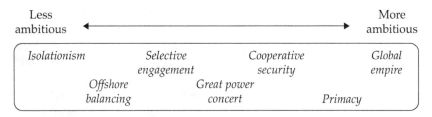

Figure 1. Continuum of grand strategies

present purposes we classify grand strategies along a single dimension: their degree of ambition. By ambition, we mean the scale and scope of the outcomes that a particular grand strategy seeks to influence. Scope here refers both to the geographic reach of a particular grand strategy and to the potential range of issue areas it addresses.

Figure 1 arranges the most familiar grand strategies along this spectrum.[29] On one end of the continuum, ambitious grand strategies seek to influence outcomes in a significant manner across a number of issue areas and geographic regions. They maintain that the security of a state depends on the maintenance of an active and engaged presence abroad. An important example of a grand strategy located on this end is primacy, in which a great power attempts to guarantee its security by establishing preponderance over all rivals.[30] A slightly less ambitious grand strategy is cooperative security, in which a great power uses standing alliances and other multilateral institutions to deter aggression and manage collective crises.[31]

On the other end of the continuum, less ambitious grand strategies seek less dramatic impacts and have more modest reach. They posit that security can be maintained through a more selective and restrained foreign policy, which seeks to influence issues closer to home or in select issue areas. One example located on this end of the spectrum is isolationism, in which a state concentrates on defending the homeland while avoiding most foreign entanglements.[32] A more ambitious but still relatively restrained grand strategy is selective engagement, in which a great power seeks to influence outcomes only in regions crucial to its security.[33]

On the most elemental level, states can expand, contract, or maintain their grand strategic ambitions. They may change their grand strategy to a greater or lesser degree using an array of tools, but the elementary distinction is whether ambitions are going up, down, or staying the same. When ambitions rise, a state is in grand strategic expansion; when they fall, it has chosen retrenchment; and when they stay the same, it is sticking to the status quo. These changes are not grand strategies unto themselves; they reflect significant and sustained trends in ambition. A state may retrench from a more to a less ambitious strategy of primacy just as it may expand from a less to a more ambitious strategy of isolationism.

At base, retrenchment is an intentional reduction in the overall cost of a state's foreign policy.[34] Conversely, expansion is an intentional increase in the overall cost of a state's foreign policy, and the status quo is maintaining the overall cost of a state's foreign policy. The cost of a state's foreign policy is a product of its expenses, risks, and burdens. To illustrate, retrenching states can economize expenses by cutting, inter alia, military spending and personnel. Retrenching states can also reduce risks by pruning foreign policy liabilities, tempering foreign policy goals in some geographic areas, and demoting the importance of some issues. Finally, retrenching states can try to shift burdens, fobbing off foreign policy obligations on allies or dependencies. All these policies allow resources to be redistributed from peripheral to core interests. Simply put, great powers retrench when they seek foreign policies that are less active, less ambitious, and less burdensome than the status quo.

Retrenchment is not synonymous with appeasement, which is narrower, or reform, which is broader. By appeasement, we mean policies of asymmetrical and sustained concessions to an adversary in order to defuse conflict.[35] Appeasement does not require retrenchment and vice versa. Retrenchment need not relate only to adversaries, nor be asymmetric or abiding. Indeed, declining powers are just as likely to offer sustained asymmetric concessions to recruit potential allies as to satiate potential adversaries. They may also use retrenchment to gather resources to confront enemies. One advantage of studying decline is that it helps identify when appeasement looks like the only way to safety.

Furthermore, retrenchment is distinct from the more generic concept of reform. By reform, we mean efforts by states to markedly change the roles, missions, standard practices, and organizational structure of prominent domestic institutions. Retrenchment can widen the possibilities for reform, but reform is not automatic. A state may decrease its overseas commitments, omit domestic reforms, and still count as a case of retrenchment. Similarly, a state may keep its overseas commitments constant while trimming back and overhauling institutions at home, and this, too, counts as retrenchment. Of course, states can also reform to maintain gains or expand assertively, but this is not evidence of retrenchment.

Grand strategy is hard in the best of times, but in many ways decline makes it more difficult.[36] Paraphrasing Alexis de Tocqueville, the most dangerous moment for a government is when it starts to reform.[37] Declining powers can face more intense and immediate threats to their security abroad and more difficulty controlling politics at home. Unable to dominate by traditional margins, they are vulnerable to challenges by potential predators and domestic groups. Procrastination is tempting. Declining powers also find it harder to command the traditional tools of statecraft. Because observers question the credibility of their commitments, they may struggle to deter potential aggressors, reassure alliance partners, and negotiate diplomatic agreements. Perhaps of greatest importance, declining powers have fewer resources to support grand strategy. Some policies are too expensive given a dwindling resource base, while others siphon funds away from pressing domestic problems.

In short, declining powers face a difficult dilemma. On the one hand, they face a more uncertain and potentially dangerous world. They fear the rise of new challengers and the potential instability created by sudden shifts in the distribution of power. At the same time, declining powers have fewer resources and more limited options available to manage these threats. They worry about the sustained erosion of their national power and the decreasing efficacy of traditional tools of statecraft. How do great powers respond to such pressures?

Plan of the Book

The remainder of this book explores how great powers deal with decline. Chapter 1 unpacks the conventional wisdom, which associates decline with paralysis at home and increased instability abroad, questioning its logic and teasing out testable implications. In chapter 2, we explain why declining powers are drawn to retrenchment during decline. We describe the various forms that retrenchment can take and why states might be drawn to different policies at different times. We also show how different structural conditions might amplify or mute pressures to retrench.

Chapter 3 looks at decline by the numbers. We identify sixteen cases of decline since 1870 and quantitatively trace the grand strategic choices that all the cases made in response. The chief findings are that retrenchment is the most common response to decline, even over short time spans, and that the depth of decline is a decent predictor of the degree of retrenchment. Compared to their non-declining counterparts, declining powers tend to spend less on their militaries and keep the size of their armed forces down, and the fastest declining states are more likely to enter alliances. We also find that declining states do not make inviting targets because, compared to non-declining states, they do not tend to lose disputes overall and tend to prevail in the disputes they initiate. This suggests that declining powers are flexible and formidable.

After this brief overview, the next six chapters provide a series of natural experiments that get inside the cases. We study three pairs of great powers, each experiencing similar depths of decline but manifesting somewhat divergent responses. Chapters 4 and 5 look at two small declines: Britain in 1872 and 1908, respectively. While geography, culture, and institutions stay constant, British policymakers retrenched in both periods, but they did so in differing manners. Policymakers in the 1870s dabbled with domestic reforms and struggled to rein in imperial proconsuls, whereas their counterparts in the 1900s embraced retrenchment at home and abroad. The latter episode elicited a more determined response because Britain had fewer reserves of power, fewer concerns of falling dominos, and access to more reliable allies. Different conditions drove different policies.

Chapters 6 and 7 compare two cases of medium decline: 1888 Russia and 1893 France, respectively. Despite radical differences in their domestic political systems, these powers espoused similar policies of retrenchment, culminating in an alliance with one another. Yet these two cases varied in key nuances: France came around to retrenchment reluctantly, while Russia took it up more eagerly, an outcome explained in part by the steady hand of successive tsars. Distant beginnings united in a common ending.

Chapters 8 and 9 pair two large declines: 1903 Russia and 1925 France, respectively. Although both states rejected preventive war as a viable option and adopted elements of retrenchment, neither limited its ambitions as much as their dire straits would have suggested. Part of this can be explained by dysfunctional domestic politics: an erratic tsar and a fractious party system. But in neither case were conditions fully favorable to retrenchment. Russia struggled to erect stable buffers along its vast and vulnerable frontiers, whereas France stumbled in its efforts to find capable, reliable allies. Their muddled responses led to morbid outcomes.

In the conclusion, we summarize findings, discuss implications, and offer predictions about the incipient Sino-American transition. To telegraph our points, we contend that China's rise is neither a historical outlier nor inherently dangerous. Consistent with other low to medium declines, we expect the United States to favor mild retrenchment aimed mostly at remedying domestic problems. The Obama administration adopted some policies from the retrenchment playbook, and we draw out the conditions that might shape whether these policies continue and where they might be prove effective. We conclude that the biggest danger may not be the impending Sino-American transition itself, but the widespread belief that it makes war more likely.

Desperate Times, Desperate Measures

Debating Decline

> The first and most attractive response to a society's decline is to eliminate the source of the problem. By launching a preventive war, the declining power destroys or weakens the rising challenger while the military advantage is still with the declining power.
>
> —Robert Gilpin

> In these more troubled circumstances, the Great Power is likely to find itself spending much more on defense than it did two generations earlier, and yet still discover that the world is a less secure environment. . . . Great Powers in relative decline instinctively respond by spending more on "security," and thereby divert potential resources from "investment" and compound their long-term dilemma.
>
> —Paul Kennedy

Since 2008, there has been vigorous argument about whether the United States is in decline. Some see clear evidence of an erosion of American power. Fareed Zakaria argues that "the distribution of power is shifting, moving away from U.S. dominance."[1] The National Intelligence Council asserts that one of the most important global trends will be the shift of power "to networks and coalitions in a multipolar world."[2] Others maintain that reports of America's demise have been greatly exaggerated. Joseph Nye contends that "describing the twenty-first century as one of American decline is likely to be inaccurate and misleading"[3] Josef Joffe reaches a similar conclusion about the "false prophecy of America's decline," noting, "The United States is the default power, the country that occupies center stage because there is nobody else with the requisite power and purpose."[4]

While there are significant disagreements about the character of American decline, there are fewer disagreements about its potential consequences. Authors across the political spectrum worry about the repercussions of ebbing U.S. influence. Robert Kagan contends that "if American power declines, this world order will decline with it."[5] And Robert Lieber declares, "The maintenance of [the United States'] leading role matters greatly. The alternative would . . . be a more disorderly and dangerous world."[6] Christopher Layne concurs: "As [its] power wanes over the next decade or so, the United States will find itself increasingly challenged."[7] Charles Kupchan echoes the point: "U.S. leadership has always faced resistance, but the pushback grows in proportion to the diffusion of global power."[8] While their policy recommendations differ, there is broad consensus that if the United States declines, this will usher in a period of greater uncertainty, complexity, and potential danger in world politics.

Why do international relations scholars assume that decline will be dangerous? This pessimism is founded in the two main theories of how great powers respond to decline. The first contends that expansion and war are the most likely responses to shifts in power. Declining states find it hard to resist the siren song of preventive war because it holds the greatest hope that they will be able to slow or stop their decline. Rather than waiting until decline has taken its toll, states prefer to confront rising challengers while the balance of military capabilities remains favorable. The second argues that, when decline strikes, great powers stick to the status quo because they struggle with domestic dysfunction. A combination of entrenched interest groups, hidebound bureaucracies, and parochial governing coalitions prevent policymakers from altering course. Paralyzed at home, declining powers cling to untenable commitments despite sharp challengers and spiraling costs. Where domestic dysfunction scholars tend to see status quo policies as imprudent, preventive war theorists tend to see those courses of action as rational, if sometimes regrettable.

In this chapter, we challenge the assumptions and logic of both of these theories. We argue that the conditions that produce dysfunctional domestic dynamics or preventive war incentives tend to be rare, and even less common when great powers are in the midst of decline. Decline creates powerful incentives for leaders to overcome domestic intransigence and push through needed reforms. Few states are so vulnerable to capture from domestic interests that they can ignore structural incentives. Decline generates equally powerful incentives for states to adjust constructively within the international order, rather than risk the grave gamble that is preventive war. Seldom are states in the position where the risks of preventive war are manageable, and yet victory will be decisive enough to solve their underlying problems. These critiques find support in the empirical record, where preventive war and political paralysis are infrequent. The true puzzle is not why states struggle to respond to decline, but why retrenchment is the most common response.

To be clear, these two theories need not be mutually exclusive: domestic dynamics can reinforce international pressures. But to simplify matters, we consider each separately. In the first section, we investigate theories of preventive war, spelling out their logics and shortcomings. In the second section, we give similar treatment to theories of domestic dysfunction. And in the final section, we summarize the debate and the gaps it contains.

International Incentives: The Lure of Preventive War

Following Thucydides, many scholars contend that decline is dangerous because it promotes war. When the distribution of national power is stable and predictable, individual states have neither the incentive nor the capacity to challenge the status quo. When the hierarchy of great powers is in flux, rising and falling powers are tempted to use force to advance their interests. Yet the two exemplars of this tradition, hegemonic stability theory and power transition theory, disagree about the precise mechanisms linking decline to war. We explain the logic of each in turn.

Advocates of hegemonic stability theory argue that declining powers have no good options to stave off defeat apart from preventive war. Robert Gilpin maintains that declining powers confront a strategic dilemma: though they would prefer to "restore equilibrium to the system" through peaceful means, there are no good policies for doing so.[9] Domestic options, such as increased taxation or institutional reform, are blocked by "vested interests."[10] International solutions, such as tighter alliances or retrenchment, are impractical and dangerous. The "utility of an alliance as a response to decline" is "severely restricted" due to free riding and cheating, while retrenchment is "by its very nature . . . an indication of relative weakness" and thus "a hazardous course" that is "seldom pursued by a declining power."[11] Unable to generate new revenues or reduce current costs, declining powers have few options short of force. "When the choice ahead has appeared to be to decline or to fight," Gilpin concludes, "statesmen have most generally fought."[12]

Dale Copeland also contends that declining powers have strong incentives to pursue antagonistic policies. When states are "declining deeply" and "will almost certainly be attacked later," preventive war is the only option that can "maximize the state's expected probability of survival."[13] Conciliatory strategies may reduce tensions, yet "sacrificing relative power in the process . . . lower[s] a state's likelihood of winning any war that does occur."[14] Attempts to "buy the rising state's goodwill" through concessions also tend to fail because declining powers cannot trust rising powers' promises to remain at peace "after preponderance has been achieved."[15] In the final analysis, "the more severe a state's decline will be in the absence of strong action, the more severe its actions are likely to be."[16] The faster and deeper great powers fall, the more likely and eager they are to fight.

In contrast, power transition theorists emphasize the incentives of rising powers to use force. A. F. K. Organski and Jacek Kugler argue that as rising challengers ascend the standings, they find that dominant powers refuse to accommodate their expanding interests.[17] Incapable of revising the status quo through peaceful means and "unwilling to accept a subordinate position," dissatisfied challengers are increasingly drawn to truculent policies.[18] It is when a rising power has "finally caught up with the dominant country" that it will use force in an "attempt to hasten [its] passage" to the top rung of the great power ladder.[19] Decline is dangerous not because leading powers will fight to defend their positions, but because rising powers will embark on destabilizing bids for hegemony.

At first glance, hegemonic stability theory and power transition theory appear to contradict one another. For Copeland, "major wars are typically initiated by dominant military powers that fear significant decline."[20] On the contrary, Organski and Kugler assert, "It is the weaker, rather than the stronger, power that is most likely to be the aggressor."[21] But in practice, the logic of each theory reinforces the other. They both agree that shifts in the balance of power are perilous but differ on who has the stronger incentives to fight. In both views, rising and declining powers are trapped in a security dilemma where one side's moves decrease the security of the other and vice versa. Initiation seldom matters in such situations. Since abrupt shifts in power heighten uncertainty, fear, and mistrust, they encourage declining powers to hold the line or expand their ambitions, which inevitably clash with those of rising powers.[22] Because both theories come out essentially the same, from this point on we will call them both preventive war theory as a shorthand. They share the same expectations: declining great powers will maintain ambitious grand strategies, in which rigid conceptions of interests foment war. The deeper the decline, the more aggressive the response will be.

Preventive war theories lay out a clear cost-benefit analysis, but their accounting is suspect in a number of respects. First, war is incredibly costly and risky. The preferred solution of preventive war theories is one of the most expensive and least predictable actions a state can take. This may be why Thucydides's prototypical example ended badly. After decisively defeating Athens, Spartan power never recovered, losing to Thebes and Macedon not long after. And modern wars are worse. Even putting nuclear weapons to one side, great power wars have been exorbitantly costly for some time.[23] As Gilpin and Copeland acknowledge, hardline foreign policies bring risks—defeat being the worst—and even victories can be pyrrhic.[24] The use of force may alienate allies, alarm neutrals, and provoke rivals. It can saddle the victor with restive populations and costlier commitments. Shallow declines are not menacing enough to warrant war, while deep declines are hard to reverse with force. Because deep declines tend to be the product of fundamental social and economic deficiencies, foreign policy fixes are seldom silver bullets. Great powers will be most willing to accept the risks of hardline policies at precisely the moments when the benefits are likely to be minimal and unattainable.

Second, and related, preventive war theories underestimate the efficacy of mutual accommodation. The assumption tends to be that war, while rare, is to a large extent inevitable. The alternatives available to declining powers, as Gilpin emphasizes, are "seldom those of waging war versus promoting peace, but rather waging war while the balance is still in that state's favor or waging war later when the tide may have turned against it."[25] But there are good reasons why rising challengers would see war as improbable. The capacity of rising powers to sustain their trajectory depends on domestic institutions, which must manage the dislocations associated with rapid growth, and the stresses of great power war are unlikely to help. Premature bids for hegemony can not only encourage the formation of hostile foreign coalitions but also upset the fragile domestic foundations of long-term growth. Windows of vulnerability rarely open as quickly or decisively as theories of preventive action anticipate, and even the most damaged declining power does not become a pushover. Rising powers have strong incentives to bide their time until they are in a decisively dominant position.[26]

On their side, declining powers have reasons to avoid confrontational responses as well. The growth of a rising challenger may slow or stall for a variety of reasons. Rising powers may acquire new and costly commitments, which can distract attention and drain resources. Domestic issues may siphon away disposable wealth and divert rising powers from challenging redoubtable great powers. While they may dominate by lesser margins, declining powers can still call upon their large and diverse economies as well as advanced and experienced militaries. They can draw on the support of longstanding allies, appeal to customary diplomatic practices and familiar rules, and concentrate resources on well-established interests. Hostile or unbending actions forfeit these advantages. Provocative actions require declining states to risk scarce resources and use dubious means in uncertain environments for quixotic goals.

Third, preventive war theories obsess over the appearance of credibility, not where it comes from or how much it is worth. For Gilpin, the "fundamental problem with a policy of appeasement or accommodation" is that it leads to "continuing deterioration in a state's prestige and international position."[27] But commitments are checks: they only cash when there is something behind them. In world politics, power is the closest equivalent to money, and as a declining state's power draws down, it has to be more frugal. Great powers cannot be fooled for long; commitments must be backed. Yet declining powers have less capability and must decide whether to keep a stronger, shorter defensive perimeter, or a longer, weaker one. Preventive war theories assert the sanctity of credibility in theory as they recommend overdrawing it in practice. And, while the debate remains lively, credibility in the abstract appears to be worth less than policymakers believe.[28] Great powers are not obligated to defend their interests with equal vigor, and accommodation in one area does not necessarily invite exploitation in others. A reputation for bluffing can be worse than a reputation for weakness.

Most important, credibility is more multifaceted and contextual than preventive war theories assume. Great powers certainly worry about their power and prestige, but their commitments are not of equal weight, and concessions in one area need not be seen as weakening commitments elsewhere. The fact that commitments are complex allows declining powers to shift burdens and concentrate capabilities at key points of challenge.[29] Tactical retreats and strongpoint defenses make deterrence more robust and threats more credible, and may help signal benign intentions.[30] The multifaceted nature of commitments also provides crafty rising challengers with opportunities to challenge the status quo in places that dominant powers are unlikely to vigorously defend. Rising powers that undertake modest challenges to the status quo in less sensitive areas send the important signal that they do not intend to forcibly overturn the existing order.[31] In this way, rising powers can take advantage of their newfound strength without generating incentives for declining powers to clip their wings.

Altogether, these points suggest that shifts in power are concerning but rarely generate strong incentives for war. Declining powers will be drawn to preventive war when uncommon stars align: if war is likely to succeed, if the consequences of war can be managed, if victory will reverse flagging fortunes, and if there are no better options. A declining power must also be confident that rising challengers will continue to ascend rapidly up the ranks, that they will fight to assure their ascendance, and that they are bent on future domination. In the absence of these conditions, pugnacious policies make little sense. Defeat in a preventive war opens the floodgates for exploitation on multiple fronts, and even a successful war can compromise a great power to the point of vulnerability. Typically, states will manage the very real, but often ambiguous, dangers that accompany decline with more caution than aggression.

Domestic Disincentives: Decentralization and Dysfunction

Another group of scholars asserts that decline begets grand strategic inertia because of domestic dysfunction. The international system may send signals for declining states to retract their grand strategic ambitions, but domestic politics intervenes to foul up the response. What these thinkers have in common is the belief that internal politics causes great powers to react to decline in an uncoordinated and unwise fashion.

Amongst themselves, though, they part company over the exact road that leads to failure. Some lay the blame squarely on the shoulders of bureaucracies while others cast it on interest groups. Regardless, the result of these domestic dynamics is that declining powers often adopt contradictory and self-defeating policies.

Starting with bureaucratic politics, the logic behind this view is that foreign policy bureaucracies have parochial outlooks and narrow interests that increasingly clash during decline. Through a careful case study of late-nineteenth-century Britain, for example, Aaron Friedberg argues that domestic political fragmentation inhibited the ability to evaluate power trends and respond properly. Friedberg shows that policymakers' recognition of decline was "disjoined and uneven" across foreign policy bureaucracies, and they were leery of recommending bitter medicine to the electorate.[32] Only sustained and unexpected external shocks, along with the presence of motivated "change agents," could alter existing images of national power.[33] Even when policymakers accepted the reality of decline, the responses taken were not "smooth, incremental, and continuous" but rather "partial, and only partially coordinated."[34] What obstructed needed reforms were divisions within and across bureaucracies and the public's aversion to bad news and belt tightening.

Mark Brawley likewise claims that declining powers often "maintain the international obligations associated with leadership, even after such policies no longer appear to be rational from a national perspective."[35] Maladjustment is primarily the result of bureaucratic competition, typically pitting those associated with international leadership, such as the central bank or military staff, against those responsible for preserving resources, notably the treasury. When bureaucracies favoring continued leadership possess intense preferences, large public constituencies, and considerable autonomy, they are able to dominate internal debates and prevent timely strategic adjustment.[36] The result of this infighting is "afterglow," the "seemingly irrational yet fairly common failure to respond appropriately to overstretch."[37]

Moving to interest groups, the logic behind this perspective is that special interests impede healthy strategic adjustment because they crowd out less myopic and less exclusive groups from government. Hendrik Spruyt, for example, argues that "veto groups"—including settler parties, business interests with foreign investments, and military organizations with a stake in the periphery—can conspire to "block territorial retrenchment."[38] When "institutional arrangements create multiple veto opportunities," interest groups can block change "even if they constitute a minority."[39] States in which "political oversight of the military is weak" or in which institutions "provide multiple partisan and constitutional veto points" are most likely to cling to costly overseas possessions, even as economic and military costs accrue.[40]

So, too, Steven Lobell contends that the grand strategy adopted by a declining power depends on the character of its domestic governing coalition. States dominated by free-trade interests will favor accommodation and "retrenching in regions with emerging liberal contenders."[41] Those in which economic nationalist interests are ascendant, in contrast, will prefer "greater military preparedness and maintaining the empire."[42] Although external conditions may not necessarily favor their preferred policy, "entrenched coalitions" will seek to "further bolster their own coalition's relative power," even when their actions "undermine the nation's interest." Such parochialism fails to slow decline and "risks shortening the hegemon's great power tenure."[43]

In the end, these arguments share the conclusion that internal groups can at least hold major issues hostage and at most hijack foreign policy. Consequently, great powers are unlikely to modify their grand strategies in a timely or effective manner. Domestic politics infects every part of the policy process: recognition of decline, identification of solutions, and implementation of policies. Democracies and other decentralized states are only more predisposed to suffer these maladies.[44] This logic culminates in a clear prediction: declining powers are unlikely to adjust their grand strategies because of domestic obstacles, and the more decentralized a regime, the greater these obstacles will be.

There can be no doubt that domestic factors influence strategic responses to decline. Nonetheless, proponents of domestic constraint arguments overstate the extent and decisiveness of these barriers. First, groups favoring ambitious foreign policies are often much less organized than these theories assume. Brawley, for example, claims that great powers that assume global leadership roles often "empower" outward-looking bureaucracies such as central banks or military staffs "during hegemonic ascendance to further policy in monetary and security affairs."[45] Spruyt points out that states that acquire overseas possessions often do so because of pressure from interest groups, such as traders or foreign investors. It is not surprising that the same groups who "advocated empire in the first place may stand to lose the most if the metropole decides to retreat from the periphery."[46]

But there are persuasive reasons to expect that great powers will be populated by bureaucracies and concentrated interests that oppose outdated policies. While great powers tend to have groups that favor continued international leadership, long periods of prosperity are just as likely to have empowered groups focused on domestic priorities. Businesses with large domestic markets, public sector unions, and advocates for social welfare spending are among the countless groups that lobby on behalf of domestic over foreign commitments. These domestic-focused interests can be just as concentrated as their foreign-focused counterparts and often have deeper pockets. To the extent that leaders find domestic interests more tangible and immediate, these groups may also have an easier time accessing the policy process.[47]

Foreign policy lobbies, moreover, do not speak in one voice; they have divisions that are exploitable. For instance, banks may lobby a government to protect their foreign investments but oppose destabilizing actions that might halt the free flow of capital.[48] Foreign policy interest groups may also be divided about how best to engage the world. As Lobell points out, some proponents of leadership may favor liberal instruments such as the promotion of free trade, a stable monetary system, and functioning international institutions, while others champion nationalist instruments like protectionist barriers, currency blocs, and militarized alliances.[49] Even within a single governing coalition, there can be differences between prominent constituencies about which interests should be protected and what regions prioritized. This disagreement permits policymakers to play groups off each other and push through policy changes.

Second, these theories downplay the benefits of domestic decentralization and assume that bureaucracies and interest groups consistently gain preferential access to the political system. "The more widely distributed decision-making power is within a political system," Friedberg emphasizes, "the more likely it is that a nation's initial response to relative decline will be fragmented."[50] Spruyt adds, "The more fragmented the decision-making process . . . the greater the resistance to change."[51] Yet the presence of multiple bodies responsible for assessment can decrease groupthink and foster a more robust marketplace of ideas.[52] Competition between bureaucracies can encourage better performance and innovation. The need for rival interest groups to accommodate one another can temper extremism and promote creative compromises.

More to the point, these theories underestimate the capacity of leaders to transcend decentralization, especially in foreign policy.[53] National leaders possess a number of advantages over even the most well organized and entrenched interest group. They have a more complete picture of the range of interest groups clamoring for attention, more experience using formal and informal channels to forge compromise, more agenda-setting powers, and more extensive patronage networks to purchase the quiescence of individual interest groups.[54] Democratic leaders have an additional set of tools to force compromise: they can use the bully pulpit to mobilize popular support, exploit cross-cutting cleavages and party rivalries, and hold out the prospects of victory in future elections as a means to convince losers to accept temporary defeats. Given that great powers have developed institutions to begin with, it stands to reason that politicians at the helm of declining powers will be well positioned to overcome all but the most determined domestic opposition.

Third, domestic dysfunction arguments soft pedal the ways in which the international environment can transform domestic political calculations.

They assume that small groups can hold a state hostage, despite mounting dangers. Brawley argues that bureaucrats are "usually able to recognize the problem" of decline but respond with a mulish refusal to change.[55] Lobell, too, acknowledges that decline can imperil the fortunes of governing coalitions but contends that politicians will react by stubbornly seeking to capture "distributional gains" and "block the opposing coalition."[56] Yet though intransigence may be appealing in the short term, it makes little sense over the long term. Bureaucracies that cling to responsibilities as resources dry up court repeated failures, public outcry, slashed budgets, less autonomy, and less prestige—and bureaucratic leaders know this.[57] Governing coalitions that force suboptimal policies on a reluctant nation tend to have abbreviated tenures. Successful policymakers cannot afford to be as parochial as domestic constraint theories suggest. External shocks and dramatic setbacks force them to accept the reality of decline and the necessity of reform.

In comparative terms, moments of decline are least favorable to parochial domestic factions. When resources are abundant, policymakers can afford to indulge domestic lobbies with minor consequences. They will have few incentives to resolve tradeoffs among competing interests or to nix foreign adventures. In contrast, policymakers in declining powers have strong incentives to sublimate private interests for the public good. The emergence of new foreign threats forces them to focus their attention, coordinate efforts among rival bureaucracies, and experiment with new policies. It is precisely in moments of decline that partisan rancor and sectoral rivalry face increasing pressure to recede.

Taken together, these points suggest that the domestic barriers to successful strategic adjustment have been exaggerated. There is no doubt that domestic politics can influence the timing and content of declining powers' strategic choices. But entrenched interest groups can completely stymie strategic adjustment only in circumscribed conditions: they must be better organized than their rivals, well positioned to take advantage of decentralized institutions, unopposed by political leaders, and insulated from the negative feedback produced by parochial policies. This final point shows an important tension in domestic constraint theories: while interest groups clamor loudest for protection during large declines, they will be in the least advantageous position to argue that status quo policies are working.

The Retrenchment Puzzle

Most international relations scholars who have written about decline are deeply pessimistic about the capacity of great powers to manage power shifts peacefully. Advocates of preventive war theories predict that declining powers will be drawn toward provocative policies that tend to culminate in war. Unable to accommodate rising rivals and unwilling to pull back, declining powers try to cow rivals while the distribution of power is favorable rather than lose later without a fight. Proponents of domestic dysfunction theories see declining powers as crippled by interest groups and self-centered bureaucracies. When reasoned assessment and hard choices are most needed, great powers struggle to transcend factional politics.

We have highlighted the weaknesses of these theories. Preventive war theories sell a skewed version of great powers' incentives during ordinal transitions. They underestimate the negative consequences of force while overselling its benefits, and they ignore the congruence of interests between rising and falling powers, which gives both sides reasons to proceed with caution. Domestic dysfunction theories overrate the ease with which parochial interests capture governments, especially during moments of decline. As the costs of maintaining the status quo rise, leaders have strong incentives to exploit their position atop the decision-making hierarchy to overcome resistance and pass reforms.

Ultimately, the issue is empirical: how do great powers actually behave? If preventive war and domestic dysfunction theories are correct, then we expect declining powers to display preferences for either expansionist or status quo policies. Rather than reduce foreign policy burdens through retrenchment, we expect them to cling to current commitments or to embrace expansionist policies. The presumed puzzle is why great powers respond to decline poorly or provocatively, and the empirical record ought to be a catalog of paralysis and calamity.

In subsequent chapters, we explain our methods in detail, but a preliminary survey of the evidence suggests that neither preventive war nor domestic dysfunction explanations receive strong support. We identified sixteen cases of great power decline since 1870 and examined whether they expanded, contracted, or maintained their foreign policy commitments in response to decline (see table 1). Of these sixteen cases, only two declining powers stuck to the status quo, while only one followed expansionist policies. The vast majority of great powers—between eleven and thirteen cases, depending on how one codes the ambiguous cases—respond to decline with retrenchment.

On its own, the table does not entirely invalidate the conventional wisdom. There are several instances where a declining state fought a major war, and at least two of these wars involved clashes between a declining power and its ordinal challenger. It may be that preventive wars are exceedingly rare but still somewhat more probable when a declining power is involved. Declining powers also appear to have a preference for milder forms of retrenchment. This could reflect the presence of dysfunctional domestic politics that constrain policymakers from retrenching as fast or as far as circumstances suggest.

Table 1 Great power responses to decline

Country year	Depth of decline	Ordinal rank	Ordinal challenger	Strategic adjustment
1879 Russia	0.36	3	Germany	low retrenchment
1873 France	0.90	3	Germany	low retrenchment-status quo
1926 United Kingdom	0.96	2	Germany	low retrenchment
1908 United Kingdom	1.41	2	Germany	medium-low retrenchment
1872 United Kingdom	1.46	1	United States	low retrenchment-status quo
1883 France	1.99	3	Germany	status quo
1930 United Kingdom	2.17	2	Soviet Union	medium-low retrenchment
1888 Russia	3.22	3	Germany	medium retrenchment
1935 United Kingdom	3.22	3	Germany	high retrenchment
1893 France	3.23	4	Russia	medium-low retrenchment
1931 Germany	3.24	2	Soviet Union	expansion
1925 France	4.00	4	Soviet Union	medium retrenchment
1903 Russia	4.22	3	Germany	medium-low retrenchment
1946 United Kingdom	5.54	2	Soviet Union	high retrenchment
1992 Japan	6.32	2	China	status quo
1987/88 Soviet Union	9.0/10.8	2/3	Japan/China	high retrenchment

A definitive assessment of the rival theories requires us to examine the data and individual cases in greater detail. Yet if this table captures the patterns accurately, the task at hand is to explain why great powers choose to retrench, rather than to lash out at their rivals or to indulge domestic factions. Why does decline create strong pressures on great powers to retrench? How might retrenchment help great powers manage the challenges created by decline? When is retrenchment most attractive to declining powers? The next chapter develops a theory to answer these questions.

Parry to Thrust

The Logic of Retrenchment

> Many who have trusted in force to gain an advantage, instead of gaining anything more, have been doomed to lose what they had. . . . The incalculable element in the future exercises the widest influence, and is the most treacherous, and yet in fact the most useful of all things, as it frightens us all equally, and thus makes us consider before attacking each other.
>
> —Hermocrates

> For one should never fall in the belief that you can find someone to pick you up. Whether it does not happen or happens, it is not security for you, because that defense was base and did not depend on you. And those defenses alone are good, are certain, and are lasting, that depend on you yourself and on your virtue.
>
> — Niccolò Machiavelli

Decline is a melancholy spectacle, and not one most care to dwell on. Yet just as doctors obsess over sickness to preserve health, international relations theorists have long fixated on the fall of great powers to preserve states. The themes of the classic writings on the subject are foresight, self-help, and prudence, but their analyses are vague and untested.[1] In the last chapter, we examined two of the best-known theories about decline and found them wanting. Domestic dysfunction theories emphasize the barriers to timely strategic adjustment but underestimate the incentives and tools policymakers have to navigate them. Preventive war theories underscore the anxieties great powers feel during decline yet misstate the utility of force and the risks of belligerence. Both schools of thought predict that retrenchment is improbable, though history suggests otherwise. This chapter develops an alternative.

We argue that declining powers will be drawn to retrenchment because, in the brutal realm of power politics, they have strong incentives to stay strategically solvent. Inside our main claim are three core contentions. First, the international system tends not to punish states that balance their means and ends, so states tend to retrench promptly and proportionately to declines. Great powers that do not react with agility and alacrity are unlikely to last long: rivals will be quick to detect and exploit incompetence, and foreign policy setbacks will mount. The faster the fall, the more likely this is to be true. Retrenchment cannot cure all ailments, but it usually beats the alternatives: depressed economic growth, sclerotic institutions, brittle defenses, provocative positions, exposed outposts, and shaky commitments.

Second, we argue that retrenchment is a multifaceted policy that declining powers tailor to circumstance because states have different assets and liabilities in different depths of decline. Leaders need to know what their options are in detail and what the likely consequences will be. Domestically, retrenchment includes reducing military spending, restructuring military forces, and reforming institutions. These policies are designed to reduce the price a state pays for its foreign policy, releasing resources for more efficient uses. Internationally, retrenchment includes redeploying forces, defusing flashpoints, and redistributing burdens. These policies can reduce the risk that a declining power will find itself embroiled in a costly foreign conflict, all while bolstering deterrence at strongpoints closer to home. Declining powers rely on a mix of domestic and international policies of retrenchment, but the mix varies based on the depth of decline. Because great powers reside in a self-help world, they prefer to minimize their dependence on others. Generally, declining powers lean most on domestic policies of retrenchment, but as declines get steeper great powers will be willing to entertain riskier international policies. The depth of decline shapes not just how much states retrench, but also how states lighten their foreign policy burdens.

Third, four structural modifiers make retrenchment more or less attractive: the declining power's relative rank, the availability of allies, the interdependence of commitments, and the calculus of conquest. Great powers at the highest ranks are more hesitant to embrace retrenchment because they have larger reserves of power and are unaccustomed to negative feedback. Great powers that have access to capable allies, in contrast, will find it easier to retrench because they can shift burdens to allies with less worry about power shifts. The nature of commitments also shapes retrenchment. When commitments are thought to be interdependent, declining powers are concerned that concessions in one area encourage demands in others, making retrenchment less likely. When the conquest calculus favors defense, declining powers can retrench with less fear of predation. The upshot is that conditions are crucial catalysts.

Stated precisely, what we are trying to explain (our dependent variable) is grand strategic responses to decline, specifically the extent and form of retrenchment. The key cause driving our model (our independent variable)

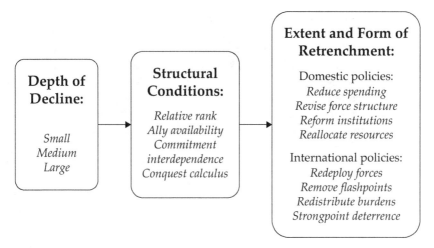

Figure 2. The logic of retrenchment

is the depth of decline. Between the two (our intervening variables) are our four structural modifiers, which, acting in concert, accelerate or decelerate the process. Figure 2 diagrams the logic of our argument.

We must make clear at the outset that our goal is descriptive. What states *tend* to do is a separate matter from what they *should* do. How attractive retrenchment is to decision makers is different from whether retrenchment brings about desirable effects, although the two may be related. We describe the logic of retrenchment, focusing on what might make retrenchment attractive to policymakers in theory. But whether retrenchment leads to its intended outcomes in practice is contingent on a whole host of factors: how well retrenchment is formulated and implemented, how allies and rivals choose to respond, and so forth. Our approach is to explain why declining powers tend to behave in predictable patterns and then to weigh and consider the merits of retrenchment compared to its rivals in the conclusion.

The rest of this chapter fleshes out the theory. In the first section, we develop the logic of why retrenchment happens. In the second section, we elaborate how retrenchment unfolds through specific domestic and international policies. And in the third section, we explain when conditions favor policies of retrenchment. We close with a summary of the theory and how it differs from its principal rivals.

Logic: Why States Retrench

The starting place for our theory is the observation that states seek security in anarchy.[2] To compete for security, states try to deter aggression and protect vital interests through a powerful military establishment, good relations with allies, and a global diplomatic presence. The tools of power politics, however, are never free.[3] Their maintenance requires considerable investment of a state's resources. There are also opportunity costs associated with spending on foreign policy: resources dedicated to ensure a state's security cannot be invested elsewhere. Ultimately, we assume that policymakers tend to be prudent and rational actors.

The crux of the decliner's dilemma is that rivals are becoming more capable and potentially threatening at the precise moment when a declining power has fewer resources to match these potential dangers. Declining powers could choose to defend existing commitments by increasing the share of resources they dedicate to foreign policy. But because decline is often driven by a dearth of domestic investment and reform, this option would accelerate negative trends and only briefly postpone the reckoning.[4] The more attractive alternative is to seek to reduce foreign policy costs while still defending vital interests against potential predators. This option necessarily curbs the ability of a state to pursue its interests and can increase risks to its security. But it has the advantage of bringing a state's strategic ambitions in line with its shrinking means while providing breathing room for potential reform and revival.

The underlying logic of retrenchment, therefore, is solvency. States, like firms, tend to go bankrupt when they budget blithely and live beyond their means, but states, unlike firms, can be subject to lethal reprisals. There is nothing wrong with pursuing bold goals when one has the resources to achieve them at an acceptable cost; yet states often find themselves overextended. When goals are too ambitious given available resources—a situation sometimes called the "Lippmann gap"[5]—states are open to predation. In the very long term, decline is inexorable, but in the near term it is anything but. To avoid insolvency, states retrench as a way to regroup and retard, if not reverse, their decline.[6]

Our chief prediction is that declining powers will promptly reduce their grand strategic ambitions proportionate to the depth of decline. The greater the decline, the more retrenchment there will be. Depth is only one way to characterize decline, of course. Declines may also vary in speed (slow versus rapid), duration (brief versus sustained), and character (economic versus military). We acknowledge these possibilities but contend that what matters most to great powers is their total base of relative national power, and that nothing captures this more than the depth of decline.

Opportunity cost is a critical factor in retrenchment. Like firms, states are capable of recovery if they make astute adjustments, but because states exist in a competitive environment, they must be careful not to waste resources when better options are available. Reorganization requires time, resources, and attention, and states need breathing room from external dangers to concentrate on needed repairs. As we saw in chapter 1, rivals have powerful incentives to be wary of declining states, but they cannot be relied upon to leave retrenching states to recuperate in undisturbed tranquility. So declining states aim to create space for internal reform at the same time they aim to seal off external vulnerabilities. Retrenchment policies can achieve this by paring back foreign policy expenditures, avoiding costly conflicts, and shifting burdens onto others. The alternatives—throwing good money after bad, resignation to continual decline, disregard of risks, unbalanced ends and means—are often much worse.

Two causal mechanisms work to push even the most hesitant of declining powers toward a strategy of retrenchment. The first is negative feedback: any state acting on an idealistic conception of what its power and goals are will soon rub up against reality.[7] Declining powers that hold fast to the status quo set themselves up for failure. In foreign policy, sagging capabilities and a sprawling defensive perimeter will court disaster. Predatory powers will probe overextended and vulnerable commitments. Tough talk will be exposed as empty boasts. Unintended crises or unnecessary conflicts will sap resources from already bare coffers. Meanwhile at home, efforts to extract resources from a diminished base will come at considerable cost. Citizens will bristle at higher revenue demands and resent the disproportionate burdens of government exactions. All the while, more pressing domestic reforms will receive limited attention and insufficient funds. The single biggest incentive to retrench is to avoid the repeated and unexpected policy failures that accompany decline.

The second incentive to change is socialization: states learn from their peers what behaviors are rewarded and punished.[8] While the range of possible foreign policies is infinite, the range of actual foreign policies is quite bounded. States are not brilliant, but they develop a fairly good idea of what policies work. Because states with good policies tend to prosper while those with bad policies suffer, states generally stick to the straight and narrow. Here retrenchment affords an opportunity to emulate—and enhance—the best practices of rivals.[9] Declining powers can improve their position by copying the successful technologies, institutions, and policies of others.

Our logic rests on two analytical bets. First, we claim that policymakers are purposive and pragmatic actors. That is to say they are mostly rational calculators who make reasonable judgments on available evidence and are sound evaluators of relative power.[10] This means that leaders tend to sensibly assess their environment, the resources available to them and arrayed against them, and the policy tools at their disposal. Individual opinion on these various issues will no doubt vary, but over time, as policymakers debate the issues, some approximation of an "official mind" will emerge.[11]

Critics might object that politicians are not known for their wisdom, coherence, or discipline. In the real world, motivated biases and cognitive limitations lead even the most careful policymaker to err.[12] Adding to these challenges is the fact that indicators of decline can be ambiguous, inviting wishful thinking and adherence to prior assumptions. Moreover, prospect theory finds that individuals become increasingly risk-acceptant when operating in the realm of losses.[13] For declining powers, this means leaders might be drawn to hazardous and desperate gambits, even if prudence dictates otherwise.

We agree that policymakers are not omniscient and are indeed prone to all manner of misperceptions. Yet these criticisms can be taken too far. Blunders receive disproportionate attention, in part because of their salience and because they provide useful object lessons.[14] Still, decision-making errors often represent minor deviations on an otherwise direct path toward a defensible decision. In addition, policymakers tend to be a select group, a fact that is especially true in the case of the great powers. Most are educated, experienced politicians who could not have risen to the top if not for a potent combination of political savvy and common sense. These personality traits do not insulate them from folly but can prevent the more deluded and rigid from achieving positions of authority. And policymakers in declining powers are in a unique position. Because decline is associated with an elevated risk of policy missteps and setbacks, leaders have strong incentives to shed motivated biases and choose pragmatic solutions.[15]

Second, we assume that policymakers seek first and foremost to further the national interest. Of course, few policymakers are so virtuous that they neglect all private interests, and coalitions of self-interested actors sometimes use foreign policy to advance parochial agendas. But in practice, there is strong continuity in the national interest, regardless of the particular individual or coalition in charge.[16] Security and prosperity are interests that can override domestic divisions, and even when interests are ambiguous, most policymakers view themselves as sitting above the partisan fray. The official mind favors technocratic approaches and resists being the cat's paw of narrow groups. Policymakers can use their institutional authority to shield foreign policy from untoward outside influences, and by and large leaders retain autonomy over vital foreign policy interests. For those issues that are subject to input from broader civil society, leaders use their political authority to break apart special interests, promote crosscutting cleavages, and forge compromises.

The picture that we are drawing is admittedly crude. All leaders face pressures from agents abroad, domestic rivals, and their own political base.[17] Bureaucracies are not merely the stewards of enlightened public policy, but also servants of their own interests, which they can pursue to the detriment of the common good.[18] States are not black boxes. Indeed, in the next section, we discuss how retrenchment provides policymakers with opportunities to tame domestic interests. But all theories simplify, and ours assumes that policymakers tend to operate with a common purpose more often than not. Domestic divisions exist, but the band of disagreement tends to be narrow and the incentives for compromise considerable.

More to the point, we have good reason to believe that domestic fissures will be least relevant in precisely the types of cases we are examining—declining powers. As threats grow more severe, the incentives to transcend domestic divisions strengthen.[19] Sometimes states choose irresponsibly or act incoherently, but usually in the near term. Imprudence usually elicits pushback from the international system, and this rebuke tends to chastise factions until they return to a soberer path. Both at home and abroad, negative feedback makes plain the considerable risks states run when they ignore structural pressures.

Forms: How States Retrench

The overriding goal of retrenchment is to avoid the negative consequences of decline. In the short run, this involves minimizing the security risks associated with the rise of new challengers and persistent gaps between ends and means. Over the long haul, retrenchment aims to slow—and reverse—the erosion of relative power. But there is no retrenchment pill to pop at the onset of decline symptoms: it is a mix of medicines, whose dosage and combinations depend on the patient. The prior section made the case that the depth of decline is the central factor to consider when treating decline. This section looks at the specific treatments within a great power's reach.

We divide retrenchment policies into two categories: domestic and international. The main domestic retrenchment policies are to reduce military spending, revise force structure, and reform outmoded institutions, while reallocating resources toward more productive investments. The key international retrenchment policies are to defuse potential flashpoints, revamp global posture, and shift burdens to allies. These policies can reduce extraneous and expensive commitments, while helping to free up resources to bolster deterrence at essential strongpoints. In the real world, specific policies from these two categories can be employed in tandem, but for clarity we discuss them separately.

DOMESTIC POLICIES

Retrenchment begins at home. Because decline is usually driven by internal factors, like an underperforming economy or military, the most reliable road to recovery is through domestic reforms. Internal reforms also have the benefit of relying less on others, and so are more attractive than measures that depend on the reciprocity of allies or adversaries.

There are four domestic options available to declining powers. First, declining states can reduce spending on the military and foreign affairs. This is one of the most obvious and most difficult courses that retrenchment can take. There is nothing inherently wrong with debt; many countries were built on it. But high and sustained debt undermines the financial foundations of any state, and marginal government expenditures are likely to face diminishing returns. As economic circumstances revive, there will be more resources for foreign policy, debt repayment, domestic investment, or whatever a government values. But until then, declining powers can slow or reduce military expenditures, trim foreign aid, and limit subsidies to restore economic vitality and generate financial reserves. It must be stressed that, to paraphrase George Washington, excessive cuts can make a state "incompetent to every exigency."[20] For instance, after the Seven Years War, Britain made deep cuts in defense spending, leaving the country in a poor position to oppose American independence a few years later.[21]

Second, declining powers can use retrenchment to revise force structure. States may not only purchase less but also invest in different instruments. Most commonly, declining powers choose to do this through revisions to the structure of their armed forces. In some cases, this can involve shifting resources from less urgent missions to more exigent ones. A declining land power might trim allocations to its navy, for example, in favor of the army. In other cases, a declining power may accept short-term tradeoffs for longterm benefits. A state might seek to limit expenditures through greater reliance on reserves rather than active-duty troops, even if mobilization is slower. States may also alter the composition of their technological investments: investing in technologies that can substitute for labor, or, more likely, purchasing older and cheaper arms. The collective impact of shifts in force structure is to make more efficient use of scarce resources and to alter foreign policy tools to combat pressing problems. Spending wisely is just as valuable as saving wisely.

Third, declining powers can use retrenchment to reform institutions. To support expansive foreign policies, great powers rely on a complex array of bureaucracies that perform a long list of tasks. Yet over time, conditions change faster than organizations. Bureaucracies become wedded to standard operating procedures, bloated by inefficiencies, and obsessed with protecting their turf.[22] This is manifest in military institutions because they are the largest, but is no less true for other bureaucracies. Bureaucratic inertia can have baleful effects on the quality of a state's grand strategy, leading it to ignore new dangers, retain unnecessary military capabilities, and cling to ineffective policies. Decline disrupts the status quo, however, and necessitates reform.

Retrenchment can spur bureaucratic reform in a number of ways. Smaller budgets prompt bureaucracies to boost organizational efficiency and integrate new innovations. To compete for scarce resources, bureaucracies must be able to prove that their missions remain relevant and to seek ways to improve their performance. Retrenchment can also discipline bureaucracies to shed extraneous missions and focus on core competencies. Reforming bureaucracies is difficult enough in normal times, and it is especially challenging when organizations are expected to perform numerous complex and onerous jobs.[23] But retrenchment can prompt bureaucracies to prioritize between competing missions, simplify assignments, and concentrate attention and resources where they are most needed. Again, excessive parsimony starves organizations of money for research and development, training, and equipment. If taken too far, retrenchment can deprive a bureaucracy of the resources for essential tasks. But when done with proportion and purpose, frugality disrupts standard operating procedures and encourages fresh thinking.

Fourth, great powers that successfully retrench can reallocate resources to non–foreign policy pursuits. Part of grand strategy involves identifying how much revenue the state will extract and how it will allocate revenue between competing needs. States face a tradeoff between guns and butter: they must choose between committing resources to foreign policy versus domestic purposes. When these tradeoffs are acute, declining powers have a strong incentive to use retrenchment to direct resources for investment elsewhere. Governments may disburse retrenchment dividends in a number of ways: tax rebates, tax cuts, entitlement benefits, and infrastructure spending, among others. For present purposes, what matters most is not the mix of methods but the relative share of the pie that foreign policy receives and the comparative return on investment.

The extent to which foreign policy spending crowds out domestic needs varies. In some cases, defense spending can aggressively displace the civilian economy. Defense spending may require high tax rates, which limit the surplus capital available to the private sector for investment. Defense spending can increase demand for strategic materials, such as iron or steel, contributing to inflation or production bottlenecks. Defense spending can also limit other types of government spending, including education or infrastructure investments that have the potential to generate greater economic returns over the long term. The Soviet Union is a cautionary case in this regard.[24] At other times, however, the domestic economic consequences of elevated foreign policy spending will be minimal or positive. When there is substantial unused economic capacity, defense spending can stimulate the economy by utilizing untapped labor or inactive capital.[25] Foreign policy expenditures, especially military spending, can generate technological spillovers that benefit the civilian economy as a whole. In the United States, Department of Defense support helped ignite a long list of civilian industries: the internet, commercial aviation, radio, computing, microwaves, semiconductors, database management, and more.[26]

The evidence shows that guns versus butter tradeoffs are real, but vary in intensity. Studies have found that a large defense burden is associated with reduced economic output, though the relationship is contingent on the absolute level of defense spending, whether the economy is in a high or low growth cycle, and the external threat environment.[27] Along the same lines, defense spending appears linked to inflation, but much depends on whether the economy is near full employment and how defense outlays are financed.[28] Yet, in the end, the latest scholarship, by J. Paul Dunne and Nan Tian, supports "strongly the view that military spending has an adverse effect on growth."[29] Reallocated foreign policy resources can play a large part in national renewal, but only a part—the same scrutiny should be applied to domestic spending, priorities, and institutions. Yet even when retrenchment dividends are small, they can add up over long time spans and have multiplier effects, which can constitute a competitive edge.

To recap, declining powers may pursue retrenchment through a variety of domestic policy options. They can slow or reduce foreign policy spending, revise their force structure toward more urgent needs, and reform institutions to boost efficiency. The resources conserved through domestic retrenchment can be recycled to reduce debt burdens or invested in more profitable pursuits. Done well, these approaches can keep expenditures down, without sacrificing effectiveness. Declining powers that ignore opportunities to retrench at home often run severe risks. Excessive military spending can cause chronic underinvestment, spiraling inflation, and sluggish economic growth. Mismatched investments can result in militaries that are poorly structured to accomplish needed missions. Unwarranted deference to ossified bureaucracies can lead to logrolling, duplication, clumsy coordination, and shoddy implementation. More broadly, excessive debt and the misallocation of resources can have deleterious consequences on economic health.

INTERNATIONAL POLICIES

Without policies to screen domestic reforms from international intrusions, retrenchment would be handicapped. Shifts in foreign policy must not antagonize adversaries, alarm allies, or disturb domestic tranquility. Four policies fit the description of decreasing commitments while limiting risks. They are redeploying forces, removing flashpoints, redistributing burdens, and bolstering deterrence at select strongpoints.

First, declining powers can redeploy forces. Large standing armies are expensive—particularly when stationed far away—so reducing forward deployed forces can save hefty sums. In some cases, these savings can be realized by abandoning inessential commitments. But more often, a declining power will attempt to defend its commitments with fewer, less expensive forces. There are a variety of techniques that fall under this rubric. Declining powers may make more use of rapid reaction forces that can quickly reinforce threatened possessions. By definition, these forces cannot respond as quickly as forward-deployed forces and are ill suited to fend off *faits accomplis*, but they bring the benefits of a less provocative, less rigid, and less expensive defense.[30] Such forces allow declining powers to move like expert fencers, giving ground to retain flexibility and strike home when an opponent overreaches.[31] Declining powers may also employ tripwire forces, which, though smaller than previous garrisons, may nevertheless credibly signal a willingness to defend exposed positions. Alternatively, declining powers may make use of regional hubs, smaller concentrations of forward-deployed forces positioned in the vicinity of exposed commitments. In all these cases, a declining power seeks to use a modified global force posture to keep costs down while maintaining credibility.

Second, declining powers can remove potential flashpoints. Flashpoints can be useful if a state has good odds of winning crises over them at acceptable cost. But over-ambitious foreign policies spark conflicts that deplete blood, treasure, and goodwill. As a result, declining powers have a strong incentive to resolve flashpoints before they ignite. Declining powers can accomplish this in a number of ways. They can seek to negotiate mutual bargains with potential adversaries to resolve an ongoing dispute. Or they may arrange spheres of influence agreements to avoid friction. By curtailing commitments in areas of marginal interest, a declining power can limit unnecessary tensions.

The obvious obstacle here is that it may be hard for declining powers to reach stable arrangements, in part because both sides may worry that possible bargains will collapse as relative power shifts.[32] Yet as Brandon Yoder argues, pulling back from extraneous commitment sends a message to friends and enemies that a declining power seeks to reduce tensions that might otherwise get out of control. Similarly, how others respond to these overtures may also be a good gauge of their designs.[33] If a potential adversary aggressively challenges a declining power, this advertises revisionist ambitions and helps rally opposition. Taken to its extreme, efforts to defuse hostility can take the form of appeasement, in which concessions are highly asymmetric. But unless a declining power is under heavy duress, it can test the intentions of potential adversaries through a series of minor concessions.

Third, declining powers can redistribute burdens. Because of their prowess, great powers have allies and political dependencies that share their interests. Rather than create power vacuums or hand over property deeds to enemies, declining powers can manipulate these relationships to sustain a favorable distribution of power. Dependencies can be granted greater autonomy in exchange for more contributions to their own defense. Retrenching powers can transfer the responsibility for upholding regional stability to what Kyle Haynes calls "successor states."[34] These are allies that can help preserve a stable balance of power in regions where a declining power has lessened its political footprint. Contrary to the claims of some critics, reducing foreign policy burdens does not require abandoning one's allies.[35] Indeed, it is when a great power is declining that allies can become useful tools to help reduce costs and shed vulnerable commitments.

Even in the throes of decline, great powers have much to offer their friends. Declining powers can use the resources gained by retrenchment to recruit new allies and reward faithful partners. They may offer potential successors an elevated share of regional spoils or better alliance terms. A declining power can also use the prospect of regional instability to encourage existing or potential partners to do more. Because retrenching states need their partners more than before, this buttresses the credibility of their commitments. Naturally, declining powers may find that successor states lack the capabilities or resolve to stand up to aggressors, possess divergent interests concerning regional order, and may harbor revisionist intentions themselves.[36] To achieve equitable burden sharing, however, declining powers may have to accept the tradeoffs that come with giving allies a greater say.

Fourth and most important, declining powers can redistribute resources to bolster deterrence at select strongpoints. If retrenchment were simply a negative process, then declining powers would do nothing but retreat. Yet declining powers often use retrenchment to shuffle resources amongst commitments, placing priority on defending vital interests. The underlying strategy here is strongpoint defense.[37] Rather than fritter away forces maintaining a sprawling and fragile perimeter, great powers can focus on protecting crucial commitments closer to home. When capabilities are concentrated, a great power will be able to respond to potential provocations from a position of strength. Furthermore, because a great power is focused on core interests, the credibility of its security guarantees will be amplified: adversaries will understand which interests a declining power values and be more likely to believe it will pay the price to defend them. Cutting the number of commitments also simplifies the strategic challenge facing declining powers: they have fewer potential adversaries to monitor, can more easily shift resources from one brushfire to another, and can more rapidly capitalize on fluid situations and adversaries' missteps. Retrenchment is a Fabian strategy designed to outlast rising challengers.

To summarize, declining powers have a variety of options to modify their external policies as part of a strategy of retrenchment. They can revamp their global posture to enhance flexibility and lighten loads, remove potential flashpoints through negotiation or cession, and redistribute burdens to subordinates and allies alike. The resources liberated from lesser commitments can be repositioned to bolster defenses at key strongpoints and deter predators. By contrast, declining powers that cling to existing commitments face a number of dangers. Adversaries may come to question both their capability and willingness to defend a brittle perimeter. Minor disputes can escalate to dangerous tests of will in which declining powers stake their reputation to defend marginal interests. Alliance partners may doubt the credibility of existing commitments, complain about a lack of voice, and entertain exit options. In such situations, declining powers are ominously overstretched; a series of local defeats has the potential to snowball into a general catastrophe. Retrenchment has its drawbacks, but properly executed it allows declining powers to reduce costs, limit risks, and promote stability where it matters most.

PRIORITIZING POLICIES

One of the most pressing questions a declining power must answer when it chooses retrenchment is the relative emphasis placed on domestic versus international policies. In general, states residing in anarchy are thought to have strong incentives to look out for themselves. When endangered by external threats, for example, states will exhibit a strong preference for self-help: they will bolster their military capabilities first before turning to allies for assistance.[38]

An analogous distinction can be made with regard to retrenchment. Domestic policies of retrenchment are most attractive because their success is less dependent on the actions of others, and because any benefits— resources allocated to more profitable pursuits—accrue solely to the declining power. International policies of retrenchment aim to reduce burdens through foreign policy changes, such as more austere global postures or more determined efforts to defuse potential flashpoints. Overall, these policies are less attractive than their domestic counterparts; both because they are more likely to require other states to honor their promises, and because they demand a declining power to relinquish something long valued.

Because declining powers are reluctant to swallow this bitter pill, they will only do so when negative trends compel them to do so. Thus, we predict that depth of decline is the primary factor influencing how great powers mix and match domestic and international retrenchment policies. For instance, great powers experiencing shallow declines will make relatively minor adjustments and rely mostly on domestic policies. Because dangers are modest and opportunities to refashion relations with external powers are minimal, declining powers in these situations rely on self-help. They will try to ease financial burdens by spending less aggressively on defense, improving efficiency, and reforming institutions. When it comes to international policies of retrenchment, however, small decliners will generally avoid major changes to their global posture. Unless they can be disposed of quickly and cheaply, they will maintain most foreign commitments. Courting new friends and foes is likely to be seen as a gratuitous burden.

Conversely, powers suffering from deep declines will make more aggressive adjustments and favor a more expansive mix of domestic and international policies of retrenchment. Significant shifts in relative power not only prompt policymakers in declining states to entertain riskier options, but they also open up opportunities to revamp foreign relations, particularly with allies. While there remain good reasons to cut spending, reallocate resources, and reform institutions, domestic policies alone are not equal to the undertaking large decliners face. Dramatic shifts in international policies must make up the difference: reorienting global posture away from forward deployments, making concessions to allies to enlist their assistance, and negotiating with adversaries—perhaps even appeasement—to stop losses before they fester.

Wrapping up, declining powers will mix and match policies of retrenchment based on the depth of their decline. Those confronted by shallow declines will employ modest shifts in policy, focused on cutting costs and domestic reforms, while those experiencing deep declines will be willing to accept major changes, including greater burden sharing and shedding foreign commitments. Declining powers will behave like doctors treating disease: if they catch it early, they will try less invasive procedures before turning to major surgery.

Conditions: How Much States Retrench

There is no single retrenchment template, and the simple fact that a state tries retrenchment does not mean it will work. Great powers reduce their grand strategic ambitions to different degrees and in different ways depending largely on structural incentives. Yet the international system evolves over time, and great powers have to regulate their behavior accordingly. Some systemic conditions favor prompt and thorough retrenchment, while others reward slower and selective retrenchment—or no retrenchment at all. As preventive war theorists warn, retrenchment brings its own set of problems. Great powers must refine their policy to reflect not just the depth of their decline but broader structural conditions as well. When does retrenchment appear well suited to circumstances?

We focus on four conditions that affect how great powers respond to decline.[39] The first is relative rank: great powers will retrench more when they are positioned lower down the great power hierarchy because they face a wider array of potential dangers. The second is ally availability: states will retrench more when they have friends to protect shared interests. The third is commitment interdependence: great powers can pull back more when peripheral concessions are believed not to undermine core commitments. And the fourth is the conquest calculus: retrenchment comes easier when taking and holding territory is harder. When these conditions obtain, security is relatively abundant, mistrust is manageable, and the risks of retrenchment are muted.[40] We detail each condition in turn.

RELATIVE RANK

If states respond to the distribution of power, then a declining power's relative rank ought to influence its choices. States near the pinnacle of power—the top two slots in our accounting—typically have fewer rivals and deeper reservoirs of power, which buffers them from blunders. Because the hegemon and its nearest competitor are more powerful, they can accept riskier ventures, think less about foreign policy, and coddle special interests.[41] For this reason, all else being equal, declining powers of higher rank are still likely to retrench, but with less enthusiasm. Naturally, with more power comes more expansive interests, and hegemonic powers may have a vested interest in defending the international order they helped to construct.[42] Yet when confronted by actual challengers, we anticipate leading states to respond to decline with less alarm. Given their position, they may believe that they can slow or reverse decline without major grand strategic changes. Given their reserves of power and prestige, they may try to mask the extent of their decline, muddle their way through crises, and temporize with hard choices.

In comparison, lower-ranked great powers will be more alert. Because they are operating with more rivals and less slack, states further down the great power hierarchy will be more sensitive to power shifts. Crises will appear more alarming, and the consequences of foreign policy failures loom larger. Declining powers with a narrower base of national power also have fewer alternatives to retrenchment. Efforts to mask their decline will be more transparent to potential predators and coveted allies. Attempts to delay retrenchment carry greater risks, given the greater number of rivals poised to capitalize on missteps. Lower ranked powers may be a few mistakes away from losing great power privileges, and, as a consequence, policymakers will be less willing to pamper lobbies or prioritize partisan interests over national ones.

Consider two cases of decline, one involving a hegemonic challenger, the other involving a state dropping from third to fourth place. The challenger confronts only one state above it, which, geography willing, may be a threat at some remove. It has deeper pockets to resist enemies, pay off allies, and strong-arm others. It sees little need for panic and so is less inclined to retrench in general and to amend international policies in particular. In contrast, a great power declining from third to fourth position has more cause for concern and more motivation to ardently implement whatever retrenchment policies it chooses. It faces multiple rivals, which may exploit its vulnerabilities individually or collectively. Its pockets are shallow, encouraging opponents, frustrating allies, and not impressing neutrals. For a top-ranked power, retrenchment is an option; for a liminal great power, it is an imperative.

ALLY AVAILABILITY

A second structural condition that shapes the attractiveness of retrenchment is the availability of allies. When a declining power can retract its forces and hand over responsibilities for maintaining the status quo to capable allies, then retrenchment becomes more likely. This is particular true when allies are located in a different region from the declining power, share common interests with the declining power, and possess the capabilities to deter regional aggressors.[43] These types of powerful regional allies can help facilitate retrenchment because they will be more capable of balancing against potential threats using their own capabilities and need not rely on cumbersome coalitions.[44] This reduces the risk that free riding or buck-passing might wreck balancing efforts.[45] Potent regional allies also require less persuading: because they are already invested in their particular neighborhood, a declining power need not shower them with spoils to secure their assistance. Capable regional allies also provide a retrenching power with future flexibility: if regional order breaks down, regional partners can help facilitate a declining power's return.

There may be some cases, however, when declining powers cannot rely on regional powers to help protect their interests as they withdraw. In these situations, retrenchment is a more forbidding prospect. Because weak regional allies lack the capabilities to safeguard the balance of power, they are more likely to bandwagon with rising great powers.[46] A declining power may not want to pull back for fear that predatory powers will fill regional power vacuums. Even if weak powers want to balance against greedy revisionists, they may find it difficult. Weak powers must be able to overcome collective action problems and are more vulnerable to divide and rule tactics.[47] To hold together regional coalitions, a declining power may retain a more robust presence than it might wish, negating the benefits of retrenchment.

Consider two worlds: one in which a declining power has access to a regional great power ally, and one where it does not. The former world is one in which balancing behavior will prevail and challengers will be punished.[48] The strong regional ally will not only have an incentive to deter local aggressors, but also be more capable of offering opposition. In contrast, the latter world is one that more resembles Gilpin's warning about declining powers and alliances.[49] Weak states abandoned by a retrenching power will either be unable or unwilling to check predators, and bandwagoning will prevail. Weak states will tilt toward rival powers, and aggressors will face only feeble resistance from fractious local coalitions. All declining powers face strong pressures to moderate their foreign policy, but some are more willing or able to get by with a little help from their friends.

COMMITMENT INTERDEPENDENCE

The third condition that affects the likelihood of retrenchment relates to the character of a great power's international commitments. At times, great powers will have international commitments that are relatively independent.[50] When commitments are independent, great power politics resembles a ship with multiple bulkheads. Great powers evaluate the credibility of international commitments on a case-by-case basis, and concessions in one area tend not to impact the evaluation of the likelihood of concessions in other areas. In such a world, declining powers will be drawn toward retrenchment. Less valuable possessions can be divested on the periphery with minimal concerns that such moves will jeopardize related commitments or sacrifice a general reputation for toughness. Because the local balance of power is most salient in any individual crisis, a policy of strongpoint defense has a higher probability of deterring challengers.

Other times, great powers will have international commitments that appear relatively interdependent. When commitments are interdependent, international politics tends to resemble falling dominoes.[51] Great powers see issues as linked across time and space, and the present credibility of commitments in one area is directly tied to past behavior in other areas. Rival claimants evaluate disputes not just in terms of local conditions but also the global balance of power and comparable commitments. Reputation concerns come to the fore, and states often fret that concessions today will spawn more and bigger demands in the future. In this sort of world, Gilpin and Copeland's concerns regarding predatory behavior become more persuasive. Declining powers will fear that retrenchment will be viewed as clear evidence of weakness, and concessions will summon circling vultures.

There is no widely accepted explanation for when commitments might be more independent or interdependent.[52] Studies of reputation have demonstrated a tenuous link between past behavior and current reputation, implying that commitments tend to be more independent than often assumed.[53] Quantitative studies have likewise found a mixed link between past concessions and future deterrence failures, which suggests the local balance of power is more important than general reputations for toughness.[54] While the fundamental character of commitments certainly varies, we contend that individual great powers also possess unique portfolios of commitments. Some great powers possess commitments that are spread across different regions and issue areas, affording them more flexibility when retrenching. Others possess clustered commitments, making them more reluctant to retrench for fear that concessions will trigger demands for more concessions.

To illustrate, consider the case of two powers: one that possesses an overseas empire with territories stretching across multiple regions, and another that is a contiguous land empire located within a single region. A case of the former might be a great power like Great Britain, the latter one like Austria-Hungary. Other things equal, the great power with an overseas empire is much more likely to view its commitments as relatively independent from one another. A commercial interest in one region is not equivalent to a strategic interest in another. Overseas empires may still worry about cascading setbacks, but they can be more assured that a challenge in one region will not spill over into another. Land empires, by comparison, are much more likely to view commitments as interdependent. A withdrawal from one territory might directly expose the flanks of a neighboring possession. Concessions to irredentist challengers in one place can fuel similar demands by minority groups elsewhere. Retrenchment will appear to be a much more hazardous course for great powers with interlocking commitments. In a nutshell, those with dispersed commitments, such as overseas empires, will find it easier to retrench than those with concentrated commitments, such as land empires.

CONQUEST CALCULUS

A fourth and related condition that influences whether declining powers are drawn to retrenchment concerns the calculus of conquest.[55] In some situations, declining powers perceive that they are vulnerable to aggression.[56] They worry that potential predators can easily overwhelm their defenses and will reap sizable rewards from doing so. In that world, declining powers will be wary of retrenchment, for the reasons that Copeland cites. They worry that withdrawing their forces will provide tempting opportunities to potential predators.[57] When militaries can promise cheap victories, declining powers will also be drawn to preventive war, not least because they expect rising challengers to launch their own bids for hegemony.

In other situations, declining powers perceive defensive military operations to be easier.[58] When this is the case, rivalries will be perceived as much more manageable: *faits accomplis* will become more difficult, garrisons can hold out longer, and great powers will have more time to respond to aggression. All of these conditions make it easier for declining powers to retrench. The harder it is for potential expansionists to overwhelm defenders, the more declining powers will be amenable to reductions in frontline defenses. The more time declining powers have to respond to aggression, the more attractive alternative global postures such as mobile reserves and tripwire forces will be.

There is no consensus on what factors might incline states to view the calculus of conquest as favoring either the offense or defense. Some scholars contend that fighting on the defense provides inherent advantages in modern warfare, and to the extent great powers accept this claim, this will increase their willingness to retrench.[59] Others point to the decreasing prevalence of territorial conquest in international politics, which suggests a more defense-dominant, retrenchment-friendly world.[60] Yet there are no standard measures of the balance between offense and defense.[61] We accept that the prevalence of conquest can vary but choose instead to examine the vulnerability of individual powers to predation. Here we make the stark but sturdy distinction between insular and continental powers.[62] Insular powers that lack land borders with rival great powers tend to be less vulnerable to offensive actions. Because their rivals usually have to project power in order to threaten them, they will have more time and latitude to respond to aggression. Continental powers tend to be more vulnerable. Their enemies are closer at hand, and they often face multiple rivals on multiple fronts.

We expect insular powers to be most likely to pursue retrenchment in response to decline because they are more immune from attack.[63] Insular powers are less alarmed that predatory powers might be able to penetrate vulnerabilities created by retrenchment. They are less likely to face threats on several fronts and will have an easier time implementing home defense. In comparison, continental powers suffering from decline will be much more hesitant to retrench. They worry they may be on a slippery slope: any gains that rising rivals obtain as a result of retrenchment can be quickly converted into capabilities to acquire more gains. Continental powers also tend to face multiple rivals on multiple fronts, which limits their ability to shift assets from one theater to another and ties down forces needed to secure the homeland. In sum, retrenchment works best when declining powers expect offensive military operations to be self-limiting, and that means retrenchment favors insular powers.

Declining powers are trapped in a dilemma: they confront rising threats but command fewer resources relative to their competitors. Fundamentally, declining states must choose between expanding, contracting, or maintaining the overall costs of their foreign policies. As we saw in the last chapter, the decline literature has clear expectations: prompt and proportionate retrenchment is the least likely outcome. In this chapter, we built the theoretical case that the literature has it backwards.

We argued that declining powers tend to retrench because international politics is intolerant of strategic insolvency. The most important factor explaining a state's behavior is relative power: the quicker a great power falls, the more it retrenches. States that fail to retrench compromise their security, sap their credibility, and encumber their economy. We agree with domestic dysfunction theorists that the international system pressures declining states to temper their ambitions, but disagree over how often domestic dynamics upstage international incentives. Our break with preventive war theorists is nearly total. We do not think that sticking to the status quo or expanding ambitions is a prudent general response to decline, and we do not think belligerence pays relative to the alternatives.

We have tried to go beyond the literature by detailing the forms retrenchment is likely to take, distinguishing between domestic and international policies of retrenchment. Domestic options include reducing spending, restructuring forces, reforming institutions, and reallocating resources. The international choices are redeploying forces, defusing flashpoints, redistributing burdens, and bolstering deterrence. Different rates of decline do not just mean more retrenchment; they also mean different kinds of retrenchment. Small declines spur self-help policies focused on domestic adjustments. Moderate declines amplify the domestic policies but turn increasingly to international policies. Large declines call for comprehensive domestic policies and heavy reliance on international policies.

Last, we identified four structural conditions that catalyze or inhibit retrenchment: relative rank, ally availability, commitment interdependence, and the conquest calculus. Low-ranked states with strong regional allies, dispersed commitments, and insular positions will take to retrenchment more energetically than high-ranked states with weak regional allies, concentrated commitments, and continental positions. Policymakers in declining states will first look at their depth of decline but then consult the prevailing conditions to see what retrenchment policies are most fitting.

We are not structural determinists; declining powers have leeway to chart their courses, and some will do so with more skill than others. Yet we are diverging from the received wisdom because we believe that during transition times the incentives of the international system are clear, those incentives push toward peace and retrenchment, and great powers generally respond rationally to them.[64] In theory, the most common response to decline should be retrenchment. The next chapter considers whether great powers actually behave this way in practice.

The Fates of Nations

Decline by the Numbers

> Everyone hangs by a thread, at any moment the abyss may open
> beneath our feet, and yet we go out of our way to invent all sorts of
> trouble for ourselves and spoil our lives.
>
> —Ivan Turgenev

> All men are inclined to adapt themselves to present circumstances and
> to assume whatever character may be demanded by the necessities of
> the moment, so that it is difficult to distinguish the real principles of
> each, and all too often the truth is obscured. But men's past actions can
> be subjected to the test of actual facts so as to reveal the true nature of
> their policies and intentions, and then we discover where we can turn
> for gratitude, kindness, and help, and where for the contrary.
>
> —Polybius

The prevailing view on great powers is that they rise, overstretch, and fall. At the root of the fall are domestic dysfunction and strategic insolvency. States could delay the inevitable if they could check their profligate tendencies, but this is a losing battle. Domestic pathologies tend to trump international pressures, and states are often trapped in downward spirals, largely of their own making. Unable to overcome entrenched interests, they embrace excessive budgets and bloated militaries. Unwilling to shed extraneous commitments, they stumble repeatedly into crises, which escalate to war and culminate in defeat.

The first chapter noted some holes in the prevailing view, and the second developed an alternative. This chapter evaluates the competing arguments through a systematic exploration of the evidence. We develop a clear measure of decline, identify a set of cases of declining powers, and consider whether these cases differ significantly from their non-declining counterparts. Granted the present chapter can only survey cases from high altitude, and the evidence presented is only indirect. But by viewing the data from different angles, we accumulate enough evidence to corroborate some claims and undermine others. In the ensuing chapters, we dive deeper to vet the arguments more thoroughly.

Our primary finding is that great powers deal with decline by retrenching promptly and proportionately. Regardless of regime type, retrenchment is the most common response to decline, and preventive wars almost never happen during decline. Retrenchment helps great powers regain their former positions with some regularity, but states that fail to retrench never recover their rank. Although decline promotes retrenchment, the rate of decline is only a rough predictor of the extent of retrenchment. Great powers have a tendency to retrench less than might be expected given underlying power trends, but most errors are modest. Without question, our theory has anomalies, but rival views are only theories of anomalies.

Secondarily, we find that states that fall at similar rates behave similarly—there is a stepwise relationship between non-decliners, small decliners, medium decliners, and large decliners. Declining powers spend less on defense and slow the growth of military personnel more than other states. They are no more likely to form new alliances, but they are less likely to participate in disputes. We also find evidence that states refine retrenchment policies to prevailing structural conditions. While our structural modifiers have modest explanatory power on their own, collectively they perform impressively. Declining powers that are most favorably positioned have almost all retrenched.

To go about testing the arguments, the first section provides an overview of our research design. It bounds the scope of our analysis, proposes a measure of decline, describes our cases, and discusses the measurement of key variables. The second section presents our initial findings. It provides a coarse-grain overview of strategic adjustment across our sixteen cases and assesses the merits of rival theories in light of the evidence. The third section buttresses this analysis with a comparison of declining and non-declining powers across a series of quantitative indicators. All in all, the empirical record suggests that moments of decline may be fraught, but that prudence tends to prevail.

Research Design

To test theories of decline, we examine the grand strategies of sixteen declining great powers since 1870. Our main unit of analysis is the great powers. Drawing on the Correlates of War (COW) Project, we identify nine states that qualify as great powers during this period.[1] Our main independent variable is the depth of decline. As defined in the introduction, acute relative decline (or simply decline from this point on) is when a great power loses its ordinal rank for at least five years. The depth of decline measures how far a state falls relative to other great powers during the transition time. In choosing to define decline in this way, we assume that what matters most is not short-term or random oscillations of power, but sustained trends that shake up the great power pecking order.

We measure relative power by examining a state's share of gross domestic product (GDP) among the great powers. Our data come from the pioneering work of Angus Maddison and date back to 1870, the first year for which we have reliable cross-national data.[2] If a country's share of great power GDP drops a rank and remains there for at least five years, we count this as a moment of decline. To count as a great power, a state must be on the COW list, but to count as a case of decline, a great power must be above a 10 percent share of total great power GDP.

We measure the depth of decline by calculating the total decline in great power share of GDP for the five years following the shift in ordinal rankings. We categorize declines that total less than a 2 percent drop in relative share of great power GDP as small; those totaling from 2 to 4 percent as medium; and those totaling more than 4 percent as large. To take a familiar example: in 1908 Germany accounted for 15.7 percent of great power GDP, surpassing Great Britain for the first time in its history. Over the next five years, Great Britain continued to lose ground to Germany, with its share of great power GDP reduced by a total of 1.4 percent. Thus, the 1908 British case represents a moment of small decline.

No measures are perfect, even when they are the best among flawed alternatives. Though parsimonious, cross-national GDP data must be viewed with skepticism, especially over long periods of time.[3] GDP was invented as a concept relatively recently, and projecting it backwards in time is an arduous art. GDP is sensitive to the domestic division of labor, culturally specific behaviors, and regulatory environments. For some countries in the data set, we have had to estimate GDP using less reliable measures of output from specific economic sectors.[4] What constitutes international power is intricate, evolving, and in part intangible. Our rebuttal is that using GDP is an elegant and conventional approach to analyzing power. Many studies operationalize power using some measure of economic output—whether energy consumption, steel production, or GDP.[5] And GDP is the most frequently used for sterling reasons: it is arguably the most comprehensive, parsimonious, and dependable measure of economic performance. No other measure offers the historical reach, analytical objectivity, and scientific comparability of GDP.

Another concern is that GDP may not be the best measure of decline. States could care more about political, military, or cultural decline—or about some dynamic basket of these.[6] Still, these indices have not been generalized across time and space, and face objections that they are arbitrary or indeterminate. We use economic data to identify decline not because we believe that policymakers are driven only by money, but because these moments are likely to correspond with crises. No other form of power is as fungible as economic power, and it can be converted into political, military, or cultural clout. Power and plenty have been closely correlated throughout history, and sustained periods of slow or negative economic growth can have profound political consequences.[7] Other more nuanced forms of decline may also encourage retrenchment, but if there is a situation that is likely to elicit a retrenchment response, economic decline is it.

A different objection is that decision-makers may not know what the great power rankings are, much less that an ordinal transition is taking place. Many policymakers had faulty or imprecise GDP data for large stretches of time, while others had no GDP data at all.[8] Yet we assume that decision makers acted as if they had access to GDP data, or something close to it. This is not unrealistic: political elites monitor a variety of economic indicators including agricultural production, industrial output, commodity prices, tax receipts, and import and export totals. Their measures may have been imperfect, but many correspond to what we now call GDP. To validate this point, we compared Maddison's measure of GDP with Arthur Banks's cross-national indicators of national performance. Although there are limitations to the Banks data, we found that GDP was highly correlated with a country's revenues, expenditures, imports, and exports.[9] These are precisely the types of indicators political elites tend to track, which gives us confidence that policymakers' perceptions of power will correlate with GDP.[10]

A final concern is that GDP is not the optimal measure for this study. GDP, like income, is a flow measure and gauges the market value of all finished goods and services produced within a country in a given year. If money were power—and it is only somewhat so—the best measure would be national wealth, a stock measure.[11] Unfortunately, no one keeps such a measure for long periods of time. In the final analysis, however, the rank ordering depends on who makes the most, year in and year out. In any given year, a lackluster income can be compensated for by a large nest egg from prior years. Conversely, poor investment, profligate consumption, or high debt can mute the advantages of an enviable income. In this sense, GDP is a leading indicator, but one whose effect can be dampened or amplified by the national balance sheet. An advantage of focusing on ordinal transitions is that they reflect sustained trends and thus dampen the downsides of using an annual flow measure. Fundamentally, states cannot maintain their position if rivals have a persistently higher economic output.

Using GDP as a measure for relative power, we identify sixteen cases of decline since 1870, the point at which reliable cross-national figures begin for all the great powers.[12] Of the nine great powers in our sample, five underwent decline at some point in their tenure. Two great powers, Italy and Austria-Hungary, remained firmly planted in the bottom rungs of the great power ladder and never experienced ordinal transitions.[13] Two other powers, the United States and China, have not experienced decline, although the former is on pace to do so sometime in the coming decade.

Great Britain was the most experienced declining power, accounting for six of the sixteen cases. In terms of rising powers, five different states managed to eclipse a rival great power. Germany dominated this list, accounting for eight of our sixteen cases.

Our sixteen cases of decline are evenly distributed in terms of depth.[14] Six of our cases were small declines, five were medium declines, and five more were large declines. The smallest decliner, 1879 Russia, involved a cumulative drop of 0.4 percent share of great power GDP over five years. The largest decliner, 1987 Soviet Union, consisted of a cumulative loss of 9 percent share of great power GDP over five years. The 1987 Soviet Union case was a notable outlier, however: the median and modal depth of decline was a 3.2 percent share of great power GDP.

One interesting feature of our cases is that the depth of decline tends to increase in more recent cases. All six cases of small declines, for example, took place prior to the First World War. In contrast, three of the five large declines took place after the Second World War. Polarity explains much of why the depth of decline has increased over time. In 1870, for example, five great powers had more than a 10 percent share of great power GDP. In 1946, in contrast, only three great powers possessed more than a 10 percent share. Given the paucity of great powers and the lofty perches that they occupied, it is unsurprising that declines in this period involved sizable shifts.

In contrast to depth, our sixteen cases of decline are not evenly distributed across time. Eight of our cases occur in the pre–World War I period; five in the interwar period; two during the Cold War; and one in the post–Cold War period. In other words, decline itself appears to be on the decline. Once again, the most plausible explanation here seems to be the shift from a multipolar to a more bipolar balance of power in the international system. During the Cold War, only three great powers other than the United States or Soviet Union ever managed to achieve shares greater than 10 percent of great power GDP, and no more than two did so at the same time. Since there are fewer great powers able to challenge on the global stage, moments of decline occur less often.

There are two ways to critique the number of our cases: one is that we have too many. Only one of our cases, 1872 United Kingdom, involves a hegemon being eclipsed by a rising challenger. Because of the impressive economic performance of the United States since 1872, no other hegemonic transitions occurred. A critic could object that this makes most of our cases irrelevant to hegemonic stability theory in general and the Sino-American transition in particular. We think that would be a big mistake. For one, it would be dangerous to focus on the top dyad when great power dynamics are systemic. For another, no theory is as hegemon-centric as the critic's case implies. Although preventive war theorists focus on the hegemon, they are promiscuous in their case selection, not just focusing on the top two powers in the system. Robert Gilpin, for instance, applies his logic to the Goths, Venice, and Austria-Hungary.[15] Lastly, there are solid reasons to suspect that hegemons are more alike than different from lesser great powers during decline, and lopping off non-hegemonic cases would obscure the patterns that studying all great power declines could teach us.

A benefit of our universe of cases is that it reveals the systemic dynamics of decline. Though we occasionally check dyadic relations to test rival views, our theory is systemic and our empirical strategies are positioned to observe the interplay between the great powers. Nearly all of our cases involve an ordinal shift from the second or third position in the great power rankings. Of the thirteen declines involving second or third ranked powers, eleven involve rival European great powers. So close together, these secondary power transitions will be highly salient to the participants, though they did not involve a hegemon and rising challenger, and may help illuminate future transitions.

Alternatively, it could be objected that we have too few cases. No selection criteria cast so fine a net that they catch all the cases of interest, and ours are no exception. A great power that experiences a sustained decrease in relative power, yet does not trade places with another power, would not appear in our cases. We accept this limitation, but choose to focus on ordinal transitions because they are most likely to prompt a response from a declining power. The emergence of a new geopolitical peer is hard to ignore and often creates security challenges that declining powers are compelled to address. It is also possible that policymakers may believe their state is in decline, even when our metrics indicate it is not. Yet that would mean leaders, selected for their political perceptiveness, were frequently out of touch with the most basic reading of relative power. The compensatory virtues of our method are that it does not rely on our own arbitrary assessments, and produces a list of plausible cases, many of which are thought archetypal.

Our primary dependent variable is the grand strategic response of declining great powers, which can fall into one of three categories. First, declining powers can expand the costs of their foreign policy. They can increase the pace of their military spending and accelerate the growth of their military. They can negotiate or strengthen offensive alliances aimed at particular targets. They can initiate fresh diplomatic crises and espouse policies that heighten the risk of war. Second, declining powers can maintain their existing foreign policy commitments in an attempt to preserve the status quo. They can continue present trends in terms of military spending and the size of their military. They can honor old alliance commitments, but not contract new ones. They can respond to potential crises in much the same manner as they have in the past. Third, declining powers can retrench and reduce their foreign policy burdens. They can slow the pace of their military spending and decelerate the expansion of their military. They can negotiate new defensive alliances to help protect vulnerable commitments. They can seek to minimize their participation in international crises, and find peaceful ways to settle those that do break out.

In practice, measuring the extent to which a great power expands or contracts its foreign policy commitments is difficult. Great powers can follow ambiguous policies, whose intent is difficult to discern. They may adopt ambivalent policies, which are pacific in some regions, but belligerent in others. Their policies may vacillate as objectives shift, assessments change, or new options become available. Even policies that achieve their objectives in seemingly reasonable ways may appear more planned and coherent than they actually were. For all these reasons, we must evaluate any shift in a great power's grand strategy with care.

Our solutions to these problems are caution and crosschecking. We use a mixture of qualitative and quantitative measures to track grand strategic adjustments over time. In terms of timing, we focus on the five years before and five years after an ordinal transition. Given our description of policymakers as rational, purposive pragmatists, this is a fair wager. Great powers helmed by far-sighted and savvy policymakers may be able to anticipate an ordinal transition and modify their policies earlier. Those with more myopic and stubborn leaders may change course only in the wake of disastrous events after rivals have overtaken them. We are agnostic as to whether great powers react at the outset, halfway through, or near the end of their decline. What matters more is whether policymakers modify their strategic approach with some proximity to the onset of decline. If strategic adjustment never takes place, or only takes place a decade or more after the fact, this would call our theory into question.

Qualitatively, we examine the foreign policy record of each of our sixteen cases for clear evidence of either the expansion or contraction of grand strategic ambitions. To keep the subject tractable, we zero in on the policy choices great powers make in the military and diplomatic spheres. For military policy, we track trends in defense spending and military manpower. How much are states spending on defense compared to previous years? We also investigate how states allocate military resources. Do they prioritize investments in certain types of capabilities? We record how states deploy their military assets. Do they position them abroad or closer to home? For diplomatic policy, we consider how a state manages its interests across regions important to its foreign policy. Which interests and which regions are stressed? We also assess the character of a great power's alliance commitments. Does it negotiate new agreements, with whom, and to what ends? We also study how a great power behaves in crises. Does it choose to confront or negotiate with rivals? What risks does it run in disputes and what settlements is it willing to accept?

We supplement these qualitative assessments with a variety of quantitative indicators. The first is the annual change in military expenditure and personnel in the declining power.[16] Combined with a qualitative analysis of acquisition, training, doctrine, and deployment, this allows us to measure military responses to decline. The second is the number of new alliance agreements signed by a declining power.[17] We couple our overview of alliances with a qualitative assessment of the substance of the agreements and how new agreements fit in a state's broader alliance portfolio. This allows us to unpack the diplomatic responses to decline. Third, we survey declining powers' behavior in militarized interstate disputes.[18] We examine how often declining powers participate and initiate disputes, as well as how far these disputes escalate. We combine this analysis with a qualitative assessment of the goals and strategies used during disputes and the outcomes of these disputes. This allows us to develop a general sense of the role of force during decline.

Our dependent variable is inescapably controversial. Great powers sometimes move forward and backward simultaneously across various spheres; these problems are inherent in any study of grand strategy. Our proxy measures are also imperfect: states reduce their military forces and contract alliances for many reasons, only some of which are the result of shifts in power. We seek to minimize these issues through transparency. Reasonable people might disagree on how to interpret a state's policy responses. We welcome these disputes, code the debatable cases within a range, and report our findings within these parameters. We include detailed information about the coding of all sixteen of our cases in an online appendix.[19]

It is very important to note that our assessments are descriptive and comparative, not normative. Though previous scholarship graded foreign policies against the threats they faced—frequently scoring them as over- or under-reacting—we take a different tack.[20] While evaluating the efficacy of foreign policy strategies is a useful exercise, for present purposes we prefer to judge foreign policies with comparable cases. The issue is not one of better or worse policies, but a relative increase or decrease in grand strategic ambition. This commitment to description brings diagnostic benefits: it sidesteps hindsight bias, groups like cases, and provides yardsticks to measure how far from the mean anomalies are.

Initial Findings

The pessimistic view of decline receives little support. A complete coding of the dependent variable for all sixteen cases of decline can be found in table 1 in chapter 1. Against arguments that retrenchment is rare, we find that declining powers retrenched in at least ten and at most thirteen of our sixteen cases, a range of 63–81 percent. On any accounting, the majority of declining powers began to retrench immediately before or shortly after their ordinal transition. We further find that great powers maintained policies of the status quo in at least two and at most five of our sixteen cases (a range of 13–31 percent). This finding suggests domestic interests can constrain retrenchment, but only in unusual circumstances. We also find that declining powers rarely take up policies of expansion. We find unambiguous evidence of expansion in only one of our sixteen cases: 1931 Germany. Aggressive responses to decline appear to be the exception, rather than the rule.

DECLINE AND PREVENTIVE WAR

First and foremost, we did not find much support for preventive war logic. Declining powers experienced war in 4.5 percent of their country-years, compared to 6.1 percent for non-declining powers. Of the sixteen cases, only six (38 percent) found themselves in an interstate war within five years of their ordinal transition. Two of these cases, however, concerned a declining great power clashing with a non-great power: Russia in the 1877 Russo-Turkish War, and France in the 1884 Sino-French War. Two additional cases involved a declining great power coming to blows with a rival great power, but not the one that had just overcome it in rank: Britain against China in the 1950 Korean War, and Russia versus Japan in the 1904 Russo-Japanese War. None of these cases resonates with the preventive war narrative, where a declining power seeks to preserve its rank through force.[21]

This leaves just two cases in which a declining power went to war with the rival that had either surpassed or was about to surpass it in ordinal rank: France in the 1870 Franco-Prussian War, and Britain against Germany in the Second World War. Neither fits the logic of preventive war. Otto von Bismarck instigated the Franco-Prussian War, and he did so more as a way to break the impasse in German affairs than because of worries about the growth of French power. For his part, Napoleon III was confident of victory and had his own domestic reasons for fighting.[22] More important, the timing of the conflict suggests the causal relationship may be backwards. A unified Germany overtook France in 1873, more than a year and a half after the Treaty of Frankfurt stripped France of Alsace-Lorraine and exacted a hefty indemnity. Decline appears more a consequence of defeat than a cause of war.[23] Also, it is hard to call British entry into the Second World War preventive. Britain famously aimed to avoid confrontation through appeasement, and, when it guaranteed Polish territorial integrity on the eve of war, the move was designed to deter German aggression, not elicit it.

A potential case is worth mentioning: 1908 Britain. Although the First World War falls outside our five-year window, it does so only barely and many scholars link the war to shifts in the balance of power. Yet once again, preventive war logic does not seem operative here. Britain worked to restrain the entente powers and mediate a diplomatic solution. When Germany dismissed these overtures, Britain sincerely sought to deter conflict with a series of warnings that it would intervene to defend its entente partners. We discuss this more in chapter 5, but the bottom line is that British policy was designed to avoid a clash of arms, not start one.

All told, evidence in favor of preventive war explanations is hard to come by. At best, declining powers embarked on preventive wars against rising challengers in two of the sixteen cases (13 percent). But the specifics of these two cases do not fit the specific causal processes asserted by preventive war theories. In one case, the declining power actively sought to appease the rising power. In the other case, the war itself appears to have been the cause of decline, rather than a consequence of it. Nor do declining powers appear more war prone as a group than their non-declining counterparts. Power shifts may still cause conflict, but the ways in which they do appears underspecified.

DECLINE AND DOMESTIC DECENTRALIZATION

Nor did we find much support for domestic dysfunction theories. While our sample of great powers is divided equally between democratic and non-democratic states, democracies were slightly overrepresented among declining powers, accounting for nine of our sixteen cases (56 percent).[24] Of these nine democratic decliners, six chose retrenchment and two followed status quo policies, while the remaining case is debatable. Declining democracies, in other words, opted for retrenchment in between 67 and 78 percent of the cases. In contrast, non-democratic countries were underrepresented in our sample, accounting for just four of our sixteen cases (25 percent). Of these, three clearly opted for retrenchment, while one case is ambiguous. Although the small number of cases makes comparison difficult, declining non-democracies retrenched in 75 to 100 percent of the cases. In short, a sizable majority of declining powers retrenched, regardless of regime type.

The three remaining declining powers in our sample experienced regime change during periods of decline. Two of these great powers democratized during decline: 1873 France and 1987 Soviet Union. Only one great power became more authoritarian in the midst of decline: again, 1931 Germany. There does not seem to be an obvious relationship between regime transitions and particular strategic responses, however. The Soviet Union retrenched and Germany expanded, while France is an ambiguous case. In short, great powers experiencing both acute decline and regime change retrenched between 33 percent and 66 percent of the time. In either case, the strong version of domestic dysfunction logic, which sees retrenchment as rare and gridlock common, receives little support.

RETRENCHMENT AND RECOVERY

Part of the reason why declining powers may sidestep conflict is the potential benefit of retrenchment. Here the data suggest that recovery is less likely than not, but the only road to recovery leads through retrenchment. Of the three states that failed to retrench, none ever regained its rank, whereas of the thirteen states that retrenched, six (46 percent) did so within a decade. This is not as heartening as it looks, and comes with two important caveats.

To begin with, two of the six cases regained their place after a world war. Both 1908 Britain and 1935 Britain reclaimed their rank from Germany, but only after waging wars that undermined Britain's long-term global position. Retrenchment may have set up Britain to fight better in these conflicts, a claim that is most plausible for the First World War but stretches credulity for the Second World War. Yet in either case, victory was the result of many factors, not just prewar policies of retrenchment.

Another caveat is that recovery tends to befall small decliners. Three of the four remaining rebounders are small declines totaling less than a 1 percent drop in share of great power GDP. This could imply that recovery is the byproduct of cyclical trends in GDP, and that may explain some of what is going on. Yet we believe an equally compelling explanation is that retrenchment is most effective for great powers facing small declines, because the challenge is modest and workable policy solutions are abundant. All three cases involve a great power declining in the aftermath of a costly interstate war: 1873 France after the Franco-Prussian War, 1879 Russia after the Russo-Turkish War, and 1926 Britain after the First World War. In each case, retrenchment and recovery are connected directly through policies designed to reduce foreign commitments, demobilize wartime military establishments, and revamp lagging domestic institutions.

Combined, these findings suggest that retrenching states rarely courted disaster and at least some were able to regain their prior position. Of course, even if we grant that retrenchment played a role in every example of recovery, a case that is hard to make for the wartime cases, the majority of declining powers still failed to recover their rank. Moreover, retrenchment appears most connected to recovery for declines that are relatively small. Only one state in a medium decline, 1888 Russia, recovered its rank. No great power experiencing a large decline has ever managed to do so. Even in cases where retrenchment failed to bring about recovery, however, this does not necessarily prove a preferable policy existed.[25] In many cases of decline, there were few restorative solutions available. Short of a miracle, it is hard to say what great powers such as France or the Soviet Union could have done to stay aloft, even with the benefit of hindsight. Yet when no plausible path to recover exists, retrenchment can still allow declining powers to manage growing dangers effectively. Whether retrenchment beats the alternatives is a subject we will take up in the conclusion. For now, we simply note that retrenching powers sometimes recovered their rank, but states that pursued policies of the status quo or expansion never did.

FORMS OF RETRENCHMENT

While it is clear that declining states retrench as a rule, support is mixed on the connection between depth of decline and extent of retrenchment. In five of thirteen cases of retrenchment (38 percent), declining powers matched their depth of decline to their extent of retrenchment. Another five cases (38 percent) are ambiguous, and a case can plausibly be made that a great power either retrenched too little or too much. A final three cases (23 percent) did not fit our expectations because they clearly retrenched too much or too little. So, depending on how one codes the half dozen controversial cases, depth of decline correctly predicts the extent of retrenchment somewhere from 38 to 77 percent of the cases. Though we believe the true figure to be at the higher end of this range, the low end is still a respectable performance for a single variable.

It is important to note that the cases that failed to fit our predictions did so at the margins. With one exception, none of the great powers facing large declines refused to retrench. And that exception, 1992 Japan, is easily explicable. Japan is not a normal great power; it has had to rely heavily on the United States for protection since 1945 because of its pacifist constitution. It should also be noted that none of the small decliners erred by conceding too much, too quickly. Great powers may not perceive decline perfectly, but they appear to have the capacity to judge the magnitude of their decline appropriately, and respond accordingly. Interestingly, there does not seem to be a significant difference between those great powers whose decline was driven by a fall in absolute economic output versus relative economic output: both retrenched at roughly the same rate.[26]

If there is a systematic tendency among those great powers that do not conform to our predictions, it is to retrench less than their depth of decline suggests. For those states that buck structural trends, under-retrenchment appears more common than over-retrenchment. All five of our ambiguous cases, for example, involve possible under-retrenchment. Of the three cases of retrenchment that clearly do not fit our predictions, two involve under-retrenchment. There is only a single case in our dataset, 1935 United Kingdom, where a great power appears to have retrenched more extensively than the underlying power trends would suggest was necessary. Perhaps unsurprisingly, this case has received a disproportionate amount of attention as a paradigmatic case of "under-balancing."[27] But in general, when confronted with decline, great powers appear to have strong incentives to adopt retrenchment but only modest incentives to match policies precisely to the depth of their decline. This finding may be a result of domestic pressures or measurement error, a topic we take up in the case studies.

Systemic pressures may vary across different depths of decline, but it is hard to say. Among great powers facing small declines, two unambiguously engaged in a low extent of retrenchment, while three cases are ambiguous, yielding a range of 40–100 percent. Among medium decliners, one clearly engaged in modest retrenchment, two cases were ambiguous but may have retrenched too little, while one retrenched too much, a 25–75 percent success rate. Among great powers confronted by large declines, two clearly engaged in significant retrenchment, while two clearly retrenched less than expected, a 50 percent success rate. These wide ranges make it hard to draw any strong conclusions about which declines elicit the most consistent responses.

Yet forced to choose amongst our three categories, the behavior of moderate decliners appears the most inconsistent. Here we observe only one clear case, 1888 Russia, of a declining power adjusting in a manner proportionate to its fall. Each of the other cases involves a great power arguably misreading its structural incentives and retrenching too little or too much. It is worth noting that the sole case of a declining power embracing a strategy of expansion, 1931 Germany, is drawn from our sample of moderate decliners. Our only clear case of over-retrenchment, 1935 United Kingdom, is also drawn from the ranks of the medium decliners. It may be that these two cases are outliers, the product of distinctive historical circumstances and structural conditions. Yet there may also be something unique about moderate decliners. When it comes to assessment, moderate decliners may be unsure whether they are experiencing a minor downturn or the early stages of a deep depression. When it comes to solutions, moderate decliners may waver between minor changes that carry fewer risks and major overhauls that promise greater rewards. The evidence suggests that great powers have a fair, but not stellar, record of matching retrenchment to depth of decline.

CONDITIONS AND RETRENCHMENT

We found mixed support for the impact of our four structural conditions on retrenchment when viewed in isolation, but stronger support when they are viewed together. None of the conditions proved dispositive alone, though some performed better than others. Consider the relative rank of the declining power. Between 63 and 75 percent of the eight cases of great powers declining from the first or second rank were coded as retrenchment. In contrast, between 75 and 88 percent of the great powers that declined from the third or fourth rank were coded as retrenchment. In addition, of the six declining powers with concentrated commitments, 66 percent were coded as having retrenched. By way of comparison, between 70 and 90 percent of declining powers with dispersed commitments were coded as having retrenched. As we predicted, both lower ranked great powers and great powers with dispersed commitments appear more likely to retrench, but the impact of each of these conditions is modest and depends on the coding of ambiguous cases.

Support for our other two conditions was less apparent. Of the six cases of declining powers with weak allies, somewhere between 50 and 83 percent were coded as having retrenched, compared with 80 percent for declining powers with strong allies. Plus, declining powers with a high degree of vulnerability retrenched in between 66 and 77 percent of the cases, compared to 71 to 85 percent for declining powers with a low degree of vulnerability. Declining powers with strong allies and those with low vulnerability appear slightly more likely to retrench, but the difference is entirely dependent on how one resolves borderline cases. No condition alone contributes extra-ordinarily to retrenchment.

The picture changes with all four conditions together. Here we developed a composite index that ranked great powers based on how many of their structural conditions favored retrenchment. Great powers that had between zero and two conditions favoring retrenchment were considered least likely to retrench, while those that had three or four conditions favoring retrenchment were considered most likely to retrench. Combined, of the nine great powers in unfavorable structural conditions, between 44 and 67 percent retrenched. In contrast, all seven—100 percent—of the great powers in favorable structural conditions chose to retrench.

There are a couple of potential explanations for this. The most straight-forward is that the index captures cross-national variation in geopolitical positions accurately. Of the seven cases of declining powers with favorable conditions, five involve Britain (1908, 1926, 1930, 1935, 1946) and all re-trenched. This suggests that there may be something inherent in Britain's insular position and dispersed imperial commitments that tended to en-courage retrenchment. Still, it is hard to tease that out from the role of do-mestic institutions and political culture.

An equally plausible explanation is that structural conditions shift together over time and prompt policymakers to act. As a country falls in the pecking order, acquires strong allies, or otherwise finds itself confronted by novel structural conditions, its willingness to choose retrenchment when confronted by decline increases. The French experience with decline offers potential evi-dence of this dynamic: the two cases that took place in unfavorable structural conditions were coded as low-no (1873) and no retrenchment (1883), while the two cases that took place in favorable conditions were coded as medium-low (1893) and medium (1925). The overarching point is that a state's relative power matters a great deal, but shifting conditions also contribute.

Descriptive Statistics

A coarse-grained overview offers general support for our predictions. Retrenchment is not rare; it is the most common response to decline. But to be sure about this finding, we need to verify it against quantitative proxies for strategic adjustment. The goal is to find out whether declining powers differed significantly from their non-declining counterparts.

We compared declining powers to their non-declining counterparts across six primary indicators.[28] These included the annual change in military expenditures, annual change in size of military personnel, total number of new defensive agreements signed, total number of militarized disputes in which a great power participates, total number of disputes initiated, and average level of hostility for militarized disputes in which a great power participates. A full summary of these indicators can be found in table 2.

Table 2 Decline and leading indicators

Country year	Depth of decline	Military expenditure (annual average change)	Military personnel (annual average change)	New alliances (annual average)	Militarized disputes (annual average)	Militarized disputes initiated (annual average)	Militarized disputes hostility (average per dispute)
Small							
1879 Russia	0.36	4.7	1.1	0.2	0.5	0.2	1.9
1873 France	0.90	-5.0	10.3	0.2	0.4	0.3	3
1926 United Kingdom	0.96	-8.0	-5.1	0.3	0.9	0.6	2.9
1908 United Kingdom	1.41	-2.3	1.5	0.3	1	0.5	2.8
1872 United Kingdom	1.46	4.0	-0.3	0.3	0.5	0.4	3
1883 France	1.99	1.9	0.9	0	1	0.5	2.3
Medium							
1930 United Kingdom	2.17	3.0	-0.4	0.3	0.7	0.5	2.6
1888 Russia	3.22	2.2	-0.1	0.3	0.4	0.3	3.3
1935 United Kingdom	3.22	47.2	16.2	0.7	2.5	1.7	2.8
1893 France	3.23	0.5	2.2	0.2	1.3	1.2	3.4
1931 Germany	3.24	39.5	22.4	0.4	0.5	0.3	1.9
Large							
1925 France	4.00	2.9	-11.6	1.0	1.2	0.9	3.1
1903 Russia	4.22	16.2	8.4	0.2	1.1	1.1	3.6
1946 United Kingdom	5.54	-4.3	7.8	1.3	2.4	1.2	2.9
1992 Japan	6.32	6.8	0.2	0	1.3	0.1	1.8
1987/88 Soviet Union	9.0/10.8	-7.1	-5.6	0.5	2.5	2	3.3
Baseline great power (with world wars)	—	27.0	10.4	0.3	1.7	0.9	2.9
Baseline great power (world wars excluded)	—	9.1	2.3	0.3	1.5	0.8	2.9

For non-declining powers, we considered two baselines: one that includes data for all non-declining powers drawn from the entire period under consideration; and a second that excludes data for the world wars. The latter is a harder test for our theory because the figures for military personnel, alliance agreements, and militarized disputes are much lower with world wars excluded. But we believe that it provides a more useful test of our theory, which is not designed to explain wartime behavior.

Similarly, we considered two comparison categories for declining powers: the first includes data for all sixteen cases; the second excludes 1931 Germany and 1935 Britain, two influential outliers.[29] Including these outliers creates a harder test for our theory, but it also raises the risk that the rapid rearmament associated with Hitler would mask more germane trends. In what follows, we focus on the results that compare declining powers with outliers excluded to the baseline category that excludes world wars, because that is the most politically relevant parallel. We also cross-check our findings to see if our findings depend on our choice to compare five-year windows on either side of an ordinal transition, as compared to three-, seven-, or ten-year windows. Our findings are generally consistent across different comparison groups and different time periods, although we note discrepancies in the footnotes.

DOMESTIC POLICIES

Beginning with military expenditure, the data strongly support the claim that declining powers prefer retrenchment. The average annual increase in military spending for declining powers was 0.8 percent, compared to 9.1 percent for non-declining powers.[30] Of the sixteen cases, only three increased military spending faster than the baseline power. Two of these cases were our outliers: 1931 Germany and 1935 Britain. The other case that spent more than we expected was 1903 Russia, though this is largely driven by a one-year spike in spending during the Russo-Japanese War.[31] In total, thirteen cases (81 percent) fit our expectations with regard to military expenditures.

A similar picture emerges with military personnel. Declining powers decreased their military personnel by an average of 1.1 percent per year, compared to the baseline that increased military personnel by an average of 2.3 percent per year.[32] Only five increased the size of the militaries faster than the baseline, and two of these were 1931 Germany and 1935 Britain. The remaining three cases—1873 France, 1903 Russia, 1946 Britain—appear to be driven by wartime mobilization, where an exceptional year doubled the size of the military.[33] For both 1873 France and 1946 United Kingdom, this outlier year preceded the ordinal transition by more than two years. When these exceptional years are excluded, all three cases fall well below the baseline.[34] At a minimum, eleven cases (69 percent) conform to our

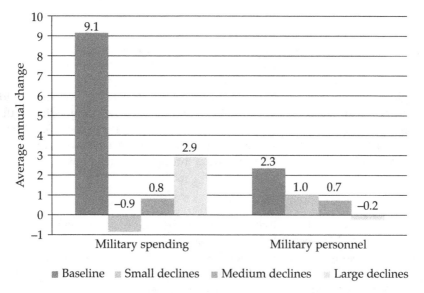

Figure 3. Depth of decline and domestic policies

Note: Baseline excludes figures for First and Second World Wars; figures for medium declines exclude influential outliers.

predictions regarding military personnel, and there are good reasons to believe that this number is actually higher.

Again, depth of decline only correlates somewhat with domestic policies (see figure 3). It is true that depth of decline and military personnel correspond to our predictions. Great powers facing small declines increase their military personnel by an average of 1.0 percent per year, compared to 0.7 percent for medium decliners, and –0.2 percent for large decliners.[35] The more states fall, the more they trim their military manpower. Yet military spending confounds our predictions. Although small decliners reduce military spending by an average of 0.9 percent per year, medium and large decliners increase military spending by an average of 0.8 and 2.9 percent, respectively.

Admittedly, our theory is not much help here, but our case studies are. Policymakers in all the cases feel the necessity of austerity, labor to keep down the number of regular soldiers, and cannot resist buying some of the latest kit. Yet as states decline more, they rely on reserves more, which leaves fewer regulars to deal with emergencies. To give the regulars a chance to succeed as both a rapid reaction and covering force, great powers invest in technology as a force multiplier.[36] In our medium and large case studies, dramatic increases in reserves went hand-in-hand with military modernization.

Overall, there is solid evidence for our theory with domestic policies: declining powers boost military spending and military personnel at slower rates than the average great power. Nonetheless, these comparisons are merely suggestive. How much a state chooses to spend on defense can be shaped by a whole host of other factors. Benjamin Goldsmith, for example, finds that a state's defense burden is shaped by a variety of factors including its level of economic development, economic growth, regime type, region, and whether it is involved in civil or interstate wars.[37] When we add a dummy variable for decline into Goldsmith's preferred model, the coefficients are negative and statistically significant.[38] This finding suggests that, controlling for other factors, declining great powers face particularly strong incentives to reduce the defense burden through retrenchment.

INTERNATIONAL POLICIES

This section analyzes two proxies for the international policies of retrenchment: alliances and dispute behavior. With respect to alliances, the evidence does not line up with our theoretical predictions. Declining powers sign an average of 0.32 new alliance agreements each year, compared with 0.27 new agreements for their non-declining counterparts, a difference that lacks statistical significance.[39] Of the sixteen cases, only five (31 percent) signed more alliances than the baseline power, while five signed as many, and six signed fewer. Contrary to our expectations, declining powers appear no more likely than their non-declining counterparts to reach out to new alliance partners to help cushion their fall in relative power.

Beneath this negative result, however, lies an interesting pattern. While moderate decliners sign an average of 0.22 new agreements, roughly the same as non-declining powers, those facing large declines penned an average of 0.58 new agreements, more than double the non-declining average.[40] Out of the five great powers facing large declines, three signed more alliances on average than the baseline power. One case, the 1946 United Kingdom, signed an average of 1.27 agreements per year, nearly four times that of the baseline power. While all declining powers do not appear more likely to sign defensive alliances, those confronted by large declines appear particularly eager to rely on new allies or partners. It may be that declining powers lean more on old allies or cooperate informally, which our measure would have trouble picking up on. Yet the snapshots of the alliance data are broadly consistent with the logic of self-help under anarchy: states prefer not to rely on others unless in desperate situations. Our findings may also be showcasing a tool declining powers can use to manage the impact of large falls. The interlocking alliance agreements embodied in institutions such as the British Commonwealth or the Commonwealth of Independent States can be seen as an effort by large decliners to brace a fall by reinforcing relationships with former possessions.[41]

An additional finding that is inconsistent with our expectations concerns the alliance behavior of small decliners. In particular, small decliners signed

THE FATES OF NATIONS

an average of 0.20 new alliance agreements, a number that is smaller than that for non-declining powers.[42] Indeed, four of our six small decliners signed fewer alliance agreements than the great power baseline. While we expected small decliners to be hesitant to rely on international policies of retrenchment, we did not expect them to be overly cautious in their behavior toward prospective allies. There are a number of possible explanations for this anomalous finding. Small decliners may have fears of being entrapped by new alliance partners, given their diminished resources. They may worry that negotiating a new alliance will alert rivals to their flagging fortunes, exposing them to predation. Whichever explanation one accepts, our theory does not predict the extreme hesitancy of small decliners when it comes to alliances.

With respect to disputes, the evidence is compelling, but with some intriguing wrinkles. Declining powers participated in an average of 1.1 militarized interstate disputes each year, compared to 1.5 disputes for the baseline power.[43] Among our sixteen cases of declining powers, only three participated in more average militarized disputes per year than their non-declining counterparts. One of these cases, 1935 United Kingdom, is an obvious outlier due to the outbreak of the Second World War.[44] Somewhat tellingly, the other two dispute-prone cases involved great powers in large declines. The 1946 United Kingdom and 1987 Soviet Union cases averaged 2.4 and 2.5 militarized disputes per year respectively, one-and-a-half times more than the baseline power. Leaving aside these anomalous cases for the moment, thirteen of the sixteen cases of declining powers (81 percent) fit our expectations with regard to participation in militarized interstate disputes.

The picture is somewhat murkier, however, with regard to the initiation of militarized interstate disputes. Here there does not appear to be an obvious difference between the willingness of declining powers and non-declining great powers to seek out new disputes. Declining powers initiate an average of 0.73 disputes per year, compared to 0.81 disputes for the baseline, a difference that does not achieve statistical significance.[45] Out of our sixteen cases, six declining powers initiated more militarized disputes on average than the baseline power. This includes the three dispute-prone cases noted above: 1935 and 1946 United Kingdom, and 1987 Soviet Union. But it also includes one medium decliner, 1893 France, and two additional large decliners, 1925 France and 1903 Russia. While our expectation that declining powers will avoid initiating militarized disputes holds for ten of the sixteen cases (63 percent), there is a noticeable difference across different depths of decline. All six of the small decliners are below the great power baseline for average disputes initiated, while four of the five large decliners are above the baseline.

Once declining powers get involved in a dispute, are they more likely to escalate? The evidence suggests not. Declining powers had an average hostility in their militarized disputes of 2.8, which compares to 2.9 for the baseline, a difference that is not statistically significant.[46] Out of our sixteen cases of declining powers, seven had an average hostility that lay above the baseline in their militarized disputes, whereas seven had an average hostility that lay below the baseline. One partial exception to this null result may be small decliners, who had an average dispute hostility of 2.6. But in general, the typical behavior of declining powers appears to resemble that of their non-declining counterparts. They tend to display or threaten to display force, rather than actually use it.

Collectively, these three sets of findings provide sturdy evidence against preventive war theories. Far from being more likely to lash out aggressively, declining powers appear no more likely to initiate militarized disputes than the average power. Nor do declining powers appear more vulnerable to scavengers. Indeed, declining powers participate in fewer militarized disputes than their non-declining counterparts. The evidence also calls into question predictions that declining powers favor do-or-die schemes. Rather, declining powers do not get involved in disputes that escalate to higher levels of hostility than the average power.

Even if declining powers are embroiled in fewer disputes, it might be the case that they perform poorly in the disputes in which they do participate. To examine this possibility, we compared how declining and non-declining great powers differed in dispute performance.[47] Surprisingly, we found that declining targets lose just 9 percent of their disputes, compared to 23 percent for their non-declining peers.[48] We also found that declining initiators are victorious in 43 percent of the disputes they start, compared to 28 percent for their non-declining counterparts.[49] It appears that declining powers tend to select themselves into disputes they are better positioned to win. How they do this is unclear, but we suspect that retrenchment may play a role. By shedding distant commitments, declining powers avoid disputes where defeat is most likely. Conversely, by concentrating capabilities to defend vital interests, declining powers can initiate disputes from positions of strength.

The evidence provides less support, however, concerning the relationship between the depth of decline and dispute behavior. Although we expect great powers facing larger declines to be especially cautious in militarized disputes, the data point to the opposite conclusion (see figure 4). Great powers experiencing low declines participated in an average of 0.78 disputes, those experiencing medium declines participated in 0.81 disputes, and those experiencing large declines participated in 1.67 disputes a year. As the magnitude of decline increases in severity, so does that propensity of great powers to participate in and initiate militarized disputes. Moreover, large decliners are actually more belligerent than the baseline across all three indicators. They participated in more militarized disputes (1.68 versus 1.46) and initiated more militarized disputes (1.04 versus 0.81) on

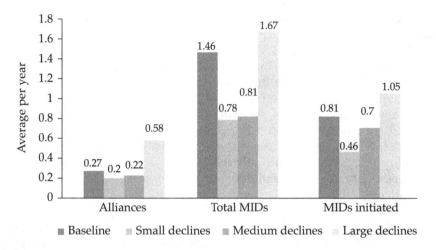

Figure 4. Depth of decline and international policies

Note: Baseline excludes figures for First and Second World Wars; figures for medium declines exclude influential outliers.

average than the baseline power, although these differences were not statistically significant.[50] While declining powers as a whole are more pacific, large decliners appear to be a noteworthy exception to this rule.

This finding represents an anomaly for our theory. Although we expected the largest declines to prompt the greatest caution, the reverse appears to be the case. Our theory does not provide clear guidance here, but there are a number of plausible explanations for these findings. One possibility is that large decliners have a harder time managing credibility crises because their Lippmann gaps are bigger. Large declines are more visible and open up more opportunities for exploitation, either by great powers rivals or former client states. The spike in militarized disputes between newly independent Russia and its former satellite states in the early 1990s, for example, can be seen as an example of this dynamic. Another possibility is that large decliners are more accident prone because they have to act in fast, drastic fashion. They tend to have less slack in terms of resources, shorter periods of time to affect reforms, and larger external threats to manage. With few attractive options, policymakers may attempt to bluff their way out of deep problems, before accepting the inevitable need for moderation. Tsar Nicholas II's mercurial behavior in the run-up to the Russo-Japanese War, and then his rapid retreat afterwards, can be seen as a possible example of this dynamic. A third possibility is that large declines necessitate home defense. Retrenchment refocuses large decliners from marginal problems in the periphery to existential threats closer to home, which often require hard-nosed crisis diplomacy. Despite efforts to lighten its imperial defense burdens, for example, postwar Britain experienced a notable uptick in militarized disputes, due in large part to the Cold War confrontation in Europe.

Altogether, the evidence on international policies provides equivocal support for our explanation. Declining powers do not appear more likely to sign new defensive alliances, but they do appear to be more pacific in terms of militarized disputes. As in the case of defense spending, however, there is an abundance of factors associated with the propensity of states to become embroiled in militarized disputes. John Oneal and Bruce Russett, for example, find strong evidence that a combination of geopolitical variables (including the contiguity, distance, shared alliance membership, and the balance of military capabilities) and liberal variables (including trade dependence, joint democracy, and shared membership in international organizations) shape the probability of dispute participation. When we added a dummy variable for decline into Oneal and Russet's model, however, the coefficient was negative and statistically significant.[51] This suggests that dyads with at least one declining power have a lower probability of experiencing a dispute.[52] Whether this finding holds because declining powers use retrenchment to minimize flashpoints and bolster deterrence or because of other causal mechanisms is unclear. But there is scant evidence for preventive war logic: on the whole, decline does not appear to be associated with an elevated risk of conflict. Rather, moments of ordinal transition increase the probability of peace, even when we control for additional factors.

RISING CHALLENGERS: BIDING TIME OR EAGER EXPANSIONISTS?

To this point, we have focused on declining powers. But this raises an obvious question: how do rising powers respond to power shifts? The question divides scholars. Some, like Jack Snyder, assert that rising powers have an especially difficult time resisting expansion.[53] Although they benefit from the status quo, rising powers resent the lack of prestige they enjoy within the existing order. Rapid growth can also generate domestic unrest, which leaders seek to manage through diversionary actions. Others, like John Ikenberry, contend that rising powers have few incentives to challenge the reigning order.[54] Because they are already benefiting from the status quo, rising powers will bide their time and avoid provocative policies. By enmeshing themselves in international institutions, rising powers can also gain access to the benefits of the existing global order, reassure other states that their ascent will be peaceful, and prevent the emergence of hostile balancing coalitions.

The theoretical framework we presented in the previous chapter provides no *a priori* reason to prefer either of these explanations. It makes sense that as great powers accumulate more power they would expand their grand strategic ambitions. Still, one of the premises of our argument is that expansion is difficult and provides circumscribed benefits. Bids for hegemony will be rare because they almost never succeed.[55] Rising powers may engage in opportunistic expansion in favorable local circumstances, but, by and large, structural incentives will encourage them to maintain moderate policies. When declining powers are willing to accommodate the legitimate interests of rising powers, then the latter have few incentives to challenge the existing international order using force.

Given our focus on declining powers, we do not examine these competing theories in any depth. But a cursory examination of the descriptive statistics yields some counterintuitive findings. Contra Ikenberry, rising powers are not resting securely, gazing lazily at their watches, luxuriating in a bountiful status quo. They increase their military spending by an average of 11.5 percent per year, compared to 7.9 percent for the non-rising baseline,[56] and expand their military personnel by an average of 3.6 percent per year, compared to 1.8 percent for the non-rising baseline.[57] Neither of these differences achieved statistical significance, however, and the differences are less noticeable when we exclude declining powers from our baseline. In terms of military spending and personnel, though, rising powers appear to have a modest preference for expansionist policies.

Yet contra Snyder, rising powers appear to favor accommodating foreign policies. They sign an average of 0.38 new defensive agreements per year, compared to 0.27 for the baseline.[58] They participate in an average of 0.92 disputes per year, compared to 1.48 for the baseline.[59] Rising powers also initiated fewer disputes, averaging just 0.57 disputes initiated per year, compared to 0.82 for the baseline.[60] Both of these figures were not only smaller than the baseline, but smaller than declining powers too. While we expected declining powers to be eager to sign alliances and avoid disputes, the evidence suggests that it is rising powers that are the most enthusiastic. Of course it may be that rising powers are signing these pacts to defend on one flank while attacking on another, or that rising powers use alliances to prevent counterbalancing coalitions, or that they favor new allies while declining powers prefer old ones. Whatever the case, the data complicate our perception of rising powers.

The overall picture is one of rising powers ready for trouble but generally avoiding it. Because we do not examine the actual policies of rising powers in detail, these findings are tentative. Nonetheless, the results are strong enough to venture some preliminary observations. Unfortunately for power transition theories, what rising powers seem most intent on preventing is war. The more common response to ordinal transitions appears to be neither gambling nor glory seeking, but wily wariness. Although declining powers worry about their flagging fortunes, they seek to smooth their descent through retrenchment at home and abroad. While rising powers flex their muscles through military investments, their foreign policies appear designed to legitimate their rise through the signing of new alliances and moderation in militarized disputes. Both rising and declining powers display pervasive caution, and transition periods are in effect less dangerous than non-transition periods.

Rising powers and declining powers, in this way, have more in common than is often thought. Declining powers fear developments that might hasten their descent before reforms resurrect their fortunes. Rising powers fret that their ascendancy may be choked by domestic instability or balancing coalitions before they peak. Neither wishes to see the status quo disrupted in abrupt or destabilizing ways. Both hope that conflicts of interest can be resolved peacefully, even though each mistrusts the other. The effect of power shifts on great powers appears analogous to that of a rainstorm on drivers: as visibility declines and the risk of accidents increases, people reduce their speed. While rising and declining powers face much different strategic challenges, both seek to manage uncertainty through moderation.

If these findings are correct, then the implication is that it is not shifts in power but moments of stability that are unduly dangerous. It is when great powers are confident in their power that they might be tempted to pick fights or complacently collide with others.[61] It is at these moments, after rising powers have ascended to the top, that they might be most tempted to embark on revisionist efforts to remake the international order. The certainty produced by the consolidation of power might be equally—if not more— dangerous than uncertainty and insecurity generated by power shifts.

This chapter has tested competing logics of how great powers respond to decline against the universe of modern cases. The findings are dramatic: declining powers are not doomed to downward spirals or destructive conflagrations. They are neither paralyzed by domestic divisions nor tempted by preventive war. Instead, retrenchment is the most common response to decline. Great powers are more likely to reduce the pace of defense spending and decrease standing militaries than other great powers. They also participate in fewer militarized disputes, and do not escalate these disputes to higher levels of hostility. The sole exception to this is alliances, where only large decliners are more solicitous of new allies than other powers.

Preventive war theories find paltry support. The overwhelming majority of declining powers do not participate in interstate wars. Those that do fight tend to do so with other great powers or minor powers, not those that eclipsed them in ordinal rank. For the small handful of cases that did fight their ordinal challenger, the casual mechanisms posited by preventive war theories do not appear to be operative. Rather than provoking conflicts, declining powers sought to avert potential clashes. There is scant evidence of declining powers engaging in provocative gambles to preserve their place.

Domestic dysfunction explanations also receive limited support. Declining powers tend to choose retrenchment regardless of regime type. Whether democratic or autocratic, declining powers have strong incentives to moderate their foreign policies. The anomaly in these findings concerns regimes in transition. Although the sample of declining powers experiencing regime change is small, their outcomes are highly variable: one opted to retrench, one to expand, a third was ambiguous. It may be that domestic tranquility, rather than a regime type, matters more for strategic adjustment.

Retrenchment is not only the most common response to decline; it is also the one with the greatest chance of success. Although the majority of declining powers failed to recover their ordinal rank, only those that chose a strategy of retrenchment were able to do so. Nevertheless, this is not as optimistic as it sounds. In some cases, retrenching powers only regained their rank after a world war. Retrenchment may have helped delay the onset of these conflicts, or put declining powers in the position to prevail, but these cases often look like pyrrhic victories. In other cases, retrenching powers recovered their rank through peacetime reforms. But almost all of these cases involved great powers experiencing small, more manageable declines. More often, retrenchment allowed a declining great power to limit the dangers associated with decline, rather than reclaim its former glory.

This may be a good vantage point to see why our study differs from its predecessors. One obvious way is definitional: we identify retrenchment as any intentional reduction in the overall costs of a state's foreign policy while others think of it as a particular grand strategy.[62] Another is focus. As we discussed above, earlier studies lavished attention on hegemonic powers and tended to consider transitions from a dyadic perspective; we do not think hegemonic transitions so unique and prefer a more systemic view.[63] Still another is normative. Previous scholarship judged grand strategic adjustment by whether states got the "right" outcome, but that underrates uncertainty.[64] Sometimes leaders get lucky or unlucky. Sometimes there may be no appealing options. Rather than judge grand strategies in hindsight, we measure state responses by their distance from an average of comparable cases. Perhaps the most important difference is methodological. Prior work tended to select cases based on the dependent variable, finding major conflicts first, then working backward to find a power transition explanation for them;[65] we have no such bias.

While the relationship between decline and retrenchment is strong, however, the one between depth of decline and extent of retrenchment is less so. Here we found that great powers had a basic sense that decline was taking place, but an uneven ability to respond proportionately. Although most responded about right to power trends, the most common error was to retrench less than was expected given external trends, and this lends some credence to domestic dysfunction theories. Great powers facing small declines frequently muddled through with the status quo, while those facing large declines often made due with minor fixes. Great powers facing moderate declines had particular problems matching their policies to their particular plight. We speculated that some of this might be due to the challenge of properly identifying moderate declines, as well as the paucity of mid-range policy options. Even then, while declining powers may have been reticent to accept their fates and reluctant to do all that was necessary, few ignored power trends altogether.

We did identify some important differences across categories of declining powers sorted by depth of decline. Small decliners tended to favor reductions in military spending over those in military personnel. They also tended to put more reliance on avoiding militarized disputes than signing new alliances. Large decliners placed greater emphasis on cuts to military personnel than military spending. They also made greater efforts to get new alliance partners, but were no more peaceful when it came to their dispute behavior. True to their name, medium decliners fell in the middle, though their actions tended to be closer to small than large decliners.

Yet on the whole, our theory of retrenchment receives the strongest support. It did the best job accounting for the general behavior of declining powers and a fair job explaining the specific form of retrenchment. Domestic dysfunction may limit the extent of retrenchment, but it does not appear to systematically prevent declining powers from engaging in strategic adjustment. Preventive war theories may help explain why large declines are somewhat more dispute prone, but this is hardly consonant with the notion that decline is a leading cause of major wars. All of this suggests that domestic dysfunction and preventive war arguments are theories of anomalies. The mechanisms they posit are plausible, just not probable. When confronted by decline, the most common response is for great powers to temper ambitions and avoid provocative policies. We also found, as a coda to these results, that preconceived notions of rising powers may need to be revised. While rising powers tend to invest in their militaries, they also seek to dissuade the emergence of balancing coalitions through new alliances and tempered behavior. States jockey fiercely for power in world politics, but during transition times, they appear to afford each other wider berths.

Studies in Revival

The moral of the story is that a loss is never the result of a single throw—nor indeed is a triumph. Success depends on seizing the opportunities of a given period, on doing so time and time again, and piling advantage on advantage.

—Fernand Braudel

Be assured, my young friend, that there's a great deal of *ruin* in a nation.

—Adam Smith

So far, we have laid out the logic for why decline leads to retrenchment and probed the universe of cases to see what state behaviors correlate with decline. At high elevation, we saw that great powers tend to respond to decline through retrenchment rather than preventive war or domestic paralysis. But the next step is to get inside the cases to see if the correlations are there for the right reasons and see what a closer view shows. In what follows, we examine six specific cases—1872 and 1908 Great Britain, 1888 and 1903 Russia, and 1893 and 1925 France—for a more detailed understanding of how states deal with decline. An overview of these cases, and their particular features, can be found in table 3.

There are a number of advantages to these particular cases. First, these cases are drawn from across all three depths of decline and showcase a spectrum of responses: 1872 and 1908 Great Britain are both small declines; 1888 Russia and 1894 France both medium declines; and 1903 Russia and 1925 France both large declines. This allows access to how decision makers in different states adapt to different pressures. If our explanation is correct, then powers that experience larger declines will be willing to retrench more aggressively than those facing smaller declines. Those facing larger declines will also be willing to accept a wider mix of policies, including negotiating new alliances and cutting deals with potential adversaries.

Table 3 Overview of the cases

Country year	Depth of decline	Relative rank	Ally availability	Commitment interdependence	Conquest calculus	Four conditions	Outcome
Small declines							
1908 United Kingdom	1.41	High	Yes	Dispersed	Less vulnerable	More favorable	Medium-low retrenchment
1872 United Kingdom	1.46	High	No	Dispersed	Less vulnerable	Less favorable	Low retrenchment—status quo
Medium declines							
1888 Russia	3.22	Low	No	Concentrated	Vulnerable	Less favorable	Medium retrenchment
1893 France	3.23	Low	Yes	Dispersed	Vulnerable	More favorable	Medium-low retrenchment
Large declines							
1925 France	4.00	Low	Yes	Dispersed	Vulnerable	More favorable	Medium retrenchment
1903 Russia	4.22	Low	Yes	Concentrated	Vulnerable	Less favorable	Medium-low retrenchment

Second, the cases are paired together by depth of decline, so we can see why states falling at nearly identical rates do not respond identically. The small cases have depths of decline of 1.41 and 1.46; the medium cases have depths of decline of 3.22 and 3.23; and the large cases have depths of decline of 4.00 and 4.21. If our theory is correct, then the structural modifiers that we identified in chapter 2 will play a prominent role here. Declining powers in more favorable conditions, such as those that have access to capable allies or possess fewer interdependent commitments, will find it easier to retrench than comparable powers situated in less favorable positions.

Third, our cases are paired together in ways that allow us to control for other factors that might shape how great powers respond to decline. Both of our small cases, for example, involve Great Britain. This allows us to control for country-specific factors such as favorable geography or decentralized parliamentary institutions that might make it easier or harder to retrench. Our two medium cases, in contrast, are drawn from a nearly identical time period, yet feature powers with much different domestic political institutions: an authoritarian Russia and republican France, respectively. If both states respond with policies of retrenchment despite these differences, then this provides additional support for our finding that regime type does not exert a strong influence on how great powers deal with decline. A drawback of our approach, however, is that we do not delve into the most recent cases, thus marginalizing the potentially pacifying effects of nuclear weapons, globalization, and international institutions. This demands more caution in exporting findings from these case studies to the present day, but it also makes for a harder test of our theory. If the incentives for preventive war and domestic dysfunction were higher before the Second World War, when great power wars were more common and state bureaucracies still in their adolescence, then the playing field should be tilted against retrenchment.

In addition to structured focused case comparisons, we also employ detailed process tracing. If our theory is correct, we need to see the following evidence in each of our cases. First, we need to see proof that policymakers recognized that their state was experiencing decline and that decline demanded a shift in grand strategy. If policymakers did not have a sense of the underlying power trends, or did not believe that these trends required a shift in policy, then this would count against our theory. To draw a sturdy sample of policymakers' perceptions, we examine the five years before and after a transition point.

Second, we need to see evidence that policymakers are embracing policies consistent with retrenchment with the explicit goal of reducing foreign policy burdens. In terms of domestic policies, policymakers may seek to reduce spending, revamp force structure, or reform institutions, the better to free up resources for more profitable pursuits. In terms of international policies, policymakers may opt to redeploy forces, defuse flashpoints, or redistribute burdens, all to help bolster deterrence at select strongpoints. The precise blend of these instruments can vary from case to case. Yet if policymakers do not adopt policies consistent with retrenchment, or do not adopt them with the explicit aim of easing the burden of their state's foreign policy, this would be contrary to our theory.

Third, we need to see indications that policymakers pay attention to structural conditions when weighing their grand strategic response. Those that perceive commitments as independent, the conquest calculus as favoring the defense, potential allies as capable, and their relative rank as low will be more willing to retrench, and will maintain policies of retrenchment longer, than those in less propitious circumstances. If these factors do not appear to shape how policymakers view decline, or if the durability of retrenchment is driven more by other factors such as domestic politics, then this would be inconsistent with our theory.

Summary of Findings

In general, our case studies provide strong evidence that decline pushed policymakers to retrench. They also show that policymakers tried to match their retrenchment policies to the depth of decline, with deeper declines prompting more far-reaching domestic reforms and dramatic foreign policy experiments. The influence of our four structural conditions, however, is more ambiguous. Structural factors do a good job accounting for variation between our two cases of small declines. But their impact is more complicated for our medium and large cases, where domestic political factors played a more prominent role. The following sections provide an overview of each case study pair.

CHAPTERS 4 AND 5: SMALL DECLINES
AS GENTLE REMINDERS

Britain dominated international politics during the nineteenth century. Its industrial economy acted as the engine of global growth. Its naval supremacy helped patrol the waves during a period of increasing globalization. Its liberal parliamentary institutions served as a model for reformers across Europe. Yet for many authors, the story of British foreign policy in the latter half of the century is not one of triumph, but of tragedy.[1] From its lofty mid-Victorian heights, Britain experienced a slow and sustained decline of its material dominance, the effects of which reverberated across its foreign and imperial relations. Rather than doing what it took to stay on top, Britain succumbed to the beguiling charms of splendid isolation.

Blinded by liberal ideology and hamstrung by sclerotic institutions, Britain proved unwilling to pay the price of leadership. The culmination of this dispiriting descent was Britain's failure to deter Germany in the First World War.

In chapters 4 and 5, we challenge this interpretation in every particular. Britain did not suffer weakness of will, sleepwalk toward liberal utopia, encourage revisionists, act capriciously, or abandon the adaptivity that made it great. Twice in this period—around 1872 and 1908—Britain had to adjust to a new rank among the great powers. Both times, it declined essentially the same depth: a 1.46 and 1.41 percent share of great power economic output, respectively. In both cases, British policymakers sensibly espoused retrenchment. They limited commitments, defused flashpoints, husbanded resources—all to bolster deterrence and gain breathing room for reform. Yet British policymakers were careful not to push things too far: they were stingy in what they relinquished, reluctant in committing to allies, and firm toward rising adversaries. As our theory predicts, Britain made minor yet significant grand strategic adjustments in response to small but genuine erosions in its relative power. Remarkably, many of the problems associated with decline should have been present in these cases, but were not. Policymakers were sensitive to their declining power and realistic about their future. Partisan differences sometimes colored policies, yet entrenched interests were often overcome.

Still, there are intriguing differences between the cases. During the 1870s, Britain joined retrenchment at home with ambiguity abroad. Domestically, policymakers cut military spending and personnel, reduced colonial garrisons, shifted increasingly to reserves, and reformed defense institutions to rehabilitate their flagging fortunes. Internationally, proconsuls and "men on the spot" expanded British commitments across the periphery, moves grudgingly tolerated by officials back home, who were working to settle flashpoints and court friendly powers. As a result, we code this case as an ambiguous case of "low retrenchment–status quo," though we believe the case for low retrenchment is more persuasive. During the 1900s, in contrast, we find convincing evidence for retrenchment in both domestic and international arenas. British policymakers not only slashed spending and embarked on a series of reform efforts in the wake of the South African War, they also recalled their naval assets to home waters, shifted burdens to new allies, and clamped down on ambitious proconsuls. For these reasons, this case falls in the "medium-low retrenchment" range of the spectrum.

This raises the obvious question: why did Britain retrench more aggressively in 1908 than 1872? We contend that the answer lies in structural conditions. Because Britain was an insular power with dispersed commitments, British policymakers found retrenchment to be an attractive option in general, yet the particular conditions in the Edwardian period favored an even more determined moderation in British foreign policy. First, Britain was falling from a lower rank in the 1900s than it was in the 1870s. As a result, Britain faced a much more complicated strategic environment. The incentives to limit commitments and minimize vulnerabilities were much greater. Second, Britain had access to more reliable allies in the 1900s than it did in the 1870s. Britain could solicit strategic partners, whether Japan in the Far East or France in the Mediterranean, to help manage its retrenchment. The support provided by these powers helped alleviate fears that pulling back from the periphery would be an invitation to predation. Third, British commitments in the periphery were perceived as much less interdependent in the 1900s than they had been in the 1870s. In the mid-Victorian period, there was a growing concern that a rival colonial power might exploit British inaction to advance colonial claims and threaten the routes to India. By the Edwardian era, Britain had largely staked out its empire and had only a modest interest in remaining areas of great power rivalry—whether China, Persia, or Turkey. The absence of serious concerns about falling dominos in the periphery allowed for the more sustained pursuit of retrenchment.

All told, British foreign policy largely conforms to our predictions: small shifts in power prompted proportionate shifts in policy, while structural conditions shaped the policy choices in different periods. Equally important, retrenchment tended to help British foreign policy rather than harm it. In the 1870s, retrenchment allowed Britain to manage tense relations with a rising United States and navigate transformative changes on the continent, while consolidating the gains of its expanding empire. In the 1900s, retrenchment helped Britain to defend a vulnerable empire, secure a threatened homeland, and preserve a fragile peace despite its eroding naval supremacy and a multiplicity of potential challengers. Those who lament Britain's lost hegemony overstate what hegemony can do and the ease with which any state can monopolize it. No policy could have made the British economy outperform the United States or Germany, or reverse the rise of Russia or Japan. But retrenchment could protect as many British interests as possible for as long as possible.

CHAPTERS 6 AND 7: MEDIUM DECLINES, MODEST OUTCOMES

In January 1871, Chancellor Otto von Bismarck stood in the Hall of Mirrors at Versailles and proclaimed the establishment of the German Empire. The creation of a populous, industrial power in the heart of Europe upended the existing balance of power. As Germany rose in the ranks of the great powers, her neighbors—in particular France and Russia—struggled over how best to respond. For many authors, neither of these states proved up to the task.[2] France struggled to manage internal divisions and wavered between those who favored overseas expansion versus revenge in Alsace and Lorraine. Russia likewise suffered due to its antiquated domestic institutions, which proved unable to manage sprawling commitments across eastern Europe, central Asia, and the Far East. The combination of decline and domestic dysfunction resulted in French and Russian responses that were incoherent at best, incompetent at worst.

In chapters 6 and 7, we offer a different interpretation of late nineteenth century French and Russian foreign policy. We accept that these two powers faced formidable strategic challenges. Both experienced repeated moments of decline in the decades following Germany unification: France declined in 1873, 1883, and 1893, while Russia did so in 1879 and 1888. Both experienced declines that increased in severity: whereas France and Russia had drops that totaled less than a 1 percent share of great power economic output in the 1870s, this had risen to more than a 3 percent share by the late 1880s and early 1890s. Both France and Russia, therefore, experienced "medium" declines according to our coding. It is also true that neither power possessed domestic institutions of considerable flexibility or coherence. Russia was in the midst of convulsive domestic reforms while France was struggling to transition into a functional republic.

Despite these constraints, we find that both France and Russia retrenched during this period. In particular, both powers sought to moderate their defense spending, reform domestic institutions, limit peripheral commitments, and bolster deterrence at exposed strongpoints. Even more important, we find that the extent of retrenchment increased over time in line with deepening decline. By the late 1880s, both France and Russia were willing to entertain much more dramatic shifts in strategy. The culmination of this process was the negotiation of the Franco-Russian alliance itself, which linked these two declining powers in common cause. Although states are reticent to rely on others for their security, the combination of timing and geography helped overcome mutual suspicions. France and Russia were falling at similar rates at roughly the same time, which helped align their interests. Distance was equally beneficial because it made it harder for France and Russia to threaten one another, which alleviated fears of exploitation. As our theory predicts, the more severe the extent of decline, the more willing great powers were to reach out to others.

Yet, at the same time, we observe notable differences in the extent to which France and Russia transformed their grand strategies. Somewhat surprisingly, Russia retrenched with greater enthusiasm and consistency. Building on an initial bout of reform following the Russo-Turkish War, Russia continued to chart a more restrained foreign policy throughout the 1880s. On the home front, Russia worked to keep budgets low, revamped its armed forces to emphasize quality over quantity, and streamlined its military bureaucracy, moves designed to reallocate resources for investment in infrastructure and industry. In its external relations, Russia moderated its provocations in the Balkans, limited itself to opportunistic grabs in central Asia, protected the Polish salient through defensive measures, and arranged alliances with a variety of partners. Based on this record, we code Russia as a clear case of "medium" retrenchment.

The record of the Third Republic, in contrast, is decidedly mixed. Although France kept a low profile in the aftermath of the Franco-Prussian War, by the early 1880s it charted a different course. Republican politicians, notably Leon Gambetta and Jules Ferry, became avowed advocates of overseas expansion, with colonial spoils being seen as critical to offset markets lost to rising protectionism. Yet French assertiveness backfired: territorial grabs in the Mediterranean drove Italy into the arms of Germany, expansion in West Africa alarmed Britain, while the public recoiled in the face of costly wars in Indochina. As a result, French policymakers reluctantly shifted course back to retrenchment. Domestically, France trimmed its military expenditures, overhauled its army to make greater use of reserves, and revamped its navy to exploit new technologies. In its foreign policy, France resisted provocations on the continent and in the Mediterranean, tempered its colonial rivalry with Britain in Africa and Southeast Asia, and courted new alliance partners. Because France continued to add to its colonial possessions, we code this later period as a case of "medium-low" retrenchment, but we believe the thrust of French policy was in line with what we expect from medium decliners.

What can explain the somewhat surprising variation between the Russian and French experiences? Here we admit that our theory is only somewhat helpful. According to our coding of the prevalent structural conditions, France was likely to retrench in the 1890s given its relatively dispersed overseas commitments and access to strong allies who could guard against potential predation. In comparison, Russia in the 1880s was unlikely to retrench due to its relatively concentrated continental commitments, long vulnerable land frontiers, and lack of reliable allies. Yet, in practice, Russia turned out to have greater geopolitical flexibility than France did, in part due to the unique nature of its empire. Whereas most continental powers tend to have quite concentrated commitments, Russia's imperial possessions stretched across the Eurasian landmass, providing it more room for maneuver. In the cases of the Far East and central Asia, Russia had commitments that were not immediately adjacent to great power rivals, and thus could be managed through opportunistic expansion and timely concessions. Russian diplomacy also benefited from the relative stability of the regimes of Alexander II and Alexander III, two tsars who possessed vastly different preferences concerning domestic reform but were united in their recognition of the need for restraint. Until the scramble for concessions in the Far East tied commitments more directly to European concerns, therefore, Russia's domestic and international conditions favored a moderate approach.

In the case of France, a curious combination of alarm regarding imperial commitments and domestic instability conspired to lead France, at least briefly, to follow policies at odds with conditions. In the early 1880s, some Republican politicians came to see France's prestige, and by extension its security, as bound up in its overseas commitments in the Mediterranean and West Africa. The willingness of a resurgent Britain to compete with France for these spoils only added to the sense that French commitments were interconnected and weak policies might invite exploitation. These perceptions were given added weight by domestic politics, in particular the belief by Republican politicians that overseas expansion could placate the working classes and restore French grandeur. What is striking is how quickly French policymakers revamped their foreign policy once they encountered negative feedback. Colonial grandstanding exacerbated France's isolation abroad and did little to mend political fences back home, and by the late 1880s, French policy began to conform more to our expectations of moderate retrenchment. France offers a cautionary tale of how imperial dreams and chronic instability can tempt declining states to entertain expansion.

CHAPTERS 8 AND 9: DEEP DECLINES AND DEATH SPIRALS

In the nineteenth century, great powers built world-spanning empires and prided themselves on how much of the globe they could claim. In the twentieth century, empires fell from grace and great powers had to withdraw from imperial commitments that once seemed unshakeable. Great powers that had enjoyed long periods of dominance were suddenly confronted by sudden, rapid, and deep moments of decline. Whether by choice or necessity, the response was often to dismantle empires that had once appeared unassailable. After the Second World War, Britain exited India, the crown jewel of its empire, and pulled back east of Suez. As the Cold War wound down, the Soviet Union curtailed its geopolitical ambitions and allowed Eastern Europe to live by the Sinatra Doctrine, letting states do socialism their way. In both cases, rapid declines disturbed regional balances, birthed new nations, and created new international orders.

At other times, large declines are not as obvious, nor as immediately transformative. Decline unfolds over many years, creating persistent dilemmas for the great powers that experience them. Even worse, prolonged moments of decline take place in the context of altered conditions, which generate unexpected challenges and countervailing pressures. Russia around 1903 and France circa 1925 fit into this category: each fell fast and hard, dropping 4.0 and 4.2 percent of great power economic output, respectively, in the wake of exhausting wars. Both grappled with large decline in the face of conflicting international conditions and tumultuous domestic politics. And perhaps tellingly, both came to ruin. Tsarist Russia stumbled into war then domestic revolution, while interwar France succumbed to the lightning offensives of Nazi Germany. Together, these cases offer dark lessons about the steepest declines.

In chapters 8 and 9, we argue that late-tsarist Russia and interwar France performed better in their foreign policies than is often assumed. Both recognized the limits of their power and lightened foreign policy burdens to bolster homeland defenses. In the case of Russia, the trauma of defeat in the Russo-Japanese war led policymakers to cut defense spending, settle long-standing colonial flashpoints, and shift burdens more assertively to friends and partners. In the case of France, the unsatisfactory end to the Ruhr crisis prompted policymakers to overhaul the French military, appease potential adversaries on multiple fronts, and search desperately for new allies. Neither France nor Russia retrenched as far as we expected: France retrenched moderately while Russia retrenched low to moderately. Yet both sought to mix domestic and international policies in inventive ways to maintain their security in the face of rising rivals and shifting circumstances.

Despite these efforts, neither tsarist Russia nor interwar France was able to use retrenchment to solve their strategic predicament. In the case of Russia, retrenchment was more brief and limited than circumstances demanded. Domestic factors, most notably the intervention of Tsar Nicholas II, resulted in distorted shifts to force structure and incomplete reforms. Yet shifting conditions, including perceptions that Russia's commitments were becoming interdependent and that the conquest calculus favored the offense, also encouraged provocative policies. In the case of France, retrenchment was beset by contradictions from the beginning and outlived the conditions that nourished it. In the 1920s, retrenchment achieved notable successes, but the absence of capable allies to help share burdens limited the ability of France to reduce defense burdens and appease adversaries. In the 1930s, the Great Depression and the ascendance of the Nazi Party necessitated a reconsideration of French policy, but France did not copy more effective policies in the teeth of negative feedback. Thus, Russia abandoned a successful policy too soon, while France clung to a successful policy too long.

Yet, on balance, retrenchment helped Russia and France fare much better than would have been the case otherwise. The shock of the Russo-Japanese war and the Ruhr occupation catalyzed a sober assessment of the limits of national power. Still, neither state was able to capitalize on the gains of retrenchment. In the Russian case, this was disproportionately due to a combination of institutional dysfunction and poor policymaking at the top. The tsar's bungling of a tough predicament contributed to domestic instability and risky foreign policy, which ultimately led to revolution at home then defeat abroad. In the French case, retrenchment ran into the Depression, a revitalized Nazi Germany, and inadequate support from allies.

Combined, the cases stress how slim the room for maneuver is in large declining states, how international circumstances can accentuate domestic weaknesses, and how important agents and structures are in shaping responses to decline. The takeaway point is that our theory is vindicated in broad brushstrokes, but the details are crucial and sometimes fatal.

For extremely coarse indicators, our four structural conditions perform fairly well across the six cases. In all the case studies, policymakers displayed a persistent talent for assessing whether they were toward the top or the bottom of the great power hierarchy. Interdependence of commitments received good backing from the cases: policymakers were attuned to spillover effects from their decisions, but they tended to worry less than our simple schema suggested. Russia in particular was less apprehensive about setting bad precedents than expected. As a variable, ally availability achieved middling success. Not only was its explanatory power modest, but the complexities of alliance politics occasionally cut against our overarching claim. With the conquest calculus, it was on leaders' minds, but had less predictable effects than expected. The upshot is that the four factors did play the catalytic role we expected, but rarely in isolation and not always to the degree that we anticipated. Having flown above the cases, we now descend to see what can be learned on foot.

A Hegemon Temporizes

1872 Great Britain

> We are not a young people with an innocent record and a scanty inheritance. We have engrossed to ourselves an altogether disproportionate share of the wealth and traffic of the world. We have got all we want in territory, and our claim to be left in the unmolested enjoyment of vast and splendid possessions, mainly acquired by violence, largely maintained by force, often seems less reasonable to others than to us.
>
> —Winston Churchill

The year 1865 represents a turning point in British foreign policy. In October, Lord Palmerston, one of the most experienced and venerated British statesmen of the nineteenth century, died at age eighty.[1] The principles of his foreign policy—including faith in British supremacy, the promotion of liberalism abroad, a desire to moderate France through friendship, the containment of Russia, and a commitment to defend the integrity of the Ottoman Empire—had become almost axiomatic.[2] At the time of his death, however, the viability of many of these principles was in doubt. Despite its putative advocacy of liberal causes, Britain had largely sat on the sidelines during Italian unification. Britain had become estranged with France over its annexation of Nice and Savoy and the handling of the Polish revolt. Russia had begun to rebound following the humiliation of the Crimean War, embracing revisionist policies in the Balkans. The ascendancy of Prussian chancellor Otto von Bismarck augured a more uncertain future in German politics. Relations with the United States were at low ebb after Britain's controversial neutrality during the American Civil War.

The conventional wisdom is that Palmerston's death and the erosion of the foundations of his policies inaugurated a new phase in British foreign relations.[3] Having suffered too many continental humiliations, Britain reverted to its traditional preference for non-intervention. As the historian Bernard Porter argues, Britain "kept to her old course of isolation and non-involvement in Europe, because the alternative was too daunting."[4] The historian René Albrecht-Carrié concludes "British policy may perhaps be described as timid at this time."[5] The death of Palmerston inaugurated a period of "splendid isolation" that was to last until the eve of the First World War, and a "tradition of appeasement" that cast a shadow over British policy until its sequel.[6]

In this chapter, we argue that British policy during this period was not driven by doctrinaire skepticism of an activist foreign policy, but by careful calculation of the balance of power. Facing the reality of decline and a transformed international environment, British policymakers opted for a strategy of retrenchment. They chose to reduce spending, adopt reforms, curtail colonial burdens, and defuse crises, while not sacrificing the defense of vital interests. Notably, retrenchment preferences transcended party lines, though they found more support during the liberal ministry of William Gladstone. Conservatives lamented Britain's sagging prestige, but their policies differed more in style than in substance.

Yet while policymakers inclined toward retrenchment, structural conditions provided limited incentives for dramatic shifts in British grand strategy. Because it was falling from the top rank of the great powers, Britain retained a sizable base of power relative to potential rivals and could draw on these resources when confronted with unexpected crises. Moreover, Britain lacked capable allies that could protect its interests in faraway regions, a fact that limited its willingness to pull back. Perhaps most important, British policymakers became alarmed at the prospect of falling dominos across the periphery. Potential threats to the routes to India stitched together commitments that might otherwise have remained independent. As our theory predicts, unfavorable structural conditions limited the extent and the durability of British retrenchment. Indeed, the accumulation of imperial crises would eventually persuade British leaders to depart from the retrenchment playbook and unintentionally set the stage for further expansion.

"Others Have Advanced": Britain Recognizes Decline

Crises test the assumptions on which policy is based, and by this measure the Schleswig-Holstein crisis dramatically exposed the limits of Palmerston's foreign policy. Both Denmark and the German powers had claims to the provinces, and matters came to a head in early 1863 when the

Danish king declared Schleswig an integral part of Denmark.[7] Although a violation of past agreements, Palmerston rose to the king's defense, declaring that the integrity of the Danish monarchy was "an important matter of British policy" and warning that any power that attempted to interfere with that independence would find "it would not be Denmark alone they would have to contend with."[8] When a joint Austro-Prussian force invaded Schleswig in February 1864, however, Britain was too weak to defend its Danish ally, and Denmark was forced to cede the whole of Schleswig-Holstein.

Britain's bluff had been called, and the blow stung. The opposition leader Benjamin Disraeli complained "the just influence of England in the councils of Europe has been lowered."[9] Lord Derby declared: "This country is now in such a position that its menaces are disregarded, its magniloquent language is ridiculed, and its remonstrances are treated with contemptuous indifference by the small as well as by the great Powers of the Continent."[10] Palmerston faced opposition from liberal and radical politicians as well. Richard Cobden observed "the present system of diplomacy has broken down. Our Foreign Office has lost its credit with foreign countries."[11] Commenting on the controversy in his diary, Gladstone concurred: "this debate ought to be an epoch in foreign policy. We all have much to learn."[12]

The Schleswig-Holstein crisis shone through as a harbinger of a shifting balance of power amidst Palmerston's "meddle and muddle."[13] The historian John Prest has described the debate over Palmerston's policy as "decisive for British foreign policy in the nineteenth century."[14] While the "pieces of the international kaleidoscope had not yet fallen into place," the historian Thomas Otte notes that among many diplomats: "widely held assumptions of British supremacy began to crumble."[15] Lord John Russell, who became prime minister following Palmerston's death, complained that all of Germany "sneers at our pacific bluster, and the harmless roar of the British lion."[16] Edmund Hammond, the permanent undersecretary in the Foreign Office, stated ominously that "England stands as isolated as she stood during the great European War [against Napoleon]."[17] The crisis also revealed the need for military reforms. Russell conceded "our force at home is miserably insufficient and in case of war would probably expose us to some great disaster in Ireland or Scotland."[18] With scattered forces and shallow reserves, Britain lacked capability to defend its interests.

These concerns only increased in coming years. Prussian victory over France and the unification of Germany were received with alarm. Disraeli warned that "the balance of power has been entirely destroyed and the country which suffers most, and feels the effect of this great change most, is England."[19] Across the Atlantic, the growing might of the United States was troubling. Disraeli noted how "the old establishments of this country, now the United States of America, throw their lengthening shades over the Atlantic, which mix with European waters. These are vast and novel elements in the distribution of power."[20] Even British economic supremacy no longer seemed assured. The panic of 1873 and the emergence of industrial competitors around the world caused much anxiety. "England is a rich country," Derby observed, "[but] I am afraid that we can hardly doubt that the United States equal or exceed us. . . . We have not gone back, but others have advanced."[21]

The reaction to this negative feedback was remarkable: successive conservative and liberal governments retrenched. Lord Derby, the conservative prime minister between 1866 and 1868, defined his policy as "to keep this country as far as possible from any entanglement in continental politics," though "not shrinking from using the moral influence of England . . . to restore to Europe the blessings of peace."[22] This policy accelerated between 1868 and 1874 during the liberal ministry of Gladstone.[23] He argued that Britain could not "foreswear her interest in the common transactions and the general interests of Europe . . . but her credit and her power form a fund which, in order that they may be made the most of, should be thriftily used."[24] The foreign secretary Lord Granville emphasized the danger of "overstating our determination whatever it may be."[25] The arrival of Disraeli's conservative ministry in 1874 altered little. Disraeli himself acknowledged "the policy of England with respect to Europe should be a policy of reserve, but proud reserve."[26] His foreign secretary Lord Derby[27] affirmed "no one is more strongly for non-intervention within all reasonable limits than I have been . . . but we must push no doctrine to an extreme."[28]

"System of Efficiency, Consistent with Economy": British Domestic Policies

We hypothesized that, on the home front, declining powers would lighten burdens by reducing spending, restructuring forces, and reforming institutions. For the most part, Britain in the 1870s conforms to these expectations. British politicians, both conservative and liberal, sought to reduce fiscal burdens, mostly in army and navy estimates, to revise force structure to make greater use of reserves, and to reform outdated institutions, notably the War Office. In many respects these reforms proved insufficient, but given Britain's relatively small decline and impressive base of national power, they reflected remarkable foresight.

First, successive ministries sought to reduce spending on national defense.[29] While military spending increased slightly during the Derby ministry, the war secretary Jonathan Peel assured parliament that the estimates had been "framed with due attention to economy."[30] The number of troops in the regular army remained flat, efforts were made to cap spending at £100 per soldier, and much of the increased expenditure can be traced to the introduction of new breech-loading rifles into service. The most significant efforts to trim expenditure, however, were advanced during the Gladstone ministry by his war secretary Sir Edward Cardwell.[31] In his 1869/70 estimates, Cardwell proposed to reduce the regular army by more than 10,000 men, withdraw a similar number of soldiers from Canada, and trim the size of garrisons in both New Zealand and the Cape Colony—changes that resulted in savings of more than £1 million.[32] In his 1870/71 estimates, Cardwell proposed to slash an additional 12,000 regulars and reduce an additional 10,000 men from colonial service, for an additional £1 million in savings. By concentrating British forces at home, Cardwell assured his colleagues that "this is an economy which is not only consistent with true efficiency, but which actually contributes to it, and adds to our power."[33]

Second, policymakers sought to revise the structure of the British armed forces to make greater use of reserves. Not only would these forces be cheaper than long-service regulars, they would provide a force that could respond rapidly to unexpected crises. Early attempts to revise force structure occurred during the conservative Derby ministry, when Peel proposed the creation of a two tiered system of reserves: the first consisting of young men liable for service overseas, the second of pensioners available for home defense.[34] In the liberal Gladstone ministry, Cardwell built on this foundation. The 1870 Army Enlistment Act introduced an option for shortened service, six years with the Colours and six with the Reserve. The purpose of this change was to form a larger reserve force, reduce the pension list, and attract "a better class of man to enter the army."[35] The 1872 Military Forces Localisation Act sought to further improve the efficiency of both the regular army and militia through the creation of sixty-six territorial districts, each of which included two line battalions and two militia battalions. One battalion would serve abroad, while the other would remain at home, training new recruits and militia forces.[36] Taken together, these reforms were designed to concentrate battalions at home, permit their rapid expansion in emergencies, and ensure more effective coordination with militia and territorial reserves. As Cardwell emphasized, the goal was "to unite all the voluntary forces of the country into one defensive army."[37]

Third, integral to raising a genuine reserve were administrative reforms designed to enhance efficiency and versatility. Whereas previously the War Office under the secretary of state and the Horse Guards under the commander in chief had been separate administrative entities, Cardwell consolidated them under a single department.[38] Cardwell also made military service less venal, moving to abolish the controversial practice of purchase, in which army officers paid for their commission up to the rank of lieutenant colonel. For his pains, he was accused of seeking to dilute the aristocratic nature of the office corps, but his main objective was to promote greater performance and professionalism.[39]

Cardwell's reforms "provided the blue-print of the late Victorian army."[40] Yet his reforms were incomplete and did not work as well in practice as on paper.[41] Short service made attracting recruits somewhat easier, but it also increased the number of new recruits required each year and did not compensate for uncompetitive salaries.[42] Localization improved readiness and helped to foster esprit de corps, but the high tempo of colonial operations skewed the balance between home and overseas battalions.[43] Most glaringly, Britain still lacked the equivalent of a General Staff and units rarely conducted exercises in large formations.

These shortcomings make sense in the context of a gradually declining state experiencing only mild negative feedback. During the alarm generated by the Franco-Prussian War, the House of Commons approved an emergency vote of credit for the War Office to increase the size of the regular forces. In the subsequent 1871/72 estimates, the economy-minded Cardwell accepted that the regular army would need to increase by some 20,000 soldiers, at the cost of more than £1 million.[44] After the crisis had passed, Cardwell resumed his efforts to reduce spending, yet costs related to his reforms—including the compensation of officers due to the abolishment of purchase, the construction of local brigade depots for his linked battalions, and upgrades to the militia—limited aggregate savings.[45] The same penchant for economy continued in the Disraeli ministry. The war secretary Gathorne Gathorne-Hardy endorsed the reforms of his predecessor and assured his colleagues that "the Army Estimates were already very large, and . . . it was his duty to keep as far as possible within those Estimates."[46] Yet he too struggled to impose economy due to the rising costs of provisions and demands for increased pay.[47] The preference for retrenchment ran deep, but the absence of urgency worked against dramatic cuts.

Fourth, the British state redistributed resources in an attempt to be more competitive. Consistent with contemporary assumptions about sound economic policy, British policymakers placed particular emphasis on reducing taxes, eliminating tariffs and duties, and paying down the national debt. The conservative Disraeli ministry put particular emphasis on reducing the debt charge, but the costs of the war in Abyssinia necessitated a two-pence increase in the income tax.[48] The liberal Gladstone ministry enjoyed much broader success. Between 1869 and 1973, it reduced the income tax by half, eliminated the corn duty, and slashed coffee and sugar duties by one-half and two-thirds respectively. It also reduced the national debt by some £36 million, while boosting spending for elementary education by £1 million.[49] Similar efforts would continue when the conservatives returned to power in 1874, but were undermined by a combination of shrinking revenues due to economic slowdown and a series of expensive overseas wars.[50]

Overall, the net effect of this period is striking. In the five years on either side of 1872, Britain spent an average of £24 million (£14 million on its army and £10 million on its navy); for all other years between 1860 and 1885, it averaged £27 million (£16 million for the army and £11 million for the navy.)[51] Fiscal retrenchment corresponded with efforts to reallocate resources and reform the military: shoring up home defense, building up reserves, and streamlining administration. As Cardwell emphasized, these changes aimed at "a system of efficiency, consistent with economy."[52] The fact that Cardwell built on the efforts of his predecessors, and that his system was accepted by his successors, demonstrates the extent to which British politicians accepted the need for retrenchment.

"Better to Promise Too Little than Too Much": British International Policies

With international policies, we conjectured that declining powers would redeploy forces, remove flashpoints, and redistribute burdens. Britain in this period conforms to some of these expectations better than others. Policymakers sought to concentrate military forces closer to home, convince colonial dependencies to pay more for their own defense, and limit intervention in dangerous continental crises. Yet these efforts were more erratic and inconsistent than one might expect, in large part because unexpected crises conspired to draw Britain back to the periphery. Although policymakers appreciated the benefits of retrenchment in the abstract, fears of falling dominoes, an absence of reliable partners, and the possession of a tremendous navy made it hard for Britain to resist responding to distant threats.

First, policymakers sought to revamp Britain's global posture. One of the lessons of the Schleswig-Holstein crisis had been the extent to which colonial obligations had constricted available manpower. Efforts to reduce colonial garrisons, therefore, were not only useful as a cost cutting measure but also freed up forces for use closer to home. During the conservative Derby ministry, the war secretary Sir John Pakington noted that the colonial "establishment might be beneficially reduced, both in regard to numbers and expense."[53] Speaking in 1873, Cardwell argued: "The essence of the retrenchment we have been able to make is that we have resorted to the policy of concentration, and have given up the mischievous and losing system of dispersion of force, not because we have given up any duty we owe to the colonies, or are less careful to discharge our duty to our colonies, but because we desire to have, at the least cost to the country, the greatest amount of power with which to discharge all our duties."[54]

In Canada, the Derby ministry lightened the imperial burden by five battalions in 1868, in spite of the continued threat of Fenian raids.[55] The Gladstone ministry maintained these trends and, save for small naval forces at Halifax and Esquimalt, had withdrawn all British troops by the end of 1871.[56] In the case of New Zealand, Britain followed a similar playbook.

Colonial garrisons fell by five regiments in 1865 and four the following year.[57] In 1870, Lord Granville completed the shift with the reduction of the last regiment of British regulars. Cardwell noted that the "withdrawal of forces from distant stations" would "not only save money, but would also permit the reorganisation of the home army."[58]

In total, colonial garrisons fell by more than half. While 49,650 soldiers were deployed in the colonies in 1868, this number had dropped to 23,941 two years later.[59] Over the same period, the number of regulars and reserves stationed in Britain but liable to serve abroad had increased from 92,574 to 106,678.[60] Just as remarkable, efforts were made to concentrate naval forces in home waters and create rapid reaction forces of "flying squadrons."[61] According to the historian Peter Burroughs, between 1865 and 1875, "the number of ships serving on non-European stations fell by 40 per cent."[62] Britain would now be in a better position to put out fires wherever they might break out.

A second—and related—effort was made to redistribute burdens. Britain strained to compel its settler colonies to contribute more to their own defenses. The belief that colonies should be self-sufficient had a long pedigree,[63] yet efforts to translate this principle into practice accelerated in the late-1860s. Speaking to parliament in 1868, Pakington declared "the policy of the present—as of the last—Government is to endeavour to make the colonies bear a fair share of the expenses."[64] In the case of Canada, British politicians recognized that a confederation involving the Maritime Provinces was a prerequisite to effective self-defense. The Colonial Office pressured local politicians to accept confederation, and in 1867, New Brunswick and Nova Scotia were joined with Canada.[65] The fruits of this policy can be observed during the 1869 Red River Rebellion: the Canadians paid three-fourths of the cost of the expedition, and London withdrew its troops on schedule.[66] A similar policy dominated in the Cape Colony, which was granted responsible government in 1872. The collective impact of these moves was not to prompt the settler colonies toward independence, though Lord Granville assumed this might be the end result.[67] Instead, according to Gladstone, these polices were intended to demonstrate that London "did not impose British connection upon the Colony, but regarded its goodwill and desire as an essential condition of the connection."[68]

Britain's willingness to shift burdens, however, was limited to negotiating new bargains with its colonial dependencies. When it came to potential allies elsewhere, British policymakers shunned firm commitments. In 1871, for example, the Austrian foreign minister, with the endorsement of the British ambassador in Vienna, proposed an alliance to work together on the Eastern Question. Lord Granville rejected the proposal, noting "the policy of successive Governments . . . has been to avoid prospective understandings to meet contingencies which seldom occur in the way which has been anticipated."[69] In 1879, Lord Salisbury rejected German alliance overtures, settling instead for a general assurance of British goodwill in the event of a Russian attack.[70] Given that Britain remained the most powerful state in Europe, policymakers saw little need to sacrifice autonomy in continental disputes.

Third, British policymakers sought to reduce the risk that they would be drawn into unnecessary and expensive conflicts with rival powers. In some cases, Britain accomplished this through a determined policy of non-intervention. In the run up to the Austro-Prussian War, Britain stood alongside France and Russia in calling for a congress to settle outstanding disputes regarding the administration of Schleswig-Holstein.[71] When this broke down, Russell was circumspect: "If you enter a war merely for the sake of preserving the general balance of power in Europe, without your interests or honour being involved, you ought to see whether you are not likely to produce much more evil than you are likely to remedy."[72] The foreign secretary Lord Clarendon concurred: "in the present state of Ireland, and the menacing aspect of our relations with the United States, the military and pecuniary resources of England must be husbanded with utmost care. The country will not tolerate any direct interference in a quarrel with which we had no concern."[73] The ascendance of the conservative ministry of Lord Derby in the midst of the crisis had little effect on the course of British policy. He declared his intention to "keep this country as far as possible from any entanglement in continental politics."[74] His foreign minister, Lord Stanley, followed suit, proclaiming: "Ours will be a pacific policy, a policy of observation rather than action."[75]

The same policy prevailed during the Franco-Prussian War. Prior to the war, Britain sought to defuse tensions between France and Prussia by brokering a French proposal for partial disarmament and warning both sides when they acted provocatively.[76] Once fighting began, Britain adhered to strict neutrality. Although Gladstone wanted to propose mediation, and was later to voice his opposition to the annexation of Alsace-Lorraine, his colleagues persuaded him to avoid steps that might entangle Britain in the conflict.[77] "We keep ourselves free," the permanent undersecretary at the Foreign Office argued, "and by so doing, preserve for ourselves an attitude more likely than any other to be useful in the end."[78] Granville argued similarly: "Palmerston wasted the strength derived by England . . . by his brag. I am afraid of our wasting that which we at present derive from moral causes, by laying down general principles when nobody will attend to them, and when in all probability they will be disregarded. We have reserved our full liberty of action."[79]

In other cases, Britain actively sought to defuse potential flashpoints through negotiation and the granting of concessions. When Russia announced its unilateral abrogation of the Black Sea clauses in October 1870, British policymakers worked to deescalate matters. The Ottomans were willing to fight and the British ambassador at Constantinople complained, "The deneutralization of the Black Sea would be a renuncia-tion of all that was obtained by the Crimean War."[80] Yet with France dis-tracted and relations with the United States strained, British policymakers had few options. With Bismarck's backing, Britain proposed the next best option: an international conference. The parties accepted the abrogation of the Black Sea clauses, yet Britain secured the essential guarantee that the Turkish Straits would remain closed to warships without the Sultan's approval.[81] As the historian Agatha Ramm argues, Britain had acquiesced, but "she gained some advantages by the way she acquiesced."[82]

The United States was arguably the most portentous instance where Brit-ish decision-makers keenly soothed frictions. In addition to perennial boundary and fishery questions, Britain and the United States were at odds over claims related to the *Alabama,* a Confederate cruiser built in Britain that had damaged Union shipping during the Civil War.[83] In 1869, Claren-don helped negotiate a draft agreement favoring arbitration, but the U.S. Senate refused to ratify it.[84] Despite the setback, patient diplomacy pre-vailed. By 1871, his successor Granville concluded the Treaty of Washing-ton, which endorsed arbitration while resolving other irritants.[85] The *Alabama* settlement had massive repercussions. The arbitration panel issued a £3 million judgment against Britain, but the payment was a third of what the Americans had demanded. The deal undercut the extravagant demands of American hawks, and Anglo-American relations improved dramatically. Granville claimed successful arbitration had resulted in "the firm establish-ment of amicable relations between two countries which have so many and such peculiar reasons to be on friendly terms."[86] More lastingly, the settle-ment "marked the breakpoint between the previous hundred years of Anglo-American strain and the subsequent century."[87]

Fourth, Britain took advantage of retrenchment to bolster deterrence at select strongpoints. Here the abiding interest was the defense of Belgium as an independent buffer state between France and Germany. In the 1867 Lux-emburg crisis, Britain opposed French efforts to secure the cessation of Lux-emburg, a move that risked a war with Prussia, which had a garrison there, and threatened Belgium's territorial integrity.[88] Disraeli observed that "France is not prepared" and "Bismarck lies to everyone," and thus "we might begin to dictate a little to Europe."[89] The result was the London Con-ference of May 1867, in which the assembled powers guaranteed Luxem-burg's territorial integrity. Britain played a similar role during an 1869 railway dispute between France and Belgium. At first, Britain sought to restrain both parties but France bridled.[90] Clarendon reported he had "never felt any confidence in the soft sayings and assurances of the French Government" but was surprised they "exposed the cloven foot so soon and completely as they have done."[91] He warned the French ambassador of "the risk of an interruption of those cordial and friendly relations between England and France."[92] France backed down, agreeing to cancel contested railroad contracts in exchange for possible future concessions. During the Franco-Prussian War, Britain exhibited similar resolve. Granville sought to secure a pledge from both France and Prussia that they would respect Belgian neutrality. Despite opposition at home, Granville insisted "this alliance will act as a powerful check on either party doing that which we wish to avoid."[93] Prussia and France signed—and observed—treaties to respect Belgian territorial integrity.

In brief, British foreign policymakers made a series of minor changes designed to corral the burdens of empire by concentrating forces closer to home, shifting defense burdens toward colonial dependencies, avoiding continental entanglements, and salving tensions with potential adversaries. With new economic and military uncertainties, greater British ambitions would have jeopardized core interests. Yet Britain did not get carried away: it neither sought to liquidate ties to its settler colonies, nor sacrifice its autonomy in far-ranging alliances with continental powers. British policy, Otte concludes, was "more than just an isolationist streak. . . . It was based on careful strategic analysis."[94]

"Float Lazily Downstream": The Limits of British Retrenchment

British grand strategy in the 1870s conforms to the expectations of a great power experiencing a small decline: policymakers placed greatest emphasis on domestic forms of retrenchment while limiting foreign policy shifts to minor moves. It is telling that one of the potential impediments to retrenchment—domestic political opposition—did not play a prominent role in this case. Most British policymakers accepted that an expensive and assertive foreign policy à la Palmerston could not be sustained, and support for retrenchment cut across party lines. When Clarendon assumed the foreign office from Stanley, for example, he reported: "I did not detect a shade of difference of opinion between us."[95] Similarly, the fall of the Russell ministry during the Austro-Prussian War did not result in any dramatic shift in approach. Nor did the ascent of the Gladstone ministry fundamentally alter the negotiations over the *Alabama* claims. Indeed, Gladstone accepted Disraeli's suggestion to appoint the conservative Stafford Northcote as one of the British commissioners, and Britain's united front in negotiations helped produce favorable terms.[96]

All policies have their detractors, and retrenchment was no exception. In particular, conservatives criticized Granville's policy of drawing down colonial garrisons. In the House of Lords, Lord Carnarvon famously declared there were "whispers abroad that there is a policy on foot [sic] to dismember this Empire."[97] Yet as historian David McIntyre points out, Granville's policies "had usually been started several years earlier, and had been endorsed by the Conservatives."[98] Cardwell, too, encountered pushback to some of his reforms, such as the abolition of purchase. But aspects of his key innovations had been initiated under Conservative rule, and subsequent Tory ministries did not try to undo his major changes.[99]

Yet while Conservative and Liberal governments alike were united on the need to limit costs and reduce risks, there were limits to the extent to which Britain was able to sustain retrenchment. Unexpected crises in the periphery consistently tempted Britain to retire retrenchment and resume a more expansionist grand strategy. Whether in Africa or Asia, British proconsuls often found themselves in a position to act assertively while policymakers at home proved unable to shackle them. For instance, the 1868 British expedition to Abyssinia experienced mission creep. Stanley favored a conciliatory approach to free a group of British captives, but pressure from the Foreign Office and men on the spot convinced him to authorize a lavish expedition that cost £8 million.[100] That same year, the British high commissioner for Southern Africa convinced a reluctant Colonial Office to annex Basutoland, in part to check expansion of the Afrikaner Orange Free State.[101]

Although liberals expressed less enthusiasm for overseas adventures, once in power they too found it difficult to control distant proconsuls. When the Ashanti invaded the Gold Coast protectorate in 1873, the colonial secretary the Earl of Kimberly observed: "if we wish to weaken ourselves we cannot adopt a better course than to spend a few millions [sic] in conquering Ashantee."[102] Yet, he conceded, "we cannot leave [the Ashanti] quietly in occupation of the Protectorate. . . . All the trade of our settlements is practically destroyed by the presence of the invading force."[103] The cabinet grudgingly consented to dispatch troops.[104] Similar pressures drew Britain into Malaya, where a series of succession crisis and clashes among Chinese clans threatened to disrupt the tin trade.[105] Kimberly believed that "it would be a serious matter if any other European Power were to obtain a footing on the Peninsula," but he urged caution.[106] The new governor immediately exceeded his instructions and compelled various Malay rulers to accept British residents.[107] Events in southern Africa traced a similar course in 1871, when the high commissioner ignored his instructions and declared a crown colony over the diamond-rich region of Griqualand West.[108] In neither case did the government disavow their agents' actions.

Why did British officials not aggressively rein in peripheral proconsuls? Part of the answers may be Britain's rank. Given its unrivaled naval supremacy and vast economic reach, British policymakers had little incentive to renounce their remote agents. Efforts were made to limit annexations and to keep administrative costs down, but it would have been absurd to expect the most powerful state in Europe to forgo potential opportunities to add to its empire. A second compelling explanation is local allies. Whether in Southeast Asia or West Africa, British policymakers saw a paucity of attractive partners. Local allies, whether the Fante in the Gold Coast or various Sultans on the Malay Peninsula, lacked military strength, and rival great powers, notably the French, were more disposed to exclude British influence than cooperate with it. Without capable intermediaries or allied powers, British policymakers faced the unpalatable choice between surrendering their interests and reluctantly protecting them.

Had these individual crises remained isolated, they would have conspired to slow, but not reverse, retrenchment. The outbreak of a more serious crisis in the Balkans, however, led British policymakers to increasingly question retrenchment. The crisis stemmed from the emergence in 1875 of an armed revolt in the province of Bosnia-Herzegovina. British policymakers were divided about how best to respond: some such as Disraeli wanted to back the Porte against outside pressure; others including Derby favored a diplomatic compromise on fresh reforms.[109] With the cabinet divided, British policy vacillated inconclusively between the two options.[110] Salisbury complained: "English policy is to float lazily downstream, occasionally putting out a diplomatic boathook to avoid collisions."[111] Yet when Russia declared war in April 1877, the collapse of the Ottoman Empire appeared imminent. Having provided half-hearted encouragement to the Turks, Britain now lacked the means to defend them.[112] British policy, however, was rescued by Russian overreaching. When the other powers learned of the harsh terms imposed on the Ottomans in the Treaty of San Stefano, they assembled quickly at the Congress of Berlin to scale back Russian gains.[113]

The impact of the Near Eastern Crisis on British foreign policy was far reaching. Although Disraeli appeared victorious, many of Britain's purported gains proved temporary.[114] The crisis also revealed the limits of retrenchment. For many policymakers, it was simply inconceivable that the world's most formidable naval power would be relegated to the sidelines of European diplomacy. Calls on British policymakers to more assertively defend British prestige became louder and more pronounced.[115] The crisis likewise displayed Britain's paucity of capable allies. Austria-Hungary no longer appeared as reliable a partner in the Balkans, while the Ottoman Empire appeared closer to collapse than ever before. Perhaps most important, the crisis served to link Britain's interests in Europe with its imperial commitments in Asia. The combination of a weakened Ottoman Empire, a revitalized Russia, and an assertive France led Britain to question the security of the routes to India. To bolster Britain's naval position, Salisbury convinced the Turks to cede Cyprus, and to purchase French acquiescence, he granted Paris a free hand in North Africa. As imperial rivalries began to heat up, British policymakers became increasingly anxious about falling dominos across the periphery. A policy of "opportunistic indecision" no longer appeared quite as attractive.[116]

As predicted, once structural conditions became more unfavorable to retrenchment, British policymakers began to shift their foreign policy in a more assertive direction. Renewed concerns over Russia's advance in central Asia, for example, tilted the balance away from those who favored a policy of "masterly inactivity" along the Indian frontier and toward those who advocated a forward approach.[117] In 1879, the governor of India Lord Lytton exceeded his instructions and attempted to forcibly compel the ruler of Afghanistan to accept a British resident, a move that ended in a disastrous war. Along the same lines, anxiety over the security of the routes to India, along with pressure from colonial officials on the spot, prompted the colonial secretary Lord Carnarvon to entertain the proposal of a closer confederation among the various states of Southern Africa.[118] The energetic pursuit of this goal by the high commissioner Sir Bartle Frere, however, backfired, when his clumsy attempt to coerce the Zulus in 1879 ended in a costly war. Even the liberals, the clearest and most consistent champions of retrenchment, would come to embrace expansion. When nationalist agitation and riots erupted in Egypt in June 1882, Gladstone authorized the dispatch of a naval squadron and then a military expedition.[119] As the First Lord of the Admiralty Earl of Northbrook concluded: "we have now been forced into the position of being protectors of Egypt."[120] The stage had been set for the Scramble for Africa and a new, more expansionist period in British foreign policy.

In sum, the limits of retrenchment in the mid-Victorian period stemmed not from domestic political factionalism but from shifting structural conditions. Pulling in one direction, Britain was an insular power with dispersed commitments. It could afford to moderate its ambitions along distant frontiers with little worry that circling predators would be able to exploit potential vulnerabilities to endanger the homeland. Pulling in the other direction, there were distinct limits to support for retrenchment. Given Britain's extensive naval reach and enviable economic influence, it was difficult for British policymakers to refrain from intervening in peripheral crises. The lack of local allies with whom Britain could manage peripheral crises, combined with the growing fear that imperial dominos might tumble, especially in the wake of the Near Eastern Crisis, put a further brake on retrenchment. By the 1880s, the politics that dominated during the 1870s was reversed. Whereas in the earlier period Conservatives and Liberals united behind the principle of non-intervention, they now were drawn to expansion. In the most surprising turn, it would be the retrenchment-minded Gladstone, who had been accused of seeking to dismantle the empire and defenestrate the army, who would lead the march into Egypt, sub-Saharan Africa, and beyond.

British foreign policy in this period closely conforms to our predictions. In response to a negative shift in the balance of power, occasioned by the unification of Germany and a rising United States, policymakers chose to move Britain's grand strategy in a humbler direction. At home, defense expenditures were reduced, military forces were restructured to emphasize reserves, and institutions were reformed to improve efficiency. Abroad, forces were pulled back from overseas garrisons, burdens were shifted to colonial governments, and potential flashpoints were resolved through tough diplomacy. Befitting a great power experiencing a small decline, Britain modified its foreign policy around the edges. It neither abandoned its colonial empire nor sacrificed its autonomy to continental allies. But because of retrenchment, Britain freed up resources to pay down its debt and reduce taxes, while defending vital strongpoints such as Belgium.

The case of mid-Victorian Britain also shows the importance of structural conditions in shaping the depth and durability of retrenchment. Because Britain remained near the top of the great power ranks, it had little incentive to dramatically overhaul its foreign policy. The absence of capable allies put a brake on the extent to which British policymakers were willing to pull back in some regions. While retrenchment could free up breathing room for reforms, it could not remove anxieties about the routes to India nor remove the temptation to intervene to tame turbulent frontiers. Retrenchment prevailed, but was undermined—and eventually undone—by recurring peripheral crises.

Perhaps most important, this case demonstrates the limits of theories of preventive war. This case is the only case of a hegemonic transition in our sample, and though the United States and Britain did clash over boundaries, fisheries, and the *Alabama* claims, at no point was there a serious risk that conflict would break out. Some of this might be explained by mutual trade ties or shared liberal values. But much of the credit must also go to British policymakers, who retrenched rather than risk an unnecessary and unprofitable clash.

A Hegemon Wakes Up

1908 Great Britain

> It has sometimes occurred to me that to a foreigner reading our press the British Empire must appear in the light of some huge giant sprawling all over the globe, with gouty fingers and toes stretching in every direction, which cannot be approached without eliciting a scream.
>
> —Thomas Sanderson

British foreign policy in the last two decades of the nineteenth century was both active and energetic. Britain played a leading role in the Scramble for Africa, pushed forward the imperial frontier across Africa and Asia, and vigorously pursued naval supremacy in the Mediterranean. By the turn of the twentieth century, however, Britain's position abroad looked precarious. In Africa, Britain suffered devastating military defeats in the opening campaigns of the South African War. In the Far East, British diplomacy appeared unable to check Russian advances into Manchuria or to forestall an impending melee over China. The situation in the Mediterranean appeared equally menacing, as growing French and Russian naval power threatened the integrity of the Turkish Straits and Britain's position in Egypt. Russian advances in Persia and Afghanistan rekindled fear about the ability of India to defend its borders. Even relations with Germany, a country that many officials in London viewed as a potential alliance partner, had become strained over naval questions and the Kaiser's erratic behavior. Splendid isolation from continental affairs no longer appeared so idyllic.[1]

The conventional wisdom is that the erosion of British power, combined with the rise of an expansionist Germany, forced a reluctant Britain to abandon isolation. Beginning with the Anglo-Japanese treaty, and culminating in the entente agreements with France and Russia, British policymakers accepted more diplomatic entanglements. "The abandonment of isolation," George Monger concludes, represented "a confession of weakness in the face of growing competition."[2] Paul Kennedy adds that "the relative decline of Great Britain . . . [was] perhaps the most critical conditioning element in the formulation of the country's external policy."[3] Slowly but surely, Britain became caught up in continental alignments and committed to military intervention to support its entente partners. This process culminated in 1914, when a hesitant Britain was drawn into a world war to prevent German hegemony in Europe.

In this chapter, we argue that decline forced British policymakers to retrench, but that the content and consequences of this shift have been misunderstood. Seeing British policy as a grand design to contain German power is hindsight bias and overlooks the complexity of British diplomacy and the coherent retrenchment policies it followed before focusing on Germany. After the calamities of the South African War, British policymakers from across the political spectrum coalesced behind retrenchment. On the domestic front, efforts were made to reduce defense expenditures, restructure the army and navy to increase flexibility, and reform the defense establishment to improve coordination, though the pursuit of economy would be hampered by the requirements of the naval arms race. In its foreign relations, Britain sought to reposition distant forces closer to home, defang peripheral disputes through timely concessions, and cultivate new friends and allies without sacrificing its accustomed autonomy.

The enthusiasm that policymakers exhibited for retrenchment during this period flowed naturally from Britain's structural position. Because it was falling from a lower rank, Britain faced a more complex array of potential rivals who themselves were more capable. The sheer number of potential dangers generated strong pressures for Britain to change its foreign policy. Yet Britain was fortunate to have plenty of latitude to chart a new course. It had strong potential allies that could help uphold a distribution of power favorable to British interests, and it had fewer reasons to fear falling dominoes in the periphery. Because the most important imperial spoils had already been claimed, Britain could afford to limit or abandon claims to the remaining scraps. In the end, the combined ability to shift burdens to distant allies and temper peripheral rivalries allowed Britain to concentrate capabilities closer to home. As the threat posed by Germany became more pronounced, retrenchment became part and parcel of a broader effort to protect British naval supremacy and preserve continental peace.

"Other Nations Have Been Creeping Up": Britain Recognizes Decline

The South African War dramatically revealed the perilous position of Britain at the turn of the century. The disastrous performance during the "Black Week" of Stomberg, Magersfontein, and Colenso highlighted the limits of the Victorian-era army in areas such as staff work, intelligence, and supply.[4] As one War Office official told the Royal Commission on the war, "Our army system is rotten. . . . We should be no good against a European power."[5]

In the diplomatic sphere, Britain's isolation was underscored by the enthusiasm with which many of the continental great powers received news of Britain's military setbacks. The British ambassador in Paris reported that he was "apprehensive as to the intentions of France and Russia to take advantage of what they consider to be England's difficulties at this juncture for their own ends."[6] The British ambassador in Vienna complained about how the foreign press "magnifies our reverses and croaks over the catastrophe in store for us," creating an "uneasy apprehension of a possible decline in our power."[7] British isolation deepened when the horrific conditions in the "concentration camps," built primarily to house displaced Afrikaner civilians, exacerbated accusations of wartime brutality.

Perhaps most important, the war revealed glaring inadequacies in Britain's military capabilities. Sustaining 250,000 troops more than five thousand miles from home had become a fiscal extravagance, costing a staggering £1.25 million per week.[8] Britain itself had been "stripped of all but a single regular battalion, leading to renewed fears of an invasion."[9] The Indian secretary Lord George Hamilton warned, "The locking-up of our troops in South Africa has so fettered our power of action that for some months to come we must lie low."[10] The war secretary St. John Brodrick confided, "The army is hopelessly disorganized and used up; everyone is stale."[11] Arthur Balfour came to the blunt conclusion: "We were for all practical purposes at the present moment only a third-rate Power."[12]

Across a range of different issues, policymakers began to accept the premise that Britain was losing ground. In naval affairs, the first sea lord warned, "The strain . . . put on our naval resources with all our wide world interest is, in view of the feverish developments of other nations, being subjected to a heavier strain than we can well bear."[13] In military affairs, the war secretary cautioned that the army was nearly fifty thousand men short of the requirements for imperial defense.[14] The Indian Office emphasized that due to railway construction the "military position of Russia grows stronger every day,"[15] while the prime minister Lord Salisbury declared, "When Russia advances we shall have to fight her on the Indian frontier" and "the strain of doing so will be enormous."[16] There was an equally palpable sense of decline on the economic front. Lord George Hamilton observed "the immense development of the material prosperity of the world and the increase of production are enabling foreign nations in all parts of the world to more effectively compete with us."[17] Sir Edward Grey worried: "Foreign competition is becoming more real: it used to be a bogey, but other nations have been creeping up to us and we shall not be able to maintain the lead, if we waste our power."[18]

None of these trends were wholly new, and on the surface, the South African War looked like a repudiation of these worries and a vindication of splendid isolation. After all, Britain had overcome tenacious opponents and global opprobrium single-handedly. Yet British politicians appreciated the negative feedback occasioned by decline. The war cost a galling £217 million, more than three times the bill for the Crimean War.[19] Worse, because only 28 percent of the war's cost was met through taxation, borrowing to pay for the war led the national debt to balloon to some £798 million.[20] "However reluctant we may be to face the fact," a Treasury official admitted, "the time has come when we must frankly admit that the financial resources of the U.K. are inadequate to do all that we should desire in the matter of Imperial Defence."[21] "This spiraling expenditure," the historian Geoffrey Searle concludes, "put ministers under intense pressure to trim their budgets."[22]

While the causes and extent of decline remained open questions, successive governments came around to retrenchment. Salisbury emphasized, "The Boer War has cost us a shilling income tax" but "a French war would cost us . . . several times as much." For this reason, "it is a matter of great importance to be very circumspect in our conduct."[23] His foreign secretary Lord Lansdowne agreed: "Our South African entanglements make it impossible for us to commit ourselves to a policy which might involve us in war."[24] Balfour, who succeeded Salisbury as head of the Unionist government in July 1902, emphasized the "particular importance" of finding plans that "shall throw a small burden on the taxpayer" largely because "the total cost of Imperial Defence threatens to become prohibitive."[25]

The push toward retrenchment gathered further momentum with the ascendancy of the Liberals under Henry Campbell-Bannerman from December 1905 and Herbert Henry Asquith from April 1908. The key figure here is Sir Edward Grey, who served as foreign secretary under both prime ministers.[26] In 1906, Grey explained to the Commons, "Our whole policy is that national expenditure has grown enormously in the last few years and that now we have reached the turning-point and there is a prospect that the expenditure can be considerably reduced without sacrificing national safety."[27] He added, "Our business is to develop what we have got, wisely and with discrimination."[28] The question was not whether Britain would retrench, but how.

"Cut Our Coat according to Our Cloth": British Domestic Policies

In the 1870s, British policymakers used an array of domestic policies to retrench, but in the 1900s success was more checkered. Although defense spending came down from South African War highs, rearmament and naval arms racing stymied deeper cuts. Greater progress was made in the realm of force structure and institutional reforms. The South African War had dramatically exposed the limitations of British strategic planning in general, and the army in particular, and provided a fillip to more thoroughgoing efforts.

First, successive governments labored to cut defense spending. Salisbury feared a "parliamentary explosion" and encouraged his war secretary to "snip down expenses."[29] Balfour likewise conceded, "The growth of the Estimates is a very serious matter."[30] The measures used to finance the war, such as an increase on the income tax and new duties on alcohol and tobacco, proved particularly controversial. Salisbury confided his hope that "paying that disagreeable Income Tax" might induce "our countrymen to believe that, in Empire as well as everything else, we must cut our coat according to our cloth."[31]

Initial efforts to realize sizable savings were thwarted, however: first by the need to rebuild and rearm the army, and second by the ambitious reforms proposed by the war secretary St. John Brodrick. In part because of these requirements, the 1903/4 army estimates totaled some £34 million, a reduction from wartime highs but still in excess of what most considered sustainable.[32] Brodrick's successor, Hugh Arnold-Forster, scrapped more expensive reforms and managed to reduce the 1904/5 estimates to £29 million.[33] But unwilling to make dramatic cuts to regular forces or to forgo the acquisition of expensive quick-firing artillery, Arnold-Forster was forced to increase the estimates by £1 million the following year.[34] Balfour warned the spending "will bitterly disappoint public opinion, and . . . in the present state of public finance the country will scarcely tolerate."[35]

While reductions to the army estimates stalled, the Unionists pursued cuts in naval expenditure, which had swelled to £37 million in the 1904/5 estimates.[36] The task fell to the dynamic new first sea lord Sir John "Jacky" Fisher. Even before he became first sea lord, Fisher had declared, "We can't go on with such increasing Navy Estimates. . . . I see my way very clearly to a very great reduction with increased efficiency."[37] Fisher decreased navy estimates by £3.5 million through a series of steps, including the decommissioning of more than one hundred and fifty obsolete ships, reductions in shipbuilding, and the shuttering of overseas stations in North America, the South Atlantic, Pacific, and China.[38] Speaking for the opposition, Grey sardonically observed that the Unionists should "be known as the Government which promised to reduce expenditure on the Army but succeeded in reducing expenditure on the Navy."[39]

After the fall of the Unionists, Campbell-Bannerman's liberal ministry renewed the push for retrenchment. The war secretary Richard Haldane declared his intention to keep the army estimates beneath £28 million, stressing the desire to "see the full efficiency which comes from new organization and no surplus energy running to waste."[40] He missed his pledge in 1906/7 but succeeded every year after until the eve of the First World War. In terms of the navy, Fisher's economizing efforts and shipbuilding reductions were extended and continued, so that naval estimates were "on average some 15 per cent below the high point that had been reached in 1904–05."[41]

Second, Unionists and Liberals alike explored ways to alter the structure of Britain's armed forces to increase their capability and flexibility. St. John Brodrick favored refashioning the British army into a force of six corps, three slated for home defense and three as a global "striking force."[42] But when it was revealed that this plan required the addition of 11,500 regulars to the roles, plus higher pay and reenlistment bonuses, it was abandoned. His successor Arnold-Forster endorsed restructuring the British army into two tiers: one consisting of long-service soldiers slated for colonial service the other of short-service soldiers available for home defense. Yet because this proposal relied heavily on expensive regular soldiers, it too was scrapped.[43] As for the navy, the first lord of the Admiralty Lord Selborne championed an ambitious slate for reforms designed to improve and standardize officer education.[44] Fisher also took important steps to improve the readiness of the Fleet Reserve through the "nucleus crew system" and greater concentration of capital ships in home waters.[45]

As for army reform, the liberals under Haldane experienced much greater success. In an early memorandum, Haldane emphasized the need for a "highly-organized and well-equipped striking force, which can be transported, with the least possible delay, to any part of the world."[46] He oversaw the creation of an expeditionary force of six reorganized divisions, and the transformation of the militia into a reserve force, which could supply drafts and other forms of support. To buttress home defense while these forces were abroad, Haldane retooled the Yeomanry, Volunteers, and portions of the militia into a new territorial force of fourteen divisions.[47] Haldane claimed his reforms would succeed in "putting a reduced Army on a business footing and producing, not only very substantial reductions in the Estimates . . . but an organization which can be . . . diminished or expanded, according to policy."[48] He largely succeeded. The British army did experience recruitment shortages, and some questioned the adequacy of the expeditionary force.[49] Still, the Haldane reforms arguably achieved more than the earlier Cardwell reforms: they raised the quality and coordination of the regular and auxiliary forces, strengthened expeditionary forces, and kept costs down.[50]

Third, British policymakers sought to reform Britain's bureaucratic institutions to enhance foreign policy planning and coordination. Balfour rued that in imperial defense "there was no co-ordination, no co-operation between the people in charge of land and sea war, and defence."[51] To facilitate cooperation between the War Office and Admiralty, he created the Committee on Imperial Defence (CID).[52] In 1904, the committee was strengthened through the addition of a permanent secretary and full-time staff, becoming the nominal center of British strategic planning. The Balfour ministry also inaugurated a bevy of reforms in the army bureaucracy: abolishing the post of commander-in-chief and creating the Army Council. Haldane built on this momentum, issuing formal orders to establish an Army General Staff.[53]

These reforms had a salutary impact on British defense institutions. The CID produced a series of influential studies on issues such as the vulnerability of Britain to invasion and the security of the Indian frontier.[54] Nevertheless, "as a device for effecting strategic unity" the committee "disappointed the hopes of its founders."[55] Civilian ministers made inconsistent use of its services, and both the War Office and the Admiralty ignored its dictates when it suited them. It was not until the eve of the war that the two services were finally forced to reconcile their strategic plans.[56]

The pace of European rearmament also conspired to limit domestic retrenchment. This was especially true when it came to the naval estimates. Concerns over French and Russian naval construction swelled the estimates during the Unionist ministry. Only after the defeat of the Russian fleet at Tsushima and the introduction of the all-big-gun battleship *Dreadnought* did British naval supremacy finally appear secure. The revelation of an expanded German naval program in late 1908, however, raised fresh concerns about the adequacy of Britain's shipbuilding.[57] To meet this challenge, the naval estimates rose from £32 million in 1908/9 to £49 million in 1913/14, an increase of more than 50 percent.[58] Although committed to retrenchment, Grey acknowledged that he "always exempted the Navy from [his] promises, and in any case promises must be subordinated to the national safety."[59]

Fourth, Britain reallocated resources with the goal of encouraging better economic performance. In the immediate wake of the South African war, Unionist governments reduced the income tax by 27 percent, repealed wartime duties on corn and tea, and paid down some £28 million in debt.[60] Subsequent liberal governments followed some of these remedies as well: they repealed taxes on coal, reduced duties on tea and sugar, and, by 1910, had paid down some £51 million in debt.[61] Yet Liberal policymakers were willing to consider more than just supply-side solutions. Liberal governments increased money for education, established labor exchanges and unemployment insurance, and inaugurated a system of old age pensions, all paid for by a combination of taxes on tobacco and spirits and new graduated income and inheritance taxes.[62] The shift in emphasis was dramatic. Between 1888 and 1913, money spent on social services went from just under £5 million to more than £35 million, an increase from 5.5 percent to 18.9 percent of total expenditures.[63]

Overall, the record of domestic policies is conflicted. In the five years prior to and after 1908, Britain spent an average of £32 million on its army and £36 million on its navy.[64] This compares to £39 million and £27 million for all other years between 1895 and 1914. Policymakers realized significant savings on the army but struggled to trim expenditures on the navy. Some increase in naval outlays was inevitable given the pace of technological change, revolutionary developments in ship design, and the challenge posed by rival powers. But the figures should not obscure the fact that slashed budgets went hand in hand with institutional upgrades: Haldane's army reforms, Fisher's modernized navy, and Balfour's restructuring of defense coordination. Because of these changes, the military that mobilized for war against Germany was far more capable than the one that struggled in South Africa.

"Limit Responsibilities while Maintaining Engagements": British International Policies

In the 1870s, Britain sought to limit foreign entanglements by shifting burdens to settler colonies and staying aloof from continental crises. In the 1900s, British external efforts were even more pronounced: British overseas garrisons were withdrawn in increasing numbers and peripheral disputes were settled more decisively, while greater burdens were shifted to distant allies and continental partners alike. Yet though the means differed, the ends remained the same. British policymakers sought breathing room to shore up defenses of high-priority interests. At first, the focus was on protecting India from the combination of France and Russia; later, attention turned to defending British naval supremacy from the challenge of a rising Germany. In both cases, retrenchment proved a useful palliative: it allowed Britain to defend its empire and its continental commitments on a budget.

First, policymakers redeployed British forces. As early as the spring of 1904, the CID declared that one of the "fundamentals of imperial defence" was the "provision of overseas garrisons at reduced establishments."[65] At the Indian Office, Lord George Hamilton concurred: "I am gradually coming round to the opinion that we must alter our foreign policy. . . . Our interests being so extended makes it almost impossible for us to concentrate sufficiently, in any one direction, the pressure and power of the Empire so as to deter foreign nations from trying to encroach upon our interests."[66] Three years later, the CID acknowledged Britain could not defend Canada, and authorized withdrawal of all British troops from Halifax and the West

Indies.[67] Haldane stressed "it is very expensive to keep troops in unnecessary colonial garrisons."[68] He trimmed seven battalions of troops from colonial garrisons in South Africa, Malta, Gibraltar, and Ceylon, saving some £2.6 million.

Although imperial garrisons were lightened, the main emphasis on British policy was the redeployment of naval assets. As Fisher bluntly put it, "We cannot have everything or be strong everywhere. It is futile to be strong in the subsidiary theatre of war and not overwhelmingly supreme in the decisive theater."[69] In 1904, Fisher reduced the strength of the Mediterranean squadron, created a Channel Fleet capable of immediate operations in the North Sea, and established an Atlantic Fleet based in Gibraltar that could "reinforce either the Channel or the Mediterranean Fleets as circumstances required."[70] Two years later, he advocated naval concentration in home waters with "ships taken from the Mediterranean, the Atlantic, and the Channel Fleets."[71] In 1909 he went further, raising the Home Fleet to "sixteen fully commissioned battleships with eight in reserve," and relocating the Atlantic Fleet from Gibraltar to Dover.[72] To offset the retraction of naval assets, Fisher endorsed the development of the armored battle cruiser, whose speed and mobility allowed it to protect distant sea-lanes.

This concentration of British naval power was completed under the reforming aegis of the first lord of the admiralty Winston Churchill. In 1912, Churchill introduced a controversial proposal to remove the final six battleships from the Mediterranean to form a new battle squadron at Gibraltar capable of rapidly reinforcing the North Sea and Atlantic squadrons.[73] "Considering you propose to send the whole Br Army abroad," Churchill explained to Haldane, "you ought to help me to keep the whole Br Navy at Home."[74] With minor modification, that is largely what happened.[75] The switch was dramatic: in 1897 Britain had eleven major ships inside home waters and twenty-four outside them; by 1912 there were 33 capital ships inside home waters and just two outside them.[76]

Second, Britain sought to shift its foreign policy burdens to others. While British policymakers continued to pressure the settler colonies to contribute more to imperial defense, they also courted the assistance of other great powers. The earliest example of this policy was the most peripheral: agreement with Japan on the Far East.[77] Although Japan had approached Britain in search of an alliance on previous occasions, Salisbury and Lansdowne preferred working with Russia and later Germany to maintain Britain's Asian position.[78] Yet neither of these diplomatic efforts bore much fruit, and the cost of maintaining the China Field Force and the Far East fleet drained Britain's already shallow resources.[79] Selborne warned that maintaining sufficient battleships to match France and Russia in the Far East would "strain our naval system greatly, and would add to our expenditure in manning the Navy."[80]

Rising Japanese capability, however, could relieve pressure on British naval resources and provide "something of a strategic umbrella protecting Britain's own interests in China."[81] The main alternative, an alliance with Germany, would not only antagonize France and Russia but also bind Britain to the fate of the Triple Alliance.[82] With some dissent in the cabinet, the Anglo-Japanese alliance was signed in 1902.[83] The two parties pledged neutrality in the event of a war with one power, and mutual aid in the event of a war with two. While some scholars characterize the agreement as a grand departure from Britain's policy of splendid isolation, the agreement is better viewed as a modest attempt to lighten the burden of protecting distant interests through the assistance of a local partner.[84]

Third, British policymakers sought to defuse potential flashpoints with rival great powers, especially in periphery. This was the logic that underpinned Britain's famous entente with France.[85] As colonial rivalries heated up in the Far East, British policymakers began to fear they might be dragged into a war with France via their alliance with Japan.[86] Growing unrest in Morocco, joined with unease over the security of Gibraltar, also raised the specter that Britain might clash with France there as well.[87] Signed in 1904, the final series of agreements were less an alliance commitment than the settlement of small disputes in Africa, Siam, Madagascar, Newfoundland, and the New Hebrides. Most importantly, the French agreed to accept British predominance in Egypt in exchange for British backing in Morocco.

Historians have emphasized that the entente with France was limited and focused exclusively on colonial affairs.[88] Yet at the time, there was recognition that the entente might have far-reaching implications. Lansdowne emphasized that the agreements should be seen "not merely as a series of separate transactions" but "as forming part of a comprehensive scheme for the improvement of the international relations of two great countries."[89] In a similar vein, the *chargé d'affairs* in St. Petersburg observed that the "next step should be . . . to use the French agreement as a stepping stone to some sort of improvement in . . . relations with Russia."[90] The entente was not a statement of attraction to a particular group of powers, but a general move to resolve present disputes, remove future clashes, and marginalize threats to Britain's Mediterranean position.

A similar desire to dampen the danger of war in the periphery drove the 1907 Anglo-Russian Convention.[91] British policymakers had long feared that their growing weakness was making it more difficult to defend against a potential Russian advance on India. Salisbury complained that the Viceroy "always wants me to negotiate with Russia as if I had five hundred thousand men at my back, and I have not."[92] As early as 1902, the CID cautioned that Britain might be unable to check Russian encroachments into Persia and Afghanistan or to prevent a seizure of the Dardanelles. Military officials concluded that a Russian advance could only be checked by massive reinforcement of at least 100,000 troops from home and an expanded railway network in India.[93] By early 1907, even these steps appeared insufficient. The General Staff warned that if Russian railway expansion continued, "the military burden of India and the Empire will be so enormously increased . . . it will become a question of practical politics whether or not it is worth [Britain's] while to retain India."[94]

Confronted by this reality, British policymakers strove to improve diplomatic relations with Russia.[95] Thomas Sanderson, the permanent undersecretary at the Foreign Office, described cooperation with Russia as "the only sound [policy]."[96] Lansdowne repudiated the controversial Younghusband mission to Tibet and sought to soothe relations in the aftermath of the Dogger Bank incident, in which Russian ships mistakenly fired on British trawlers.[97] When the liberals came to power, Grey concluded that the only alternative to rapprochement with Russia was the "intolerable increase of the military responsibilities of India and the Empire."[98] Sanderson's successor, Sir Charles Hardinge, pleaded that Britain must find a way to "limit our responsibilities . . . while maintaining our engagements."[99] The final convention appeared to square this circle: it secured joint recognition of Chinese suzerainty over Tibet, neutralized Afghanistan, and divided Persia into spheres of influence.[100]

British policymakers did not just attempt to remove flashpoints in the periphery, however; they also sought to reduce tensions in Europe. While some viewed the entente agreements as an attempt to encircle Germany, Grey never viewed rapprochement with either Paris or St. Petersburg as incompatible with improved relations with Berlin.[101] British policymakers reserved the right to check aggression, but they consistently claimed the entente agreements did not commit them firmly to one continental bloc or another. Instead, successive foreign ministers hoped to use the entente agreements to deter aggression *and* restrain partners. An early example of this delicate balancing act can be seen during the First Moroccan Crises. Initially, Lansdowne promised diplomatic support to the French but was careful to emphasize that Britain would use force only in circumscribed circumstances.[102] The liberal ascendancy changed little: Grey warned the Germans that British opinion would not tolerate the crushing of France while simultaneously encouraging the French to make reasonable compromises.[103] Grey shepherded both sides to the Algeciras conference and worked behind the scenes to engineer a compromise on the internationalization of the police at Moroccan ports.[104]

Britain played a similar role during the 1908 Bosnia crisis. Despite suggestions he exploit rifts between the Dual Alliance powers on Balkan questions, Grey refused to adopt a strident policy. He explained to the Russian ambassador "the absurdity of trying to make mischief between Germany and Austria-Hungary."[105] He also cultivated Berlin's assistance to help mediate the crisis. Simultaneously, Britain worked to support Ottoman claims and maintain Russian friendship.[106] Ultimately, Britain gained compensation for Turkey from both Austria-Hungary and a newly independent Bulgaria, but Russian demands for compensatory concessions on behalf of Serbia failed.[107] Hardinge confessed that British retreat on this issue "might be a climb-down," but it had "the advantage of showing to the whole world that [Britain is] ready to stretch a great many points to secure European peace."[108]

British policy during the Second Morocco Crisis in 1911 exhibited similar flexibility. Grey warned the French that they could not partition Morocco without reasonable compensation for Germany.[109] Britain would not "go to war in order to set aside the Algeciras Act and put France in virtual possession of Morocco."[110] When Berlin attempted to extract the entirety of the French Congo, however, Grey warned the German ambassador that Britain would not permit its entente partner to be exploited.[111] Lloyd George echoed this point in his famous Mansion House speech, declaring, "Peace at that price would be a humiliation intolerable for a great country like ours to endure."[112]

The First Balkan War represents the quintessential example of British efforts to cultivate peace through a great power concert. The primary goal of Grey's diplomacy was to keep the conflict localized. At the London Conference, he worked closely with Germany to oppose Russian efforts to extract large concessions on behalf of Serbia and Montenegro, as well as to restrain Austria-Hungary from using force to expel the Montenegrins from Scutari.[113] This diplomatic triumph proved short-lived, with the Second Balkan War between Bulgaria and her former allies breaking out a year later. Yet Grey again showed Britain's willingness to balance entente obligations with concert diplomacy.[114]

British accommodation was, however, not appeasement. Britain consistently used retrenchment to defend its core interests, especially its naval supremacy, and its concessions were neither asymmetric nor sustained. Whether it was France and Russia in the first half of the 1900s or Germany in the latter half of the 1900s, no one could be permitted to out-build Britain.[115] In 1908, Grey bluntly warned, "If the German Navy ever became superior to ours, the German Army can conquer this country. There is no corresponding risk of this kind to Germany: for however superior our fleet was, no naval victory would bring us nearer to Berlin."[116] Foreign office clerk Eyre Crowe's famous memorandum underscored the same danger.[117]

Yet repeated diplomatic efforts to end the naval race failed.[118] German policymakers were only willing to consider a relaxation in the pace of shipbuilding in exchange for significant British concessions. But Grey refused to accept any political formula "which would separate us from Russia and France, and leave us isolated while the rest of Europe would be obliged to look to Germany."[119] Although Britain was willing to promise to "neither make nor join in any unprovoked attack" in exchange for reductions in German shipbuilding, policymakers in Berlin insisted on a formal declaration of neutrality.[120] Grey went to great lengths to improve relations with Germany, offering terms on future spoils from the Portuguese empire, the extent of the Baghdad railway, and the status of advisors in Constantinople.[121] Yet Britain refused to budge either on its entente agreements, which safeguarded the empire, or on naval supremacy, which secured the homeland.

On balance, British policymakers made a number of changes in external politics as part of a strategy of retrenchment. They continued to remove troops from distant colonial garrisons and concentrate manpower and naval assets closer to home. They accelerated efforts to shift burdens to colonial partners while also reaching accommodations with new allies, like Japan. They also sought to remove dangerous flashpoints in the periphery through a series of interlocking agreements with France and Russia. Through a more restrained foreign policy, Britain sought to remove threats to the empire, secure its homeland from invasion, and preserve its freedom of action to manage continental crises. As Nicolson noted, "In present circumstances we are certainly not strong enough to stand alone."[122] This required delicate balancing acts: accommodating rivals without sacrificing vital interests, supporting partners while restraining them, and defending the homeland without denuding the empire.

"Curbing the Empire of Swagger": The Strength of British Retrenchment

In broad brushstrokes, British grand strategy in the 1900s tends to conform to our predictions. Having experienced a small decline, Britain adopted a series of modest changes to its domestic and foreign policies designed to bring ends and means in alignment. Yet one of the salient features of this period is the urgency and consistency of British efforts. In particular, domestic resistance to retrenchment was more muted and peripheral pulls less prominent than in prior periods.

On the home front, there was greater consensus in favor of a restrained foreign policy. Prior to entering office, Grey gave a prominent speech pledging continuity in foreign policy.[123] The liberals also invited members of the opposition, including Balfour himself, to participate in the activities of the CID.[124] "The appearance of an understanding between the two front benches on major foreign policy questions," the historian Keith Robbins concludes, "frustrated those who wanted to see a distinct 'Liberal' foreign policy."[125] Chamberlain concludes that British foreign policy was "more bipartisan in the decades before the First World War than it had been a generation earlier."[126]

There were nuances between Lansdowne and Grey concerning their interpretation of the role and purpose of the entente with France.[127] Yet for the most part Grey, "like Lansdowne," was "acutely aware of Britain's diplomatic weakness and isolation."[128] The most consistent source of opposition to British foreign policy came not from across the aisle, but from the radical wing of the Liberal party.[129] Radical members criticized the government for excessive naval estimates, the abandonment of liberal principles in Persia, and the failure of negotiations with Germany. Radical pressure did lead to minor concessions, such as the Haldane Mission to Berlin, yet it "did not fundamentally affect its content."[130]

Bureaucratic rivalries played an equally small role in policy outcomes. Foreign Office officials certainly tended to be more anti-German than members of the cabinet, and senior officials in the Admiralty and War Office often held divergent views of Britain's preferred strategy in a continental war. Yet, in the end, Grey designed a foreign policy that reflected his own preferences rather than those of his more hawkish advisors, and with the appointment of Churchill as first lord in 1911, the cabinet forced a reluctant navy to accept the planned dispatch of a continental expeditionary force.[131]

When it came to the empire, policymakers in this period proved more adept at limiting peripheral proconsuls. Both Unionist and Liberal ministers, for example, refused to endorse a forward policy along the Indian frontier. Lansdowne disavowed the controversial Younghusband mission in Tibet, with Balfour stating, "[I] strongly deprecate permanent entanglements in Tibet, partly because I think we have as much on our hands as we can look after."[132] Grey also approved withdrawal from the Chumbi Valley even before the 1907 convention with Russia had been finalized. The Indian secretary Viscount Morley noted with satisfaction the ability of the liberal cabinet to curb the "empire of swagger."[133]

British officials also avoided being drawn too deeply into the affairs of Persia, despite Russian encroachments and the protestations of radicals in parliament. Between 1907 and 1911, Persia experienced no less than four coups and counter-coups involving the Russian-backed Shah and nationalist forces. Throughout these repeated crises, Grey resisted calls for British naval demonstrations and stuck to a policy of working with Moscow. "If there is one thing more than another that I have striven to secure," Grey declared, "it is that we should not incur any increase of Imperial liabilities."[134]

Why then did Britain retrench more during this period? The answer can be found in profound shifts in Britain's structural position in the 1900s. To begin with, Britain was falling from a lower rank among the great powers, from the number two to three spot. Confronted by an increased number of potential rivals, British policymakers had narrower margins within which to operate. In naval affairs, the first lord of the Admiralty questioned whether the "two-power standard" for capital ships "will any longer serve, considering that within the last five years three new navies have sprung into existence—those of the United States, Germany, and Japan."[135] Adding to the potential alarm was the fact that the great power overtaking Britain,

Imperial Germany, was situated in Europe and posed a greater threat to the balance of power. "The real isolation of Germany would mean war," Grey lamented, but "so would the domination of Germany in Europe."[136] This dilemma did not make the Anglo-German antagonism inevitable, but once the naval race heated up, it added urgency to London's efforts to bring resources home.

At the same time, structural conditions afforded Britain greater leeway to moderate its foreign policy. The presence of Japan as a potential ally especially helped buttress retrenchment in Asia. Japan had the advantage of being a capable power with interests that were aligned with Britain and was unlikely to entrap Britain in a dangerous war or exploit Britain in the foreseeable future. For Lansdowne, this was a key argument in favor of aligning with Japan rather than Germany: "The area of entanglement [is] much more restricted."[137] The nature of Britain's peripheral commitments also put it in a favorable position to retrench. Aside from Persia, China, and portions of central Asia, there were few peripheral areas where great power rivalries were present. Even these regions were considered by many to be minor sideshows irrelevant to the defense of the empire. The Indian secretary described great power rivalry in Tibet, to take one example, as a "battle over a shadow."[138] There were also persuasive geopolitical reasons to preserve the independence between peripheral and core commitments. Were Britain and Russia to compete for influence in Tehran, Grey concluded, "everything would be worse both for us and for Persia."[139]

In short, while the depth of British decline in the 1900s mirrored that of the 1870s, structural conditions pushed Britain toward more vigorous retrenchment. The combination of urgent threats closer to home, more capable and dependable allies in the periphery, and the absence of strong fears of falling dominoes smoothed the path toward retrenchment. While retrenchment had begun as a response to fiscal crises and global uncertainty in the balance of power, the emergence of Germany as a naval threat added fresh urgency to these efforts. A modest adjustment had become a major reorientation in British foreign policy, although British policymakers still hoped flexible diplomacy could preserve a fragile peace.

"Lamps Are Going Out": British Retrenchment and the First World War

For critics of British foreign policy, the outbreak of the First World War is taken as persuasive evidence of the bankruptcy of retrenchment. Some claim that Britain's unwillingness to make firm and formal commitments to its entente partners weakened the credibility of its defensive guarantees, undermined deterrence, and encouraged German opportunism.[140] Others—somewhat contradictorily—argue that Britain's search for peace at any price with France and Russia encircled and inflamed Germany, alienated a potential partner in Austria-Hungary, and deprived Britain of a free hand in continental crises.[141]

We find both of these arguments unpersuasive: there are no doubt many causes of the First World War, but retrenchment is not one of them. For starters, Britain's approach to the July Crisis was strikingly similar to its handling of prior diplomatic crises that had resolved peacefully. As had been the case during the Balkan War, Grey initially sought to work with Germany to restrain their respective protégés, France and Austria-Hungary.[142] What Grey did not anticipate, and what German diplomats actively tried to obscure, was that Berlin was not interested in defusing the crisis but was instead encouraging Vienna to take a hard line.[143] Britain's cautious tone in the early part of the July crisis, therefore, stemmed not from naïveté or a hesitancy to act, but from a conviction that reassuring Germany would reduce fears of encirclement and give time for concert diplomacy to work.[144]

Following Austria-Hungary's provocative ultimatum, Britain focused its diplomacy on limiting the crisis. Here Grey deployed the diplomatic formula he had used to great success during the two Moroccan crises. On the one hand, he discouraged France and Russia from escalation. On July 29, Grey told the French ambassador that Britain was "free from engagements," and that he "should have to decide what British interests required [him] to do."[145] On the other hand, he warned Germany that Britain would back its entente partners. That same day, Grey explained to the German ambassador that "if [Germany] and France should be involved, then the situation would immediately be altered. . . . It would not be practicable to stand aside and wait for any length of time."[146] Further, British officials rejected a clumsy effort by the German chancellor Theobald Bethmann-Hollweg to purchase British neutrality and insisted that the great powers convene a conference to manage the crisis.

British preferences were clear, and the Germans knew it. By July 30, Bethmann-Hollweg conceded that "the hope for England [was now] zero."[147] Yet German leaders still refused to accept collective mediation, to press the "halt in Belgrade" proposal on their ally, or to delay mobilization in response to Russian military preparations. For its part, the German military had long expected British intervention and modified the Schlieffen Plan to anticipate it.[148] Germany, as Chamberlain concludes, "had determined to go ahead in any case."[149] There were no good options: Germany could not be deterred and Russia refused to be restrained. "The lamps are going out all over Europe," Grey said, but Germany and Russia put them out.[150]

More important, retrenchment meant that Britain entered the war in a much stronger military position than would have been the case just a decade earlier. Had the First Moroccan Crisis ended in war, for example, Haldane estimated that it would have taken the British army two months to land a mere 80,000 troops on the continent.[151] This force would have been dispatched without a clear objective, with limited means of sustaining itself in the field, and with no predetermined means of coordinating with its ally. Nor was it clear that the Royal Navy could have assembled the transports necessary to cross the Channel.

Contrast this state of affairs to the one in August 1914. Due to the Haldane reforms, Britain possessed an expeditionary force of six divisions—some 150,000 men—five of which would eventually be dispatched to the continent. Thanks to formal staff talks, which had been inaugurated in 1906 and conducted in earnest since 1911, Britain and France had joint plans governing the expeditionary force's landing, movement, concentration, and tactical employment.[152] Similar discussions between the French and British navies had resulted in coordination on sharing of signals, division of patrol zones, and joint operations.[153] Meanwhile, the CID had compelled the navy to harmonize plans with the committee's preferred continental strategy. Doubtless not all of these changes were the direct result of retrenchment, yet retrenchment afforded policymakers valuable breathing space, which they used to react to improve their preparedness.

Put simply, retrenchment neither hastened the onset of the war nor inhibited Britain's fighting ability. Indeed, it is hard to argue that any of Britain's policy alternatives would have fared better. An Anglo-German alliance would have exposed a vulnerable British Empire to French and Russian predation, while an Anglo-French alliance would have fueled German fears of encirclement and invited an earlier test of arms when Britain was less prepared. Despite its best efforts, Britain simply lacked the capability to deter a highly motivated Germany or rein in an equally determined Russia.[154] Considering the massive land forces of Germany and Russia did not deter each other, this is no indictment of Britain.

It is worth noting that the First World War fails to fit the predictions of preventive war theories. Britain had no desire to engage in preventive war to stop Germany's ascent: its diplomacy was aimed to reducing the likelihood of war. Nor did Germany initiate the war to overturn British hegemony: its revisionist aims were centered on the continent, and it hoped up until the last moment—despite compelling evidence to the contrary—that Britain might remain neutral. The First World War is more wisely seen as the historian Joachim Remak sees it: "a modern diplomatic crisis gone wrong, the one gamble that did not work out, the one deterrent that did not deter."[155]

Twice in the fifty years prior to the First World War, Britain was confronted by a small decline in its national power. As predicted by our theory, British policymakers responded with a strategy of retrenchment in both cases. In the 1870s, Britain made a series of modest changes at home and abroad to consolidate its empire and manage unexpected shifts in the balance of power. In the 1900s, Britain made more far reaching shifts in both its domestic and foreign policies in order to defend an overstretched empire and meet nearby challenges to its naval supremacy. In neither case did Britain seek to abandon its empire, surrender autonomy to allies, or appease adversaries. Whatever challenges it faced, Britain remained an intimidating great power, a fact policymakers used successfully.

Although Britain retrenched on both occasions, it trimmed its policies to prevailing structural conditions. Take relative rank. In the 1870s, talk of rank is conspicuous by its absence, but by the 1900s leaders such as Balfour were concluding that Britain was "for all practical purposes . . . only a third-rate Power."[156] As for ally availability, Britain could conciliate Japan and the United States at the turn of the century in ways that looked impossible in the early 1870s, and the rise of Germany made Russia and France more amenable to aligning with Britain as well. With respect to commitment interdependence, first sea lords complained of the strain on naval resources, but that did not prevent them from calling home capital ships without the belief that defeats on the periphery would cascade into a flood at home. The conquest calculus changed over time, from the limited aims wars of the late nineteenth century to the total wars of the early twentieth, and Britain was affected by the arms races leading into World War I. Yet in both cases, Britain availed itself of its insular geography to moderate costs and maintain the smallest great power army in Europe.[157]

In light of the last two chapters, a few final points are worth emphasizing. First, domestic politics played a more tangential role than we predicted. Although it makes deductive sense that small decliners would be more susceptible to interest group and bureaucratic pressure, we did not find persuasive evidence of these dynamics. Policymakers disagreed about the extent and cause of decline, but there was consensus about the underlying trends. And though there were slight differences in stress and shading, policymakers tended to agree about the necessity of retrenchment. At the end of the day, the difference between Gladstone's "thriftily used" power and Disraeli's "proud reserve" was more rhetorical than substantive. It may be that the similar backgrounds of British policymakers limited disagreement. There might also be something in Britain's parliamentary institutions that afforded flexibility to forge consensus and circumvent veto players. Or small decliners might simply be better positioned than we assumed: because they are not falling by much, policymakers do not need to force through the types of ambitious reforms that elicit domestic backlash.

Second, the management of peripheral crises shaped retrenchment in both these cases in substantial ways. In the 1870s, peripheral crises served to slow—and eventually reverse—retrenchment. In the 1900s, policymakers worried about how peripheral disputes might undermine core defenses. This suggests that striking a balance between commitments across regions is a central element of retrenchment. Structural conditions, like commitment independence, play a prominent role, but astute policymakers can also build bulkheads between regional commitments. For instance, the 1907 convention with Russia was both a reflection of the marginal importance of British commitments in places such as Persia, and an attempt to preempt potential crises by demarcating spheres of influence. The British cases suggest that retrenchment is most sustainable when policymakers enforce clear priorities and engineer agreements that not only defuse current flashpoints but anticipate future ones as well.

Third, these cases highlight the limits of hegemony in general, and the potential benefits of rising powers in particular. In spite of being near the pinnacle of international power, British policymakers in each of our cases were painfully aware of the issues they could not change. In the 1870s, Britain could neither impose a favorable settlement of the *Alabama* claims nor prevent Bismarck from redrawing the map of Europe. In the 1900s, Britain played more of a spectator role in the scramble for concessions in China and the dismantlement of Ottoman influence across the Balkans. Despite deep and diverse resources, Britain's ability to influence events on its own did not live up to expectations. An irony of the British cases is that decline actually made this situation better in many respects. In the 1870s the paucity of allies limited how much Britain could pull back, but a stronger Japan in 1900 created opportunities for Britain to do more with less. This dynamic would become even more pronounced with the United States' backing of a humbled Britain in the mid-twentieth century. Life can be lonely at the top, but not necessarily. Rising powers can help as much as hurt.

A Descending Whirligig

1888 Russia

> Russia is not sulking, it is recovering its strength.
>
> —Alexander Gorchakov

From the time of Peter the Great, Imperial Russia added an average of 55 square miles a day to its dominions.[1] Russia accumulated territory like no other state in history and looked inveterately expansionist to neighbors and supporters alike. As one Russian observer reported, "No one knows why or for what purpose . . . there is a wanton element in everything that is going on in the borderlands of our empire."[2] Yet this general pattern masks considerable variation in Russian foreign policy. Following victory in the Napoleonic Wars, Russia stood alongside Britain as one of the most commanding states in all of Europe. Yet after the calamity of the Crimean War, Russia struggled to maintain its position among the great powers.[3] It sought to balance the urgent need for domestic reform with the constant temptation of imperial expansion. It sought to break out of the restrictions imposed by the Treaty of Paris without provoking hostile coalitions or precipitating costly conflicts. The result was a strange mixture both of expansion and contraction, provocation and retreat, which characterized Russian foreign policy in the closing decades of the nineteenth century.

For many, Imperial Russia becomes a tragic story of unmet expectations: a state flush with manpower and natural resources that failed to adapt rapidly to a changing world.[4] It is tempting to chalk up the uneven character of Russian diplomacy to domestic factors, whether fractious bureaucracies or erratic tsars. Yet, in this section, we contend that Russian foreign policy, while far from perfect, did follow a recognizable pattern. Beginning as early as the 1860s, but accelerating in the wake of foreign policy setbacks in the

1870s and 1880s, Russian policymakers espoused retrenchment policies designed to minimize conflicts and free up space for domestic reforms. Acknowledging that Russia was not keeping pace with the competition, policymakers searched for alternatives. Domestically, policies centered on reducing spending to restore fiscal health, modernizing armed forces to meet new threats, and reforming sclerotic institutions to improve performance. Internationally, policies were designed to shift burdens to new allies and settle peripheral disputes, all while defending vital interests in Europe. There were gaps in these efforts, and Russian policymakers often missed opportunities to push reforms as far as necessary, but the thrust of Russian foreign policy was one of *recueillement*—relative quiet abroad to facilitate recovery at home.[5]

Russia's approach to retrenchment was not uniform, however. The wave of reforms that took place in the 1860s and 1870s were focused mainly on domestic policies. Policymakers hoped social and military reforms alone would restore Russian greatness. In the wake of Russian failures in the Near Eastern and Bulgarian crises, policymakers were willing to entertain even more dramatic steps. International policies, notably greater reliance on alliance partners, assumed a more important role, culminating in the transformative Franco-Russian alliance. This embrace of retrenchment was especially surprising given Russia's structural position. As a continental power with concentrated commitments, Russia had good reasons to fear retrenchment might damage its reputation or increase its vulnerability. These concerns sometimes put a brake on retrenchment, especially in the periphery where distant proconsuls could cite them to justify pushing forward the imperial frontier. But it was not until the turn of the century, when the appearance of great power rivals in Asia linked peripheral and European concerns, that these factors proved powerful enough to finally undermine the consensus around retrenchment.

"We Need Peace and Quiet": Russia Recognizes Decline

The seminal shock to Russian foreign policy in the mid-nineteenth century was its performance in the Crimean War.[6] Not only did Russia's military perform poorly, but the conflict left the government deeply in debt.[7] Russia had to slash expenses without sacrificing security. That task fell to the war minister, Dmitry Miliutin, a giant among Russian reformers until his retirement in 1881. The historian Bruce Menning observes, "Above all he was concerned with reducing state expenditures while simultaneously closing the gap between Russian military potential and the reality of Russia's international position."[8] The broad outlines of Russia's dilemma were clear: an agricultural economy and a large uneducated population provided a poor foundation for national power compared to emerging industrial powers with their vibrant middle classes and technologically advanced militaries. The challenge became freeing up the time, resources, and focus needed to invest in domestic reform at a time of looming security threats and ballooning imperial obligations.[9]

In the following decades, Russia would encounter periodic foreign policy crises that would remind it of its persistent vulnerabilities. In the 1863 Polish Uprising, Nikolai Miliutin, the war minister's brother, wrote him, "I cannot tell you what a pitiful impression is produced here [in Warsaw] by our failure to act against a half-armed mob of priests, kids, and every kind of bastard."[10] The wars of German unification worried military strategists to such an extent that they began calling for radical changes to deal with the impending danger in the west.[11] Most dramatically, in the three decades prior to the turn of the century, Russia would experience two moments of ordinal decline. The first, small in depth, occurred in 1879 and gained salience with Russia's setbacks in the Russo-Turkish War. The second, moderate in depth, occurred in 1888 and became most apparent in Russia's failure to impose its preferences during the Bulgaria crisis. Both episodes prompted Russian policymakers to rethink their domestic priorities and foreign commitments.

In the Great Eastern Crisis of 1875–78, Russian leaders were well aware that adventures abroad might lead to revolution at home.[12] Miliutin warned, "The internal and economic transformation of Russia has reached a stage where every external disruption could lead to long-lasting disorder in the organism of the state."[13] The foreign minister Alexander Gorchakov lamented, "We are a great and powerless country. . . . One can always dress up finely, but one needs to know that one is dressing up."[14] Nevertheless, bargaining collapsed and the Russo-Turkish War ignited in 1877, dragging into the following year and draining Russia's coffers. In 1876 and 1877 alone, Russian expenditures related to the war totaled "a shocking 888 million rubles."[15] General Nikolai Obruchev admitted, "We do not have the resources for a second [campaign], and, moreover, because then we would have to fight not only with Turkey but with all those who are only waiting for our exhaustion."[16] Peter Shuvalov, Russia's plenipotentiary to the Congress of Berlin, observed, "We can fight no longer. Neither financial nor military considerations allow it. . . . Defend positions which you consider possible to defend, and yield, better yield everything."[17] Militarily successful but financially compromised, Russia was forced to pare back its inflated aims. At the Congress of Berlin, Russian diplomats abandoned battlefield gains but realized they had no better options.[18] Gorchakov called Russia's diplomatic defeat "the darkest page of my life."[19]

A similar sense of decline gripped Russian policymakers following the 1885–88 Bulgarian crisis. Russia's aims were primarily defensive: to prevent the establishment of an anti-Russian regime in an expanded Bulgarian state. Yet Russia was opposed by Britain and received only tepid support from its partners in the Three Emperors' League. To intervene in Bulgaria meant risking war with Turkey and European powers, and the tsar and all his ministers agreed that the empire's financial and economic state was "catastrophic."[20] Policymakers believed Russia was "not even strong enough to resist an invasion *by Austria, acting independently of its German ally.*"[21] Lacking military muscle or diplomatic backing, Russia sat on the sidelines, watching in horror as Eastern Rumelia was united with Bulgaria and a pro-Austrian prince placed on the throne.[22] The foreign minister Nicholas de Giers acknowledged, "We have submitted, and we are submitting, to the deepest humiliation."[23] "In the entire history of Russian diplomacy," the historian George Kennan concludes, "one searches in vain for any failure more spectacular, and more searing, to the sense of Russian prestige."[24]

In short, in both the late 1870s and late 1880s, Russia experienced a profound foreign policy crisis, which could be connected to its troubled financial situation and unprepared military. The consequences of these setbacks were dramatic: in both cases, Russian policymakers advocated for retrenchment. As Gorchakov explained to the tsar, the Russian state would "have to focus persistently on the realization of [its] internal development and the entire foreign policy [would] have to be subordinated to this main task."[25] Alexander Jomini, one of Gorchakov's chief advisers, likewise argued, "The development of [Russia's] internal life, her productive resources, her prosperity, her culture, her commerce, her industry—[are] all things which require peace. Her foreign policy should thus be purely preventative and defensive."[26]

Similar sentiments prevailed after Russian failures in the Bulgarian crisis. Giers pledged to follow a simple principle: "Above all, avoid unnecessary and untimely complications."[27] In 1888, Jomini reiterated his previous position: "You will not make people like you by using force. It is time to finish with that system."[28] Veteran diplomat Vladimir Lamsdorf, writing in 1890, similarly stressed, "We need peace and quiet in view of the miseries of the famine, of the unsatisfactory state of our finances, of the uncompleted state of our armaments program, of the desperate state of our transportation system, and finally of the renewed activity in the camp of the nihilists."[29] The main debate among policymakers was not whether Russia would retrench, but how it would do so.

"Observation of the Strictest Economy": Russian Domestic Policies

For domestic policies, we ventured that medium decliners would make modest strides in four areas: they would reduce spending, restructure armed forces, reform institutions, and reallocate resources toward more profitable pursuits. Russia followed some, but not all, of these policies. Greatest strides were made on the budgetary front: Russia aggressively trimmed its military expenditures and reallocated resources toward domestic development. The record on reform is less impressive. Policymakers sought to make better use of reserves and incorporate new military technologies, but pushback from entrenched interests blocked progress in crucial areas such as military education. Overall, retrenchment contributed to Russia's fiscal and economic health, but there were missed opportunities to put the Russian military on a stronger footing.

First, Russian policymakers kept military expenditure under control. To address a national debt totaling some 4.9 billion rubles following the Russo-Turkish War, Russian policymakers reduced money for the army from 255 million rubles in 1881 to below 200 million in 1884.[30] The war minister Peter Vannovski reported "the necessity in all measures related to military affairs observation of the strictest economy."[31] Expenditures for the army would not reach 1881 levels again until 1891.[32] These savings were facilitated by cuts in end strength. Between 1881 and 1884, the standing army was "reduced from 863,000 to 756,000 men.[33] Despite twin war scares in 1885 and 1887, austerity remained unshakable. The budget share claimed by the military steadily declined over the last decades of the nineteenth century, from 41 percent in 1855–59 to 24 percent in 1895–99.[34] The army's share of the budget fell by nearly half: from 30 percent in 1881 to 18 percent in 1902.[35] Vannovski complained, "[We are] supposed to be ready to prepare weapons, rations, and food, and they don't even give us kopecks for these things."[36] Yet as the finance minister Alexander Abaza explained to the tsar in 1881, "even though our foreign policy has resumed its peaceable directions . . . it is urgent to take measures to reduce the sacrifices of the country for her armed forces."[37]

Second, Russian policymakers made modest efforts to revamp force structure, making better use of reserves and new technologies. These efforts had a long pedigree. When Miliutin became war minister in 1861, he discovered that Russia had great reserves on paper, but in reality they were "imaginary," fictions based on outdated data and wishful thinking.[38] He capped the regular army and began patiently ramping up reserves. In 1862, he inherited an army with active forces of 793,000 soldiers; he left office in 1881 with 844,000 soldiers. Reserve forces fared differently: in 1862 effective reserves numbered around 100,000, whereas by 1881 they totaled approximately 1.6 million.[39] To help fill the ranks, Miliutin oversaw the adoption in 1874 of universal military service, which increased available conscripts while decreasing the length of service, promoting literacy, and expanding the territorial militia.[40] Alongside these new manpower policies, Miliutin took modest steps toward military modernization, introducing a new breech-loading rifle as well as breech-loading artillery.[41] Miliutin's reforms gave Russia a "smaller, better-trained standing army with large reserves and much improved morale."[42]

Russian performance in the Russo-Turkish War validated some of Miliutin's efforts but exposed other liabilities.[43] Despite Miliutin's best efforts, the Russian army still fielded a hodgepodge of inferior weapons, relied on outdated tactics, and possessed poor logistical and medical support.[44] Further reforms were urgently needed, but the ascendance of the more conservative Alexander III to the throne, combined with the dismissal of the energetic Miliutin, conspired to slow progress. New regulations in the 1880s did restructure the infantry reserves into larger formations, improve training, and strengthen reserve cavalry forces.[45] The army also continued to update its stocks of arms, introducing steel field guns and mortars in the 1880s, a new magazine rifle in the 1890s, and quick-firing artillery in the 1900s.[46] Yet the paucity of railway lines combined with disorganized planning meant that Russia lagged behind its rivals in its ability to deploy its reserves quickly.[47] Writing in 1883, Obruchev lamented that Russia's rivals could "mobilize and concentrate their armies on the frontier much more rapidly than we. Our borders are completely open."[48] Similarly, Russia's technological investments were often tardy and incomplete. The army acquired magazine rifles six years later than other powers and had not acquired modern heavy field artillery by the turn of the century.[49]

Third, Russian policymakers approved some institutional reforms, although the record here is less impressive. The most important military reforms date back to Miliutin's tenure in the 1860s. On the administrative front, Miliutin streamlined the War Ministry, created the Main Staff, rationalized the flow of information, improved the use of military statistics, and reorganized the empire into thirteen military districts.[50] In terms of the officer corps, he made military education a requirement, promoted more meritocratic paths to commissions, and improved the curriculum and prestige of the Nicholas Academy.[51] For the common soldier, he upgraded rations and uniforms, instituted regular target practice, liberalized military justice, and raised medical standards. Miliutin accomplished all this while keeping budgets a third lower than Russia's nearest peer, Prussia.[52]

The essence of these reforms survived into the 1870s and 1880s, but the pace of progress slowed, and there was pushback from entrenched interests.[53] The Main Staff continued to exercise an important planning role, and made greater use of war games, staff rides, and strategic studies, but proposals to expand its size and authority were squashed.[54] New regulations were issued to improve wartime coordination between frontline units and support elements, but there remained a surprising lack of coordination among the various military districts.[55] Perhaps most important, Alexander III "reversed many of Miliutin's educational reform priorities," constricting the pathways to commissions for candidates from non-gentry backgrounds and diluting the quality of officer education.[56] As a consequence, the character and professionalism of the officer corps atrophied, and the gulf between paper plans and actual preparedness grew.[57]

Fourth, Russian policymakers reallocated resources away from the military pursuits and toward domestic development. Particular emphasis was placed on improving Russia's infrastructure and promoting industrial growth.[58] In 1885, for example, the Ministry of Transportation received 2.5 percent of the budget; ten years later it claimed 11 percent, and that figure would nearly double in another ten years.[59] A series of finance ministers embraced various development schemes—Nikolai Bunge (1881–86) revamped the tax system; Ivan Vyshnegradski (1887–92) expanded railroads, grain exports, and protective tariffs; and Sergei Witte (1892–1902) bet heavily on railroads, put Russia on the gold standard, and aggressively pursued foreign investment—and all were given remarkable resources to develop the economy.[60]

Witte in particular adopted American and British approaches of "peaceful penetration" and using economic tools for political influence.[61] Russia's railway network increased from roughly 11,200 kilometers of finished track in 1870 to more than 32,000 kilometers by 1890.[62] Despite the urgings of the Main Staff, however, most of Russia's railroads were built along economic rather than strategic lines.[63] Yet beginning in the mid-1890s, Russia experienced a remarkable period of economic growth. Between 1890 and 1900, "the production of iron and steel, crude oil, and coal all roughly tripled, the length of railway track increased by 50 percent, and the overall value of industrial output doubled."[64] Although the causes of economic expansion remain controversial, Witte's policies correlate with Russia's revenues rising 43 percent.[65]

In sum, the record of Russian domestic retrenchment in this period is inconsistent. On the one hand, Russia made sizable cuts to its defense expenditures. In the five years on either side of 1888, Russia spent an average of 274 million rubles on defense; for all other years between 1870 and 1900, it averaged 298 million rubles.[66] These reductions freed up resources for investment and helped contribute to Russia's surprising economic performance. On the other hand, policymakers made limited progress in the realm of military reforms. The historian William Fuller characterizes this period as one of "squandered opportunities."[67] Yet the 1880s also saw the Russian Main Staff perfect its first modern war plan, and as the historian David Alan Rich concludes, "under no circumstances could the Central Powers muster a force of sufficient preponderance to confidently undertake a strategic offensive."[68] Starved for resources and lacking political backing, Russian military reformers failed to make the most of retrenchment. But retrenchment did not leave empire exposed and helped strengthen the domestic foundations of Russian national power in vital areas.

"Feign Power and Hold Tight": Russian International Policies

In terms of international policies, we expect medium decliners to aggressively redeploy forces closer to home, offer larger concessions to defuse potential flashpoints, and make more sustained strides to share burdens with potential allies, all with the aim of defending core strongpoints. We see solid evidence of each of these approaches in Russian foreign policy during this period. Despite widespread imperial commitments, the Russian military reinforced forces in the west to defend the Polish salient. Russian diplomats strove, with varying success, to temper rivalries with Austria-Hungary in the Balkans, Britain in central Asia, and China in the Far East. And facing the prospect of isolation following the lapse of the Reinsurance Treaty, Russian policymakers went to considerable lengths to cultivate France as an unexpected alliance partner. Distant proconsuls and peripheral crises conspired to periodically disrupt these efforts, yet until the late 1890s, there was consistent and broad support among Russian policymakers in favor of a more restrained foreign policy.

First, policymakers revamped Russia's global posture to concentrate military forces in core theaters. As early as 1873, Russian military officials recognized the vulnerability of the Polish salient to either German or Austro-Hungarian offensives.[69] Given the sluggish pace of Russian mobilization and paucity of strategic railways, planners worried that frontier forces would be overwhelmed before reserves arrived. In an influential 1885 memo, Obruchev compared Russia to a comet with an underdeveloped European core and "a horrifying Asiatic tail, stretching from Tiflis to Vladivostok" that frittered away Russian power.[70] The long-term solution lay in the construction of new fortifications and more railway lines, but in the short term, policymakers endorsed a redeployment of Russia's forces. Forces in the Warsaw, Kiev, and Vilnius districts rose from 227,000 in 1883 to 610,000 in 1893. By 1894, almost half of the regular army had been concentrated in the western military districts.[71] Given limited resources and incomplete reforms, the military was forced to alter its global posture to reflect a more constrained reality.

Second, Russian policymakers sought to avoid crises with potential rivals and to settle disputes nonviolently. For example, in the Balkans, Giers worked with Germany and Austria-Hungary to limit tensions. The treaty that revived the Three Emperors' League in 1881 required the signatories' approval for any territorial changes in the Balkans. A separate protocol encouraged the parties to restrain their local Balkan agents in order to avoid possible collisions of interests. The Bulgarian crisis exposed the weakness of these paper pledges, but at no point did the tsar seriously entertain war. "It would be inexcusable and even criminal," Alexander III argued, "to expect Russia to fight a war with Turkey and possibly Europe [over Bulgaria]."[72] Once the crisis had passed, Russia reverted to its policy of being "relatively inactive in the Balkans."[73] In 1897, unrest in Crete led some Russian policymakers to advocate seizing the Turkish Straits,[74] but Lamsdorf slapped the idea down, arguing that "this unsuccessful and hare-brained attempt would inevitably lead to war and to countless miseries for us."[75] That same year, with trouble brewing in Macedonia, Russia and Austria-Hungary signed a compact to uphold the status quo, a pledge that held for almost a decade.[76]

Russia made similar, albeit belated, efforts to manage tensions with Britain in central Asia. During the 1860s and 1870s, Russian expansion had followed a familiar pattern: Russian military agents would push forward the frontier, Britain would protest vigorously, and the Russian foreign ministry would disclaim any aggressive intentions but refuse to abandon fresh annexations.[77] Following the Russo-Turkish War, however, Russian expansion took on a different dynamic. In 1878, when the British invaded Afghanistan, Russia chose to abandon the Emir Sher Ali Khan to his fate, despite having cultivated his friendship and encouraged his resistance.[78] In 1881, Russian forces captured Goek Tepe, yet in order to smooth relations with London, Moscow dismissed the famous expansionist General Mikhail Cherniaev from his post as Governor of Turkestan.

The most dramatic case of defusing tensions occurred during the 1885 Panjdeh crisis. When a Russian detachment defeated an Afghan force near their disputed border, a war involving Britain appeared likely. Yet a council advised the tsar that "the moment was not opportune for the beginning of a great war. The Russian army was in the midst of reorganization, the navy and the coast defences were unprepared, and the treasury was empty."[79] Russia instead opted to negotiate a new treaty that demarcated the contested Afghan border and acknowledged clear spheres of influence.[80] Ambitious plans to occupy Herat and menace British India were tabled, with the tsar allowing, "We have no use for colonialism."[81] Thus, when a Russian force occupied passes in the Pamir Mountains in 1892, the imperial government disowned the move and ordered a rapid evacuation.[82] As Lamsdorf explained, the "immoderate development of military forces in our central Asian territory would hardly facilitate the preservation of calm and peace necessary for Russia."[83]

Russia favored conciliatory policies in the Far East as well. In 1878, for example, Russia occupied portions of the Ili valley after a local Muslim revolt called into question the firmness of Chinese rule. But when China dispatched a force to suppress the rebellion, Russia had few options. As the historian Sarah Paine emphasizes, "war with Turkey had also financially burdened an already faltering Russian economy and a highly indebted government, all of which served to feed the growing public unrest. The tsarist government was in no position to embark on another war in the Far East."[84] In 1881, Russia signed a treaty in which it agreed to abandon the Ili valley and pay China an indemnity of 9 million rubles.[85] The British ambassador to Russia took note: "China has compelled Russia to do what she has never done before, disgorge territory that she had once absorbed."[86] Russia showed similar willingness to retreat in Korea. In 1884, after Britain and Germany signed treaties with Korea, Russia seized Port Lazarev, prompting Britain to claim Port Hamilton in retaliation. Alarmed, China and Japan successfully pressed the two countries to relinquish their new ports, and the status quo was reestablished.[87]

Third, Russian policymakers cultivated Russia's alliance relationships to reduce its defense burdens. This process unfolded in two distinct stages. At first, Russia sought to tie down Germany with diplomatic agreements, hoping that friendship with Berlin would limit Moscow's defense requirements. A new Three Emperors' League had many potential benefits: it would prevent Russia's isolation and reduce fears that Germany and Austria-Hungary might conspire to threaten Russian interests in Poland and the Balkans, and it could provide opportunities to check British moves in the Near East.[88] Although Russia bristled at Germany's protectionist tariffs and penetration of its domestic markets, the tsar consented in 1881 to a revived alliance.[89] The alternative, being left out of—or left alone to face—a hostile alliance of Germany and Austria-Hungary, was worse.[90] "This is why the Imperial Cabinet has joined the entente established between Germany and Austria," Giers explained in 1883. "Our adherence has given it a negative and defensive character which has blunted the point that was ultimately directed against us."[91] Lamsdorf made a similar argument: "In order to calm things down, at least for a time, we need to repair as far as possible our relations with Germany."[92]

But there were increasing indications that the *Dreikaiserbund* was insufficient. By the mid-1880s, Russia had become so estranged that the tsar proposed a toast to "Russia's sole ally in Europe, the prince of Montenegro."[93] Failure in the Bulgarian crisis was only one indication of Russia's isolation.[94] In the Mediterranean Agreement of 1887, the United Kingdom, Austria, and Italy committed to managing the region, shutting out Russia.[95] When Sir Henry Drummond-Wolff's mission miscarried that same year, the British presence in Egypt appeared indefinite, dealing Russia a further setback.[96]

The most disquieting development was Germany's growing estrangement. While the Triple Alliance of Germany, Austria, and Italy was renewed in 1887, there was too much tension between Austria and Russia to continue the *Dreikaiserbund*. Russia could only get Germany to commit in secret to limited neutrality in the form of the three-year Reinsurance Treaty, but

Russian anxieties were high enough to accept these conditions. Then in 1887 Bismarck added to Russia's woes with the *Lombardverbot*, an order that the Reichsbank take no more Russian securities as loan collateral.[97] Even Russia's friends were not being friendly.

Alienated from most of the great powers and in need of allies, Russia turned to France. The French had been interested in allying with the Russians for years, but the tsar was put off by what he perceived to be French atheism and republican principles.[98] His position softened as Russia's position eroded. Russia needed credit and France was happy to extend it; the first major loan came in 1888, and five more would follow in the subsequent two years.[99] When groups competed to finance the Baghdad Railway, German and British interests lined up against Russo-French interests.[100] When the Russians requested the state-of-the-art Lebel rifle, the French were swift to supply it.[101] At the dawn of the 1890s, Russia was reluctantly moving away from Germany. The foreign minister Giers earnestly hoped for continued connection to the Germans, and the tsar was not far behind him.[102] Yet the Germans remained cool, and with the rise of a new Kaiser and the fall of Bismarck, the Reinsurance Treaty was allowed to expire and Germany steadily signaled that it was more interested in supporting others over Russia.[103] Diplomacy may have been more fluid than usual during this period in part because the great power hierarchy was in considerable flux.

France and Russia began negotiating a secret military convention to defend each other in case of German attack. The French had no desire to get involved in a war with Germany over the Straits, and the Russians had no interest in supporting a land grab for Alsace-Lorraine.[104] In 1892 both sides agreed to a military convention stipulating that if Germany attacked France or Russia, both would employ "all available forces" against Germany, and that German mobilization meant French and Russian mobilization.[105] By 1894 the alliance became official. To be sure, the Russians remained touchy about how committed they were to the French; they signed a commercial treaty with Germany not long after, and it was only after Alexander III's death at the end of the year that the word "alliance" was used.[106] But it was undoubtedly a commitment to mutual defense against German aggression.[107] The deal's consummation, along with the achievement of no major wars on his watch, earned Alexander III the nickname "the Peacemaker" among conservatives.[108]

Fourth, Russian decision-makers sought to bolster deterrence through strongpoint defenses. The most important of these was Russia's western front, especially the Polish salient. We have already noted the shift of military forces into forward positions along the western front. Modest efforts were also made to improve fortifications after tests in 1886–87 found Russia's forts outmoded and defenseless. Russian engineers strengthened the forts, but strategists refused to rely on static positions, designing a flexible defense in depth "built around concealed and mobile guns and requiring elaborate communications."[109] Russia also revised its mobilization plans in light of the French alliance, which had "rescued the entire process of Russian war planning by granting it a foothold in the world of the feasible."[110] Through these moves, Russian policymakers sought to protect the one place where, according to Obruchev, Russia could be dealt a "mortal blow."[111]

In brief, Russian policymakers retrenched during this period. Global posture was modified to concentrate soldiers in vulnerable western military districts. Efforts were made to temper colonial rivalries and settle disputes short of war. And perhaps most dramatically, Russia reached out to potential alliance partners to help reduce burdens, initially by binding itself to Germany, later by aggregating capabilities with France. As Fuller observes, Russian foreign policy in the 1880s "sought to avoid overt clashes with other Great Powers and equally tried to employ diplomacy to paper over military weakness."[112] "The economic crisis eliminated any real possibility of an aggressive foreign strategy," the historian Dietrich Geyer concludes, so Russia's "only recourse was to feign power and hold tight."[113]

"Interests Grow More Intense": The Breakdown of Russian Retrenchment

Throughout this period, Russian foreign policy broadly conformed to our expectations. When confronted by clear evidence of decline, Russian policymakers embraced policies of retrenchment. This pattern is striking for two reasons. First, the Russian state is not held up as a paragon of functionality, modernity, or bureaucratic rationality. Entrenched interests certainly conspired to limit the depth and extent of needed reforms. When Alexander III became tsar in 1881, for example, he commissioned a hostile group to review Miliutin's reforms, and they favored tearing them down. Yet economic and strategic realities prevailed and most of Miliutin's reforms endured.[114] The tsar grumbled but did not repeal the Great Reforms. Vannovski was not an enthusiastic reformer but he maintained Miliutin's right-hand man Obruchev and main strategist Genrykh A. Leer in high authority. A reactionary tide nibbled at the edges of the prior generation of reforms, but could not undo them—they were too vital to the regime's survival. The fact that substantial progress was also made in modernizing the Russian economy during this period is a laudable achievement.

Second, Russian retrenchment is surprising because structural conditions did not appear to favor it. As a continental power with vast interconnected commitments, exposed and difficult-to-defend positions, and fleeting and unreliable partners, Russian policymakers could have viewed restraint with deep suspicion. For their part, Pan-Slav ideologues and peripheral proconsuls frequently invoked images of falling dominos. The governor general of Turkestan observed, "Asia knows that Turkey and England are

125

watching us. The slightest concession and we will . . . risk losing all that we acquired."[115] The Main Staff warned that the calculus of conquest was shifting against Russia. "When powerful neighbors arm themselves, furnish themselves with improved arms, provide themselves with strategic railway lines, and become capable of hurling armies of millions of men," Obruchev declared, Russia could be "wiped off the earth by history."[116] But the very nature of Russia's liabilities and vulnerabilities meant that these constraints could only slow, not reverse, retrenchment. The sheer distance between Russia's core European possessions and its central Asian outposts muted concerns of falling dominos. Modern militaries with strategic railways were a feature of Russia's western front, not the Balkans or central Asia. Indeed, Russia's possession of distant and defensible peripheries, alongside a compact yet vulnerable core, reinforced, rather than undermined, retrenchment.

By the mid-1890s, however, Russian retrenchment began to break down. In particular, despite continued weakness at home, Russia embarked on a series of provocative, wasteful, and ultimately calamitous moves in the Far East. In 1895, with German and French backing, Russia forced Japan to renounce gains it had acquired in its successful war against China. Witte, having "virtually taken over the conduct of Russian foreign policy in the Far East," pressed China to accept a French loan and to grant a secret railway concession in Manchuria.[117] Two years later, the German seizure of Tsingtao left the Russians feeling betrayed and vulnerable.[118] In response, Russia seized Port Arthur and demanded a twenty-five year lease of the entire Liaotung peninsula, embittering Japan and violating Russia's former policy of only taking contiguous, defensible territories.[119]

From this point forward, Russia's Far East policy became increasingly contradictory. On the one hand, Russia took steps to allay Japanese anxieties in the 1898 Nishi-Rosen Agreement, which vowed not to block Japanese commercial penetration, to leave alone Korean domestic politics, to consult Japan before sending military advisors, and to acknowledge Korea as a Japanese sphere of influence in return for Manchuria being a Russian sphere of influence.[120] In the Scott-Muraviev Notes of 1899, Russia also reached an accommodation with Britain to divide China into railway spheres.[121] And Russia joined the other great powers in suppressing the Boxer Rebellion, and paid lip service to the United States' Open Door Notes.[122]

On the other hand, in 1903, the tsar embarked on the "new course," the stated purpose of which was "no penetration of foreign influence into Manchuria . . . in any form whatsoever."[123] The prior year, a courtier named Alexander Bezobrazov had presented the tsar with his report, *A Humble Memorandum*, which argued that war with Japan was inevitable and must be prepared for. He explained how Russian interests "grow more intense, *through the sheer expanse of its territory*," how Russia could use its size as a lever in Europe and Asia, and how the decisive rule world politics.[124] The tsar funded Bezobrazov's clique lavishly,[125] exiled Witte to a ceremonial post, increased military forces in the Far East, and halted the planned evacuation of Manchuria.[126] The war minister Alexei Kuropatkin complained that "the Sovereign had taken the 'new course' without consulting his ministers," and Lamsdorf threatened to resign.[127] Even proponents of the "new course" were perplexed by it: the interior minister Vyacheslav Plehve acknowledged that he did not know where Russian leaders were going.[128] The culmination of these policies was the outbreak of the disastrous Russo-Japanese War in 1904.

What can explain the breakdown of Russian retrenchment? Partially it was a product of Russia's fortunes reviving: cushioned by French military and financial support and somewhat protected in the west, Russia increasingly eyed sideshows in the east.[129] Still, many senior advisors appreciated the marginal importance of the Far East. As the Chief of Staff Viktor Sakharov explained, "It is essential to give priority to the main danger . . . the power of the Triple Alliance. They threaten Russia with the greatest loss, having the capacity . . . to deliver a blow to the very center of our might."[130] Partially it was a product of poor judgment: the ascension of the inexperienced and erratic Nicholas II to the throne accentuated many of the inherent defects in Russia's autocratic system. Whereas Russia had three foreign ministers since 1815, for example, "no less than nine men held the post between 1894 and the dynasty's collapse."[131] Absent consistent direction from the tsar, control over Russian policy in the Far East wandered from Witte in the Finance Ministry to Kuropatkin in the War Ministry to the shadowy Bezobrazov clique. The empowerment of Admiral Yevgeni Alekseev, the hawkish man-on-the-spot in Port Arthur, to lead negotiations only accentuated the fissiparous tendencies in Russian policy.

Yet more generally, shifts in structural conditions also reduced support for retrenchment and empowered those calling for expansionist policies. The appearance of rival great powers in the Far East, combined with the continued decline of the Chinese empire, increased the perception that Russian commitments were becoming interdependent. In an influential memorandum, for example, Prince Volkonskii warned that if Russian passivity in Asia "continues for many more years then Vladivostok [will be] threatened with the fate of Sevastopol."[132] After Germany seized Tsingtao, Lamsdorf fretted that "within days England will appear in Port Arthur" and Russia would never get a warm-water port.[133] In early 1903, Tsar Nicholas II reiterated his intention to withdraw from Manchuria but simultaneously declared, "We will upgrade our armed forces in the Far East as soon as possible, and without regard to budgetary prudence . . . thereby proving to the world our steadfast determination to defend our right to exclusive influence over Manchuria."[134] The apparent ease in which Russian military forces had overrun the Boxers reinforced these arguments. Given the efficacy of force, Russia could resist any armed opposition to its presence.

Conversely, if Russia were to withdraw, other powers could quickly fill the void. As Plehve bluntly observed, "Russia has been made by bayonets, not diplomacy . . . and we must decide the issue with China and Japan with bayonets and not with diplomatic pens."[135]

The fact that Russia embraced retrenchment with such consistency during the 1880s and early 1890s is surprising. As a continental great power with vast and vulnerable possessions, it was predisposed to be reluctant to risk retrenchment. Yet policymakers across the board were grim in their assessments of Russia's relative standing. The sheer size of the Russian empire combined with the relative insularity of its particular commitments afforded Russian policymakers greater latitude to experiment with retrenchment than we anticipated.

Support for retrenchment wavered, however, once imperial rivalries began heating up in the Far East. The fear of falling dominos, combined with the perceived efficacy of faits accomplis, led an inexperienced tsar to embrace a contradictory and ultimately disastrous policy. Russia's actions in the Far East, the historian David MacKenzie concludes, "constitute the exception to generally prudent external policies in the post-Crimean era."[136] Ultimately, the costs of this adventurism proved "staggering."[137] "Neither the army nor the treasury could keep pace," Menning concludes, and "once again a dangerous gap opened between state policy and military capacity."[138] After defeat, Russia again found itself in the throes of decline and domestic upheaval, forcing another round of retrenchment.

"Les Jeux Sont Faits"

1893 France

> We dream of an alliance for revenge, and we get an alliance for peace, and must bury our hopes.
>
> —*Le Rappel*

As in the Russian case, French foreign policy in the late nineteenth century was profoundly shaped by the experience of military defeat. Yet the debacle of the Franco-Prussian War far surpassed that of Crimea. The unexpected defeat of the French army at Sedan, the traumatic siege of Paris, and the bloody purge of the Paris Commune generated a profound sense of crisis in French politics and society.[1] In the wake of these events, French politicians faced a number of challenges. At home, the fledgling institutions of the Third Republic needed to be consolidated and defended against the forces of reaction on the right and revolution on the left. Abroad, France needed to break out of its isolation and restore its place among the ranks of the great powers, all while avoiding a premature war of revenge with Germany.

Unlike Russia, French policymakers adopted a more varied range of policies in response to decline. Initially, French policymakers favored retrenchment. In the 1870s, France avoided escalating disputes with its European rivals, limited its colonial adventures, and rebuilt and reformed its army. At other times, however, French policymakers flirted with expansionist policies. In the early 1880s, France raced to acquire new colonies, advanced competitive commercial policies, and fought a series of costly wars in the periphery. The inconsistent character of France's foreign policy during this period would seem to reflect the unsettled state of its domestic politics. Frequent changes of government, turmoil in key ministries, a fractious parliament, contested elections, and a series of domestic crises conspired to degrade the quality and coherence of French foreign policy.

In this chapter, we argue that France was much more sensitive to external constraints than is commonly understood. Rather than being driven by domestic upheaval or the vain pursuit of prestige, French foreign policy was fundamentally pragmatic and defensive in character. Military expenditures were kept at manageable levels, the armed forces were modernized and reformed, and efforts were made to promote industrial growth and overseas trade. French policymakers also sought to deescalate crises with more capable rivals, manage colonial rivalries through negotiation, and cultivate new alliances. There were moments when colonial escapades captured policymakers' attention, but unbridled expansion tended to do France more harm than good. Overseas adventures sapped blood and treasure, alienated other great powers, and failed to garner widespread domestic support. France continued to dabble in the colonial sphere, but its foreign policy in the 1890s was far more consistent with retrenchment than anything else.

France stuck to retrenchment, despite the troubled politics of the Third Republic, in part because of favorable structural conditions. Situated in a relatively low rank and confronted by declines of increasing magnitude, France had strong incentives to rethink its approach to foreign affairs. As a continental power surrounded by capable neighbors, France might have feared that retrenchment would expose it to predation. Yet with minor exceptions, Germany and France did not compete directly in the colonial sphere, and, even if they had, the victor could not have used the spoils to dominate the other. Moderating ambitions in the Mediterranean or Southeast Asia did not dilute France's standing or boost Germany's; it freed resources that shielded vital interests. What ultimately undermined French retrenchment was less shifting external circumstances than chaotic internal ones. Whereas the Fashoda crisis confirmed the frivolousness of colonial scrambles, the Dreyfus affair injected poisonous domestic politics into debates over military reform. External moderation endured, but army modernization stalled and in some cases reversed.

"Immobility Becomes a Veritable Decline": France Recognizes Decline

The turning point for France's foreign policy in the late nineteenth century was its traumatic defeat in the Franco-Prussian War. German victory was so decisive, and the indications of rising German strength so clear, that reality was too obvious to deny. As one editorial observed, "What we bitterly deplore is not so much France's weakened position as its spontaneous and satisfied acceptance by public opinion. . . . But we must confess . . . our humiliation and agree that it conforms exactly with the spirit of the chamber and of the country."[2] Joseph Chailley-Bert, a member of the Chamber, recalled, "We had been beaten in 1870. We had been demoted . . . from our position as the dominant power in Europe and almost master of the world to the status of a second-class power."[3]

The war also revealed fundamental defects in France's political and military institutions.[4] The leaders of the Second Empire were revealed as incompetent, the military as inadequately trained and poorly led. The British ambassador to France Lord Lyons reported that "the dread that an attack from Germany may come before France is ready to meet it still weighs upon men's minds."[5] The Republican statesman Léon Gambetta likewise observed, "Having watched the maneuvers of every branch of [Germany's] army, I entreat my country more than ever to remain completely apart from the quarrels of Europe, for unfortunately, we do not possess any forces which can compare with the troops I have just seen."[6] More generally, observers interpreted the defeat as "a sign of political and social malaise."[7]

This pervasive sense of weakness endured in the decades after the war. When the prime minister Jules Ferry fell from office due to criticisms of his expansionist colonial policies, the veteran diplomat Paul Cambon reported, "The general impression is that the Republic is at the end of its tether."[8] In 1886, a prominent retired general observed, "It is high time to call the attention of the country to the constantly growing state of disorganization in which our army finds itself."[9] In a speech to the Chamber the following decade, the veteran politician Théophile Delcassé stated, "On whatever side we look, grave subjects for reflection force themselves upon us. Foreign trade has ceased to expand, industrial production is at a standstill, the population is no longer growing. . . . This immobility, which is already disquieting in itself, becomes a veritable decline when we consider the audacious and self-confident growth and the continuous ascent of our most redoubtable neighbours."[10]

While there was broad recognition of the reality of decline, French policymakers responded to these trends with varying policies. In the immediate aftermath of the Franco-Prussian war, French politicians favored a more modest foreign policy. The president of the republic Adolphe Thiers advocated maintaining a position as "friends of all the world," arguing that "for some time yet [this would be] the conduct that serve[d] France's interests."[11] So, too, Gambetta observed that "the supreme art will lie in keeping France free in her movements, reserved in the midst of the general agitation, able to defend her own territory without giving herself up to suspect alliances or to unfounded illusions."[12] To put France back in the position to compete with Germany, politicians acknowledged that ambitions must "necessarily [be] modest."[13] Gambetta famously declared, "Let us not speak of *revanche*, let us not utter rash words, let us keep silence. When we have completed this essential regeneration time enough will have passed for there to have been changes in the world around us."[14]

Under the governments of Ferry in the early 1880s, however, French foreign policy moved in a different direction. Ferry characterized his foreign policy as "a pacific policy," but added, "A pacific policy is not necessarily an inactive policy. . . . In all questions where our interests or our honor are involved we shall maintain for France the rank that belongs to her."[15] Ferry focused his efforts on the colonial sphere. Thus, in 1881, he authorized military intervention in Tunisia, nominally to protect the Algerian border but in the context of growing Franco-Italian rivalry.[16] When locals resisted, France suppressed them and declared a protectorate.[17] In 1883, Ferry endorsed the explorer Pierre Savorgnan de Brazza's efforts to extend French influence into the Congo River basin. That same year, he authorized a punitive expedition against Madagascar to defend French rights on that island. Most significantly, in Indochina, Ferry pressed local officials to extend French influence into Annam and Tonkin, moves that sparked a war with China in 1884.[18]

Ferry offered many justifications, both contemporary and in hindsight, for his policies.[19] He stressed the economic advantages of colonial outlets in a time of rising protectionism, famously declaring, "Colonial policy is the daughter of industrial policy."[20] He characterized colonialism as a duty all civilized nations should perform. But most important, he emphasized the prestige to be gained from colonial conquests. "To have influence without acting," Ferry concluded, "is to abdicate, and in a shorter time than you can believe, it is to descend from the first rank to the third or fourth."[21] Yet in practice, Ferry's policies received little support, either at home or abroad. The annexation of Tunisia soured relations with Italy, incited a revolt among members of the Chamber, and led to the fall of the first Ferry government. The scramble for concessions in the Congo River basin strained relations with Britain, as well as Belgium and Portugal, and encouraged Germany to jump into the colonial race. The war with China in Tonkin dragged on for half a year, and when an overblown report of a military setback reached Paris, Ferry was again thrown from office, never to return.[22]

The final fall of Ferry represents a turning point in French foreign policy. As the diplomat Frederick Quinn put it, Ferry's enthusiastic pursuit of colonial prestige encountered "few followers, a hostile press, and an indifferent public."[23] France could not abandon existing colonies or abstain from imperial competition, but nor could it ignore the threat posed by Germany's rise in Europe.[24] The primary response was to return to retrenchment. The incoming cabinet of the prime minister Henri Brisson set the tone: "The Republic desires nothing but peace, peace accompanied by the dignity which a nation like ours demands, peace assured by a solid army of defense."[25] The minister of war General Jean-Baptiste Campenon added, "We have only one course to follow, to wait and to struggle, not in distant quarters of the world, but in Europe; you know against whom."[26] In an 1887 newspaper article, Delcassé similarly observed, "Let us . . . settle our internal problems as quickly as possible in order that we may devote all our attention to the enemy. Let us hold ourselves in readiness."[27] It remained to be seen how Ferry's successors would balance competing pressures at home and abroad.

"Behind that Décor were Chaos and Waste": French Domestic Policies

For Russia, domestic responses were blurry: budgetary burdens were lightened and resources reallocated, but military reforms languished. In the case of France, domestic responses also conflicted, but in a different way. Efforts were made to cap spending increases, but the need to keep pace with Germany meant that France was often obliged to spend significant sums for its defense. It was in the area of force structure and institutional reform, in contrast, where France made the greatest strides. France slowly transitioned from a small professional army into a modern mass conscript army, armed with the advanced weaponry, and commanded by a core of well-educated staff officers. Given its commitment to civilian supremacy, France could not simply copy the German General Staff system, but it revamped its institutions to enhance strategic planning and coordination. Scholars debate whether these changes would have been sufficient to defeat Germany in an actual war, but the bottom line is that the French military had been rebuilt into a more capable and credible force.

First, the French made significant exertions to lower the financial burdens of their foreign policy. In financial terms, the Franco-Prussian war cost France some 16 billion francs, an amount "ten times France's budget for 1870 and one-tenth of France's total capital."[28] Policymakers recognized the importance of parsimony: only if military spending were controlled could France then pay off its war indemnity and reduce the national debt. Gambetta contrasted the Third Republic's policy with that of its predecessor, when France had "a sumptuous military décor, but as experience has so terribly demonstrated, behind that décor were chaos and waste."[29] The ordinary army budget fell from 600 million francs in 1882 to just 550 million francs in 1888, although extraordinary budget requests frustrated the pursuit of economy.[30] Parallel efforts were made to limit waste and abuse, and in part through these efforts, the cost of provisioning a French infantryman fell from 447 francs in 1878 to 394 francs in 1890.[31] Understandably, the navy felt the biggest pinch. In 1872, the minister of marine Admiral Louis Pierre Alexis Pothuau consented to a 25 percent cut in his budget, stating that the navy had "to sacrifice itself on the altar of the nation."[32] Some members of the Chamber clamored for increased shipbuilding but acknowledged that "there is a fact of *force majeure* that dominates the whole question, the lack of resources to meet the augmentation of expenses."[33]

Nonetheless, rising rivalries in the 1890s conspired to push French military expenditures higher. The share of the national budget spent on defense crept up slowly from 23 percent in 1872 to 26 percent in 1880 to 30 percent in 1890 to 38 percent in 1900.[34] And after 1900, French military expenditures swelled to more than 1 billion francs. Policymakers were under immense pressure to keep pace with Germany. As the radical deputy Camille Pelletan declared in 1891, "The budget for the Ministry of War is the sacred treasure of the country."[35] Despite considerable investments between 1890 and 1914, special military appropriations ran double in Germany what they were in France.[36]

Second, France sought to restructure its military forces to reduce costs and boost effectiveness. In particular, policymakers transformed the army from a professional force consisting of long-serving soldiers to a mass army comprised of a mix of short-serving regulars and reservists. In 1872, the Chamber passed a law establishing universal conscription, although Thiers insisted on a five-year term and the maintenance of certain exemptions. This system persisted until the late 1880s, when the growth of German military capabilities prompted policymakers to reconsider the length of service. The French war minister Charles de Freycinet concluded, "We cannot remain faced with such an increase in forces without taking similar measures."[37] In 1889, the Chamber passed a new law that reduced service to three years and eliminated most exemptions. The cumulative impact of these bills was to expand the number of people trained and swell the size of the reserves.[38] In 1870, the French army numbered 404,000 on a peacetime footing and 758,000 on a wartime footing, but by 1885 those figures had ballooned to a regular army of 525,000 with 2.5 million men including reserves.[39]

The underlying logic was the same as Russian strategy: France could not afford to keep massive armies at the ready, so it maintained an active force large enough to train the nation-in-arms and provide a covering force (*couverture*) to buy time for full mobilization.[40] The military brass initially put little stock in reserves, but that began to change in the late 1880s.[41] In particular, the chief of staff General Joseph de Miribel led the push for an increasing role and reliance on reserves in the face of burgeoning German power.[42] Realizing it could never outnumber the Royal Navy, the French Navy, too, turned to reserves and mobilization as the keys to safety. Although some ministers of marine, like Admiral Théophile Aube, tried to keep as many ships in commission as possible, the trend was unmistakable by the late 1890s. Naval planners relied increasingly on faster ships and faster mobilization to make up for inferior numbers and inferior finances.[43] Defeat was also a boon to the adoption of new technology. Napoleon III had to push the generals to use the chassepot rifle or rifled artillery, but now technological change met little resistance.[44] A long list of military improvements and reforms came on line shortly after 1888: widespread use of the Lebel magazine-loading rifle, adoption of high explosives and smokeless powder, advanced fortifications, and better conditions for soldiers.[45]

Third, policymakers implemented a number of institutional reforms designed to improve the performance of the French military. In terms of the army, the Franco-Prussian War had revealed all manner of problems related to organization, logistics, officer quality, and command. As one prominent post-war commission concluded, "One cannot improvise either generals or armies."[46] Over the course of two periods of intense reform, French policymakers sought to redress these defects.[47] The first surge of reforms took place in the early 1870s, and featured conservative but nevertheless important changes to organization.[48] Peacetime command structures were established for all units up to the corps level to smooth mobilization. The size and composition of French formations were reorganized along German lines to increase their striking power. Staff officers were required to attend the newly christened École Supérieure de Guerre and then serve in greater variety of assignments to improve their quality and experience.[49] The army's supply services were brought under the direct command of field officers to ensure greater coordination.

These reforms improved the quality of the army, but the rapid turnover of personnel in the War Ministry created a persistent leadership vacuum.[50] The second surge of institutional reforms in the late 1880s, therefore, focused on strengthening planning and command. Freycinet elevated the position of the chief of the General Staff in both rank and prestige, a move he hoped would insulate the position from ministerial instability.[51] Freycinet also revived the Conseil Supérieur de la Guerre (CSG), an advisory body of prominent officers established in the early 1870s that had become moribund from disuse.[52] By establishing regular positions on the council, streamlining its size, and requiring it to meet monthly, Freycinet encouraged the CSG to evolve from a consultative body into what the historian Douglas Porch describes as "a de facto high command."[53] Freycinet also upgraded army depots, raised soldier pay, and eliminated salary differentials between branches.[54] The French army even developed annual maneuvers along the German model, albeit not as good.[55] By way of contrast, the pace of reform in the French navy was slower and less consistent than that of the army.[56] Yet a French naval General Staff was established in 1881, consistent naval maneuvers were adopted in 1887, and an École Supérieure de la Marine was proposed in 1881, although not established until 1895.[57]

Fourth, France reallocated resources to slow its slide. Cost-saving measures paid significant dividends. In part by keeping its military spending to under 650 million francs from 1870 to 1875, France was able to quickly pay off its 5 billion franc war indemnity.[58] The percentage of government expenditures devoted to debt interest fell from 38 percent in 1872 to just 28 percent by 1900.[59] Meanwhile, government investment in education and science increased from 2.3 percent of expenditures in 1872 to 7.4 percent in 1900.[60] French growth rates were not as blistering as German rates, but this was in part due to birth rates—French per capita GDP stayed on par with German per capita GDP through the turn of the century.

On balance, the record of French domestic retrenchment in this period is promising, yet incomplete. On the positive side, French policymakers made substantial progress in the area of military reform. As Porch underscores, "In the two decades following the Franco-Prussian War, France had undergone a military renaissance."[61] France's "organization, construction, and strategic planning before Freycinet had been extremely wasteful," the historian Allan Mitchell observes.[62] Following these reforms, the French military improved not only in quantity but also in quality. Indeed, the German military attaché in Paris went so far as to report in 1891 that "the French army was superior to ours for the moment."[63] At the same time, France struggled to keep its defense expenditures under control. In the five years on either side of 1893, France spent an average of 888 million francs on its military; for all other years between 1875 and 1905, it averaged 868 million francs, a nearly identical, if not smaller, sum.[64] The pressure to match German expenditures combined with the need to acquire the latest weapons worked to limit potential savings. Yet the periods when French expenditures were lowest, the early 1870s and late 1880s, roughly correspond to the most salient moments of decline.

"We Must Proceed with Great Prudence": French International Policies

Whereas Russia clearly favored retrenchment in its international policies, the case of France is more ambiguous. After the fall of Ferry, French policymakers did incline toward retrenchment in a number of key areas. They slowed the pace of imperial expansion and entered into negotiations to eliminate potential colonial flashpoints. They cultivated allies who could help share the burden of checking German ambitions in Europe. And they invested in capabilities designed to improve France's capacity to defend the homeland from external aggression. Yet at the same time, the siren song of colonial expansion was tempered, but never eliminated. Expansionist proconsuls exploited poor oversight and local opportunities to push forward the colonial frontier across the periphery, while a small but vocal colonial party rose to defend expansion back in the metropole. As a result, France's global posture remained curious and contradictory: it pulled back ships from imperial commitments at a time when overseas forces were expanding in size and stature. Its foreign policies were sensibly designed to soothe tensions, yet its colonial policies unintentionally provoked dangerous crises.

First, France sought to revamp its global posture by concentrating forces closer to home. It was most successful in these endeavors in terms of its fleet. The Third Republic gradually demoted high seas operations and winnowed down its naval stations, although the process was not linear.[65] The trend, however, was to bring the best ships home and the number of coaling stations down. By the 1890s, the historian Theodore Ropp observes, "nobody cared whether the colonies were defended or not." And "even if France had had some coaling station overseas, there would have been no ships to use them. . . . The Chamber vigorously protested any policy that would catch good ships away from home in case of war."[66] There were no modern ships abroad and dwindling numbers of coaling stations; in 1890 the Navy proposed ten but by 1900 they were down to five.[67] Rather than invest in battleships, the Jeune École called instead for a system of fast commerce raiders, torpedo boats, and small rams, which exploited telegraph and semaphore communications to quickly concentrate, disperse, and reconcentrate. Although defense was supposed to be a springboard for subsequent offense, the French were well aware of their inferiority against the British and the ideas of the Jeune École waxed and waned from the mid-1880s until the turn of the century.[68]

Curiously, at a time when France was concentrating its navy at home, it was expanding its ground forces overseas. Both the Armée d'Afrique and the Troupes de Marine, which were responsible for garrisoning North Africa and the colonial empire, respectively, increased in strength. The Armée d'Afrique, for example, added two battalions of infantry, two regiments of light cavalry, and doubled the size of its *tirailleurs* battalions from twelve in 1875 to twenty-four in 1898.[69] As a consequence, French forces in North Africa increased from approximately 52,000 troops in 1879 to more than 65,000 in 1900.[70] The Troupes de Marine similarly swelled in size from four regiments in 1870 to eighteen regiments in 1900, as well as adding three regiments of *tirailleurs*.[71] Thus, French forces responsible for the rest of the empire quadrupled from approximately 16,000 troops in 1880 to more than 68,000 by 1900.[72] All told, France went from having roughly 14 percent of its land forces committed to its empire in the early 1880s to around 20 percent by the late 1890s. Yet several caveats are in order. Algeria was considered a department in France, and thus its garrisons might properly be considered as being stationed at home rather than abroad. In addition, the majority of the white regiments in the Troupes de Marine were based in France, and much of the duty of imperial policing fell upon local indigenous forces. But perhaps most important, colonial units could be sent to the metropole in time of crisis, as was that case for thirty-two of forty *tirailleurs algériens* and *tirailleurs tunisiens* battalions at the outbreak of the First World War.[73]

Second, French policymakers aimed to eliminate potential flashpoints with rival great powers. In Europe, the main goal was to prevent a minor crisis from escalating into a general war given France's isolation and continued military weakness. An early example of this policy can be seen in the 1875 "War in Sight" crisis, when a series of minor events made it seem as if Germany might be contemplating a preventive war.[74] Rather than exploit this opportunity to build the case for revenge, however, France sought instead to soothe tensions. French policymakers avoided any actions that had escalatory potential, and pressed the other powers, notably Britain and Russia, to exercise restraint with Germany. Despite the thirst for *revanche* in many quarters, French policymakers refused to support anti-German movements in Alsace-Lorraine. "The true *revanche* of which we are thinking," Thiers emphasized, "is the reconstitution of France."[75]

In fact, the period following the War in Sight Crisis was marked by Franco-German rapprochement.[76] Periodic crises would continue to flare, but French policymakers obstinately defused tensions. In the 1887 Schnaebelé Affair, for example, German police officers arrested an obscure French official under controversial circumstances. The French war minister General Georges Ernest Boulanger was making waves at the time with defiant rhetoric about standing up to Germany. Yet even the organ of Boulangisme, the *France Militaire*, concluded, "Whatever happens, we will not declare war."[77] Boulanger was chased into exile and Franco-German relations repaired.

In the colonial sphere, France sought to expand its colonial possessions while avoiding unnecessary clashes with rival powers.[78] Even before his fall from power, Ferry consented to an international conference in Berlin to manage disagreements concerning the Congo and Niger River basins.[79] After Ferry's departure, France opted to avoid further provocations and recalled the latest Brazza expedition.[80] The departure of Ferry also led French policymakers to reconsider the wisdom of military intervention in Madagascar. French forces were withdrawn, and in December 1885, a new treaty was signed that granted France more limited territorial concessions and an ill-defined claim of a protectorate.[81] In Indochina, even the expansionist undersecretary of state for colonies Eugène Etienne remarked that "[we must] proceed with great prudence."[82] France avoided moves that might provoke China, and French forces in Cambodia fell back to more defensible lines.

French colonial activity ticked up in the 1890s, but expansion was over by 1893. As undersecretary of state for the colonies Delcassé declared, "The period of conquest and territorial expansion must be considered as definitely over."[83] When authorizing a military expedition to conquer portions of Dahomey, Delcassé emphasized to the commanding officer "our strict duty . . . not to impose upon the country any sacrifice which is not absolutely necessary."[84] Similar efforts were made to manage tensions with rival colonial powers. In 1890, France and Britain signed a convention confirming colonial possessions in East Africa and demarcating boundaries in West Africa up to Lake Chad.[85] According to William Langer, "A whole literature advocating Franco-German rapprochement had sprung up during 1890."[86] In 1895, France and Britain worked together to manage the question of Siam. French policymakers resisted the rush to conquest, opting instead for coercion and a naval blockade of Bangkok.[87] They then worked with the British to negotiate a treaty that ceded portions of Siam to France while establishing a buffer state above the Mekong.[88]

Third, France toiled incessantly to attract allies and share burdens with them, culminating in the Franco-Russian alliance. The 1875 "War in Sight" crisis was the seed of that union.[89] It illuminated to France its isolation and, to Bismarck, a latent Russian sympathy for France. But matters were slow to develop and France found sufficient safety for the time being in placating Germany. The Schnaebelé and Boulanger affairs a decade later signaled the increasing peril of France's diplomatic isolation. As a result high-level French officials stepped up their efforts toward Russia, making no less than five overtures to get an alliance with the tsar that year.[90] France had been trying to use its economic levers on Russia for some time, but the overtures only began bearing fruit when Germany restricted Russian access to its capital markets.[91] France was also more of what Bismarck called *Bündnisfähig* (alliance worthy) by this time; she was militarily stronger, diplomatically more active, financially generous, and a desirable source of arms.[92] France also bent over backwards to appear more ideologically palatable, reassuring the tsar about the French governmental system and cracking down on Russian revolutionaries in France.[93] France and Russia also worked jointly to keep open the Egyptian question and increased their activities in Abyssinia.[94]

Russia was not the only state France courted at this time. French diplomacy tried to break up the Triple Alliance, by dangling a commercial treaty in front of the Italians, and made overtures to the United Kingdom as well.[95] Yet while France and Russia made overtures to others, it made sense that they ended up together. No two states were more diplomatically isolated.[96] The Triple Alliance was renewed again in 1891, and British flirtation with Germany correlated with the inauguration of formal cooperation between France and Russia.[97] Both states were similarly menaced by the same countries in the same places. As Delcassé declared, "To France and to Russia alike, a common peril calls imperatively for the closest co-operation. . . . Each acts as a counterweight in Europe . . . to the Teutonic giant, just as they act as bulwarks in Asia . . . against the encroachments of China and Great Britain."[98] And both states signaled that they were not committed to provocative policies: French designs on Alsace-Lorraine had greatly abated, and Giers emphasized that Russia had status quo policies in the Near East.[99] As decline became more pronounced France grew more interested in allies and Russia was perfectly positioned to help compensate for France's weakness.

Fourth, the French committed their scarce resources toward homeland defense in order to deter a German attack. In the 1870s, the most visible manifestation of this effort was the evolution of French fortresses. When General Raymond Adolph Séré de Rivières became secretary of the Comité de Defense in 1873, he moved to construct an extensive and expensive system of defenses—numbering almost 200 forts.[100] From the start, his forts were envisioned to enhance mobility and counterattack.[101] Although Séré de Rivières aimed to defend all of France's borders, he concentrated on the front from the English Channel to the Mediterranean, predominantly along potential routes of German attack, seeking to shield Paris and pen in invading armies. By the late 1880s, however, advances in explosives, particularly the invention of Melinite, threatened to render many of these forts obsolete. The French high command was quick to see the danger of wasting money on too many forts of too weak design, which might be circumvented. Their solution was to upgrade a small number of forts to the best of their ability, increase strategic depth, and to improve army mobility.

Part and parcel with these efforts were French investments in the area of strategic railroads. In 1870, Germany had nine lines to the French border while France had only four. By 1886, Germany still had nine while France had twelve. By 1913, the rail ratio still favored France, sixteen to thirteen. And the French continually elevated the quality of their lines: smoothing gradients, adding junctions and watering points, upgrading signals, and multiplying tracks at congested points. In fact, during the transportation revolution, between 1870 and 1914, Germany's ability to move men and horses along its rail lines improved by a factor of four, while France's ability improved by a factor of six to seven.[102]

Taken in full, French foreign policy during this period is consistent with retrenchment with some exceptions. In the core of power politics, the main current of French foreign policy flowed toward retrenchment policies, but on the periphery there were undercurrents flowing in the opposite direction. In Europe, French policymakers sidestepped clashes with rival powers, concentrated naval assets closer to home, improved homeland defense, and courted allies that could augment French capabilities. As the historian Robert Anderson concludes, "France's role in continental affairs remained essentially passive."[103] In the colonial sphere, however, French policymakers proved willing to accept more assertive policies. Although they sought to minimize colonial flashpoints, they tended to acquiesce to the expansionist projects of distant proconsuls. As the colonial frontier expanded, so too did the size of overseas garrisons. Bismarck may have been correct that "France has colonies but no colonists,"[104] but a combination of official indifference and administrative confusion encouraged a colonial policy that was occasionally at odds with the central push toward retrenchment.

"More Worthy of an Opéra-Bouffe": The Fragility of French Retrenchment

In contrast with Russia, France's response to decline was much more erratic and varied during this period than one might expect given underlying structural conditions. France experienced a series of declines in short succession and was falling from a relatively low rank. It shared a border with the great power that was surpassing it in rank and thus had strong incentives to concentrate its assets and attention closer to home. Because it possessed a dispersed global empire, moreover, France was more likely to have considerable latitude to moderate its behavior in the periphery without compromising the security of the core. Yet despite these factors, France seldom implemented retrenchment continuously. Policymakers such as Ferry rejected retrenchment in the early 1880s, hoping that imperial expansion would reap economic rewards and restore France's prestige. When these policies failed, policymakers pursued policies largely consistent with retrenchment, but defense expenditures continued to increase while colonial expansion never entirely halted.

It is hard not to lay part of the blame for this inconsistency on the vagaries of French domestic politics. Between 1871 and 1914, the Third Republic had no less than sixty governments, which lasted an average of eight months.[105] These ministerial crises brought no less than thirteen different foreign ministers to power before 1890, "with all the obvious drawbacks for a consistent and stable foreign policy."[106] The War Ministry changed hands more than any other ministry in the Third Republic. General du Barail angrily complained that "three-quarters of [the war ministers] did not have the time to apply the reforms which they had to prepare, nor dispose of the funds which they had requested."[107] Yet the ways in which domestic factors influenced French policy were distinctive. Entrenched interest groups did not force policymakers to reject retrenchment. Political parties in the Chamber did not pressure policymakers to embrace expansionist policies. Rather, it was precisely the apathy and inattention that many domestic actors showed toward events overseas that allowed contradictions to creep into foreign policy.

The most obvious place where this can be seen is in French colonial policy. There were organized pressure groups such as the *parti colonial* that sought to promote overseas expansion, yet one ought not overstate their influence. In 1893 the colonial lobby could count on perhaps 91 out of 576 votes in the Chamber.[108] The first reference to the *parti colonial* is in 1894, and it did not come into widespread use until 1897—when most of French colonial acquisition was over.[109] As the historian Henri Brunschwig observed, "The movement had no executive committee, no organised sections, no clearly defined program, no electoral platform, and no discipline."[110] Membership "never reached 10,000 and was probably below 5,000 in 1914."[111] In short, the *parti colonial* was more a product of French colonialism than a driver of it.[112]

Rather, French colonial expansion was facilitated by potent combination of administrative confusion, official indifference, and local initiative. Responsibility for colonial matters was vested in an undersecretary post, which shuffled between the ministries of foreign affairs, commerce, and the marine. The Armée d'Afrique answered to the War Ministry, and the Troupes de Marine to the Naval Ministry, neither of which cared much about colonial affairs. It was not until 1894 that a cabinet-level position overseeing the colonies was established, and until 1900 that responsibility for the various colonial forces were centralized under the War Ministry.[113]

Amid this administrative uncertainty, colonial governors and local military commanders had considerable license. They routinely ignored their instructions, dispatched military expeditions, and pushed forward the colonial frontier. For their part, French policymakers back home rarely disavowed these initiatives, so long as conquests were successful and costs kept under control. Given the relative weakness and indifference of French cabinets, pro-colonial ministers faced little pushback.[114] When imperial-minded ministers occupied key positions, as was the case when Delcassé and Gabriel Hanotaux were appointed heads of the Colonial and Foreign Ministries respectively in 1894, French foreign policy became less restrained and more contradictory.[115]

The apotheosis of these dynamics can be seen in the ill-fated Fashoda expedition. Delcassé approved an expedition from the French Congo to the Nile headwaters in early 1893, but a combination of logistical challenges and Belgian opposition meant the project had to be abandoned. After Anglo-French negotiations on the upper Nile broke down, Delcassé resuscitated French efforts to reach the headwaters. In 1895, the French cabinet approved the dispatch of two expeditions advancing along separate lines, but "once the decision had been taken to send [Major Jean-Baptiste] Marchand to the Nile, the purpose of his expedition was—incredibly—never discussed again by the French government until after its arrival at Fashoda."[116] Fashoda ended up "as great a humiliation to the French as any in the history of the Third Republic."[117] Now foreign minister, Delcassé ordered Marchand's unconditional withdrawal, admitting "the necessity of avoiding a naval war which we are absolutely incapable of carrying on, even with Russian help."[118] The British man on the spot, General Herbert Kitchener, denigrated the Marchand expedition as "more worthy of an *opéra-bouffe* than of the outcome of the maturely considered plans of a great government."[119]

Although Fashoda appeared to be a repudiation of retrenchment, it ironically set the stage for more consistent moderation in French foreign policy. In March 1899, Eugène Etienne, the leading colonial spokesman in the Chamber, declared, "It is necessary to say clearly, especially after the unhappy Fashoda affair, that France has . . . a desire for conciliation and peace."[120] France moved to win over Spain and mollify the United States by hosting the peace conference following the Spanish-American War and seeking bilateral deals with both states.[121] With Italy, one of Delcassé's first moves in office was to cut a trade deal in 1899, ending a long tariff war and mending relations between the two states. He followed up with a 1901 colonial deal that traded Tripoli for Morocco and a 1902 neutrality deal.[122] With the bait of African concessions, France pried apart the Triple Alliance.[123]

But the most dramatic and far reaching consequence of Fashoda was the shift in France's approach to Britain. Delcassé laid out his vision: "This liquidation [of our colonial problems] should lead us . . . to a political alliance with England. . . . If we could lean both on Russia and on England, how strong we should be in relation to Germany."[124] In 1904, following two years of negotiations, France and Britain signed the *entente cordiale*, what the historian Phillip Bell called a "mixed bag of bargains over territory in Africa and Asia and regulations about fishing for bait off Newfoundland."[125] France had come full circle: whereas Ferry's colonial adventurism had estranged France from other great powers, Delcassé's colonial moderation split hostile coalitions and mended broken relationships.

Domestic political factors introduced periodic contradictions in French foreign policy but did not reverse retrenchment. The same cannot be said for domestic military affairs, where a political firestorm centered on the Dreyfus Affair created a crisis in civil-military relations that unraveled previous reforms.[126] To a certain extent, the crisis was unexpected: for most of the 1880s and 1890s, the Chamber showed it was inefficient in dealing with military matters, and ministers routinely worked around it while the Chamber looked the other way.[127] Yet after the Dreyfus affair, politicians swooped in to reform a military that looked insulated and unrepresentative. The goals of the reformers were laudable, but their means were crude and costly. Army service would be further reduced and democratized,[128] but promotion became a political process with advancement going only to candidates suitably republican in their views.[129] General Louis André was likewise put in charge of the army to clean house in 1900, and his vigorous reforms degraded army performance, depressed applications to military schools, sunk military educational standards, made a mockery of merit-based promotion, cut training time, abolished inspections, and stifled military pay and pensions, which were a fraction of the German equivalents.[130]

When the 1905 Moroccan crisis broke out, French military leaders found the army unready for war.[131] French generals complained that there were too few training camps and firing ranges, and that political machinations were undermining eastern defenses.[132] The army was increasingly used to suppress labor unrest; morale plunged and antimilitarism rose. This period also incubated France's disastrous shift to *offensive a l'outrance*. Daunted by German material superiority and concerned that their conscripts were unprepared for war, French planners began to see rapid offensives and

French morale as decisive.[133] Although mostly tactical, these beliefs were to have pernicious consequences when the war came.[134]

In sum, France adopted retrenchment, but with less consistency than other states in medium declines. As French decline became more pronounced, it did exhibit a willingness to entertain more dramatic shifts in policy, including greater reliance on alliance partners. Yet given its relatively low rank and the existence of pressing threats close to home, it is surprising that France kept expanding its colonial empire throughout this period. Not until after Fashoda did French policymakers finally acknowledge the benefits that could come from moderation and settling disputes with colonial rivals. Domestic politics plays an important role here, but not in the way that is often assumed. It was not pressure from domestic interests, but rather official indifference and bureaucratic confusion that allowed a relatively small number of pro-colonial ministers and men on the spot to drive French policy. These actors helped slow French retrenchment, but could not reverse it. French colonial expansion remained opportunistic, public enthusiasm was limited, and risky and expensive ventures were either avoided or disowned. Not until the Dreyfus Affair did the domestic divisions that had lain dormant during the Third Republic finally spring forth to reverse the benefits of retrenchment.

In the late nineteenth century, Russia and France were confronted by a surprisingly similar dilemma. Both experienced repeated moments of decline, and both were confronted by declines of increasing depth. Both were surpassed and menaced by a strong continental power located along their vulnerable frontiers. Both felt isolated in an increasingly eat-or-be-eaten world. But most important for our purposes, both Russia and France opted for policies that conformed more to retrenchment than the alternatives. In broad brushstrokes, that meant early efforts at domestic retrenchment policies followed by growing reliance on international retrenchment policies. In finer detail, that meant sustained efforts to trim military expenditures, ambitious programs of domestic reform, diplomatic moderation, and a greater willingness to share burdens. Eventually, these declining powers would link arms, setting aside ideological differences to address a common geopolitical challenge.

Despite the similarities of these cases, there were key differences. Russia enjoyed greater success in its international policies: it reoriented its global posture toward defending its frontiers in Europe, reached important colonial deals to resolve potential flashpoints, and signed an alliance that helped ease a desperate military situation. Yet with its domestic policies, Russia had much more modest success: it kept defense burdens light and made valuable investments in infrastructure and industry but struggled to sustain desperately needed military reforms. The French pattern is almost the exact opposite. At home, reforms led to a renaissance in the capability and prestige of the French military. But abroad, France pursued an erratic policy that mixed caution in Europe with recklessness in Africa and Asia.

There is some evidence that structural conditions played a role in retrenchment policies. As we have seen, policymakers appeared well aware of their poor relative standing, and policy change was motivated by fear of falling further. Russians in the late 1880s knew they were barely a match for the Austrians, and no match for the Germans, while French politicians were very sensitive that their role as a great power was in jeopardy.[135] Although France had more and better allies available than Russia, both eventually found each other. With regard to commitment interdependence, Russia should have worried about precedents, but seems not to have, abandoning the Emir Sher Ali Khan, backing out of the Panjdeh crisis, evacuating the Pamir mountains, and retiring from the Ili valley and Korea with minimal concerns that these moves would snowball. France had more dispersed commitments and acted accordingly: recalling the Brazza expedition, withdrawing from Madagascar, and reversing course in Southeast Asia. The calculus of conquest militated against retrenchment for both.[136] Still, at bottom, structural modifiers made little difference in these cases. Russia faced more restrictive geopolitical conditions than France, but retrenched no less for that.

In the end, domestic political factors provide the most plausible explanation for the variation in these two cases, but not for the reasons given by domestic dysfunction theorists. In both cases, the story was less about the bureaucracies and interest groups exploiting leaders than leaders exploiting bureaucracies and interest groups. There was little inherently institutional and nothing inevitable about this. Heads of state played off interest groups and exploited bureaucratic loopholes to advance their preferred policies. It is hard to say why the substance of the two states' policies differed, but it appears that, in Russia, a deeply ingrained culture of autocratic privilege contributed greatly while in France individual idiosyncrasies were the prime suspects. What is particularly striking in each of these cases is less that domestic politics mattered and more that the cumulative impact of domestic factors was so muted.

Stepping back, there are a number of broader lessons one can draw about retrenchment from this pair of unlikely partners. First, these cases suggest that military reforms are one of the most challenging aspects of domestic retrenchment. For Russia, the military struggled to adopt needed reforms at a time of limited resources, before buckling in the face of tsarist opposition. For France, ideological differences between radicals, moderates, and conservatives delayed the pace of initial reform efforts before torpedoing the project in the wake of the Dreyfus affair. The process of reforming military institutions appears to balance on a knife-edge. Moving too quickly can disrupt proven practices, but moving too slowly can compromise security. Showering outdated institutions with resources can reward incompetence, but starving organizations of needed resources can undercut performance. Challenging conservative cultures can lead to fresh ideas, but intervention from above can politicize the military in dangerous ways. The skill that policymakers exhibit when navigating these tradeoffs can make a critical difference.

Second, these cases suggest that retrenchment requires a firm bureaucratic hand, especially in peripheral regions. France's moderation in the wake of the Franco-Prussian War was derailed by imperial expansion in Africa and Southeast Asia throughout the 1880s. Russia's retrenchment was similarly undermined by the lure of expansion in East Asia in the 1890s. Ultimately, Russia's departure from the retrenchment playbook proved more disastrous, because it precipitated a clash with a strong rising power in Japan. Yet in both cases, a combination of administrative confusion, official indifference, and grasping proconsuls lured great powers into peripheral areas, often with negative consequences. This suggests that it is not enough for key policymakers to accept the principles of retrenchment; they must make the bureaucratic changes to follow through their priorities in practice.

Third, these cases sketch some limits of allies. If alliances are too effective at reducing burdens, they raise incentives to free-ride, squander resources in marginal areas, and accept frivolous risks. This can be true even when allies place clear bounds on the assistance they are willing to offer, such as Russian signaling over Alsace-Lorraine and French signaling over the Balkans. With Russia, the French alliance made some policymakers feel safer in Europe, encouraging expansionist ventures in Asia. For its part, France appeared more willing to run risks in its colonial rivalry with Britain in Africa once assured Russia might apply parallel pressure on India. Yet the cases also suggest the difficulty of transforming defensive alliances into offensive instruments. The Franco-Russian alliance could not save France from humiliation at Fashoda nor Russia from defeat at Tsushima. In World War I, the alliance proved its worth; outside that war, its worth is hard to prove.

CHAPTER 8

Tsar Power

1903 Russia

Concessions always lead to concessions.

—Tsar Nicholas II

The popular view of Russian foreign policy during this period is of serial blunders: Russia stumbled into a disastrous war in the Far East, sparked embarrassment in the Balkans, and floundered in the opening campaigns of the First World War, before finally succumbing to domestic revolution. There is truth in this view: the tsar bungled many aspects of Russian foreign policy, while the tsarist state proved incapable of adapting quickly to shifting circumstances. Yet Russian grand strategy in this period was not nearly as deficient as is often assumed. Diplomatically, Russian officials doused fires across the empire and solidified alignments with great power allies. Economically, the Russian state would bounce back from major defeat in the Russo-Japanese War and domestic revolution. Militarily, Russian performance in the First World War was as good as—and in some respects even better than—many of its great power peers.[1] The eventual collapse of imperial Russia should not obscure the genuine progress made during this period.

The foundations of Russian success can be found—to a significant degree—in its pursuit of retrenchment. For a brief period of time following the calamity of the Russo-Japanese War, Russian foreign policy adhered closely to the retrenchment playbook. At home, it sought to cap defense spending, modernize its armed forces, and reallocate resources toward economic investments. Abroad, it tempered expansion in the periphery, worked assiduously to defuse flashpoints with potential rivals, and deepened its cooperation with allies and partners. These efforts were not always as consistent or as far-reaching as they could have been, especially when it came to domestic reforms. Nor were these policies maintained for as long as might have been prudent. The bulk of Russian retrenchment occurred between 1905 and 1908, when the obvious calamity of the Russo-Japanese War focused attention on the need for domestic reform and diplomatic caution. By 1908, however, Russia began to entertain policies at odds with retrenchment, especially in the Balkans, a trend that would further accelerate after 1912. Despite its large decline, Russia chose to move away from retrenchment, and tensions began to creep in and eventually overwhelm Russian grand strategy.

Why did Russian policymakers choose to abandon retrenchment? Part of the answer lies in structural conditions. The conquest calculus during this period appeared to shift toward the offense, which increased the allure of more aggressive war plans and stoked fears of predation if Russia stayed on the defensive. Russian commitments also came to be seen as more interdependent. As Germany and Austria tightened their alliance, the stability of the Polish front became intertwined with events in the Balkans and the Ottoman Empire. Especially after the humiliation of the 1908 Bosnian crisis, Russian policymakers feared that the mere appearance of weakness in one area might invite predation in the other. But of equal importance were Russian domestic politics. The institutions responsible for guiding Russian foreign policy were riddled with divisions—between one another, between internal factions, and between authorities in the capital and the provinces. Adding to this confusion was the tsar. While he was not bereft of good intentions or good ideas, his preferred policies were a central source of domestic instability and foreign policy incoherence. Nicholas II's resistance retarded needed reforms; his decisions abetted dysfunction; his insistence on living in the past impeded his advisors from bringing Russia into the future.

"Some Political Nonentity": Russia Recognizes Decline

Russia's position appeared precarious even before the calamity of the Russo-Japanese War. The Russian economic situation was deteriorating in the first years of the new century, and the country remained uncomfortably dependent on foreign markets and credit.[2] Furthermore, social stability was deteriorating. From 1901 to 1905, four high-level officials were assassinated.[3] In an unusually explicit 1900 policy paper, the war minister Alexei Kuropatkin offered a bleak strategic assessment, stressing the need to avoid war and expansion.[4] Although he had contributed to expanding Russia's Far Eastern footprint, the finance minister Sergei Witte loudly warned that Russian impotence meant the country must walk more softly and avoid trouble.[5]

Despite these pleas, Russia stumbled into war with Japan and paid a heavy price. At the Battle of Tsushima alone, Russia lost 12 capital ships, with 4,380 sailors killed and 6,000 prisoners of war. The cumulative losses were much greater: for 2.2 billion rubles in military expenses, plus 4 billion rubles in debt service, Russia accumulated 270,000 casualties and not a single victory in 18 months.[6] On his way to negotiate the peace treaty, Witte felt scorned: "In the French capital my feelings as a Russian patriot were hurt at every step. The public treated me, the chief plenipotentiary of the autocrat of all the Russias [sic], as a representative of some political nonentity."[7] Witte's successor, Vladimir Kokovtsov, asserted in no uncertain terms that "Russia cannot be a great power with an economy in ruins."[8]

The impacts of the war were far reaching. Both Russia's finances and its military capabilities were devastated. In 1907, the war minister Alexander Rödiger warned, "At the present moment after the war and the current upheaval the condition of our armed forces is such that it is extremely desirable for us to avoid foreign entanglements for some time to come."[9] A 1908 meeting of the army and navy chiefs of staff concluded that if St. Petersburg were attacked, the capital might fall.[10] That same year, the deputy minister of war Alexei Polivanov conceded, "Our army was incapable of fighting."[11] A 1909 report glumly noted, "Even Great Powers must necessarily conform their political objectives with an understanding of available means and the present situation."[12] In staff talks with the French in 1911, the foreign minister Alexander Izvolsky told the French, "We are in no state to participate in a European war. We still need at least two years to reorganize our forces."[13]

In response to this obvious fall in standing, Russian policymakers urged retrenchment. The new chairman of the Council of Ministers observed, "Our internal situation does not permit us to conduct an aggressive foreign policy."[14] Izvolsky argued that Russia must renounce "fantastical" schemes of imperial expansion.[15] Veteran statesman Sergei Sazonov stressed, "It was essential for the Russian government to placate German hostility for a long time to come by means of all possible concessions in the economic sphere."[16]

In brief, Russia's performance throughout this period flagged, and Russian leaders noticed. All the top ministers knew how precarious the state's position was, and they roundly and repeatedly urged retrenchment: Russia must pull its forces back, focus on core interests, and reform the country to avert stiffer censure. Unfortunately for all involved, one of the authorities most resistant to this message was the person with the most authority.

"Down with the Army": Russian Domestic Policies

We expect large cases to look like the medium cases of the last chapter but stronger: declining powers will make large cuts to military spending and personnel, overhaul their forces to meet urgent vulnerabilities, embark on massive reforms to learn from their mistakes, and pour resources into new investments to spark economic revivals. Russia reformed along all these avenues, but did not go far enough in many of them. Spending cuts and resource reallocation put the Russian state on firmer financial footing over the next decade, but force restructuring and institutional overhauls were stunted, both by bureaucratic intransigence and the tsar's conservatism. Somewhat surprisingly, economic issues appeared to be the easier road to reform.

First, constrained military spending was a main goal under several ministers, and they mostly achieved it. Witte and Kokovtsov kept military spending on a short leash, and "retrenchment" was a watchword.[17] The Russo-Japanese War and the disturbances that followed raised defense spending for three years, but from 1907 to 1911, Russian military expenditures stayed essentially flat—averaging 15 percent less than German military spending—at a time when there was a genuine need to replace heavy wartime losses.[18] With economic recovery[19] and growing danger from Germany and Turkey,[20] total military spending jumped from 669 million rubles in 1911 to 815 million rubles in 1912 and 962 million rubles in 1913.[21] Of course, these figures are only crude indicators that obscure both the division between army and naval spending and the return on investment for various projects. We will explore these qualitative factors shortly, but for now it is sufficient to note that military austerity was real and sustained following Russia's ordinal transition.

Second, Russia sought to restructure its forces to boost reserves and use existing reserves more efficiently. In 1900 the peacetime strength of the army was 896,000 with wartime strength of 3.5 million men, while the navy stood at 45,000.[22] By 1905, though the data are somewhat shaky, those figures stood at 1.1 million men on a peace footing and 4.6 million men on a war footing, with a 60,000-man navy.[23] But a 1906 law shortened active service from six to three years—the first such shortening since 1874—plus recruitment loopholes tightened, raising reservist numbers by 25 percent.[24] Defeat in the 1908 Balkan crisis bestirred Russia to ramp up its military reforms and to transform its "reserves into a useful force rather than a liability."[25] As the historian Norman Stone puts it, "In the First World War, it was the great profusion of reserves that counted for most."[26]

Parallel to these efforts, Russia took major steps to enhance efficiency and equipment. The 1906 service law raised pay and streamlined reserve mobilization.[27] After the Bosnian annexation crisis, the War Ministry emphasized modernizing, procuring high quality weapons and more of them: machine guns, howitzers, artillery, and mobile artillery; it also built up its domestic arms industry using foreign technology.[28] It cut inessential privileges and the number of officers' servants, freeing up more soldiers for regular duty.[29] The army increased by 13 percent without additional cost and created a central supply service "from virtually nothing."[30] Mobilization times improved significantly.[31]

Nevertheless, these improvements were not enough. The War Ministry had to cut too many corners, often gratuitously.[32] Troops were given raw materials to make their own uniforms, and often boots, too. They had to bring or find their own soap, spoons, boot brushes, polish, oil and rags for rifle cleaning, bed linen, shirts, and often blankets and beds. Moreover, soldiers were paid so poorly, and units were so cash-strapped, that soldiers had to work the fields to make ends meet, much to the annoyance of the generals.[33] Between having to work outside jobs and suppress internal unrest, the army was inadequately trained and staffed, much to the annoyance of the war minister.[34] Worse, the war ministers Rödiger and Vladimir A. Sukhomlinov wanted to scrap exposed border fortresses to pull back to a more defensible line with more mobile units, but the tsar watered down their plan and required an upgrade to one of the forts.[35] The opportunity cost ended up being the heavy artillery that Russia needed.[36]

Exacerbating matters was the tsar's naval fetish, which diverted valuable resources from the army for years, and those resources were not well spent. The tsar generously supported the navy, over objections from the State Defense Council, the war minister, the French military, and the chairman of the Duma and the Committee of Imperial Defense, Alexander I. Guchkov.[37] The tsar was more interested in smart-looking ships than highly functional crews, and sailors were not well trained. He quashed any serious inquiry into the naval disasters of the Russo-Japanese War for fear it would unearth embarrassing details about his family and his decision making, so naval progress had to be made from the grassroots.[38] By the First World War, the navy had but four capital ships, was superior only to the Austro-Hungarian navy in tonnage, and was of little strategic benefit.[39] The end result was that there were improvements in army reserves and equipment but they were not sufficiently supported, and prudent force structure was undermined by unnecessary fortresses, underinvestment in artillery, and excessive shipbuilding.

Third, after getting burned in the Russo-Japanese War, Russia was under pressure to drastically reform its military institutions, sack incompetent officers, and revise its logistics, revamping its planning, training, and command. That is in fact largely what happened. After 1905 the Russian military implemented extensive reforms under very different war ministers, Rödiger and Sukhomlinov.[40] But both made deep reforms in the same directions. The historians Bruce Menning and John Steinberg argue that "the far-reaching changes of 1905–12 . . . rivaled, if not exceeded, the heralded reforms of D. A. Miliutin a half century earlier."[41]

Institutionally, authority was further centralized under the war minister in 1909.[42] The War Ministry overhauled regimental purchasing, boosted

pay, enhanced pensions, tightened performance reviews, promoted com-
moners, and retired dead wood.[43] This last point was critical; observers
thought that the biggest contributor to Russian defeat had been the lackluster Russian officer corps.[44] More than 2,000 under-performing officers
were let go, and the army became a much more attractive prospect for tal-
ented Russians. Officers had been in chronic short supply. By 1907 the
army was still running 20 percent below capacity, but by 1910 there was an
officer surplus.[45] After 1908, the War Ministry found the funds to double
the funding for military maneuvers, which would again double by 1913.[46]
It also advanced artillery and gunnery, upgraded sapper units, adopted
wireless communication, homogenized unit organization, and built the
world's second largest air force.[47] Intelligence reform was also a success. In
1908, the German general Helmuth von Moltke the Younger sent a memo
to his foreign ministry warning: "The Russian intelligence machinery com-
prises a well-ordered, widely dispersed system, which has considerable
financial resources."[48] Russian bureaucracies in general, and the military
in particular, continued to become larger, more inclusive, and more
professional.[49]

Alas there was reform from below, but rot at the top. Indeed, the two are
causally linked; the historian Bruce Menning states, "Persistent failure at
higher levels had prompted Russians to evolve a reasonably efficient military administration, perhaps the most efficient since the era of Miliutin."[50]
Yet both war ministers warned that the reforms did not go far enough: there
was too much interference from the tsar's family, too many fortresses, too
little training, speed, and concentration, all of which would produce hor-
rendous consequences in the First World War.[51] But the tsar was the prover-
bial dog in the manger, unable to use central authority or let others use it.
He obstructed attempts to learn from the Russo-Japanese War, interfered
with efforts to modernize military education, and had an immense talent
for promoting mediocrities and demoting the gifted.[52]

Russian reformers sought to corral the tsar after 1905 by creating the
Council of State Defense (GSO) and an independent Russian General Staff
(GUGSh).[53] But the tsar sought to elude any encroachment on his authority.
In 1908, he abolished the GSO, declaring, "I intend to take military affairs
more into my own hands."[54] As Fuller observes, this meant that "for all
practical purposes, … issues of defense would not be coordinated at all."[55]
The GUGSh lived on, but never lived up to reformers' hopes because the
tsar thwarted institutions that limited his prerogatives.[56] Civil-military relations were "profoundly dysfunctional."[57] All told, after the Russo-Japanese
War, the Russian military made huge leaps in morale, supply, mobilization,
reserves, weapons, logistics, maneuvers, and education, but there remained
a toxic stratum of institutional dysfunction above.[58]

Fourth, Russia reallocated resources to raise growth and improve efficiency. Witte remarked, "Among those factors that retard growth, the first

place is occupied by militarism," and, "My motto is—up with trade and industry, down with the army!"[59] And Kokovtsov maintained similar policies until he was sidelined around 1912. Russian priorities drifted increasingly to non-military projects. In 1891, 30 percent of central government expenditure was for defense, but by 1903 that had fallen to 21 percent and would hover there until 1913, when it would bounce back to 29 percent with the Big Program.[60] Meanwhile, 10 percent of Russian spending went toward government enterprises like railroads in 1891, and that quadrupled to 39 percent by 1903 before declining to 35 percent by 1910. Even as the bureaucracy grew, administrative costs dropped from 25 percent in 1891 to 19 percent in 1903 to 17 percent in 1913, and debt charges halved from 26 percent in 1891 to 14 percent in 1903 to 13 percent in 1913.[61]

On balance, the reallocation worked. Estimates differ, but growth was around 3 percent from 1885 to 1914 and was accelerating before the First World War.[62] Russian industrial growth, the explicit aim of the government to be a stronger strategic competitor, was 8 percent from 1890 to 1899 and 6.3 percent from 1907 to 1913.[63] By 1913, Russian industry was 5 percent of the labor force but 20 percent of the gross national income.[64] Railroad mileage doubled from 1890 to 1904, and thereafter management improved and the lines became profitable.[65] In addition, Russia had one of the world's fastest growing populations—and the few countries doing better were taking large numbers of Russian immigrants.[66] In the First World War, Niall Ferguson's marvels that Russia "had the most successful war economy."[67]

To be sure, Russia misallocated massive resources on corruption and graft, useless forts and ships, and ill-conceived economic and social policies. Furthermore, many policies over many ministers and many years aided the multifarious sources of Russian growth, and the state was withdrawing from direct industrial promotion after 1900.[68] But there is some consensus among economists that the Russian government's stringent fiscal policies, high tariffs, low taxes, stabilization of the ruble, domestic infrastructure investments, and encouragement of foreign financial inflows to Russian capitalists were major contributors to higher growth rates.[69] The economist Olga Crisp comments, "The total of new capital which entered the Russian market on account of government policies had reached the enormous sum of over 3000 million roubles, a sum exceeding the yield of the war indemnity which the Germans received from France in 1870."[70] Absent those policies, Russia would have done worse.

In sum, Russian domestic retrenchment was only a partial success. Uneven progress was made across time and issue area, but Russia tried to rein in expenses during a time when Europe was in an arms race. In the five years on either side of 1903, and excluding the cost of the Russo-Japanese War, Russia spent an average of 498 million rubles on defense; for all other years between 1895 and 1913, it spent 602 million rubles.[71] Russia's achieve-ments were more ambivalent in force restructuring and institutional reforms. For force structure, policymakers bulked up reserves and armed them better but siphoned off needed resources for unnecessary fortresses and battleships. For institutional reforms, a bevy of measures were employed to fix the glaring errors showcased by the Russo-Japanese War, but the tsar steadily blunted them. The bottom line is that there was much more reform than counterreform, but there was not as much retrenchment as our theory expects.

"Being on Good Terms with Everybody": Russian International Policies

We expect that large decliners will rely on international policies to an unparalleled degree: calling home most of their forces, desperately extin-guishing flashpoints even if it means appeasement, fervently shedding bur-dens to others, and focusing intensely on homeland defense. This is what Russian policy did until 1912, with some minor exceptions. Legions came home, but they did not fall as far back as war ministers would have liked. Diplomats raced to avert escalation, but they sometimes tried swagger, to unhappy outcomes. Russia secured allies and aid galore without taking on new commitments. Homeland defense was in much better shape after retrenchment than before. Russia's record is far more congruent with retrenchment here than in the domestic realm.

First, Russia redeployed forces away from the periphery. The orientation of Russian foreign policy rushed to the core after 1905, then began seeping back to the periphery around 1912.[72] After the war, Far Eastern forces were drawn down to help suppress civil unrest in Russia's core. As those embers cooled, homeland concentration was institutionalized in Plan 19 of 1909/10. Despite beliefs that offense was the best form of war, Russian generals abandoned much of the Polish salient to avoid a pincers attack and agreed to mobilize in rear areas with less *couverture*, or covering force.[73] To this end, forces in the Warsaw and Vilna military districts were slashed by 91 and 37 battalions, respectively, while the Moscow and Kazan districts gained 28 and 51 battalions, respectively.[74] Plan 19 also focused Russian efforts on the German threat in East Prussia while maintaining a holding action against Austria-Hungary.[75] The historian John David Walz summa-rizes, "Whereas 70 [percent] of Russia's infantry had been deployed west of the line St. Petersburg-Moscow-Kharkov before the change, only 59 [per-cent] remained there afterwards."[76] According to the political scientist Jack Snyder, it "was more defensive and more oriented toward Germany than any other Russian plan made between 1880 and 1914."[77] Meanwhile, naval forces clung to coastal defense.[78] Altogether, from 1905 to 1912 Russia recalled its forces to the core to a degree not seen in decades.

Second, Russian policymakers sought to defuse flashpoints, at times to the point of appeasement. After the Russo-Japanese War, the new foreign minister Izvolsky saw his task as "being on good terms with everybody."[79] He openly ruled out force: "We ought not, we cannot undertake anything that would lead to an armed conflict with anybody, for Russia needs peace above all, needs restoration of its strength after the external and internal shocks of the last years."[80] The primary focus of Russian efforts to defuse flashpoints was the periphery, with the banner event being the 1907 Anglo-Russian Convention.[81] Having previously struggled to reach an acceptable deal with Britain in the Middle East, the task became much easier after the *annus horribilis* of 1905.[82] At a 1907 special conference, Izvolsky stated: "We must put our interests in Asia in their proper place otherwise we would ourselves become an Asiatic state, which would be the greatest calamity for Russia."[83] The tsar was emphatic that "the agreement *must* be made."[84] When Britain objected to the proposed spheres of interest, Russia duly moved them back, and tension ebbed for years.[85] And with Turkey, Russia made few waves.[86]

Russia adopted a similar policy in the Far East, seeking to placate Japan. Even though the Portsmouth peace conference was barely successful,[87] and Russia had not forsaken the possibility of renewing war with Japan, policymakers quickly came around to the need to improve relations.[88] In 1907, Russia and Japan came to terms on fisheries, railways, commerce, the Open Door, Chinese integrity, and spheres of influence.[89] As one scholar notes, "The Russo-Japanese Agreement was proposed by Russia because of a shift of emphasis in her foreign policy from Asia to Europe. However, the final Agreement itself was closer to conditions desired by Japan than those desired by Russia."[90] Because of its weakness, Russia accepted concessions, though they heavily favored Japan.

Russia not only sought to limit disputes in the periphery, it also sought to resolve tensions with adversaries in the core. Although the French alliance was the foundation of Russian policy, policymakers sought to soothe tensions with Germany when possible. In the First Moroccan Crisis, Russia verbally supported France, but steered clear of conflict and capitulated to French demands that Russia drop clauses in the Franco-Russian military agreement that contemplated war with Britain.[91] Although Russia aligned with Britain in 1907, Izvolsky kept Berlin apprised and sought German approval of the deal.[92] The German and Russian emperors met for the same purpose at Swinemünde, and a Russo-German understanding was also reached on the Baltic territorial status quo some months later. Russia also reluctantly consented to German plans for the Baghdad railway. The historian Firuz Kazemzadeh puts it this way: "It is abundantly clear that, given freedom of choice, the Russian government would have preferred to keep Persia without railways. However, fearing a further deterioration of her relations with

Germany, Russia felt compelled to placate her powerful western neighbor."[93]

There were exceptions to Russian passivity, but they only revealed the futility of bluff. Izvolsky searched for a redemptive diplomatic victory to wash away the stains of the Russo-Japanese War, but Russia lacked the capability to win one. Over the Åland Islands, his awkward attempt to bully Sweden was easily blocked by other powers.[94] In 1908, Izvolsky and the Austro-Hungarian foreign minister Alois Aehrenthal secretly discussed a quid pro quo for Austrian annexation of Bosnia-Herzegovina.[95] But the Austrians, and more important the Germans, were confident that Russia was too weak to put up resistance, and so the annexation was done without any offer of compensation. Rödiger remarked: "It is out of the question for Russia to fight a war on account of the Serbs."[96] Russian military leaders, according to the historian David Herrmann, "begged the civilian authorities not to get the country involved in a war."[97] Without consulting their allies, the Russians humiliatingly gave way, demoted Izvolsky the following year, and nursed the wound for some time.[98] The new foreign minister, Sazonov, aimed to avoid another such debacle by appeasing Germany in the Potsdam agreement, which extracted a German promise not to support Austrian aggression in the Balkans in exchange for a Russian promise not to support British policy hostile to Germany.[99]

When the Second Moroccan Crisis occurred in 1911, Russia not only failed to offer firm support for its ally, it suggested France should back down and surrender the port of Agadir to Germany.[100] In 1912, the French were alarmed by reports of the German and Russian emperors meeting in the Gulf of Finland. According to the political scientist Glenn Snyder, the French prime minister Raymond Poincaré "asked Sazonov for formal assurance that no political discussions would be discussed and for a public declaration of Russia's allegiance to the Triple Entente. Sazonov refused both requests."[101] Throughout the government, Russia's war aversion remained strong. As the historian Dietrich Geyer concludes: "There is no doubt . . . that both Foreign Ministers in this period . . . preferred to avoid war. They adopted a defensive strategy for securing Russian interests and thus tried to take into account the Empire's limited military margin for manoeuver."[102]

Third, Russia looked to distribute defense burdens to others as its power faded. The French alliance shouldered the bulk of what Russia could shed.[103] French diplomatic cables reveal that the French realized they were stuck on the short end of an asymmetric relationship.[104] Economically, although the Russians gestured toward French interests, they typically spent French loans on Russian priorities.[105] Russia used French loans to build rail lines along economic corridors rather than strategic lines to the German front, though that shifted as war neared.[106] At sea, the Franco-Russian naval convention of 1901 attempted to coordinate navies by dividing labor and theaters, and

Russia said it was building its navy to help the French.[107] Yet France disliked Russian naval spending because it detracted from investment in the Russian army, and anyway Russian naval investments came too late to be a factor in the First World War.[108] On land, France demanded Russian offensives at the earliest possible moment, but until 1912 Russia was largely bluffing when it said it would oblige.[109] A series of meetings between the military staffs of both countries coordinated plans and underscored the need for quick and complete mobilization if Germany mobilized against either country. But more was expected of France than Russia. In the 1913 military agreement, France consented to mobilize 1.3 million men to Russia's 700,000–800,000, which represented only 20 percent of Russian soldiers.[110] And when Russian war plans turned aggressive, it was not because of French requests. Russian policymakers were increasingly pessimistic that France would be knocked out of the war quickly and needed immediate help to stand a chance.[111]

As mentioned, after 1907 the Franco-Russian alliance was augmented by agreements with the British and Japanese, which eased the defensive burdens of the Russian empire and allowed greater concentration on Europe. The Anglo-Russian entente settled disputes over Tibet, Persia, and Afghanistan, bringing the decades of rivalry in "the Great Game" to an apparent close.[112] As for Russo-Japanese relations, the two states signed a series of deals—in 1907, 1910, 1912, and 1916—to give Russia peace on its eastern flank and Japan freedom with China. The 1910 deal was a stronger version of the 1907 deal, but omitted mention of the Open Door or Chinese integrity, and transformed a consultative pact into something closer to a defensive alliance.[113] The 1912 Sazonov-Motono agreement extended spheres of influence to Mongolia and turned the country into a buffer state.[114] The 1916 treaty was a defensive agreement for five years to keep third parties out of China. In total, Russian diplomats found multiple capable allies to help carry the country's burdens, which they did when war struck.

Fourth, Russian policymakers sought to bolster homeland defense. We have already noted how the Sukhomlinov reforms concentrated troops in the core, and how, though the war minister was compelled to upgrade a fortress in the Polish salient, Russia's strategy shifted increasingly toward defense in depth. To the tsar's credit, he also reoriented Russia's railroad building priorities. Before 1908, they were predominantly along economic corridors, but afterward they were directed toward strategic corridors.[115] Before 1912, railways in Poland had been neglected for fear of German invasion, but after 1912 increasing confidence meant that railways in Poland were much improved.[116]

To recap, Russian international policies made great strides in recovering from the damage wrought by the Russo-Japanese War. Forces were redeployed to the interior of the country to buttress homeland defense. Diplomats toiled to button down points of friction to keep Russia out of fights it could not win. Perhaps most helpful, Russia diplomacy calmed its periphery by cooperating with the British and Japanese and did an astute job exploiting the French alliance for all that could be extracted while committing nothing that was outside narrow self-interest. When war returned to the continent, Russia was a formidable part of a formidable coalition.

"Victory and Cataclysm": The Extremes of Russian Retrenchment

Russian foreign policy in the immediate aftermath of the Russo-Japanese War conforms closely to one of retrenchment. Russia dampened defense spending, at least until the pressure of European rearmament drew it into the continent-wide arms race. It revamped its force structure and reformed its military institutions, although investments in fortresses and battleships made little sense and reforms were not as thorough as one might have hoped. It sought to defuse flashpoints, although the pleas of Balkan Pan-Slavs occasionally drew Russia into unwanted and unwinnable crises. Finally, it retrenched in critical areas, yet its pursuit of retrenchment was both inconsistent and incomplete. For this reason, we code Russian retrenchment as modest, a surprising outcome given the large depth of Russian decline.

To a certain extent, it is surprising that Russia retrenched at all. Late-tsarist Russia was no paragon of functionality, rationality, or modernism. Yet internal faction can seldom explain Russia' foreign policies during the period. The key cleavages were largely over domestic policy, and there was wide agreement about a less ambitious foreign policy.[117] Public opinion and business interests were not influential in tsarist Russia, and there was not a groundswell of support in either for assertion abroad.[118] The Duma was typically tame and supported the military's funding requests, pushing back only slightly on the most dubious programs like massive naval rebuilding.[119] Even the archconservative Nicholas II succumbed to the pull of retrenchment. He brought in reformers known to be conservative, like Rödiger, and, when the tsar found him insufficiently conservative, he brought in Sukhomlinov to undo the damage, only to find Sukhomlinov following his predecessor's policies.[120]

After 1912, however, Russian retrenchment began to break down. In 1913, Russia inaugurated the so-called Big Program, which looked to expand peacetime military forces by 40 percent and double the number of artillery batteries.[121] By 1914, the regular army had swelled to some 1.4 million soldiers, with active reserves and various militia formations contributing an additional 2.6 million and 6 million respectively.[122] Russian war plans also shifted in a more offensive direction. In 1912, military planners adopted Plan 20, which included offensive options against both Austria-Hungary (Plan A) and Germany (Plan G).[123] It was not French but

Russian generals that were calling for more ambitious policies, and indeed Plan A alone, which was the default plan, would have left the French in the lurch.[124] When war erupted in 1914, Russia implemented Plans A and G simultaneously, with no real oversight from the tsar or war minister, to terrible results.[125]

Russian diplomacy also became more confrontational. Russia became more assertive in the Far East, central Asia, and Persia, even when such moves antagonized its would-be entente partner Britain.[126] Russia also began to entertain revisionist schemes in the Balkans, even though such moves risked war at a time when Russian rearmament was incomplete.[127] Rather than defuse flashpoints, Russia seemed willing to provoke them. Key stepping stones on the road to war were the Balkan Wars of 1912–13, where four Balkan states seized almost all of Turkey's possessions in Europe. The wars seemed to vindicate Russian perceptions about the importance of the offense, the need to back allies such as Serbia, and the connection between the German and Austrian fronts. Pan-Slavism, already a force to be reckoned with, intensified in part through Russian encouragement.[128] Allies in the Balkans went from being seen as defensive tools to offensive instruments.

What can explain this dangerous shift in Russian foreign policy? To a certain degree, Russia became more ambitious because it could afford to be: war stocks had rebounded, stability had returned, the economy rallied, and concessions had secured diplomatic flexibility.[129] Structural conditions also appeared more conducive to an aggressive foreign policy. The tightening of the alliance between Germany and Austria-Hungary led to the impression that Russian commitments in Europe were much more interdependent then had been the case in the past. As the historian Alex Marshall observes, "By the end of the Tsarist period . . . [the southern frontier] was seen implicitly in the eyes of many Tsarist officers as part of a long single 'causal chain', in which events in one theater would carry inevitable political repercussions elsewhere along the line."[130] Technological changes also seemed to have pushed the conquest calculus in the direction of the offense. Military officials worried that fighting on the defensive might leave Russia exposed, while the perceived efficacy of the offense increased the attraction of aggressive moves into the Balkans. Fuller finds that none of the defense planners' "scenarios posited any intermediate outcomes between victory and cataclysm . . . [Defeat meant Russia] would be utterly destroyed or so crippled that that an eventual total collapse would not be far away."[131] Even though reforms were incomplete, Russian policymakers increasingly looked to turn the army from a "purely defensive weapon" to a "first-class offensive" tool.[132]

Yet structural conditions are only part of the story: equal blame must be laid on the dysfunctional character of Russian domestic politics. In particular, while there is plenty of blame to go around, no one was more instrumental in thwarting sound policy than the well-intentioned but overwhelmed tsar.[133] This is in part a product of his cultural and educational background.[134] But many Russian elites who had similar backgrounds were vociferous in lobbying for greater reforms, while Nicholas II stubbornly shunted them aside.[135] Not only did the tsar fail to charm the masses, both traditional and new elites in Petersburg and Moscow disliked him. He lived in an unusually tiny bubble compared to his British and German counterparts.[136] His poor personnel decisions—including most disastrously Rasputin and Sukhomlinov—helped undermine the coherence of the state.[137] There was a proliferation of bodies that worked at cross-purposes, and the tsar neither provided a unified policy nor allowed anyone else to furnish central direction, keeping total control over foreign and defense policy.[138] The tsar had ample room to play court factions off against each other, but he seldom refereed ruinous fights between his ministers, and his handiwork was a triumph of mindless traditionalism over substantive conservatism.[139] Unlike most heads of state, he tended to operate without a personal secretary or office staff, which mired him deeply in trivia.[140] The ramshackle character of the tsarist state was exacerbated by the tsar's decisions.[141]

Paradoxically, the tsarist system was both too centralized and too decentralized. When the tsar was motivated, he would often intervene in a capricious and uninformed manner. Yet when the tsar was distracted or overwhelmed, he ceded the initiative to a dysfunctional bureaucracy filled with ambiguous and overlapping lines of authority, personal rivalries, and tensions between center and regions. In the final analysis, however, the correlation between Russian foreign policy success and how involved the tsar was with foreign policy is striking. Early in his reign, the country made impressive strides as his ministers directed the ship of state. From 1903 to 1905, the tsar unceremoniously dumped Witte, used the Bezobrazov faction to do his bidding, then sidelined its figurehead, and drove the country into an ignominious war. From 1906 to 1911, Nicholas was more passive and the country recovered.[142] After 1912, he grew increasingly assertive, and, when war came, there was negligent oversight, no unified doctrine, poor command and control, and little flexibility. At the decisive hour, Russia was helmed by a leader whose competence was in serious question.

Despite its defects, we should not be blind to the accomplishment of the late-tsarist state. Prior to 1912, Russian policymakers reacted to deep decline with a combination of fiscal prudence, sensible reforms, and politic diplomacy. Although incomplete, late imperial defense efforts produced a military that could credibly defend the nation.[143] For all their contradictions, late imperial diplomatic initiatives knitted Russia into a diplomatic system where its interests were protected by allies in both Europe and

Asia. Even with their many limitations, late imperial economic reforms helped spark a period of unprecedented economic growth. Retrenchment worked, but in the end, a combination of new circumstances and old leadership meant that reforms neither went far enough nor endured long enough. Instead, Russia was overtaken by arms races, crises, war, and revolution.

The Utopian Background

1925 France

> I won't hide from you that in making foreign policy I ask myself what
> French resources are, from the financial and military standpoints. You
> must not be megalomaniac. You must have the foreign policy that
> your country's finances and ability to use force allow. The day you go
> beyond them, it leads to Sedan.
>
> —Aristide Briand

Familiar images of France before the Second World War come in two contradictory varieties. One is a country stubbornly clinging to its power
through vindictive and provocative policies, refusing to accommodate Germany's rise.[1] The other is a country characterized by divisions, delusions,
and decadence. "In a mere twenty-two years," Randall Schweller argues,
"France went from hegemonic grandeur to humiliating defeat. The primary
cause of French decline was that, while Germany rearmed, France was
wholly distracted by internal troubles."[2]

In this chapter, we argue that French foreign policy was not remotely as
self-defeating or incoherent as these images contend.[3] French policymakers
had no illusions about their country's fading power, broadly agreed on foreign policy aims, and accepted most reasonable remedies. At times, policymakers flirted with a more independent policy, but when that experiment
failed with the Ruhr occupation, they gravitated to a more collaborative
and restrained foreign policy that curbed costs, dampened flashpoints,
courted allies, and fortified deterrence. And, in general, French retrenchment in the 1920s did a good job of putting the military on a solid footing,
calming diplomatic tempests, wooing friends, and spurring economic
revival. In the round, French policy in the early interwar period was consistent, practical, and inventive.

Yet as circumstances changed, France struggled to change with them. The same policies that served France so well in the 1920s were worse than ineffective in the 1930s. The Great Depression was slow to hit the French economy, but when it did the impact was immense, and the maintenance of austerity policies in the teeth of epic dislocations was a mistake. The shortage of strong regional allies was less of an issue when Germany was weak, but it put France in a terrible position as Germany revived. Domestic divisions, muted in the early interwar period, flared up in the 1930s, paralyzing reforms and poisoning negotiations with potential partners. As a consequence, French foreign policy became increasingly contradictory and inconsistent, until its independence was extinguished in defeat.

"Breathing Space if That Is at All Possible": France Recognizes Decline

Despite its victory in the First World War, French policymakers were agonizingly aware of their country's precarious position. No great power suffered more than France during the Great War. Of every 1,000 inhabitants, France had mobilized 168 and lost 34; fully 27 percent of its 18- to 27-year-old men were dead, and its industrial heartland was ravaged.[4] It took substantial support from allies to remove German soldiers from French soil, and Germany had a population of 63 million and growing to France's 39 million and falling.[5] The prime minister Aristide Briand declared, "I am pursuing the policy dictated by our birthrate,"[6] adding, "Germany in a few weeks can raise an army of six to seven million men. . . . The danger is there. It is on the prowl. It is just above our heads."[7] The opposition politician Henry Franklin-Bouillon echoed, "We cannot forget that our weak birthrate governs and governs more strongly every day our general policy."[8]

Even with Germany beaten, French government officials knew their reprieve was temporary. A 1920 report to the French Senate stated, "The Germany of Versailles is doubtless a conquered Germany, but also a Germany retaining, even enhancing, its unity; this Germany is powerless today, but capable of becoming fearsome tomorrow."[9] A French expert on Germany concluded, "France is a finished country."[10] The statesman Jules Cambon commented that "in the immediate future the difficulty will be to slide France reasonably smoothly into the ranks of the second-rate powers to which she belongs."[11] Retrenchment was the answer. General Noël Édouard de Castelnau admitted, "I should not like to carry for thirty years a burden that weighs heavily on my shoulders, in order to forestall an eventuality that will materialize in fifty years; I shall simply ask you for a 'breathing space' if that is at all possible."[12] In 1922, Chief Lieutenant

Colonel Charles Fournier of the Deuxième Bureau (military intelligence) gave France a mere ten years to cobble together a coalition to stop Germany.[13]

The turning point of French foreign policy in the early 1920s was the Ruhr occupation crisis.[14] The crisis came about due to Germany's failure to pay reparations on schedule. One solution was to occupy the Ruhr valley and forcibly requisition payment in raw materials. The French statesman Jacques Seydoux trumpeted the advantages of such a move: "It is a violent solution, but it will settle everything. We will become masters of Germany, independent of England, and an industrial power of the first rank."[15] Neither the French prime minister Raymond Poincaré nor his ministers were eager to occupy the Ruhr to secure reparations,[16] yet with no alternative left, all political parties backed the policy.[17] French and Belgian forces moved into the Ruhr in 1923.

The Ruhr occupation marked a fundamental shift in France's diplomatic strategy. Financially, the French turned a nominal profit on the occupation.[18] But the operation poisoned relations with Germany, Britain, and Czechoslovakia, and that was intolerable.[19] The franc fell dramatically, potential allies were antagonized, and German public opinion turned against France.[20] By 1924, in the words of the historian Jon Jacobson, "France was insolvent," unable to uphold its military or financial goals without the help of other powers. The historian Stephen Schuker adds that French weakness "rendered the pursuit of a genuinely independent foreign policy by France impossible."[21] These setbacks culminated in the surprising electoral victory of the Cartel des gauches in 1924. The historian Richard Challener chronicles how this was "a dramatic reversal of French political fortunes which accurately reflected popular dissatisfaction with the economic disorders resulting from the Ruhr occupation and with Poincaré's policy of 'going it alone.'"[22]

Whatever uneasy postwar optimism there had been about France's falling power was punctured by the reality of the Ruhr crisis. Afterwards, French officials saw that they must retrench more actively. There was a purge of senior officials at the Quai d'Orsay, making 150 personnel changes and ending several high-profile careers.[23] In 1925, the Counseil Supérieur de la Defense Nationale (CSDN) was candid about why it had to appease allies: "Our inability immediately to fill in the gaps in our national defense preparations make all the other contributions to security we can command absolutely indispensable: conclusion of a security pact guaranteeing the automatic, or at least very rapid, determination of the aggressor and the equally rapid beginning of coercive measures."[24] The council concluded that since France did not have the military means to fit its diplomatic goals, France needed to retrench more.[25] If confrontation was not the solution, what was?

"Reduction in the Budget as National Defense": French Domestic Policies

Large decliners ought to retrench in decisive and dramatic fashion: large spending cuts, substantial restructuring of forces, and major military reforms, all yielding a sizeable redistribution of resources. There is evidence that French policy advanced strikingly along all these courses except institutional reform. Spending was slashed, the army was radically revamped, and institutional reforms were significant, but the French army did not evolve fast enough. The country was in improved economic health by the end of the decade and in much better military shape as well, but these advantages were undermined by deeper institutional problems.

First, France shed expenses energetically. The war had left the country heavily indebted and its currency vulnerable. Taxes had not been increased immediately following the war, but to stabilize the franc, France shed tens of thousands of public employees starting in 1922, raised taxes, and took out loans, and by 1925 the budget was back in surplus.[26] Government spending as a percentage of GDP halved from 29 percent in 1922 to 14 percent in 1926.[27] At the highest levels, the French government took austerity seriously.

The military was not exempt from this push, and there was great desire to minimize defense burdens. The war minister Louis Barthou told the Finance Commission that he considered "reduction in the budget of the War Ministry . . . a form of national defense."[28] In nominal sums, French defense spending dropped from 6.1 billion francs in 1920 to 4.1 billion francs in 1924.[29] In real terms, military spending sloped gently downwards from 1921 to 1926 and was the lowest of any great power save Germany.[30] As a share of French GDP, military spending fell precipitously around 1924, from 10.4 percent in 1922 to 3.4 percent in 1926.[31] The overall pattern is of aggressive belt tightening around the transition point.

Second, France revised its force structure, stressing the army over the navy and low-cost reserves over expensive regulars. What resources there were went to the army, not the navy, and the air force was for most of the period the army's neglected stepchild.[32] At the Washington Naval Conference of 1921/22, Briand declared, "If France had not for forty years worked up a strong army what would have happened to the peace of the world in 1914?"[33] France reluctantly acceded to the most stringent tonnage limits, behind Japan and on a par with Italy, a marginal great power.[34]

With its army, France continued to move toward a nation-in-arms concept and away from a standing army of professionals.[35] Those plans developed in the wake of the Ruhr occupation. When the Cartel des gauches assumed power, it aimed, in the words of the historian Irving Gibson, to "reorganize the entire military system of France, carrying out the principle of the nation-in-arms to the last letter."[36] The war minister General

Charles Nollet introduced new plans for faster mobilization and better training in 1924, but these were rejected as too hastily drawn up.[37] The next year, the prime minister Paul Painlevé developed the main lines of Nollet's recommendations, and they were implemented in the years following. Painlevé's plan legally tied service reductions to the retention of a cadre of professional soldiers sufficient to act as a *couverture* and organize a surge in forces as necessary, created mobilization centers, readied for a system of frontier defenses (soon to be the Maginot Line), and reduced active army divisions at the same time as developing quick-mobilizing units in between active and reserve forces, called *disponibles*.[38]

In 1920, the Counseil Supérieur de la Guerre (CSG) had unanimously approved a model of forty-one active divisions on national territory and eight colonial divisions, but with reduction in conscription terms from twenty-four months in 1921, eighteen months in 1924, and twelve months in 1928, active divisions on national territory fell to twenty by the late 1920s.[39] Gibson notes, "The French army henceforth was to exist only as a reserve, if we use the old vocabulary. In reality it was a new conception, a nation-in-arms created in conformity with geographical limitations and other circumstances beyond the control of France."[40] France also sought to increase the number of indigenous troops serving in its armed forces so it could shift regular units back to France, and it sought to increase civilians in non-military jobs that were previously performed by army personnel.[41] These were the blueprints for French pre-war defenses. As Challener puts it, "none of the later legislation produced any significant change in the fundamental military pattern established in the twenties."[42] The state traded a larger army of professionals more capable of offense for a larger army of reservists more capable of defense.[43]

Third, France seriously reformed its military institutions, with a particular emphasis on organization and command. Administratively, the CSDN was reconstituted in 1921 with more ministers, more meetings, and more authority.[44] Hughes describes how the "interlocking crises in finance, the colonies, morale, and recruitment had both heightened the military's sense of urgency about establishing a functioning army organization and forced them to fashion the new military machine under severely straitened circumstances. Although the actual reorganization legislation was not enacted until 1927–1928, the outlines of the army's new structure became clear during 1925."[45] The French Air Ministry was also born in 1928, and it would grow into the French Air Force in 1933.[46]

French military training and education notched notable successes. From 1920 to 1927, France made great progress experimenting with mobile, mechanized warfare.[47] As two military historians of the period put it, "The conference chambers of the Ecole de Guerre and the training grounds of Coetquidan, Mailly, and Mourmelin were alive in the 1920s to the sound of the theory and practice of mobile experimentation."[48] Viewing France's large-scale maneuvers in 1930, the British attaché was impressed "by the improved methods of movement and concealment of tanks which had hitherto usually been puerile." The French had "really woken up" to modern mobility.[49]

Nonetheless, it is plain that French reformers made grave errors. The political scientist Barry Posen suggests that structural conditions were the main contributor: when innovators like Charles de Gaulle proposed more thoroughgoing reforms, they were ignored because they "undercut the broader purposes of French grand strategy."[50] A highly trained, innovative military would have looked like a sharp, offensive instrument and would have alienated sorely needed allies.[51] Beyond this, however, French civil-military relations were not healthy. The standing army had little faith in the reservists, the military bureaucracy shielded senior officers in need of retirement, and the command structure was unwieldy at making and executing decisions.[52] These were unnecessary weaknesses in a country facing dire threat. The upshot is that French reformers made good faith efforts to improve their military institutions, but they were hamstrung by the desire to attract allies and by poor civil-military relations.

Fourth, France reallocated resources to revive its economy. The war had revealed serious problems in the banking sector, and the French state gradually became a large bank to remedy these deficiencies.[53] Defense declined as a share of government expenditures. While total expenditures stayed roughly flat from 1920 to 1925, defense's share fell from 42 percent to 28 percent, and rose above that share only twice before 1937. Some of the retrenchment dividend was spent paying off debts, which consumed 23 percent of government expenditure in 1920, but 44 percent in 1926, falling back to 23 percent by 1930. Meanwhile, education and science received a progressive infusion of funds, growing from 3.7 percent share of expenditures in 1920 to 8.1 percent in 1930.[54]

How much these priorities contributed to French economic performance is debatable, but policymakers succeeded in putting France on sound financial footing by the late 1920s. The French economy was booming by 1929, reaching levels it would not see again until the 1950s.[55] Total French tax yields went from 22.5 billion francs in 1920 to 50.8 billion francs in 1930, with the biggest jump occurring between 1922 and 1926.[56] France posted high growth rates for years, and this was not simply a function of recovering from war. French per capita GDP was higher than the German equivalent until well into the 1930s, and France's average annual growth rate in the 1920s was 5.2 percent—the highest of any great power.[57] The franc stabilized by 1927, stayed stable for a decade, and became one of the strongest currencies in the world.[58] In liquid assets, the historian David Landes notes, "France was the richest country in Europe. . . . The reserves of the Bank of France, in gold and foreign exchange (*devises*), had risen from some 20 billion (milliard) francs at the end of 1925 to 67.5 billion at the end of 1929."[59]

On the whole, French domestic policies dealt with decline capably in almost every category. Austerity in the defense budget was a hallmark of French policy in the 1920s. In the five years on either side of 1924, France spent an average of 8 billion francs on its military; for all other years until 1938, it averaged 16 billion francs.[60] Policymakers kept budgets down via smaller end strength, shorter service terms, larger reserves, and quicker mobilization. They reoriented forces in an increasingly defensive direction to attract allies, but the goals of defending the country and attracting allies were in tension with one another. France could not reform to the full extent demanded by its decline without estranging potential allies, and bad civil-military relations damaged the nerve center of the French state. Yet this must be kept in perspective. At the time, no other state had a better-trained army, and French doctrine was no worse than that of its counterparts. The government managed to reallocate resources, which appears to have boosted its growth rate and kept the door open for allied aid. In the 1920s, French domestic retrenchment was a success, but its success would lay the groundwork for failure in the 1930s.

"Sacrifices to Its Allies": French International Policies

France was falling too fast for domestic policies alone to manage the problems of decline, so we expect policymakers to redeploy forces, remove flashpoints, redistribute burdens, and bolster deterrence more than states in medium declines. This is pretty much an accurate portrayal of events, but the tensions between these policies were acute. France zeroed in on homeland defense, practiced appeasement, and resolutely shifted burdens to allies wherever it could. But France reached a point where it could not defuse flashpoints without losing allies to whom it desperately wanted to shift burdens. Furthermore, there was a paucity of capable allies available. French policymakers struggled to resolve these problems, which may well have been insoluble.

First, France was most successful at redeploying forces to concentrate on homeland defense. It drew down in the colonies, built up fortifications, and built around counterpunching defensive plans. At sea, the French navy focused on home waters and assuring access to its colonies, but these aims were a distant second to territorial defenses.[61] On land, it is difficult to neatly categorize French actions in part because of accounting ambiguities (e.g. some French colonial forces were stationed in metropolitan France) and some conceptual ambiguities (e.g. France's often large Army of the Rhine was stationed abroad but was seen as contributing directly to homeland defense.) Nevertheless, fewer and fewer French forces were stationed abroad as the 1920s wore on. In Germany, France evacuated the Ruhr in 1925 and the first Rhineland zone in 1926, followed by several more waves from 1928 to 1930. In the colonies, France was eager to scale back its forces, though two rebellions in Syria and Morocco, both beginning in 1925, temporarily reversed this trend. In 1921, French colonial forces stood at 251,000, but by 1929 they had declined to 151,000.[62] The prime minister Édouard Herriot declared, "My country has a dagger pointed at her breast, a centimeter from the heart."[63] In such an environment, core defenses naturally took priority over peripheral concerns.

Second, French policymakers desperately sought to remove potential flashpoints. However, this varied over space and time: French retrenchment was faster in the colonies than in Europe, and greater after the Ruhr occupation than before. In the colonies, France increasingly worked to eliminate areas where great power conflicts might flare up. Initially, however, this was not the case.[64] According to the historian Zara Steiner, "Clemenceau cared little about colonial issues," but was not averse to easy acquisitions.[65] The 1920 Treaty of Sévres settled the end of the First World War with Turkey, and France claimed swaths of the Ottoman Empire—to such an extent that the British were irritated by how "rabid on the subject" the French were.[66] When Britain backed Greek territorial claims, France took Turkey's side because "neither parliament nor public opinion [will] accept the continuance of costly and bloody fighting on the frontiers of the Syrian mandate."[67] The British felt betrayed.[68] French officers exceeded their authority and instigated conflicts in Syria, Morocco, and Indochina. This exacerbated manpower shortages and alarmed officials in Paris.[69]

France swiftly repented of its adventures abroad. In 1921, France renounced its occupation of Cilicia.[70] It also retrenched in Syria. A British observer remarked gleefully, "The French do not realise that they have got to cut their coat according to their cloth, and they have got very little cloth."[71] This was an uncharitable reading; even Georges Noblemaire, a member of the *groupe colonial*, said that "public opinion has been more or less spontaneously alarmed by the prospect of large and costly expeditions. People have spoken of [the prospect of] . . . the disastrous and unlimited expenditure of money."[72] As the historian Dennis William Brogan observes, "That France, out of all the kaleidoscopic changes of the years between 1916 and 1923, got no more than Syria, was not surprising; what was surprising was that she got so much, for at no time was she ready to spend the men or money required to gain more."[73] By the Ruhr occupation, French imperial expansion was over.[74]

In Europe, the tone and tempo of French concessions changed over time. Before the Ruhr occupation, France grudgingly gave ground and made few big compromises, but after 1924, appeasement switched into high gear. For instance, France was willing to risk German and British opposition early on. In a 1921 German-Polish dispute over Upper Silesia, Britain backed Germany's claim and France backed Poland's. A plebiscite of the Silesians found that 60 percent wanted to remain part of Germany, yet, at France's suggestion, the issue was kept alive by referring it to the League of Nations, which defused the situation by siding with France and Poland.[75]

And France was willing to negotiate hard over reparations at first, but it increasingly gave way.[76] At the San Remo Conference of April 1920, France capitulated to Britain, promising not to act without allied support in the future.[77] At the Hythe, Bologna, and Spa Conferences in the months following, the historian Walter McDougall describes how the French "entered as supplicants."[78] At the London Conference in 1921, the allies issued the London Schedule of payments. Steiner notes that they were "not a good bargain for France."[79] At the Cannes Conference of 1922, French firmness and accommodation failed to bring better results. The Genoa Conference that same year was a disaster. France insisted that the Soviet Union assume Russia's prewar debts to France, and that Germany pay reparations to the USSR. The Germans and Soviets departed to the nearby town of Rapallo to sign their own agreement.[80]

French appeasement accelerated after the debacle of the Ruhr occupation. To win Anglo-American support, France accepted the American diplomat Charles Dawes's "independent inquiry" into reparations.[81] Herriot bemoaned that his foreign policy tools were "few and feeble," but French policymakers used what they had to detach the Soviet Union from Germany, allow German revisionism, and knit allies into multilateral agreements.[82] Herriot granted diplomatic recognition to the Soviets and normalized relations. At a meeting of the CSDN, Herriot, Briand, and Joseph Paul-Boncour shot down the objections of some of France's most celebrated soldiers to France's new diplomacy.[83] Defense would dominate French strategy, and diplomacy was going to keep the next war off French soil.[84]

The Locarno Treaties of 1925 represent the zenith of French diplomacy in the interwar period but also a new nadir of French aims.[85] To protect borders in Western Europe, the French accepted the probability of revision in eastern Europe.[86] In Herriot and Briand's words: "We do not have an option."[87] Most legislators saw no alternative either, and the Chamber voted 413 to 71 to pass the measures.[88] The historian Piotr Wandycz captures the shift that Locarno signified: "Paris had originally regarded a threat to the Polish borders as tantamount to a threat on the Rhine. Then voices began to be heard that France would accept a freely negotiated German-Polish border settlement. Finally, the French government was giving the Germans to understand that it would actually welcome it."[89]

After Locarno came a Franco-German steel entente in 1926,[90] a commercial agreement in 1927, and a similar agreement with Belgium in 1928.[91] The 1926 Mellon-Bérenger agreement settled French war debt repayments to the United States.[92] And the Kellogg-Briand Pact, signed by fifteen powers, condemned "recourse to war for the settlement of international differences," outlawed war "as an instrument of national policy," and would resolve disputes "by peaceful means only."[93] In 1929, the Dawes Plan was morphed into the more lenient Young Plan for German reparations at the Hague Conference. Wandycz states, "The Hague conference was Stresemann's victory and Briand's defeat. Germany had reached its goal, an early evacuation of the Rhineland, in exchange for the Young Plan, which would shortly turn out to be a scrap of paper."[94] As the 1920s wore on, France switched from resentful concessions to widespread appeasement to stifle flashpoints, and the same trends continued into the 1930s.[95]

Third, interwar France fought feverishly to export burdens onto allies, primarily Britain and the United States but secondarily eastern European states. Yet France was caught in a vise: Britain and the United States had little desire to underwrite France's defense and eastern European states had little capability to help defend France. Worse, the two groups of potential allies had contradictory preferences; Britain and the United States wanted a softer line against Germany while the eastern European states wanted a harder line. And then there were irreconcilable interests and collective action problems within each group. For example, French designs for a "Slav corset" to restrain Germany's girth were thwarted by infighting and territorial disputes among the states that wanted to balance Germany.

France knew from the start it could neither defend itself nor rely mostly on others to defend it. After the First World War, the prime minister Georges Clemenceau explained to his ministers the choice they faced: "Stand alone on the Rhine against a vengeful Germany, or rely on distant allies. The foreign minister [Stéphen Pichon] was skeptical of alliances . . . yet he did not see how the offer could be refused."[96] But Britain and the United States were opposed to what France saw as its minimum requirements for its safety.[97] Clemenceau confessed to Poincaré, "We will not perhaps have the peace that you and I would like. France will have to make sacrifices, not to Germany but to its allies."[98] French policymakers agreed that British support was the indispensable element in French security.[99]

But France struggled to win the trust of the British or the Americans because it was the strongest state on the continent. The veteran British statesman George Curzon observed before the Versailles conference: "I am afraid that the Great Power from whom we have most to fear in the future is France."[100] As the historian Robert Boyce details, the British prime minister Lloyd George "acknowledged to Clemenceau after the peace conference that France and Britain would always remain enemies."[101] The French perceived British antipathy and took steps to reassure them, offering to cut French armaments in proportion to international assistance given, but to no avail.[102] During the Ruhr crisis, Curzon publically accused the Poincaré government of "striving for European domination."[103] At the British foreign office, Eyre Crowe detected that the highest levels of the British government leaned "towards the substitution of an *Entente* with Germany in place of that with France."[104] France looked no better in the United States.

President Herbert Hoover confided to his secretary of state, Henry Stimson, who recorded, "France always goes through this cycle. After she is done and begins to recuperate . . . she gets rich, militaristic, and cocky; and nobody can get on with her until she has to be thrashed again. And in this matter he [Hoover] saw nothing in the future but a line-up between Germany, Britain, and ourselves against France."[105]

With Britain and the United States suspicious, France fell back on whatever non–great power allies were available. In 1920, France signed a military convention with Belgium and hoped to pull Luxembourg into its orbit.[106] French policymakers made multiple attempts to shed their defense burdens by advocating Rhenish autonomy movements, but all were abject failures.[107] When policymakers considered a permanent French presence in the region, the idea died for predictable reasons.[108] One staffer wrote in the margin of the proposal, "Admirable project, if Britain did not exist."[109] That left eastern Europe as the most fertile ground for allies.

Because of France's falling power, the search for eastern European allies went from cautious in the early 1920s to eager in the mid-1920s. The defeat of France's allies in the Russian civil war opened the door for a Franco-Polish alliance in 1921.[110] Yet though the high-ranking foreign ministry official Philippe Berthelot wanted Poland as an ally in 1920, even he thought it was a strategic liability.[111] When Poland and the USSR fought in 1920, France was stingy in its aid to the Poles because of British disapproval.[112] Another possibility was to ally with the successor states of the Austro-Hungarian Empire. Initially, this took the form of trying to forge what the historian Piotr Wandycz calls "a French-oriented Danubian union including and based on Hungary."[113] The plan was a non-starter, however, because France could not support Hungary's desired border changes without alienating other allies.[114] A 1921 report by the Foreign Affairs Committee regretted the lack of counterweights on the Danube, which would be "vigorous and powerful, capable of checking German ambitions."[115] France saw that devotion to eastern allies risked alienating Britain, enabling its eastern allies to take reckless positions, and diluting its ebbing strength.[116]

Negative feedback after the Ruhr occupation inaugurated another round of ally searching. From 1924 to 1927, France penned consultative, defensive, or non-aggression pacts with Czechoslovakia, Romania, and Yugoslavia. The historian Peter Jackson contends, "Balance-of-power calculations determined virtually every aspect of security policy in the east."[117] Briand emphasized to skeptics, "It's necessary to make up our minds to have some friends, however painful that might be."[118] This was a diplomatic outreach but also a retreat. France had little interest in defending its partners but hoped they would contain Germany with limited obligations on France's part.[119] For this reason, it was foreboding that the Quai d'Orsay underscored that none of the existing Franco-Polish agreements guaranteed current borders.[120]

Fourth, France not only tried to deflect Germany's attention to eastern allies it had little intention of defending, it also revised strategic plans to boost homeland defense through fortification, internal lines of communication, and flexible defense.[121] Again, the period following the Ruhr occupation was most fertile for change. Hughes chronicles, "With each successive revision of French mobilization plans, the scope of offensive operations from the Rhineland base had progressively diminished."[122] From 1921 to 1923, Plan P had aimed to advance on the Ruhr and Main valleys. In 1924, Plan A attempted to learn the lessons of the Ruhr occupation with a less ambitious but still multi-prong advance into Germany. That plan was obsolete within the year. In 1926, Plan A-bis called off early offensives and was replaced the same year by the more defensive Plan B, which stressed defense of French territory above all.[123] This was uncontroversial: "Even the right stood generally for a reduction of military service and a defensive strategy."[124]

To boost homeland defense, defense planners looked to improve fortifications, interior lines of communication, and flexible defense. Around the same time as Plan B, the French general staff started planning what would become the Maginot Line.[125] Tactically, the fortifications were designed to facilitate mobility, but strategically their purpose in the opening phases of combat were defensive.[126] It is no coincidence that the Maginot Line was timed to become effective as the French completed their withdrawal from Germany.[127] The defensive works were designed to protect lines of communication and aid flexibility under fire. There was little dispute that the strongpoint defenses would be the Metz, Lauter, and Belfort regions because the hope was to channel a German attack through Belgium and guarantee British support.[128]

In sum, French foreign policy attempted retrenchment policies early and often, but increased its efforts in the mid-1920s. France restructured its global posture by concentrating forces at home and reconfigured its war plans to privilege homeland defense. The most agonizing issues of interwar French strategy involved tradeoffs between cultivating allies and defusing flashpoints. With German capability capped by the Versailles treaty, Britain and the United States felt they had more to fear from unchecked French military power. France was happy to facilitate an anti-German coalition in eastern Europe, but not if doing so estranged Britain or required any diversion from defense of the French homeland. Too much appeasement would lose valuable friends, but so would too little appeasement. Not only were there too few friends available, none of the prospective suitors seemed capable or willing to lighten France's defensive burdens on their own. France managed these contradictions as well as it could in the 1920s, but they would become overwhelming as conditions shifted in the 1930s.

"A Firm Hand on the Scruff": The Limits of French Retrenchment

Despite its large decline, France, we contend, attained only modest levels of retrenchment. French retrenchment in the 1920s has much in common with French retrenchment in the 1890s: domestic differences over foreign policy narrowed, colonial conflicts were reined in, eastern fortifications were resurrected, the search for allies was intensified, and conscription cast a wider net. The problem is that France in the interwar period was experiencing a much deeper decline, and the allies available to France were much less willing to help share defense burdens. Thus while modest policies of retrenchment helped secure important breathing space early in the interwar period, French foreign policy became increasingly incoherent as circumstances altered.[129]

These later developments, however, do not diminish the important accomplishments of French policy. As the historian Anthony Adamthwaite, no admirer of interwar French politics, writes, "If the Third Republic had ended in 1931, it would have been celebrated as a success."[130] Domestic reforms put France's fiscal house in order after a devastating war. Military reforms tied the armed forces to a sustainable vision of the nation-in-arms, and a sensible strategy of blunting any invasion with a covering force while mobilizing for a long-term total war. Diplomatic moves kept France on good terms with most states, and Germany was being rehabilitated into the world order.

Not only was French foreign policy in the 1920s effective, it was also free from domestic dysfunction. There were cleavages between the left and right, but these were more over domestic than foreign policy. The seeds of poor civil-military relations were sown before the Second World War, but there is little indication of them in the 1920s. In the words of Challener, apart from the debate over military service terms, there were "no serious parliamentary debates on military policy" for much of the 1920s, and that debate was hardly divergent; the argument was between twelve- or eighteen-month terms, no one questioned absolute service equality, the eighteen-month party was apologetic, and the measure passed in a record two days.[131]

Briand and Poincaré were emblematic of this consensus. While Briand was known as the dove and Poincaré the hawk, both worked together, served together, and complemented each other. The two had differences, but international incentives homogenized their behavior. During the more autonomous period in the early 1920s, Briand not only agreed with the harder line but implemented it, ordering the occupation of some Ruhr towns in 1921 because Germany deserved "a firm hand on the scruff of the neck."[132] Likewise, Poincaré bought into accommodation and cooperation with Germany long before Locarno, and not only went along with the policies but was instrumental in effecting them.[133] At the Cannes

Conference, the French public saw Briand as insufficiently standing up for French interests and replaced him as prime minister with Poincaré.[134] Poincaré retained most of Briand's ministers, but he came to talks with a tougher attitude.[135] An ally of Poincaré thundered in the French daily *Le Figaro*, "As soon as we invoke our rights in a voice that no longer trembles and with gestures that do not fumble, we will see an end to the moral isolation of France."[136] Foreign leaders were unimpressed.[137] Poincaré was forced back toward the policies of his predecessor.[138] Negative feedback from the system was visible to voters and politicians, and that constricted policy options.

Tellingly, foreign policy continuity was not due to interest group politics or domestic political stability. In his masterly study, Wandycz finds that interwar French alliance politics and foreign policy were based on top-down decision making, not lobbying.[139] And French governments were hardly lasting. In the interwar period, the only major European country with more annual cabinet changes on average was Spain.[140] Between 1920 and 1930, France had fifteen different ministries and ten different prime ministers, but only six individuals served at the Quai d'Orsay. Challener discerns, "Actually, despite chronic French ministerial instability, from January 1921 until March 1932 . . . with the exception of two short interludes . . . French foreign policy was in the hands of but two men."[141] Similarly, there was great stability at the CSG from 1920 to 1940: only three individuals led it.[142] A long roster of preeminent scholars finds continuity the dominant trend in French foreign policy at least through the early 1930s.[143]

The interwar French case also spotlights the important role played by structural modifiers. In most respects, structural conditions mostly favored French retrenchment, but the one exception was crucial. Favoring retrenchment were France's low rank, the apparent dominance of the defense, and the separation of colonial and continental commitments. Falling from a low rank appears to have given French policy a fillip; we have seen evidence that policymakers were aware that their status as a great power was in jeopardy unless they made astute adjustments. In the wake of the First World War, almost everyone saw defense as the dominant form of war going forward. And French colonial commitments were not thought to be test cases of resolve for European crises; retrenchment on the periphery would not vitiate protection of the core.

Yet in this case, the availability of capable, reliable allies appears to be the central structural feature that complicated French retrenchment. Challener captures the leitmotif of interwar French security: "It was impossible for France to enlist Britain as an ally in the East; on the other hand, it was impossible to get along without England. But to follow her meant that French ties with Central Europe were increasingly worthless, while to rely on continental allies alone was to have no real strength. French foreign policy . . . was throughout the 1920s caught on the horns of a dilemma."[144]

France managed these contradictions as well as it could in the 1920s, but in the following decade, circumstances outran French foreign policy. One tension was that there was only so far France could cut military spending without having sufficient forces for homeland defense and reserving the option to aid allies in the future. But if France overspent on defense, the perception was that budget deficits would hurt the country's ability to fight a protracted war. Another tension was the familiar one that cultivating forces to help eastern allies would estrange Britain, but cultivating Britain would entail estranging eastern allies. Not feeling able to rely on either strategy, French diplomats lobbied for alliances with the Soviet Union and Italy. A final tension was that, as Germany gathered strength, France wanted more allies but could not offer enough to keep them. The foreign minister, Louis Barthou, tried to curry favor with the Soviet Union by advocating for their admittance to the League of Nations and bringing about the Franco-USSR Treaty of Mutual Assistance in 1935.[145] Yet as before, any French treaty with the USSR was not very useful because Poland and Romania were explicit about not wanting the Soviets traversing their territory.[146] When war approached, France again made overtures to the USSR—this time with Britain—but they possessed nothing to match Germany's offer to the Soviet Union of huge swaths of eastern Europe.

With Italy, France struck an agreement in 1935: Italy would give up claims on French Tunisia, and France would give Italy a free hand in Ethiopia.[147] In April, Britain joined France and Italy in the short-lived Stresa Front, agreeing to "oppose, by all suitable means, any unilateral repudiation of treaties which is liable to endanger the peace of Europe" and affirm the independence of Austria.[148] This ushered in talks in June, broaching the possibility of using Italian soil to provide military aid to France's eastern allies.[149] All of this placed France in an awkward position when Italy invaded Abyssinia in October. France eventually tried to appease Italy, but the invasion hurt France's domestic consensus. The historian Jacques Néré observes that until 1936 French leaders "had succeeded in coming to an agreement on a common policy, by putting the national interest before any ideological preference and in making it acceptable to the country. The Ethiopian war was the first occasion on which the two Frances confronted each other, with an unyielding violence in the field of foreign policy."[150] Italy would never amount to much of an ally, but French offers were not enough to entice meaningful cooperation from the Italians.

In brief, around the time that France was falling in the great power ranks, French policymakers returned with urgency to earlier retrenchment recipes: the nation-in-arms, eastern fortifications, and alliances.[151] The French were amply alert to their decline and responded in a swift and sizeable manner.[152] Yet France did not retrench enough because alone it was too weak to deter Germany, and no combination of allies was willing to try until it was too late. The result—tough talk blended with appeasement—only inflamed the situation.

From high up, our theory gets a number of factors right in the large cases. Russia and France clearly saw their declines, moved aggressively to remedy their problems, and were in better shape to compete as a result. Up close, however, our theory does not do justice to significant facets of the cases. Both countries retrenched less than expected. In Russia, this had much to do with a maladroit leader and dysfunctional domestic system that put Russia on collision courses the country was not prepared for. In France, this was due largely to wrenching structural dilemmas: it could not defend against Germany on its own, but it could not secure effective, reliable allies. Whatever the reasons for their lapses, both states were crushingly punished for their inadequacies.

There is sound evidence that structural conditions played a significant role in both cases. Relative rank was low, and policymakers in both states knew it. Witte, Kuropatkin, Lamsdorf, and their successors were outspoken in how precarious Russia's standing was. French policymakers made similar statements, and at the Washington Naval Conference they accepted the same limits as Italy, a liminal great power. Both states had available allies, though the tradeoffs in Russia's options were less unsavory. The interdependence of commitments was a problem for both countries and contributed to war. As for the conquest calculus, both nations felt deeply vulnerable and couched their policy options in existential language.[153] Conditions favored French retrenchment more than Russian retrenchment, and that appears to match their relative performance as well.

There are a few final points to make about the two large cases studies. First, they demonstrate how international policies of retrenchment can conflict with one another. For example, sometimes the cultivation of allies and efforts to defuse flashpoints worked at cross-purposes. Russia's settlement of disputes with Britain and Japan inadvertently caused problems with Germany and Austria. French policies designed to appease Germany in eastern Europe raised serious questions about the credibility of its commitments to potential alliance partners. Domestic and international retrenchment policies need to be harmonized with each other and with themselves. When this cannot be done, leaders must accept the least bad as good.

Second, these cases highlight the difficulties and dangers of deep declines. There is a good case to be made that Russia departed too much, too soon from the retrenchment policies that could have been its salvation. The days of tsarism may have been numbered, but it is not hard to imagine them stretching out longer with leadership that was not so dogmatically resistant to reform nor willing to indulge expansionist temptations. The flipside of that coin is that France stuck to the same policies as the world rapidly changed in the mid-1930s. When the skies darkened, France did not respond with its vaunted *souplesse*, quick-witted adaptability.[154] Unable to attract firm commitments from a capable ally until virtually the eve of war, France did not develop policies that would help its less capable allies maintain pressure on Germany or the military institutions to react nimbly to German attack. Best to avoid large declines, of course, but, if unavoidable, better to be aware that such situations have narrow tolerances and demand acuity as well as agility. In retrenchment as in life, timing is everything.

Conclusion

Retrenchment as Reloading

Mistakes in operations and tactics can be corrected, but political and strategic mistakes live forever.

—Allan Millett and Williamson Murray

Everything dies baby that's a fact, but maybe everything that dies someday comes back.

—Bruce Springsteen

How do great powers respond to decline? The prevailing wisdom among international relations scholars is pessimistic; decline invites preventive war and domestic dysfunction. Reluctant to surrender their dominant positions, declining powers will be tempted to use force to sustain the status quo and fend off potential predators. Flush with new capabilities and entranced by myths of empire, rising powers will be drawn to aggressive policies. All the while, domestic political dynamics will diminish the prospects for peace. Parochial interest groups and hidebound bureaucracies will encourage declining powers to clutch indefensible commitments despite gathering storms. Nationalist parties and offensive-oriented militaries will pressure rising powers into expansionist ventures even as costs mount and benefits dwindle. Great powers are caught in what Graham Allison calls the "Thucydides Trap": one state overtaking another makes war highly likely.[1] And preventive war and domestic dysfunction are not the only potential consequences of decline. All states will look for loosely held claims and power vacuums, stirring vortices of regional instability. When the international distribution of power is in flux, the world is up for grabs.

For many, this sounds like current events. As the United States retreats from global affairs, rising powers and revisionist states are taking advantage. Walter Russell Mead declares that the unipolar moment has given way to a "return of geopolitics," where "U.S. presidents no longer have a free hand as they seek to deepen the liberal system."[2] Robert Kaplan adds that: "for the first time since the Berlin Wall fell, the United States finds itself in a competition among great powers."[3] These challenges might be surmountable if there were consensus on how to respond. Yet as Michael Cohen argues, "At no point in recent American history has the country's politics been more polarized and less primed to dealing with serious national challenges."[4] Pessimism is a staple in political discourse, but seldom has there been so much of it surrounding America's role in the world.

We have argued that the prevailing wisdom about the dangers of decline is misleading. Relative decline is common; war and death spirals are not. These facts alone should discourage panic or overreaction. Even beyond war, decline has the opposite effect to that which scholars have posited over an array of measures. Instead of pushing states to belligerence in disputes short of war, decline is one of the most powerful forces pulling states to peace. The case studies have shown that there is a great deal of ruin in nations, but serious reforms have regularly surmounted setbacks and dysfunction. In fact, recovery is a real possibility. States have healthy competitive instincts and decline opens space for institutional overhauls. Rather than being puppets of structural forces, declining powers have room to shape their policies in ways that make them more viable, but less violent.

In short, there are good grounds for optimism in decline. Declining powers are not inclined to unleash violence, nor are they tied up by competing bureaucracies, interest groups, or parties. The most frequent response to decline is not belligerence but retrenchment. Great powers align their ends and means to better defend core interests, refit and refuel institutions, and reallocate resources for more productive investment. Retrenchment does not always lead to recovery, but under a wide variety of conditions it is preferable to the alternatives: expanding out, lashing out, or holding on. If this argument is correct, then the deep and abiding pessimism about the capacity of the United States to manage the rise of new great power rivals is misplaced. Pundits have it backwards: if power politics is returning, those forces are more likely to preserve peace than preclude it.

This chapter reviews and extends the analysis. In the first section, we evaluate the main theories and findings. In the second section, we use our framework to examine the implications of our theory for the impending Sino-American transition. We conclude with some observations about the prospects for peaceful change in world politics.

Arguments and Evidence: Assessing the Decline Debate

International politics is a complex environment in which structural pressures and individual choices combine in unexpected ways to produce a range of outcomes. It is not surprising then that none of the theories in this book fully account for how great powers deal with decline. Yet on balance, we find the strongest and most consistent support for the logic of retrenchment. Simply put, the most common responses to decline are not expansionist policies designed to risk war, but retrenchment policies intended to secure peace. This does not mean that retrenchment is embraced with a smile, or that it always works. It requires declining powers to relinquish things they value, redistribute risks, and bristle at strongpoints. But if leaders are responsible for protecting the national interest, then retrenchment is usually the most attractive option.

The next best theory is domestic dysfunction. Internal factors can illuminate how declining powers choose to retrench, but only in unusual circumstances do they overwhelm the structural pressures on declining states. The theory that fares the worst is preventive war. Declining states almost never follow the logic of preventive war, and even weaker versions of that explanation show the folly of war as a solution to decline. Below we survey what the theories can and cannot explain.

THE STRUCTURAL DETERMINISM TRAP: PREVENTIVE WAR REVISITED

Thucydides is notoriously hard to pin down, but there is one argument he makes his own. "The real cause [of the Peloponnesian War] I consider to be the one which was formally most kept out of sight. The growth of the power of Athens, and the alarm which this inspired in Sparta, made war inevitable."[5] Ever since, advocates of preventive war logic have argued that declining great powers are drawn to major war like moths to a flame.[6] At base, declining powers suffer from a commitment problem; they cannot be sure that rising powers will honor promises they make once they become more powerful. As a result, war in the near future becomes enticing. If true, then declining powers will rarely retrench, and they will participate in armed conflict at higher rates than other states.

Preventive war may have made sense in ancient Greece, but it does not today. Most declining powers do not fight interstate wars; the few that do fight interstate wars do not fight with the rising power that overtook them. For preventive war to work, the odds of victory have to be good, the spoils of war have to exceed the cost, and the alternatives—diplomacy, reform, or inactivity—have to be worse. But nothing is more expensive and uncertain than war. Perhaps for these reasons, war is more likely to cause decline than arrest it. Rational, security-seeking states are not perfect, but they tend to be far more cautious than preventive war theorists suggest.

We find little support for preventive war logic in our universe of cases. In only two of the sixteen cases did a declining power fight its ordinal challenger, and both cases cut against preventive war. In one, 1873 France, war was more the cause of decline than a consequence. In the other, 1935 Britain, war was desperately avoided for as long as possible. Nor do we find much support for preventive war theory in our descriptive statistics. Declining powers were less likely to initiate, participate in, and be targeted in disputes. The claims that declining powers use force to retain their rank or that they are attractive prey was not borne out by the evidence.

There is only one area with potential support for the preventive war hypothesis. In a subset of the data, large decliners, we find a slightly increased incidence of militarized dispute participation and initiation—more than either non-declining powers or small and medium decliners. It might be that decline sometimes prompts aggression in the most desperate situations. Yet this result is driven by only two cases, 1946 Great Britain and 1987 Soviet Union, which participated in disputes at nearly twice the rate of other large decliners. The bulk of large decliners participated in disputes at lower rates than non-declining powers. Of equal importance, neither of the dispute-prone large decliners escalated to major war, despite ample opportunities. And in neither case were elevated levels of disputes strong evidence of an aversion to retrenchment. Britain participated in a number of early Cold War crises as it was withdrawing from imperial commitments; the Soviet Union became embroiled in crises in its near abroad at the same time that it was pulling back from Eastern Europe.

A proponent of preventive war theory might retort that examining militarized disputes or interstate wars is an unfair test. Power transition theories aim to explain large "system changing" wars, not disputes, skirmishes, or minor conflicts. Britain declined vis-à-vis Germany in 1908 on the eve of the First World War and then did so again in 1935 in the run-up to the Second World War. These facts alone could suggest that decline is a leading contributor to major wars. Yet in neither of these cases are the mechanisms posited by preventive war logic operative. Before both world wars, Britain went to great lengths to avert war and the second time around went so far as to appease Hitler. Had Britain intended to keep its position with force, then it would have angled for offensive alliances with continental powers and picked fights early, either over Morocco prior to the First World War or over the Rhineland before the Second World War.

A more tenable interpretation is to recast Germany as the declining power. Had the war not intervened, imperial Germany was poised to decline at the expense of Russia in the late 1910s, and interwar Germany declined relative to the Soviet Union in the early 1930s. Still, even here, neither of these cases represents a clean-cut example of a preventive war. In the case of the First World War, there were certainly those in Germany who made "better war now than later" arguments, but there is little evidence that German policymakers urged on Austria-Hungary with the intention of sparking a war with Russia.[7] The case of the Second World War is even harder to characterize as a preventive war. By our coding, interwar Germany was overtaken by the Soviet Union in 1931; it would be another ten years before Hitler turned his armies on Stalin, and the Second World War would start with these two powers joined as allies.

Further, the policymaking processes found in these cases do not match preventive war theory. Preventive war scholars contend that policymakers choose war because they have little choice: trends in structural power make conflict the most rational choice.[8] But in their bids for continental hegemony, Wilhelmine and Nazi Germany were not models of rational deliberation or success.[9] Policymakers were bitterly divided. Many vacillated wildly and put forward sharply contradictory images of themselves and their adversaries. Germany was at once weak and vulnerable, but also assured of success in war. Her enemies were united and growing stronger, but also easy to divide and conquer. It is intriguing that prior to the world wars—and only prior to the world wars—Germany was both rising against one rival and declining against another. Thus, it may not be conventional preventive war logic that led to conflagrations, but the torsion of structural cross-pressures. Tensions between existing structural trends may have found their way into the contradictory images policymakers held, and the conflicted policies they pursued, both of which failed horrendously.

We are not arguing that policymakers never draw on preventive war logic in their political deliberations. The argument that fighting will be easier now rather than later can be appealing, especially for leaders that are risk acceptant or are already resolved on war. But there are many reasons why policymakers might be drawn to preventive war logic, only some of which are connected to trends in the balance of power. There may be domestic political reasons to act now rather than later. There may be temporary, tactical vulnerabilities that a military organization seeks to exploit. There may be cultural or ideological biases. Yet such incentives have little to do with decline.

Overall, preventive war theory fares the worst. Decline is a frequent feature of international politics, but preventive wars almost never happen. Advocates of preventive war logic underspecify their theory and overpredict their outcome. Where decline and war correlate, preventive war mechanisms are hard to find, so it may get these cases right for the wrong reasons. Most importantly, there is no modern case of a preventive war reversing decline, and every violent bid for mastery ended in misery. No mildly rational actor could view preventive war as the least bad option.

PRESENT BUT NOT PARALYZING: DOMESTIC
DYSFUNCTION REVISITED

Domestic dysfunction theorists assert that internal politics interferes with a timely and coherent response to decline. This could be a product of domestic factions or myopic bureaucracies, but in either case the matter boils down to subnational groups putting their interests ahead of the national interest. If these theories are true, then declining powers will systematically under-retrench, rarely recover, and be less likely to retrench the more decentralized they are.

The evidence in this book suggests that the domestic dysfunction hypothesis receives some support, but not in its present incarnations.[10] From recognition to policy implementation, domestic political factors were rarely significant enough to block strategic adjustment, though they did shade how retrenchment unfolded in some cases. There was a marked tendency for the declining powers in our dataset to under-retrench. In only five of our thirteen cases did retrenching powers unambiguously match their policies to the depth of decline. The cases show instances of policymakers disregarding systemic pressures for domestic reasons. Jules Ferry's pursuit of overseas colonies was driven in part by his desire to secure new markets and restore the prestige of the Third Republic. Tsar Alexander III's watering down of badly needed military reforms reflected his close ties to a conservative corps of aristocratic army officers.

Nevertheless, the importance of domestic politics should not be oversold. Declining powers responded to systemic pressures promptly, and the tendency to under-retrench was not a strong one. If one takes a forgiving view of the marginal cases, then great powers matched the extent of retrenchment to the depth of decline in ten of the thirteen cases. While we expected domestic politics to play a prominent role in small decliners, the cases of Britain in the 1870s and 1900s shows the bipartisan consensus that often accompanied retrenchment. In cases where errors were made, it is difficult to disentangle domestic dynamics from structural ones. Both Russia in the 1900s and France in the 1920s retrenched less than their depth of decline would suggest, but neither of these powers was situated in a favorable structural position. Russia feared growing interdependence of its commitments along a long and difficult to defend border, while France struggled to find reliable and capable allies.

Where domestic barriers were present, their influence was often evanescent and limited. Interest groups seldom hijack foreign policy because policymakers devoted to special interests tend to have shabby results and short tenures. In Jules Ferry's case, his colonial policies were deeply unpopular; they led him to be thrown from office, and very nearly into the Seine.[11] Nor did bureaucratic factors consistently undercut retrenchment. Where heads of bureaucracies stood on an issue was only somewhat related to the post in which they sat. Finance ministers were predictably opposed to greater spending in straitened circumstances, but they opened state coffers when defense necessitated it. Military chiefs were not consistently opposed to smaller budgets, and they understood that economy was "a form of national defense."[12] Nor is there much evidence that military leaders willfully ignored decline to push for war. The Russian war minister Alexei Kuropatkin offered gloomy assessments before the Russo-Japanese War, and his successor continued to do so afterward.[13] Expansion-minded groups seldom had the upper hand and seldom got their way.

Proponents of the domestic dysfunction hypothesis might respond that internal factors can still have profound political consequences. Mid-Victorian policymakers in London may have appreciated the need to conserve resources, but expansion-minded proconsuls in the periphery consistently undermined, and eventually overturned, retrenchment. The majority of the tsar's ministers may have wanted to extinguish flashpoints with Japan, yet a small faction was able to block concessions until Russia stumbled into a disastrous war. Fair points. However, even in these cases, subnational groups gained purchase because they could point to structural conditions unfavorable to retrenchment. British proconsuls justified imperial expansion by emphasizing the interdependence of Britain's commitments along the routes to India. Russia could meddle in the Far East because retrenchment generated resources and allies to guard its European flank. Domestic politics is not independent of international conditions but intimately bound up in them.

Neither decentralization nor regime type explains domestic dysfunction well. British domestic politics was more decentralized than those of the French in the late nineteenth century, but Britain retrenched with more speed and steadiness than their continental counterpart. Tsarist Russia was in theory a highly centralized system, but it responded to decline better in some cases than others. A variety of regimes confronted ordinal transitions and, though there was a small number of cases, the evidence suggests that democracies, non-democracies, and regimes in transition all reacted to decline in similar fashion. Regime type appears marginal in explaining whether states respond consistently to decline.

To the extent that domestic dysfunction hampered retrenchment, it had more to do with poor institutional design and imprudent policy implementation than interest group interference or bureaucratic bungling. Turn-of-the-century Russia is an outstanding example. The same institutions in one tsar's hands had a much different impact in the hands of another. With backing from above, bureaucracies could modernize and improve dramatically, as they did under Alexander II. But with ambivalent or indifferent support from the top, those same bureaucracies stagnated and faltered, as they did under Nicholas II. The latter saw himself as above bureaucracies and domestic politics, and his poor judgment harmed both.

All this suggests that domestic dysfunction may have more to do with oversight and competence than centralization, regime type, bureaucratic infighting, or interest group politics. All leaders and governments make mistakes, and all receive systemic feedback, but rarely are leaders or governments immune to the outside world for long. Rarely is not never, of course, and low-quality leadership can have gruesome repercussions. Thus, domestic dysfunction is real and present, but rarely ruinous or persistent.

HOW STATES DEAL WITH DECLINE: RETRENCHMENT REVISITED

Our theory contends that declining states retrench because retrenchment represents the most rewarding response. Declining powers that live beyond their means become strategically insolvent and forfeit the better opportunities that come with adaptability. Romanticizing one's strength is a recipe for fossilized institutions, inflexible defenses, skeptical allies, unimpressed neutrals, and eager enemies. If this hypothesis is right, retrenchment will be the most common response to decline.

Across a spectrum of states and conditions, the logic of retrenchment was vindicated. The vast majority of states undergoing decline retrenched, many of them recovered their rank, and no state that failed to retrench recovered its rank. Retrenchment is the only known road to recovery. Yet retrenchment is no fairytale ending; most declining states never recovered their rank and retrenchment requires giving up valued commitments and possessions at least temporarily. Most declining states continued declining, which implies that foreign policy often buys breathing room, but not resurrection.

In a nutshell, whether a great power is in an ordinal transition is a powerful predictor of whether it will retrench. The depth of a state's decline is the single best indicator of how much that state will retrench and what policies it will use. Domestic retrenchment policies are the best options for states in small and medium declines, but international retrenchment policies become the dominant options for states in large declines. There is ample evidence that policymakers have an accurate sense of their state's relative power and know that bad consequences await if they make claims beyond their capabilities. Secondarily, our four structural modifiers began clarifying the conditions that catalyze and inhibit retrenchment. Relative rank and commitment interdependence fared better than ally availability and the conquest calculus, but ideally all should be used together as a rough index.

While our arguments on retrenchment got the broad brushstrokes right, we missed key details. Although the rate of decline was a strong predictor of state behavior, states tended to under-retrench. There are several plausible explanations for this pattern. The most obvious is that under-retrenchment represents a rational risk. Power is composed of imprecise quantities of various elements whose importance shifts over time; leaders may be wagering that the ambiguity of power favors inertia. Or measurement error is always a possibility. Another explanation comes from prospect theory: people value what they have more than what they want. This will make leaders especially reluctant to part with long-held possessions, and we see evidence of this in some of our cases. But not all of this may be due to psychological propensities: international conditions and diplomatic gambits can also play a role. France in the 1920s may have been averse to retrenchment not because it could not find allies or because it overvalued its commitments, but because it did not trust its allies to provide timely support.

Moreover, what form retrenchment takes was mostly captured by our logic, but the anomalies are numerous and fascinating. There are objective differences between how small, medium, and large decliners behave, and they tend to vary in a stepwise function. But those differences are not always substantial and sometimes work in the direction opposite to what was anticipated. In general, declining states are much more likely than other great powers to cut military spending and personnel. But small decliners are more likely to cut military spending than large decliners, and large decliners are more likely to cut military personnel than small decliners. With international policies, only large decliners are more likely to contract alliances, indicating that serious alignments are predominantly the tools of states in extremis. Dispute data show that decline tends not to be linked with military tensions. Declining states are less likely than other great powers to participate in disputes, and no more likely to initiate or escalate disputes. Large decliners are an exception to this rule and tend to be slightly more dispute-prone. This may be because they are defending truly vital interests that cannot be compromised.

The case studies support the quantitative findings. In the 1872 and 1908 British cases, small decliners were adept at timely and successful retrenchment, focusing primarily on domestic policies. In the 1888 Russia and 1893 France cases, medium decliners focused on domestic policies as well but had a more difficult time and relied increasingly on international policies. In the 1903 Russia and 1925 France cases, large decliners adopted domestic and international policies, but both came to grief: Russia for lack of good leadership, and France for lack of good options. The case studies also underline the challenges policymakers face when crafting retrenchment policies. They must harmonize domestic policies so defense cuts do not starve reformers of needed resources. They must balance international policies so shifts in global posture do not alienate allies. Yet declining powers find solace in unexpected places. In some cases, rising powers became unexpected partners, as Japan did with Britain. In other cases, the sheer extent of their interests provided declining powers with unexpected flexibility, as tsarist Russia found as it managed challenges along its vast frontier. In almost all cases, politicians found it relatively easy to sell retrenchment to domestic audiences. Interest groups might grumble and bureaucracies might bristle, but the public tends to prioritize expending precious resources at home rather than squandering them abroad.

A critic could counter that our view is too narrow. In focusing on how states deal with decline, we miss how the system fares. What about regional power vacuums, land grabs, and arms races? The case studies suggest these outcomes are rare. When Britain reduced its colonial ambitions in the 1870s, its competitors largely accepted the status quo. When Russia moderated its expansion in central Asia in the 1880s, relations with rivals such as Britain improved. Indeed, the evidence suggests it is the abandonment of retrenchment that is often responsible for regional instability. For instance, in the 1880s, Britain's renewed activism abroad spurred rivals to scramble into Africa in search of compensation. Russia's embrace of expansion in the Far East in the 1890s unleashed a similar rush for concessions.

A different critique is that our cases are too antiquated. Retrenchment may have made sense in the nineteenth century when the great powers could sacrifice metaphorical pawns on the geopolitical chessboard, but the contemporary international order is too interconnected. States depend on shared rules and common institutions to a much greater degree, and reputations carry more easily from one region to another. Yet on the whole, our structural modifiers would appear to be moving in directions that favor, rather than inhibit, retrenchment. Nuclear deterrence and economic interdependence have raised costs of conquest in ways that make predatory behavior less attractive for rising powers. Standing alliances with formal decision-making processes make it easier for declining powers to share burdens with others. Institutions that can foster cooperation and promote shared rules have reduced the need for a single hegemon to police the world. A great power's prestige is no longer as tightly bound up in the extent of its territory or the grandeur of its empire. Declining powers today can moderate their grand strategies with less fear of circling predators, power vacuums, falling dominos, and calamitous conflicts.

All told, the evidence suggests that declining powers favor retrenchment more often than not. This does not mean that policymakers are enthusiastic about retrenchment. They hope that trends will reverse and other states will fail to appreciate the extent of their plight. They are more willing to avoid new burdens than abandon current ones. They prefer to rely on self-help before relying on others. Declining powers are cautious in more ways than one: they are just as wary of imbalanced ends and means as they are of retrenchment's hazards. Nonetheless, when structural pressures create incentives to change course, policymakers typically retrench rather than gambling or pandering.

Peaceful Fall? Implications for the Sino-American Transition

The argument that decline is dangerous has important implications for the potential Sino-American power transition. For some scholars, the fact that China might overtake the United States raises the likelihood for conflict. "To put it bluntly," John Mearsheimer concludes, "China cannot rise peacefully."[14] For others, war does not have to be the inevitable result of the impending power shift. "The rise of China does not have to trigger a wrenching hegemonic transition," John Ikenberry argues, "because China faces an international order that is fundamentally different from those that past rising states confronted."[15] Scholars not only differ in their assessment of the prospects for peace, they also differ in their recommendations for U.S. policy. Those that take a darker view of Chinese ambitions, such as Robert Blackwill and Ashley Tellis, propose "a new grand strategy toward China that centers on balancing the rise of Chinese power."[16] In contrast, those that take a brighter view, like Michael Swaine, encourage a transition "from U.S. predominance toward a stable, more equitable balance of power in the western Pacific."[17]

In this section, we spell out the implications of our argument for these debates. We make three claims. First, we argue that the United States will probably experience a moment of decline sometime in the next decade, with China in the role of challenger, but the magnitude of this decline is likely to be modest and manageable. Second, we contend that the United States has already adopted elements of retrenchment in anticipation of this transition. This is most noticeable in the domestic sphere, where the Obama administration made initial efforts to reign in defense spending and push for defense reforms. Third, we maintain that there are good grounds for optimism in the Sino-American transition, and that policies of retrenchment can play a role in reducing the risk of hostilities.

"NEW OPPORTUNITIES BUT ALSO NEW DANGERS": IS THE UNITED STATES IN DECLINE?

Scholars have offered conflicting assessments about the trajectory of American power. Some contend that China's rise is inexorable and that the United States is already in decline. "There is abundant evidence that American global hegemony is steadily eroding," Martin Jacques observes, adding, "The rise of China will change the world in the most profound ways."[18] Arvind Subramanian concludes, "The economic dominance of China relative to the United States" is "imminent" and will be "broad-based."[19] Others argue that China's ascendance is fragile and that America's exceptional features will insulate it from decline. "China is rising, but it is not catching up," Michael Beckley maintains, in large part because "trends favor continued U.S. dominance."[20] Joseph Nye similarly argues, "China is nowhere near close to the United States," warning that "the greatest danger we have is overestimating China."[21] Politicians echo this skepticism. In a 2014 speech at West Point, President Barack Obama declared, "America has rarely been stronger relative to the rest of the world. Those who argue otherwise—who suggest that America is in decline, or has seen its global leadership slip away—are either misreading history or engaged in partisan politics."[22]

There are many complex issues bound up in this debate. Scholars differ on what metrics to use, what timeframes to examine, and what comparisons to make. We follow the method that yielded the most commonsense cases: lasting ordinal transitions involving relative shares of great power gross domestic product (GDP). Using this approach, the United States is on pace to enter acute relative decline sometime in the next decade.[23] To be perfectly clear, this prediction depends on a number of factors that are hard to predict. Extrapolating out from present trends is notoriously unreliable, and much depends on the baseline year one chooses to begin with. There will be shocks and surprises, and it is impossible to know their frequency, magnitude, or direction. Yet using our terminology, the United States is likely to face a decline that is small or medium in magnitude. This is good news for the United States and for China, since it affords both powers the time and space to manage the impending transition. It deserves emphasis that China is no world-beater, the United States is no weakling, and American decline is likely modest.

As always, much depends on the measures used. Power is an intricate concept and sensitive to context. Every measure of power has its drawbacks, and we already detailed many of the flaws of using GDP in chapter 3. We agree that GDP trends mask a great deal of nuance, cross-national GDP figures are imprecise, and China's figures are more suspect than most. Yet GDP is determinate and correlates with a number of compelling metrics, many of which suggest that China is indisputably gaining ground on the United States. Over the past decade, the United States has experienced a decline in global share of high technology exports, trademark applications, market capitalizations of its publicly traded companies, and renewable energy production. Meanwhile, China has gained relative to the United States in terms of patent applications, high technology exports, and information and communication technology service exports.[24] Even when it comes to GDP per capita, which many claim provides "a much more robust indicator of national power," China is gaining ground.[25] China's GDP per capita has tripled over the past decade, and the U.S. advantage has declined as a result.

Naturally, these are not the only indicators one could point to, and economic measures may lose traction on the political consequences of China's rise. Yet experts come to similar conclusions: Thomas Christensen finds China's rise very real, though the United States retains a commanding lead on many measures, and Jonathan Kirshner sees American economic advantages fading.[26] Even U.S. policymakers, who reject the term decline, nevertheless acknowledge that the distribution of international power is shifting. In his West Point speech, President Obama observed, "The world is changing with accelerating speed. This presents new opportunities, but also new dangers."[27] Former Secretary of State Hillary Clinton conceded, "The Asia-Pacific has become a key driver of global politics. . . . Harnessing Asia's growth and dynamism is central to American economic and strategic interests."[28] Whether one prefers the term "rising power" or "emerging power," the implication is the same: the geopolitical landscape is shifting, and U.S. policymakers must plan accordingly.

"OUR POWER GROWS THROUGH PRUDENT USE": HOW WILL THE UNITED STATES RESPOND?

If our theory is correct, then the United States will respond to its impending decline by retrenching. It will move away from a grand strategy of primacy or liberal hegemony and toward a grand strategy that is less burdensome and more selective. Because its decline is moderate, the United States will seek to reduce the costs of its foreign policy in measured ways, not through isolationism. We predict American policymakers will focus on domestic over international policies of retrenchment to gain time for domestic reforms to bloom. Yet retrenchment will be mild and war very unlikely.

This prediction is based on a cautious application of history. We have sixteen comparable cases, only three of which happened after World War II, and only one of which happened after the Cold War. Applying findings from these cases to the present demands delicacy. For most of our cases, the major forces for peace—democracy, international institutions, globalization, and nuclear weapons—either did not exist or were not very strong. That has paradoxical implications for our argument. The good news is that these factors probably make retrenchment a more palatable alternative for declining powers. If nuclear weapons alter the conquest calculus in ways that make it harder for aggression to pay, then they make it easier for states to retrench without fear of putting their survival at risk. To the extent international institutions can foster durable cooperation absent hegemonic leadership, they can reassure states that retrenchment will not lead to a collapse of the global order and a revival of interstate competition. The bad news is that, with less chance of violent negative feedback, the cost of foreign policy errors is low and the pressures to retrench diminish. A declining power might hope it can hold its alliances together using nuclear weapons and extended deterrence, even as its conventional capabilities atrophy and these guarantees become less credible. In this way, the current system is a bit like a nuclear power plant with many safety systems: they help prevent accidents, but they can lead to accidents if the glut of safety systems makes the operators complacent or risk acceptant. But overall, contemporary structural conditions make retrenchment easier and less hazardous, if somewhat less urgent.

Accepting these caveats, there are signs that retrenchment has already started. During the Obama administration, policymakers emphasized the need to reduce the burden of U.S. foreign policy. In his 2009 inaugural address, Obama argued explicitly that "[U.S.] power grows through its prudent use."[29] In his introduction to the 2010 National Security Strategy, the president declared, "The burdens of a young century cannot fall on American shoulders alone. . . . Our adversaries would like to see America sap our strength by overextending our power."[30] As Colin Dueck observes, "American grand strategy under Barack Obama [emphasized] international retrenchment and accommodation."[31]

Moving beyond rhetoric, many of the Obama administration's policies were drawn from the retrenchment playbook. In terms of the budget, the Obama administration fought to reduce the defense burden. As Secretary of Defense Robert Gates argued in 2009, "The United States cannot expect to eliminate national security risks through higher defense budgets, to do everything and buy everything."[32] In 2011, Gates proposed to trim defense spending by $78 billion over the next five years. The Budget Control Act, passed that same year, placed new caps on security-related spending, and resulted in an additional $24 billion being trimmed from the base defense budget. Matters came to a dramatic head in March 2013 when the failure to pass a deficit reduction bill triggered sequestration, which threatened to strip some $600 billion from defense over the next nine years. As a result of these changes, defense spending has slowed: where the Pentagon planned for an average base budget of $582 billion between 2011 and 2015, the actual average was $509 billion.[33]

The Obama administration also endorsed changes in force structure consistent with retrenchment. Most obviously, the Pentagon made wide-ranging reductions in end-strength. Between 2011 and 2016, the Army and Marine Corps trimmed their active duty forces by 91,000 soldiers and 17,000 marines, respectively.[34] These cuts allowed the Pentagon to shrink its budget while preserving funds for acquisition and modernization. The administration has also emphasized investments in the navy and air force. Between 2011 and 2016, the navy's share of the discretionary defense budget rose from 26 to 29 percent, while the air force's share increased from 24 to 29 percent.[35]

Investments in the navy and air force are not the only ways the military sought to improve flexibility and frugality. The administration pushed to increase the ratio of reserve to active duty forces in the army from around 49 percent in 2010 to 54 percent by 2017.[36] Special operations forces have also gained in prominence. From 2004 to 2014, the number of special operations forces positions has grown from roughly 45,000 to 63,000, while during the same time span funding rose from $6 billion to $10 billion.[37] As a result of these changes, the secretary of defense Leon Panetta stated, "The military will be smaller and leaner, but it will be agile, flexible, rapidly deployable, and technologically advanced."[38]

Other domestic reforms met with checkered success. On the positive side, there were small steps toward improving the military acquisition system. In 2009, President Obama signed the Weapon Systems Acquisition Reform Act into law, which provided better oversight and more rigorous monitoring of weapons purchases. And in 2010, then-undersecretary of defense for acquisition Ashton Carter inaugurated the first of a series of better buying power initiatives to boost efficiency. Less positively, congressional opposition impeded more thorough reforms. Despite multiple attempts, the Obama administration was unable to convince lawmakers to authorize another Base Realignment and Closure round, which could save upward of $2 billion a year.[39] Progress was made on military compensation, with a new retirement system slated for introduction in 2018, but Congress nixed broader changes to military salaries, housing allowances, commissaries, and health care. Congressional opposition also stymied progress on the "Force of the Future" initiative, the ambitious plan Carter introduced as secretary of defense to improve military personnel policies.[40]

In terms of international policies, some of the Obama administration's efforts resembled retrenchment, but events often pulled in other directions. In terms of force posture, the Obama administration advocated a shift away from Europe and the Middle East and toward the continental United States and Asia-Pacific region. In Iraq and Afghanistan, the president reduced the presence of American combat troops by 142,000 and 90,000 respectively, though small numbers of U.S. forces have flowed back with the rise of the Islamic State and the return of the Taliban.[41] In Europe, the Pentagon announced in 2012 the elimination of two forward-stationed army brigades, though Russia's annexation of Crimea has prompted reconsideration.[42] But the signature change to global posture has been the so-called "pivot" or "rebalance," which seeks to orient American diplomatic and military attention toward the Asia-Pacific region. A new rotational force of marines was added to Australia, while Pentagon officials committed to deploying 60 percent of air force and navy forces by 2020 to the Asia-Pacific region.[43]

When it comes to burden sharing, the Obama administration placed increasing weight on a reinvigorated NATO, more assertive Japanese Self Defense Forces, and regional partnerships with Australia, Singapore, and Thailand. Few allies assumed these burdens eagerly, however. As of 2010, only four of NATO's twenty-eight member states met the collective goal to spend at least 2 percent of GDP on defense, and in almost every major European state that line has trended downward.[44] The situation is not much better among America's bilateral partnerships: after the Cold War, Pakistan, South Korea, and Australia cut defense spending as a share of GDP by 54 percent, 39 percent, and 14 percent, respectively.[45] The approach of "leading from behind" (a phrase coined by one official to describe the Obama administration's policy in Libya) presumed greater participation by allies and partners, but in some cases, these contributions were not forthcoming or proved insufficient.[46]

Perhaps most controversially, the Obama administration resisted being drawn into new disputes. The administration refused deep military involvement in Syria and limited its involvement in Ukraine. It also sought to defuse flashpoints with potential adversaries, most notably in the multilateral deal to address Iran's nuclear program. In defending these decisions, President Obama warned of the "Washington playbook," whose preference for "militarized responses" can be "a trap that can lead to bad decisions."[47] Yet despite the reluctance to become embroiled in new conflicts, the administration authorized the use of military force in 2014 to "degrade, and ultimately destroy" the Islamic State.[48] The administration also resumed freedom-of-navigation patrols in the South China Sea in late 2015, in part to signal opposition to Chinese land reclamation and military activities on disputed islands in the area.[49]

In sum, American foreign policy under President Obama began to tilt in favor of retrenchment. The combination of costly wars in the Middle East, a crippling financial crisis, and the rise of China prompted policymakers to reduce America's foreign policy burdens. For the most part, Obama achieved this through domestic policies such as defense cuts and force reductions. Some savings also accrued from alterations in global posture and the avoidance of militarized disputes. Still, there were limits to this initial round of retrenchment. Congressional opposition stymied ambitious efforts to reform military compensation, personnel policies, or basing infrastructure. Allies did not always cooperate in assuming greater leadership roles or sharing defense burdens. The need to respond to revisionist challenges and regional instability also slowed efforts to draw down in regions such as the Middle East.

A skeptic might argue that President Obama's embrace of retrenchment reflected his personal preferences rather than structural constraints. The fact that Congressional Republicans bitterly opposed elements of retrenchment, such as the Iranian nuclear deal, highlights the importance of party rivalries in shaping foreign policy. Nevertheless, the cases in this book demonstrate that messy and acrimonious domestic politics need not bar retrenchment, and there are elements of contemporary retrenchment that have proved popular with both parties. The drawdown of forces in the Middle East, after all, began in the second term of George W. Bush's presidency. The person responsible for overseeing Obama's initial slate of defense reforms was Secretary of Defense Gates, a Republican appointed by Bush. Prominent Republican lawmakers, such as Senator John McCain, have been strong supporters of acquisition reform. The Budget Control Act received bipartisan support, although neither side desired that sequestration actually be imposed. Since then, Republicans and Democrats have twice raised defense budget caps, although to levels below what the military requested, proving there are deficit hawks in both parties. Despite the rancor that surrounds foreign policy, there appears to be a broad consensus that the high budgets, unilateralism, and nation-building missions that defined the Bush presidency are no longer viable.

With a new administration in Washington, will the United States continue to embrace retrenchment? During the campaign, Donald Trump made statements that appeared to endorse a less active foreign policy.[50] He expressed doubts about the wisdom of foreign interventions, such as the Iraq War. He raised questions about the costs and benefits of America's military alliances. He accused other countries of taking advantage of the United States, especially in the realm of trade. At the same time, Trump called for increases in defense spending and a larger, more capable military. He endorsed more aggressive policies to defeat terrorist groups such as the Islamic State and to confront rogue states such as North Korea. His rhetorical rejection of the Iran deal seemed to reflect a willingness to create—rather than defuse—flashpoints. Complicating any assessment is the fact that the new president lacks experience in foreign affairs and does not seem to have consistent or deeply held opinions on the subject.[51] The upshot is great uncertainty: time will tell if "America First" will usher in a more isolationist and disengaged grand strategy, or a more aggressive and unilateral approach toward foreign policy.[52]

Unless trends in relative power reverse, however, our theory suggests the incoming administration will find it difficult to abandon retrenchment. Given the sluggish performance of the American economy relative to its rivals, continued deficits, and concerns about the national debt, there will be limits on the ability of the incoming administration to ramp up defense spending. Already, there have been clashes between deficit and defense hawks in Congress over the size and method of funding Trump's proposed defense increases.[53] The continued increase of Chinese economic influence and military capacity in Asia presents analogous geopolitical constraints on U.S. policy in that region. Despite tough talk on the campaign trail, the reality is that any lasting solution to the North Korean nuclear program, maritime disputes in the South China Sea, or the status of Taiwan will require some accommodation of Chinese interests. More broadly, efforts to remake failed states or underwrite stability in regions such as the Middle East are likely to be met with skepticism. There is little enthusiasm within either Congress or the public to undertake such ambitious projects, and it seems likely that the favored counterterrorism instruments will remain the familiar ones: standoff airpower, assistance to local allies, the selective use of special operations forces, and regional diplomacy. Given the limits on America's resources, time, and attention, the new administration will probably imitate the old, seeking to keep existing wars contained, while looking to fight them on the cheap.

Naturally, trends may not be linear and incentives do not always point in the same direction during individual crises. But given the slow but steady erosion in its relative rank, the United States should continue to seek to reduce its foreign policy burdens in a prompt but proportionate manner, focusing its resources away from the Middle East and Europe and toward East Asia. These outcomes are not inevitable, of course. As our case studies have shown, erratic and unpredictable leaders can produce unanticipated outcomes. If negative feedback is ambiguous or if the new president chooses to ignore it, it is possible Trump could reverse course and ramp up the scale and scope of America's foreign policy ambitions. We turn to the question of what is at stake if he chooses to do so.

"ANOTHER FIFTY YEARS AS LEADER": THE CONSEQUENCES OF U.S. RETRENCHMENT

This book has made the case that states *tend to* react to decline with retrenchment, but it has largely sidestepped whether they *should*. In this section, we address the "should" issue in the context of debates over whether the United States should have a more or less ambitious grand strategy. Some say the United States should maintain the status quo. "Retrenchment would in essence entail a massive experiment," Brooks, Ikenberry, and Wohlforth assert, one that "would present much greater risks and costs."[54] Beckley seconds this view: "Advocates of retrenchment assume, or hope, that the world will sort itself out on its own. . . . Order and prosperity, however, are unnatural."[55] Others counter that pulling back would be better. "Shifting to a more restrained global stance," Barry Posen contends, "would yield meaningful benefits for the United States, saving lives and resources and preventing pushback."[56] John Mearsheimer concurs: "It is time for the United States to show greater restraint. . . . That means putting an end to America's pursuit of global dominance."[57]

We dissent from both positions. Contrary to the position of Brooks, Ikenberry, and Wohlforth, retrenchment is not the devil great powers don't know, but the devil they know best. Decline happens commonly and retrenchment is the most common response to it. More to the point, retrenchment gets better results than sticking with the status quo. Declining states that did not retrench are not paragons of success nor good models for the United States. Retrenchment may not have always led to recovery, but it was a necessary condition for it, and retrenching helped skirt the sinkholes of losing fights. Nostalgia is no solution to decline, and the small decline the United States is poised to experience is precisely the challenge retrenchment has proven most adept at meeting.

Every event is unique, but we have seen hegemonic decline before, and retrenchment worked out fairly well the last time we saw it. In the 1870s, the United States and United Kingdom had numerous conflicts of interest—the *Alabama* claims, contested boundaries, maritime disputes— yet British retrenchment managed these problems efficiently and sustained immense influence for decades. Similar opportunities present themselves in the Sino-American relationship. Beijing and Washington have common interests in areas such as non-proliferation, climate, and trade, but disagreements over maritime security, currency manipulation, and intellectual property rights. If the United States uses the same firmness and flexibility Britain did, even thorny issues can be kept in perspective and managed. Moreover, maintaining high defense budgets would not bankrupt the United States, but it is hard to argue that more military spending is the shrewdest investment, especially if it is used to boost end strength rather than spur innovation and reform. After all, the Bush administration lavished record sums on defense and had little to show for it.

These authors also mischaracterize retrenchment as the complete repudiation of leadership. Brooks, Ikenberry, and Wohlforth define retrenchment as a policy in which the United States would "eliminate or dramatically reduce its global security commitments," while Beckley characterizes retrenchment as "the divestment of all foreign policy obligations save those linked to vital interests."[58] Yet this erroneously equates retrenchment with isolationism. As our case studies show, retrenching countries rarely renounced most—let alone all—of their foreign policy commitments. Usually, retrenchment involves a shift in emphasis away from some issue areas or regions and toward others. Resources flow from the military to the civilian economy; reserve forces receive more attention than active-duty ones; military assets migrate from distant frontiers toward central strongpoints. None of the great powers we surveyed viewed retrenchment as a renunciation of leadership, and all continued to play a prominent role after retrenchment. The same is likely to be true of the United States. By virtue of its innovative economy and military reach, there is no reason why Washington cannot exercise leadership as it diverts resources from costly quagmires in the Middle East to the more promising states of Asia. Toughness and unpredictability is a poor grand strategic substitute for a clear assessment of one's interests and the prioritizing of commitments.

While we think retrenchment matches the current strategic environment, we do not advocate retrenchment for retrenchment's sake.[59] Contrary to what Posen claims, retrenchment is not a set policy whose benefits are predictable and enduring. Policymakers have to mold policies to conditions, which can make retrenchment more or less successful. Here it is worth emphasizing that the external environment confronting the United States does not favor retrenchment as consistently as Posen assumes. On the one hand, because nuclear weapons and nationalism make the taking and holding of territory extremely difficult, the conquest calculus tends to favor greater retrenchment. So, too, America's maritime geography and dispersed commitments incline toward retrenchment: there are plenty of marginal interests the United States could sacrifice without serious repercussions. Posen is on firm ground when he emphasizes how these conditions favor retrenchment.[60] On the other hand, the allies available to the United States are a mixed bag. European states have been neglecting investments in defense for some time, and Asian states do not combine power and proximity to effectively check China on their own. America's high rank also militates against retrenchment. Insulated by deep and diverse reservoirs of power, the United States can afford to temporize, to wait and see if China's economy falters or its own economy rebounds. Thus, there are convincing reasons for the United States not to pull back too far, too fast, especially in regions where allies are unable or unwilling to uphold a favorable distribution of power.

We also disagree with Mearsheimer that retrenchment requires the complete repudiation of American dominance in international politics. If retrenchment helps facilitate recovery, it can protect the foundations for future leadership. As the former deputy national security advisor Ben Rhodes explained, "We're not trying to preside over America's decline. What we're trying to do is to get America another fifty years as leader."[61] As we saw in the case studies, retrenchment comes in waves. Declining powers oscillate between retrenchment and non-retrenchment, typically abandoning restraint as their fortunes revive or structural conditions change. This is often sensible; when the world changes, great powers have to change with it, and retrenchment affords the flexibility to do so more effectively. In the Sino-American case, retrenchment can reduce the perception of Chinese encirclement and create opportunities for mutual accommodation. Simultaneously, by saving resources and avoiding quagmires, retrenchment enables the United States to adopt a more confrontational approach in the event China behaves aggressively. Retrenchment can be a repudiation of global leadership, but it can also be a precursor to it.

In all, the evidence in this book suggests that Washington and Beijing have compelling incentives to avoid confrontation and resolve their disputes diplomatically. Declining powers that fail to draw in their horns tend to fall further faster, while rising powers that launch violent bids for hegemony have always come to ruin. But what if President Trump or his successors choose to ignore these precedents? What happens if the United States expands its foreign policy ambitions at a moment when the distribution of power in international politics is in flux?

We predict the rejection of retrenchment would result in foreign policy crises of escalating frequency and severity. Rising powers or regional aggressors would be more likely to call the United States' bluff, and deterring these adversaries would require greater commitments of resources and more dramatic demonstrations of resolve. Foreign interventions would be more likely to turn into quagmires, as American ambitions escalate and local opposition hardens. The gap between foreign commitments and available resources would widen, requiring growing deficits and crash rearmament programs rather than steady budgets and sensible reforms. The evidence suggests that declining powers throughout history have tried to avoid this dismal fate, but that they are not always able to do so. Minor disputes can spiral into major confrontations; domestic rancor can get out of hand; leaders can make poor decisions; things fall apart. Whether current U.S. policymakers will dodge these dangers depends on how well they learn the lessons of retrenchment.

Coda

International relations thinkers are rightly obsessed with rise and fall, war and peace. To date, most of them have looked at the historical record and not seen much cause for optimism. As new powers rise and old powers fall, the prospects for peace diminish because aggression pays and domestic politics is rife with dysfunction. Long placid periods are punctuated by thunderous bursts of war and change. Fear, honor, and greed come to the fore, and the tragedy of great powers politics repeats once more.

In this book, we developed a dissenting view. Starting from standard assumptions, we reasoned that the world is harsh enough to discipline domestic faction but not so harsh as to regularly demand aggression. Leaders have an array of policy tools to react in their own ways to shifting conditions, and states can seize control of their fates. Decline encourages retrenchment, but this is no bad thing and seldom a belligerent one. Past policymakers have done an admirable job keeping their ships of state from running aground, and today's policymakers have better ships, better gauges, and better weather.

There is no sense in exacerbating decline by indulging delusions of everlasting grandeur, coddling ossified institutions, and living in the past. The United States has been the world's largest economy for over a century. It has seen off numerous challengers before and can do so again. But the best chances for success are to keep one's perspective, patience, and prudence intact. The United States is declining, but not much, and China is preoccupied by its own rise. This is no reason for preventive war or gratuitous malice. The odds are good for peace and prosperity, but there are non-negligible risks that domestic politics or unexpected crises could derail events. If the

United States gives the mistaken impression that it is seeking to contain a rising China, whether through a rapid military buildup or intransigent diplomacy, this would empower hardline factions, stoke fears of falling dominos, and raise the stakes of minor crises. It is the American rejection of retrenchment, and the alarm this inspires in China, that could make war appear inevitable.

Notes

Introduction

1. Thucydides, *The Landmark Thucydides: A Comprehensive Guide to the Peloponnesian War*, trans. Richard Crawley (New York: Free Press, 2008), 16 [1.23.6–1.23.7]. See also Graham Allison, "The Thucydides Trap: Are the U.S. and China Headed for War?" *Atlantic* (September 24, 2015), https://www.theatlantic.com/international/archive/2015/09/united-states-china-war-thucydides-trap/406756/; T. V. Paul, "The Accommodation of Rising Powers," in *Accommodating Rising Powers: Past, Present, Future*, ed. T. V. Paul (New York: Cambridge University Press, 2016), 7; and the various sources cited in chapter 1.

2. See, most famously, Paul Kennedy, *The Rise and Fall of the Great Powers: Economic Change and Military Conflict from 1500 to 2000* (New York: Random House, 1987), xxii; Paul Kennedy, "Conclusions," in *The Fall of Great Powers: Peace, Stability, and Legitimacy*, ed. Gier Lundestad (New York: Oxford University Press, 1994), 374.

3. See Robert Gilpin, *War and Change in World Politics* (Princeton: Princeton University Press, 1981), 10–11, 156–57; Robert Gilpin, "The Theory of Hegemonic War," *Journal of Interdisciplinary History* 18, no. 4 (Spring 1988): 591–613.

4. See A. F. K. Organski and Jacek Kugler, *The War Ledger* (Chicago: University of Chicago Press, 1980), 19–22; Douglas Lemke and Jacek Kugler, eds., *Parity and War: Evaluations and Extension of the War Ledger* (Ann Arbor: University of Michigan Press, 1996), 7–12.

5. See Arnold Wolfers, *Discord and Collaboration: Essays on International Politics* (Baltimore: Johns Hopkins University Press, 1962), 118; Inis Claude, *Power and International Relations* (New York: Random House, 1962), 42.

6. See James Fearon, "Rationalist Explanations for War," *International Organization* 49, no. 3 (Summer 1995): 379–414; Robert Powell, "War as a Commitment Problem," *International Organization* 60, no. 1 (Winter 2006): 169–203.

7. See Deborah Welch Larson, "Bandwagon Images in American Foreign Policy: Myth or Reality?" in *Dominos and Bandwagons: Strategic Beliefs and Great Power Competition in the Eurasian Heartland*, ed. Robert Jervis and Jack Snyder (New York: Oxford University Press, 1991), 85–111; Jennifer Milliken, "Metaphors of Prestige and Reputation in American Foreign Policy," in *Post-Realism: The Rhetorical Turn in International Relations*, ed. Francis Beer and Robert Hariman (East Lansing: Michigan State University Press, 1996), 217–38.

8. See Jack Snyder, *Myths of Empire: Domestic Politics and International Ambition* (Ithaca: Cornell University Press, 1991), chap. 2; Charles Kupchan, *The Vulnerability of Empire* (Ithaca: Cornell University Press, 1996), 3–8.

9. See Robert Lieber, *Power and Willpower in the American Future: Why the U.S. Is Not Destined to Decline* (New York: Cambridge University Press, 2012), 3–5; Robert Lieber, *Retreat and Its Consequences: American Foreign Policy and the Problem of World Order* (New York: Cambridge University Press, 2016), 9–12; Robert Kagan, *The World America Made* (New York: Knopf, 2012), 133–39.

10. Robert Kagan, "No Time to be Cutting the Defense Budget," *Washington Post*, February 3, 2009.

11. Robert Kaplan, "Where's the American Empire When We Need It?" *Washington Post*, December 3, 2010.

12. Quoted in Scott Shane and Jo Becker, "After Revolt, a New Libya 'With Very Little Time Left'" *New York Times*, February 29, 2016.

13. Leon Panetta, "Speech on Al-Qaeda," Center for New American Security (November 2012).

14. Rex Tillerson, "Statement Before the Senate Foreign Relations Committee" (January 11, 2017), https://www.state.gov/secretary/remarks/2017/01/267394.htm.

15. Graham Allison, "The Thucydides Trap: Are the U.S. and China Headed for War?" *Atlantic*, September 24, 2015.

16. Aaron Friedberg, "Hegemony with Chinese Characteristics," *National Interest* 114 (July/August 2011), 18.

17. Quoted in Max Fisher, "Trump's Military Ambition: Raw Power as a Means and an End," *New York Times*, March 3, 2017.

18. For similar definitions, see George Modelski, *Principles of World Politics* (New York: Free Press, 1972), 149; Jack Levy, *War in the Modern Great Power System, 1495–1975* (Lexington: University of Kentucky Press, 1983), 16–17; Karen Rasler and William Thompson, *The Great Powers and Global Struggle, 1490–1990* (Lexington: University of Kentucky Press, 1994), 15–16.

19. See Gilpin, *War and Change*, 28–30; Organski and Kugler, *War Ledger*, 52.

20. For similar definitions, see Aaron Friedberg, *The Weary Titan: Britain and the Experience of Relative Decline, 1895–1905* (Princeton: Princeton University Press, 1988), 17; Dale Copeland, *The Origins of Major War* (Ithaca: Cornell University Press, 2000), 41; Alex Weisiger, *Logics of War* (Ithaca: Cornell University Press, 2013), chap. 2.

21. See Kenneth Waltz, *Theory of International Politics* (New York: McGraw-Hill, 1979), 105; Joseph Grieco, "Anarchy and the Limits of Cooperation: A Realist Critique of the Newest Liberal Institutionalism," *International Organization* 42, no. 3 (Summer 1988): 498; Robert Powell, "Absolute and Relative Gains in International Relations Theory," *American Political Science Review* 85, no. 4 (December 1991): 1303–20.

22. See Christopher Layne, "The Unipolar Illusion: Why New Great Powers Will Rise," *International Security* 17, no. 4 (Spring 1993): 10–12; John Matthews, "Current Gains and Future Outcome: When Cumulative Relative Gains Matter," *International Security* 21, no. 1 (Summer 1996): 112–46.

23. See G. John Ikenberry and Charles Kupchan, "Socialization and Hegemonic Power," *International Organization* 44, no. 3 (Summer 1990): 283–315; Stacie Goddard, "When Right Makes Might: How Prussia Overturned the European Balance of Power," *International Security* 33, no. 3 (Winter 2008/09): 110–42.

24. For similar definitions, see Barry Posen, *Sources of Military Doctrine: France, Britain, and Germany Between the World Wars* (Ithaca: Cornell University Press, 1984), 13; Richard Rosecrance and Arthur Stein, eds., *The Domestic Bases of Grand Strategy* (Ithaca: Cornell University Press, 1993), 4; Kupchan, *Vulnerability of Empire*, 3; Christopher Layne, *The Peace of Illusions: American Grand Strategy from 1940 to the Present* (Ithaca: Cornell University Press, 2006), 13; Hal Brands, *What Good is Grand Strategy? Power and Purpose in American Statecraft from Harry S. Truman to George W. Bush* (Ithaca: Cornell University Press, 2014), 2–6.

25. For similar definitions, see Arnold Wolfers, "'National Security' as an Ambiguous Symbol," *Political Science Quarterly* 67, no. 4 (December 1952): 484; Waltz, *Theory of International Politics*, 126; Andrew Kydd, "Sheep in Sheep's Clothing: Why Security Seekers Do Not Fight Each Other," *Security Studies* 7, no. 1 (Fall 1997): 125–26.

26. See Williamson Murray and Mark Grimsley, "Introduction: On Strategy," in *The Making of Strategy: Rulers, States, and War*, ed. Williamson Murray, MacGregor Knox, and Alvin Bernstein (New York: Cambridge University Press, 1994), 1–23; Williamson Murray, "Thoughts on Grand Strategy," in *The Shaping of Grand Strategy: Policy, Diplomacy, and War*, ed. Williamson Murray, Richard Hart Sinnreich, and James Lacey (New York: Cambridge University Press, 2011), 1–33.

27. The term comes from the seminal work by Ronald Robinson and John Gallagher, *Africa and the Victorians: The Official Mind of Imperialism* (New York: Macmillan, 1961).

28. For various ways to distinguish grand strategies, see Robert Art, *A Grand Strategy for America* (Ithaca: Cornell University Press, 2003), 43–46; Peter Trubowitz, *Politics and Strategy: Partisan Ambition and American Statecraft* (Princeton: Princeton University Press, 2011), 15, 31; Colin Dueck, *Reluctant Crusaders: Power, Culture, and Change in American Grand Strategy*, (Princeton: Princeton University Press, 2007), 12–20; Kevin Narizny, *The Political Economy of Grand Strategy* (Ithaca: Cornell University Press, 2007), 11–12.

29. For overviews, see Barry Posen and Andrew Ross, "Competing Visions for U.S. Grand Strategy," *International Security* 21, no. 3 (Winter 1996/97): 5–53; Dueck, *Reluctant Crusaders*, chap. 5.

30. See, for example, Walter Russell Mead, *Power, Terror, Peace, and War: America's Grand Strategy in a World at Risk* (New York: Vintage, 2005); Timothy Lynch and Robert Singh, *After Bush: The Case for Continuity in American Foreign Policy* (New York: Cambridge University Press, 2008).

31. See, for example, Claude, *Power and International Relations*, chap. 4; Charles Kupchan and Clifford Kupchan, "Concerts, Collective Security, and the Future of Europe," *International Security* 16, no. 1 (Summer 1991): 114–61.

32. See, for example, Eric Nordlinger, *Isolationism Reconfigured: American Foreign Policy for a New Century* (Princeton: Princeton University Press, 1995); Christopher Preble, *The Power Problem: How American Military Dominance Makes Us Less Safe, Less Prosperous, and Less Free* (Ithaca: Cornell University Press, 2009).

33. See, for example, Robert J. Art, *A Grand Strategy for America* (Ithaca: Cornell University Press, 2003); Stephen Walt, *Taming American Power: The Global Response to U.S. Primacy* (New York: Norton, 2006), chap. 5; Barry Posen, *Restraint: A New Foundation for U.S. Grand Strategy* (Ithaca: Cornell University Press, 2014), chap. 2.

34. See Paul MacDonald and Joseph Parent, "Graceful Decline? The Surprising Success of Great Power Retrenchment," *International Security* 35, no. 4 (Spring 2011): 11. For similar definitions, see Trubowitz, *Politics and Strategy*, 13; Dueck, *Reluctant Crusaders*, 115–17; Stephen Brooks, G. John Ikenberry, and William Wohlforth, "Don't Come Home America: The Case Against Retrenchment," *International Security* 37, no. 3 (Winter 2012/13): 8–9.

35. See Norrin Ripsman and Jack Levy, "Wishful Thinking or Buying Time? The Logic of British Appeasement in the 1930s," *International Security* 33, no. 2 (Fall 2008): 148–81; Stephen Rock, *Appeasement in International Politics* (Lexington: University Press of Kentucky, 2000), 10–14; Daniel Treisman, "Rational Appeasement," *International Organization* 58, no. 2 (Spring 2004): 345–73.

36. On the dilemma facing declining powers, see Harold Sprout and Margaret Sprout, "The Dilemma of Rising Demands and Insufficient Resources," *World Politics* 20, no. 4 (July 1963): 660–93; Arthur Stein, "The Hegemon's Dilemma: Great Britain, the United States, and the International Economic Order," in *Theory and Structure in International Political Economy: An International Organization Reader*, ed. Charles Lipson and Benjamin Cohen (Cambridge: MIT Press, 1999), 312–13.

37. Alexis de Tocqueville, *The Old Régime and the French Revolution*, Stuart Gilbert, trans. (New York: Anchor Books, 1983 [1856]), 177 [III.4.]

1. Desperate Times, Desperate Measures

1. Fareed Zakaria, "The Future of American Power: How America Can Survive the Rise of the Rest," *Foreign Affairs* 87, no. 3 (May/June 2008): 18–43.

2. National Intelligence Council, *Global Trends 2030: Alternate Worlds* (December 2012), 7, see also 9, 12, https://www.dni.gov/files/documents/GlobalTrends_2030.pdf.

3. Joseph Nye, *Is the American Century Over?* (Malden, MA: Polity Press, 2015), 116.

4. Josef Joffe, "The Default Power: The False Prophecy of America's Decline," *Foreign Affairs* 88, no. 5 (September/October 2009): 21–35.

5. Robert Kagan, "Not Fade Away: The Myth of American Decline," *New Republic*, January 11, 2012, 19–25.

6. Robert Lieber, *Power and Willpower in the American Future: Why the U.S. Is Not Destined to Decline* (New York: Cambridge University Press, 2012), 4.

7. Christopher Layne, "The End of the Pax Americana: How Western Decline Became Inevitable," *Atlantic* (April 26, 2012), https://www.theatlantic.com/international/archive/2012/04/the-end-of-pax-americana-how-western-decline-became-inevitable/256388/.

8. Charles Kupchan, "The Decline of the West: Why America Must Prepare for the End of Dominance," *Atlantic* (March 20, 2012), https://www.theatlantic.com/international/archive/2012/03/the-decline-of-the-west-why-america-must-prepare-for-the-end-of-dominance/254779/. See also Charles Kupchan, *No One's World: The West, the Rising Rest, and the Coming Global Turn* (New York: Oxford University Press, 2013), 3.

9. Robert Gilpin, *War and Change in World Politics* (New York: Cambridge University Press, 1981), 187. See also Robert Gilpin, "The Theory of Hegemonic War," *Journal of Interdisciplinary History* 18, no. 4 (Spring 1988): 601–3.

10. Gilpin, *War and Change*, 189.

11. Gilpin, *War and Change*, 193–94. For similar arguments, see Harold Sprout and Margaret Sprout, "The Dilemma of Rising Demands and Insufficient Resources," *World Politics* 20, no. 4 (July 1963): 661.

12. Gilpin, *War and Change*, 191. Less known is that Gilpin softened his position subsequently. See Robert Gilpin, *Global Political Economy: Understanding the International Economic Order* (Princeton: Princeton University Press, 2001), 146.

13. Dale Copeland, *The Origins of Major War* (Ithaca: Cornell University Press, 2000), 53. See also Jack Levy, "Declining Power and the Preventive Motivation for War," *World Politics* 40, no. 1 (October 1987): 82–107; Stephen Van Evera, *Causes of War* (Ithaca: Cornell University Press, 1999), chap. 4.

14. Copeland, *Origins of Major War*, 40. See also Dale Copeland, *Economic Interdependence and War* (Princeton: Princeton University Press, 2015), chap. 1.

15. Copeland, *Origins of Major War*, 49. See also Robert Powell, "Uncertainty, Shifting Power, and Appeasement," *American Political Science Review* 90, no. 4 (December 1996): 749–64; James Fearon, "Rationalist Explanations for War," *International Organization* 49, no. 3 (Summer 1995): 405–7; Alex Weisiger, *Logics of War* (Ithaca: Cornell University Press, 2013), chap. 2.

16. Copeland, *Origins of Major War*, 41.

17. See A. F. K. Organski and Jacek Kugler, *The War Ledger* (Chicago: University of Chicago Press, 1980), 19; Jacek Kugler and Douglas Lemke, "The Power Transition Research Program: Assessing Theoretical and Empirical Advances," in *The Handbook of War Studies II*, ed. Manus Midlarsky (Ann Arbor: University of Michigan Press, 2000), 174–75.

18. A. F. K. Organski, *World Politics* (New York: Knopf, 1968), 367; see also William Thompson, *On Global War* (Columbia: University of South Carolina Press, 1988), 14–15.

19. See Organski and Kugler, *War Ledger*, 28.

20. Copeland, *Origins of Major War*, 3.

21. Organski and Kugler, *War Ledger*, 19.

22. For similar arguments, see Geoffrey Blainey, *The Causes of War* (New York: Free Press, 1988), 122; George Modelski, *Long Cycles in World Politics* (Seattle: University of Washington Press, 1987), 35–36; Karen Rasler and William Thompson, *The Great Powers and Global Struggle, 1490–1990* (Lexington: University of Kentucky Press, 1994), 1.

23. See Robert Jervis, "Theories of War in an Era of Leading Power Peace," *American Political Science Review* 91, no. 1 (March 2002): 1–14; John Mueller, "War Has Almost Ceased to Exist: An Assessment," *Political Science Quarterly* 124, no. 2 (Summer 2009): 297–322; Carl Kaysen, "Is War Obsolete? A Review Essay," *International Security* 14, no. 4 (Spring 1990): 42–64.

24. See Gilpin, *War and Change*, 203; Copeland, *Origins of Major War*, 42–46.

25. Gilpin, *War and Change*, 201. See also Copeland, *Origins of Major War*, 20, 40–41.

26. As Oneal, de Soysa, and Park also point out, rising powers are the least likely to be dissatisfied, because they are benefiting disproportionately from the status quo. See John Oneal, Indra de Soysa, and Yong-Hee Park, "But Power and Wealth *Are* Satisfying: A Reply to Lemke and Reed," *Journal of Conflict Resolution* 42, no. 4 (August 1998): 517.

27. Gilpin, *War and Change,* 194.

28. See Jonathan Mercer, *Reputation and International Politics* (Ithaca: Cornell University Press, 1996), 10, 67; Daryl Press, *Calculating Credibility: How Leaders Assess Military Threats* (Ithaca: Cornell University Press, 2005), 32. See also Alex Weisiger and Keren Yarhi-Milo, "Revisiting Reputation: How Past Actions Matter in International Politics," *International Organization* 69, no. 2 (Spring 2015): 473–95.

29. As Lobell points out, great powers rarely experience declines that are "global, rapid, and uniform," which allows a declining power to "tailor its responses across locales." Steven Lobell, *The Challenge of Hegemony: Grand Strategy, Trade, and Domestic Politics* (Ann Arbor: University of Michigan Press, 2003), 4.

30. For similar points, see Charles L. Glaser, *Rational Theory of International Politics: The Logic of Competition and Cooperation* (Princeton: Princeton University Press, 2010), 109–10; Andrew Kydd, "Trust, Reassurance, and Cooperation," *International Organization* 54, no. 2 (Spring 2000), 325–57.

31. A point emphasized by Stacie Goddard, "When Right Makes Might: How Prussia Overturned the European Balance of Power," *International Security* 33, no. 3 (Winter 2008/09): 110–42.

32. Aaron Friedberg, *The Weary Titan: Britain and the Experience of Relative Decline, 1895–1905* (Princeton: Princeton University Press, 1988), 286. British decision makers were averse to offending public preferences about more government involvement in the economy, higher taxes, larger military expenditures, and some form of conscription. See Friedberg, *Weary Titan,* 302–3; cf. 133–34, 289–90.

33. Friedberg, *Weary Titan,* 286–87.

34. Friedberg, *Weary Titan,* 288, 290.

35. Mark Brawley, *Afterglow or Adjustment? Domestic Institutions and Responses to Overstretch* (New York: Columbia University Press, 1999), 2. See also Paul Kennedy, *The Rise and Fall of the Great Powers: Economic Change and Military Conflict from 1500 to 2000* (New York: Vintage, 1989), xxiii.

36. See Brawley, *Afterglow or Adjustment,* 35–36, 38, 280.

37. Brawley, *Afterglow or Adjustment,* 7.

38. Hendrik Spruyt, *Ending Empire: Contested Sovereignty and Territorial Partition* (Ithaca: Cornell University Press, 2005), 10, 26–28.

39. Spruyt, *Ending Empire,* 7.

40. Spruyt, *Ending Empire,* 265.

41. Lobell, *Challenge of Hegemony,* 22.

42. Lobell, *Challenge of Hegemony,* 24.

43. Lobell, *Challenge of Hegemony,* 26, 37.

44. For related concerns, see Friedberg, *Weary Titan,* 291; and Spruyt, *Ending Empire,* 6, 29–31. It is odd that whereas Friedberg considers Great Britain to be a highly decentralized polity, Spruyt considers the Westminster system to have "few constitutional and partisan veto points." Compare Friedberg, *Weary Titan,* 18–19, 302–3; and Spruyt, *Ending Empire,* 32.

45. Brawley, *Afterglow or Adjustment,* 15, 28.

46. Spruyt, *Ending Empire,* 26–27.

47. Ironically, a persistent theme of Friedberg's critique of British foreign policy is that domestic-oriented lobbies proved more powerful than international-focused ones. See Friedberg, *Weary Titan,* 133–34, 289–90, 302–3.

48. See, for example, Jonathan Kirshner, *Appeasing Bankers: Financial Caution on the Road to War* (Princeton: Princeton University Press, 2007), chap. 1.

49. See Lobell, *Challenge of Hegemony,* 22–24.

50. Friedberg, *Weary Titan,* 291.

51. Spruyt, *Ending Empire,* 6.

52. See Irving Janis, *Groupthink: Psychological Studies of Policy Decisions and Fiascoes* (Boston: Wadsworth, 1982), 260–76; Alexander George, *Presidential Decisionmaking in Foreign Policy: The Effective Use of Information and Advice* (Boulder: Westview Press, 1980), 204–5.

53. See, for example, Stephen D. Kranser, "Are Bureaucracies Important? (Or Allison Wonderland)," *Foreign Policy* no.7 (Summer 1972): 159–79.

54. In Friedberg's own narrative, for example, we observe Prime Minister Salisbury forming a royal commission to study British trade and industry, as well as Prime Minister Balfour using his place on the Committee of Imperial Defence to press for his preferred policy on Indian defense. See Friedberg, *Weary Titan*, 39–40, 240–41.

55. Brawley, *Afterglow or Adjustment*, 2, 35–36.

56. See Lobell, *Challenge of Hegemony*, 37, 26.

57. For examples, see Richard Betts, *Soldiers, Statesmen, and Cold War Crises* (New York: Columbia University Press, 1991), 153–60; Stefano Recchia, *Reassuring the Reluctant Warriors: U.S. Civil-Military Relations and Multilateral Intervention* (Ithaca: Cornell University Press, 2015), 6–8.

2. Parry to Thrust

1. See, for example Niccolò Machiavelli, *The Discourses on Livy*, Harvey Mansfield and Nathan Tarcov, trans. (Chicago: University of Chicago Press, 1998), book III, 209–310; Montesquieu, *Considerations on the Causes of the Greatness of the Romans and Their Decline*, trans. David Lowenthal (Indianapolis: Hackett, 1965), 91–96, 167–74; Edward Gibbon, *The Decline and Fall of the Roman Empire* (New York: Everyman, 1993), vol. 1: chap. 2, 65–68; vol. 3: chap. 31, 327–28; vol. 4: chap. 38, 117–27.

2. On the central importance of anarchy in international politics, see Kenneth Waltz, *Theory of International Politics* (New York: McGraw-Hill, 1979), 88; Robert Jervis, "Cooperation Under the Security Dilemma," *World Politics* 30, no. 2 (January 1978): 167.

3. On resource tradeoffs as a critical constraint, see Robert Gilpin, *War and Change in World Politics* (New York: Cambridge University Press, 1981), 19; Stephen Brooks, "Dueling Realisms," *International Organization* 51, no. 3 (Summer 1997), 459–63.

4. Much remains unknown about the causes of decline, but the best works tend to attach primacy to internal factors. See, for example, Roger Fouquet and Stephen Broadberry, "Seven Centuries of European Economic Growth and Decline," *American Economic Review* 29, no. 4 (Fall 2015): 227–44, esp. 240; Daron Acemoglu and James Robinson, *Why Nations Fail: The Origins of Power, Prosperity, and Power* (New York: Crown Publishers, 2012), chaps. 3–4; Dani Rodrik, "Where Did All the Growth Go? External Shocks, Social Conflict, and Growth Collapses," *Journal of Economic Growth* 4, no. 4 (December 1999): 385–412; Joseph Tainter, *The Collapse of Complex Societies* (New York: Cambridge University Press, 1990), chap. 6.

5. From Walter Lippmann, *U.S. Foreign Policy: Shield of the Republic* (Boston: Little, Brown, 1943), 7–8.

6. See Kevin Narizny, *The Political Economy of Grand Strategy* (Ithaca: Cornell University Press, 2007), 301.

7. For similar discussions of negative feedback, see Waltz, *Theory of International Politics*, 118; Gilpin, *War and Change*, 121; Robert Jervis, *Systems Effects: Complexity in Political and Social Life* (Princeton: Princeton University Press, 1997), chap. 4.

8. For the importance of socialization, see Waltz, *Theory of International Politics*, 116–22; Gilpin, *War and Change*, 85–87; G. John Ikenberry and Charles Kupchan, "Socialization and Hegemonic Power," *International Organization* 44, no. 3 (Summer 1990): 238–315.

9. For a discussion of emulation, see Waltz, *Theory of International Politics*, 127–28; João Resende-Santos, *Neorealism, States, and the Modern Mass Army* (New York: Cambridge University Press, 2007), 5–6.

10. For a similar approach, see Charles Glaser, *Rational Theory of International Politics: The Logic of Competition and Cooperation* (Princeton: Princeton University Press, 2010), 20–33. See discussion in Miles Kahler, "Rationality in International Politics," *International Organization* 52,

no. 4 (Autumn 1998): 919–41; Jonathan Mercer, "Rationality and Psychology in International Relations," *International Organization* 59, no. 1 (Winter 2005): 77–106. Humans are not the only ones adept at assessing power and avoiding costly battles. See Lawrence Freedman, *Strategy: A History* (New York: Oxford University Press, 2015), 4, 8.

11. The term comes from Ronald Robinson and John Gallagher, *Africa and the Victorians: The Official Mind of Imperialism* (New York: Macmillan, 1961), 19. For a useful discussion, see Thomas Otte, *The Foreign Office Mind: The Making of British Foreign Policy 1865–1914* (New York: Cambridge University Press, 2011), 2–6.

12. See, for example, Robert Jervis, *Perception and Misperception in International Politics* (Princeton: Princeton University Press, 1976), 3–10; Richard Ned Lebow, *Between Peace and War: The Nature of International Crises* (Baltimore: Johns Hopkins University Press, 1981), chap. 6.

13. See, for example, Robert Jervis, "Political Implications of Loss Aversion," *Political Psychology* 13, no. 2 (June 1992): 187–204; Rose McDermott, *Risk-Taking in International Politics: Prospect Theory in American Foreign Policy* (Ann Arbor: University of Michigan Press, 1998), 42–43; Jack Levy, "Loss Aversion, Framing Effects, and International Conflict," in *Handbook of War Studies II*, ed. Manus Midlarsky (Ann Arbor: University of Michigan Press, 2000), 193–221.

14. Misperceptions can also lead states to cooperate and avoid conflict. See Arthur Stein, *Why Nations Cooperate: Circumstance and Choice in International Relations* (Ithaca: Cornell University Press, 1990), chap. 3.

15. See Jeffrey Taliaferro, "Security Seeking Under Anarchy: Defensive Realism Revisited," *International Security* 25, no. 3 (Winter 2000/1), 141.

16. For similar claims, see Waltz, *Theory of International Politics*, 134; Stephen Krasner, *Defending the National Interest* (Princeton: Princeton University Press, 1978), 11–12.

17. See Narizny, *Political Economy of Grand Strategy*, chap. 2; Peter Trubowitz, *Politics and Strategy: Partisan Ambition and American Statecraft* (Princeton: Princeton University Press, 2011), chap. 2.

18. See Morton Halperin and Arnold Kanter, *Bureaucratic Politics and Foreign Policy* (Washington: Brookings Institution Press, 1974).

19. See, for example, Arnold Wolfers, *Discord and Collaboration: Essays on International Politics* (Baltimore: Johns Hopkins University Press 1962), 16.

20. George Washington to John Hancock (December 16, 1776), in *The Papers of George Washington, Vol. 7, Revolutionary War Series*, ed. Philander Chase (Charlottesville: University of Virginia Press, 1997), 352.

21. See Williamson Murray, "Grand Strategy, Alliances, and the Anglo-American Way of War," in *Grand Strategy and Military Alliances*, ed. Peter Mansoor and Williamson Murray (New York: Cambridge University Press, 2016), 31. Alternatively, see Geoffrey Parker, *Global Crisis: War, Climate Change, and Catastrophe in the Seventeenth Century* (New Haven: Yale University Press, 2013), 123.

22. See Graham Allison and Philip Zelikow, *Essence of Decision: Explaining the Cuban Missile Crisis* (New York: Longman, 1994), chap 3; James March, *How Decisions Happen* (New York: Free Press, 1994), chap 4.

23. See Richard Betts, *Enemies of Intelligence: Knowledge and Power in American National Security* (New York: Columbia University Press, 2009), 142–46; Robert Jervis, *Why Intelligence Fails: Lessons from the Iranian Revolution and the Iraq War* (Ithaca: Cornell University Press, 2011), chap. 4.

24. A point emphasized by Aaron Friedberg, *In the Shadow of the Garrison State: America's Anti-Statism and Its Cold War Grand Strategy* (Princeton: Princeton University Press, 2000), 75–77.

25. See Benjamin Fordham, "Paying for Global Power: Assessing the Costs and Benefits of Postwar U.S. Military Spending," in *The Long War: A New History of U.S. National Security Policy Since World War II*, ed. Andrew Bacevich (New York: Columbia University Press, 2007), 382–83.

26. See Bruce Cumings, *Dominion from Sea to Sea: Pacific Ascendancy and American Power* (New Haven: Yale University Press, 2009), 430–70; also Mark Zachary Taylor, *The Politics of Innovation: Why Some Countries are Better than Others at Science and Technology* (New York: Oxford University Press, 2016), 5, 225.

27. See Jesús Crespo Cuaresma and Gerhard Reitschuler, "A Non-Linear Defence-Growth Nexus? Evidence from the U.S. Economy," *Defence and Peace Economics* 15, no. 1 (February 2004): 77–80; Joshua Aizenman and Reuven Glick, "Military Expenditure, Threats, and Growth," *Journal of International Trade and Economic Development* 15, no. 2 (June 2006): 129–55.

28. See Harvey Starr, Francis Hoole, Jeffrey Hart, and John Freeman, "The Relationship Between Defense Spending and Inflation," *Journal of Conflict Resolution* 28, no. 1 (March 1984): 103–22; Gordon Adams and David Gold, *Defense Spending and the Economy: Does the Defense Dollar Make a Difference?* (Washington: Center on Budget and Policy Priorities, 1990), 6–11, 55–56.

29. See J. Paul Dunne and Nan Tian, "Military Expenditure, Economic Growth and Heterogeneity," *Defence and Peace Economics* 26, no. 1 (2015): 29–30. See also Daniel Drezner and Nancy F. Hite-Rubin, "Does American Military Power Attract Foreign Investment?" in *Sustainable Security: Rethinking American National Security Strategy*, ed. Jeremi Suri and Benjamin Valentino (New York: Oxford University Press, 2016), 65.

30. One of the most durable pieces of military advice is to hold formidable forces in reserve to be able to react to the ineluctable surprises of conflict. See, for instance, Carl von Clausewitz, *On War*, trans. Michael Howard and Peter Paret (Princeton: Princeton University Press, 1976), 210–11; Parker, *Global Crisis*, 497.

31. For a good example of asset shifting in a different context, see Ira Katznelson, "Flexible Capacity: The Military and Early American Statebuilding," in *Shaped by War and Trade: International Influences on American Political Development*, ed. Ira Katznelson and Martin Shefter (Princeton: Princeton University Press, 2002), 82–110.

32. See Robert Powell, "Uncertainty, Shifting Power, and Appeasement," *American Political Science Review* 90, no. 4 (December 1996): 749–64; Patrick McDonald, "Complicating Commitment: Free Resources, Power Shifts, and the Fiscal Politics of Preventive War," *International Studies Quarterly* 55, no. 4 (December 2011): 1095–1120.

33. See Brandon Yoder, "Power Transitions and Uncertainty of Intentions: A Dynamic Model of Belief Formation," paper presented at the Annual Meeting of American Political Science Association, Seattle (September 2011). See also Evan Braden Montgomery, *In the Hegemon's Shadow: Leading States and the Rise of Regional Powers* (Ithaca: Cornell University Press, 2016), 8, 11, 20.

34. Kyle Haynes, "Decline or Devolution: The Sources of Strategic Military Retrenchment," *International Studies Quarterly* 59, no. 3 (September 2015): 490–502.

35. See Stephen Brooks, G. John Ikenberry, and William Wohlforth, "Don't Come Home, America: The Case Against Retrenchment," *International Security* 37, no. 3 (Winter 2012/2013): 15.

36. On the challenge of unreliable allies, see Waltz, *Theory of International Politics*, 163–72; Thomas Christensen and Jack Snyder, "Chain Gangs and Passed Bucks: Predicting Alliance Patterns in Multipolarity," *International Organization* 44, no. 2 (Spring 1990): 137–38; James Morrow, "Arms versus Allies: Trade-Offs in the Search for Security," *International Organization* 47, no. 2 (Spring 1993): 207–33.

37. See John Lewis Gaddis, *Strategies of Containment: A Critical Appraisal of Postwar American National Security Policy* (New York: Oxford University Press, 1982), chap. 4.

38. Often referred to as the difference between internal and external balancing. See Waltz, *Theory of International Politics*, 163–72; Resende-Santos, *Modern Mass Army*, 66–69.

39. For other views on structural modifiers, see Glenn Snyder, "Process Variables in Neorealist Theory," *Security Studies* 5, no. 3 (Spring 1996): 171–72; Joshua Itzkowitz Shifrinson, "Dilemmas of Decline, Risks of Rise" (PhD diss., MIT, 2013), chap. 2; Peter Toft, "The Way of the Vanquished" (PhD diss., University of Copenhagen, 2006), 88–117.

40. See Glenn Snyder, "Mearsheimer's World: Offensive Realism and the Struggle for Security," *International Security* 27, no. 1 (Summer 2002): 153–58.

41. For similar claims, see Kenneth Waltz, *Realism and International Politics* (New York: Routledge, 2008), 134; Kenneth Waltz, "The Continuity of International Politics," in *Worlds in Collision: Terror and the Future of Global Order*, ed. Ken Booth and Tim Dunne (New York: Palgrave Macmillan, 2002), 348–54; Robert Jervis, *American Foreign Policy in a New Era* (New York: Routledge, 2005), 92–96.

42. See Michael Mastanduno, "System Maker and Privilege Taker: US Power and the International Political Economy," in *International Relations Theory and the Consequences of Unipolarity*, ed. John Ikenberry, Michael Mastanduno, and William C. Wohlforth (New York: Cambridge University Press, 2011), 144.

43. See Haynes, "Decline or Devolution," 492–93; Glenn Snyder, "The Security Dilemma in Alliance Politics," *World Politics* 36, no. 4 (July 1984): 469.

44. See James Morrow, "Alliances and Asymmetry: An Alternative to the Capability Aggregation Model of Alliances," *American Journal of Political Science* 35, no. 4 (November 1991): 920.

45. On buck-passing, see John Mearsheimer, *The Tragedy of Great Power Politics* (New York: Norton, 2002), 157–59.

46. See Glenn Snyder, "Alliances, Balance, and Stability," *International Organization* 45, no. 1 (Winter 1991): 121–42; Randall Schweller, "Bandwagoning For Profit: Bringing the Revisionist State Back In," *International Security* 19, no. 1 (Summer 1994): 72–107.

47. See Timothy Crawford, "Preventing Enemy Coalitions: How Wedge Strategies Shape Power Politics," *International Security* 35, no. 4 (Spring 2011): 155–89; Yasuhiro Izumikawa, "To Coerce or Reward? Theorizing Wedge Strategies in Alliance Politics," *Security Studies* 22, no. 3 (August 2013): 498–531.

48. The tendency to balance, of course, does not mean that the distribution of power in the system will be distributed equally, or that an individual challenger will inevitably fail in its efforts to dominate its rivals. See Jack Levy, "Balances and Balancing: Concepts, Prospects, and Research Design," in *Realism and the Balancing of Power: A New Debate*, ed. John Vasquez and Colin Elman (New York: Prentice-Hall, 2002), 128–53; Daniel Nexon, "The Balance of Power in the Balance," *World Politics* 61, no. 2 (April 2009): 338–40, 351–53.

49. See Gilpin, *War and Change*, 193–94.

50. For similar distinctions, see Paul Huth, "Reputations and Deterrence: A Theoretical and Empirical Assessment," *Security Studies* 7, no. 1 (Autumn 1997): 72–99; Paul Huth, "Deterrence and International Conflict: Empirical Findings and Theoretical Debates," *Annual Review of Political Science* 2 (1999): 32–33.

51. For applications of this analogy, see Thomas Schelling, *Arms and Influence* (New Haven: Yale University Press, 1967), 124; Robert Jervis, "Domino Beliefs and Strategic Behavior," in *Domino and Bandwagons: Strategic Beliefs and Great Power Competition in the Eurasian Rimland*, ed. Robert Jervis and Jack Snyder (New York: Oxford University Press, 1991), 22.

52. Compare Jervis, "Domino Beliefs," 39–40; and Dale Copeland, "Do Reputations Matter?," *Security Studies* 7, no. 1 (February 1997): 50–53. For systemic conditions that might favor interdependent commitments, see Jervis, *Systems Effects*, 118–22; Robert Jervis, "Was the Cold War a Security Dilemma?" *Journal of Cold War Studies* 3, no. 1 (Winter 2001): 44–45.

53. See Jonathan Mercer, *Reputation and International Politics* (Ithaca: Cornell University Press, 1996), 10, 67; Daryl Press, *Calculating Credibility: How Leaders Assess Military Threats* (Ithaca: Cornell University Press, 2005), 32. For a contrasting view, see Anne Sartori, *Deterrence by Diplomacy* (Princeton: Princeton University Press, 2005), 5.

54. See Paul Huth, "Deterrence and International Conflict," 43–44; Vesna Danilovic, "The Sources of Threat Credibility in Extended Deterrence," *Journal of Conflict Resolution* 45, no. 3 (June 2001): 341–69. States may not develop reputations for weakness, but leaders can develop reputations for dishonest bluffing. See Alexandra Guisinger and Alastair Smith, "Honest Threats: The Interaction of Reputation and Political Institutions in International Crises," *Journal of Conflict Resolution* 46, no. 2 (April 2002): 175–200; Mark Crescenzi, "Reputation and Interstate Conflict," *American Journal of Political Science* 51, no. 2 (April 2007): 382–96; Alex Weisiger and Keren Yarhi-Milo, "Revisiting Reputation: How Past Actions Matter in International Politics," *International Organization* 69, no. 2 (Spring 2015): 473–95.

55. Here we draw on the controversial literature on the office defense balance. See, for example, Jervis, "Cooperation Under the Security Dilemma," 186–213; Jack Levy, "The Offense/Defense Balance of Military Technology and the Incidence of War," *International Studies Quarterly* 28, no. 2 (June 1984): 219–30; Charles Glaser and Chaim Kaufman, "What is the Offense-Defense Balance and How Can We Measure It?" *International Security* 22, no. 4 (Spring 1998): 44–82.

56. On the effects of offense dominance, see Stephen Van Evera, "The Cult of the Offensive and the Origins of the First World War," *International Security* 9, no. 1 (Summer 1984): 63–66; Robert Art, "American Foreign Policy and the Fungibility of Force," *Security Studies* 5, no. 4 (Summer 1996): 7–42.

57. See Dale Copeland, *The Origins of Major War* (Ithaca: Cornell University Press, 2000), 40.

58. On the effects of defense dominance, see Charles Glaser, "Realists as Optimists: Cooperation as Self-Help," *International Security* 19, no. 3 (Winter 1994/95): 67–70; Charles Glaser, "The Security Dilemma Revisited," *World Politics* 50, no. 1 (October 1997): 185–93.

59. One familiar, albeit controversial, claim contends that armies fighting on the tactical offensive need a three-to-one superiority in numerical strength to succeed. Others note that in order to overcome the defensive advantages offered by improved firepower, modern militaries have had to master the complicated features of combined armed warfare. See Stephen Biddle, *Military Power: Explaining Victory and Defeat in Modern Battle* (Princeton: Princeton University Press, 2004), chap. 1.

60. See, for example, Tanisha Fazal, *State Death: The Politics and Geography of Conquest, Occupation, and Annexation* (Princeton: Princeton University Press, 2007), 53–54; Boaz Atzili, *Good Fences, Bad Neighbors: Border Fixity and International Conflict* (Chicago: University of Chicago Press, 2011), 23–27.

61. A central finding of Keir Lieber, *War and the Engineers: The Primacy of Politics over Technology* (Ithaca: Cornell University Press, 2005), 149–58.

62. By insular powers, we mean those great powers that do not share a land border with another great power. For similar definitions, see Mearsheimer, *Tragedy of Great Power Politics*, 126–28; Jack Levy and William Thompson, "Balancing on Land and at Sea: Do States Ally against the Leading Global Power?" *International Security* 35, no. 1 (Summer 2010): 13–14, 16–19. The usual caveat applies: insular great powers are seldom completely insular. For example, Britain maintained a large land army in India, though most of the forces were not British regulars.

63. An insular power, as Layne argues, "enjoys a wider range of strategic options." Christopher Layne, "The Unipolar Illusion: Why New Great Powers Will Rise," *International Security* 17, no. 4 (Spring 1993), 49.

64. For the received wisdom, see William Wohlforth, *The Elusive Balance: Power and Perceptions During the Cold War* (Ithaca: Cornell University Press, 1993), 299, 306–7; Norrin Ripsman, Jeffrey Taliaferro, and Steven Lobell, *Neoclassical Realist Theory of International Politics* (New York: Cambridge University Press, 2016), 2, 21–22, 31.

3. The Fates of Nations

1. They are Austria-Hungary (1870–1918); China (1950–present); France (1870–1940, 1945–present); Germany (1870–1918, 1925–45, 1955–present); Italy (1870–1943); Japan (1870–1945, 1952–present); Russia/Soviet Union (1870–1917, 1922–present); United Kingdom (1870–present); and United States (1870–present). See Correlates of War Project, "State System Membership List, v2008.1." We make three minor changes to the start- and end-dates used by the Correlates of War project. First, rather than code the United States as a great power beginning in 1898, we code it as one for our entire dataset, which dates back to 1870. We think this coding better reflects the influence of the United States after the Civil War. Second, we code Imperial Japan as a great power beginning in 1870, rather than in 1895. We contend this coding more accurately captures the ascendance of Japan as a regional power following the Meiji Restoration. Third, rather than code postwar Japan and Germany as great powers only after 1991, we code these countries as great powers following the negotiation of treaties granting them formal independence in 1952 and 1955 respectively. We believe this coding closely corresponds to the important role each of these powers played in shaping the Cold War international system. These coding decisions result in the addition of just two cases of decline to our dataset, and do not substantially affect our primary findings. For similar lists, see J. David Singer and Melvin Small, *The Wages of War, 1816–1965: A Statistical Handbook* (New York: Wiley and Sons, 1972),

23–24; Jack Levy, *War in the Modern Great Power System, 1495–1975* (Lexington: University of Kentucky Press, 1983), 10–19; Daniel Geller and J. David Singer, *Nations at War: A Scientific Study of International Conflict* (New York: Cambridge University Press, 1998), 177.

2. Our data come from Angus Maddison, *Monitoring the World Economy, 1820–1992* (Paris: Development Centre of the Organisation of Economic Cooperation and Development, 1995); Angus Maddison, *Contours of the World Economy, 1–2030 AD: Essays in Macro-Economic History* (New York: Oxford University Press, 2007). Maddison does his best to measure GDP neutrally and non-imperially, so India does not count toward British GDP, nor do Finland and Poland count toward Russian GDP.

3. A theme found in Diane Coyle, *GDP: A Brief but Affectionate History* (Princeton: Princeton University Press, 2014), 81–82; Joseph Stiglitz, Amartya Sen, and Jean-Paul Fitoussi, *Mismeasuring Our Lives: Why GDP Doesn't Add Up* (New York: Free Press, 2010), chap. 1.

4. Maddison's series for Imperial Russia, for example, omits certain years. Maddison includes data for Russia in 1870, 1900, 1913, and 1928–2008. We filled these gaps using the industry of origin method, which measures output based on volume estimates of physical indicators such as agricultural and industrial production. We interpolated missing data for forty-six years: 1871–99, 1901–12, and 1923–27. For a description of the method, see Maddison, *Monitoring the World Economy*, 141–42. The historical data come from Raymond Goldsmith, "The Economic Growth of Tsarist Russia, 1860–1913," *Economic Development and Cultural Change* 9, no. 3 (April 1961): 450, 462–63; and Robert Davies, ed., *From Tsarism to the New Economic Policy: Continuity and Change in the Economy of the USSR* (Ithaca: Cornell University Press, 1990), 279.

5. See, among many examples, Emerson Niou, Peter Ordeshook, and Gregory Rose, *The Balance of Power: Stability in International Systems* (New York: Cambridge University Press, 1989), 223–34; Stephen Brooks and William Wohlforth, *World Out of Balance: International Relations and the Challenge of American Primacy* (Princeton: Princeton University Press, 2008), 30.

6. See Michael Beckley, "China's Century? Why America's Edge Will Endure," *International Security* 36, no. 3 (Winter 2011/2012): 41–78.

7. See, for example, Ronald Findley and Kevin H. O'Rourke, *Power and Plenty: Trade, War, and the World Economy in the Second Millennium* (Princeton: Princeton University Press, 2007), 216, 264, 465.

8. See, for example, Allan Mitchell, *The German Influence in France after 1870: The Formation of the French Republic* (Chapel Hill: University of North Carolina Press, 1979), 119; Aaron Friedberg, *The Weary Titan: Britain and the Experience of Relative Decline, 1895–1905* (Princeton: Princeton University Press, 1988), 44–50, 67, 81.

9. The main limitation of the Banks data is missing values: data for state revues, for example, were available for just 66 percent of the country-year observations in our dataset. Despite these gaps, GDP had correlation coefficient of 0.83 for revenues, 0.85 for state expenditures, 0.87 for exports, and 0.80 for imports across our entire sample of great powers. See Arthur Banks, "Cross National Times Series, 1815–1973," ICPSR 5701 (Ann Arbor: Interuniversity Consortium for Political and Social Research, 1999), http://www.icpsr.umich.edu/icpsrweb/ICPSR/studies/7412.

10. Measuring decline with GDP has advantages over well-known alternatives. The Correlates of War project's Composite Index of National Capabilities (CINC) score, for example, is often used to track the balance of power among the great powers. By aggregating measures of economic production with military strength, however, this index conflates the causes of decline with its consequences. A decision by a great power to reduce its military expenditures may reflect a decision to retrench, and thus be a consequence rather than a cause of decline. CINC scores are also poorly correlated with most other indicators of national power, including economic output (0.2301), state revenues (0.3181) and expenditures (0.3255), imports (0.1299) and exports (0.2139). When using CINC scores, therefore, we must make even more heroic assumptions about how policymakers generated perceptions of their relative position. Correlation coefficients reported; GDP data come from Maddison; data for revenues, expenditures, imports, and exports from Banks; CINC data from J. David Singer, "Reconstructing the Correlates of War Dataset on the Material Capabilities of States, 1816–1965," *International Interactions* 14 (1987): 115–32.

11. See William Grampp, "What Did Smith Mean by the Invisible Hand?" *Journal of Political Economy* 108, no. 3 (June 2000): 441–65.

12. Due in part to data availability but also the unreliability of wartime figures, we exclude transitions that took place during the two world wars.

13. Between 1870 and 1914, Austria-Hungary's share of great power GDP remained fixed around 1.6 percent; Italy's share fluctuated between 5.4 and 8.4 percent, with no clear pattern in one direction or the other.

14. In a previous article, we made an error in calculating the GDP of postwar West Germany, which led us to incorrectly identify two additional cases of decline: 1956 United Kingdom and 1967 West Germany. See Paul K. MacDonald and Joseph M. Parent, "Graceful Decline? The Surprising Success of Great Power Retrenchment," *International Security* 35, no. 4 (Spring 2011): 28. We exclude these two cases here, a decision that does not significantly impact our findings. We are grateful to George Peden for bringing this mistake to our attention.

15. See Robert Gilpin, *War and Change in World Politics* (Princeton: Princeton University Press, 1981), 190–94; also Ronald Tammen et al., *Power Transitions: Strategies for the 21st Century* (New York: Chatham House, 2000), 49.

16. We use military personnel data from Correlates of War, *National Material Capabilities* data set, ver. 3.02. See Singer, "Material Capabilities of States," 115–32.

17. We use alliance agreement data from the Alliance Treaty Obligations and Provisions Project, ver. 3. See Brett Ashley Leeds, Jeffrey Ritter, Sara McLaughlin Mitchell, and Andrew Long, "Alliance Treaty Obligations and Provisions, 1815–1944," *International Interactions* 28, no. 3 (July 2002): 237–60.

18. We use data from Correlates of War, *Militarized Interstate Disputes* data set, ver. 3.1. See Daniel M. Jones, Stuart A. Bremer, and J. David Singer, "Militarized Interstate Disputes, 1816–1992: Rationale, Coding Rules, and Empirical Patterns," *Conflict Management and Peace Science* 15, no. 2 (Fall 1996), 163–213.

19. The online appendix can be found at http://politicalscience.nd.edu/faculty/faculty-list/joseph-m-parent/.

20. See, for example, Jack Snyder, *Myths of Empire: Domestic Politics and International Ambition* (Ithaca: Cornell University Press, 1991), 2–21; Jeffrey Taliaferro, *Balancing Risks: Great Power Intervention in the Periphery* (Ithaca: Cornell University Press, 2004), 40–54.

21. For similar findings, see Dan Reiter, "Exploding the Powder Keg Myth: Preemptive Wars Almost Never Happen," *International Security* 20, no. 2 (Fall 1995): 25–28; Richard Betts, "Suicide from Fear of Death?" *Foreign Affairs* 82, no. 1 (January/February 2003): 34–43.

22. See, for example, Michael Howard, *The Franco-Prussian War: The German Invasion of France, 1870–1871* (New York: Fontana, 1967), 40–42, 54; Otto Pflanze, *Bismarck and the Development of Germany* (Princeton: Princeton University Press, 1990), 1:451.

23. This suggests a more general problem with power transition theories—in many cases transition is produced by war rather than vice versa. See Richard Ned Lebow and Benjamin Valentino, "Lost in Transition: A Critical Analysis of Power Transition Theory," *International Relations* 23, no. 3 (September 2009): 389–410.

24. Democracies accounted for 50 percent of great power country-years across our sample. Based on coding in Monty Marshall, Ted Robert Gurr, and Keith Jaggers, "Political Regime Characteristics and Transitions, 1800–2012," Polity IV Project (April 2013), http://www.systemicpeace.org/polity/polity4.htm.

25. See Jack Snyder, "Review of *The Weary Titan: Britain and the Experience of Relative Decline, 1895–1905*, by Aaron Friedberg," *American Political Science Review* 84, no. 2 (June 1990): 719.

26. Eight of our cases involved a great power whose economic output was shrinking in absolute terms, six of which retrenched. Of the eight cases of great powers that were losing out in relative terms only, between five and seven retrenched.

27. See Randall Schweller, *Unanswered Threats: Political Constraints on the Balance of Power* (Princeton: Princeton University Press, 2006), chap. 3; Jeffrey W. Taliaferro, Norrin M. Ripsman, and Steven E. Lobell, eds., *The Challenge of Grand Strategy: The Great Powers and the Broken Balance between the World Wars* (New York: Cambridge University Press, 2012), chaps. 6–7.

28. We note that our approach here differs from an earlier version of this project, where we compared strategic adjustment in the five-year periods following ordinal transitions with five-year periods that did not. We improve that approach in two ways. First, we make our unit of analysis individual country-years, rather than five-year periods. Second, we examine both the five years prior to and the five years following an ordinal transition. These changes did not alter our main findings, but the additional observations allow us to be more confident in our results. Compare to MacDonald and Parent, "Graceful Decline?," 30–31.

29. Between 1932 and 1936, for example, Germany increased its military personnel five-fold and its military spending fifteen-fold. British defense spending likewise increased by 324 percent in 1939, and its military personnel ballooned by 159 percent in 1940.

30. This difference is significant at the $p<0.01$ level, $p=0.0038$, $t(2.6981, 190.966df)$. We use a one-tailed t-test for unpaired samples with unequal variance for all of the following tests. This finding held for three of our four comparisons. The only comparison for which this finding did not hold was when we included outliers, but excluded world wars from the baseline category. This finding also held for all four of our time windows.

31. Russian defense spending increased by 16.2 percent during its decline, but much of this is the result of a 238 percent spike in defense spending in 1905. When this outlier year is excluded, Russia averages –6 percent for the ten remaining years surrounding its ordinal transition.

32. This difference is significant at the $p<0.1$ level, $p=0.0531$, $t(1.6223, 229.55df)$. This finding held for three of our four comparisons. The only comparison for which this finding did not hold was when we included outliers, but excluded world wars from the baseline category. This finding also held for three of our four time windows.

33. France increased its military personnel by 121 percent in 1871 during the Franco-Prussian War, Russia increased its military personnel by 104 percent in 1905 during the Russo-Japanese War, and Great Britain increased its military personnel by 125 percent in 1941 during the Second World War.

34. With 1871 excluded, 1873 France averaged a –5.5 percent annual change in military personnel during its decline. With 1905 excluded, 1903 Russia averaged a –1.2 percent annual change in military personnel during its decline. With 1946 excluded, 1946 United Kingdom averaged a –3.9 percent annual average change in military personnel during its decline.

35. In what follows, we exclude the two influential outliers—1935 United Kingdom and 1931 Germany—from figures for medium decliners.

36. This echoes the discussion of capability versus capacity cuts in contemporary American defense planning. See Department of Defense, "Press Briefing by Secretary Hagel and Admiral Winnefeld" (July 31, 2013), http://archive.defense.gov/news/newsarticle.aspx?id=120560.

37. Benjamin Goldsmith, "Bearing the Defense Burden, 1886–1989: Why Spend More?" *Journal of Conflict Resolution* 47, no. 5 (October 2003): 551–73. For similar findings, see William Nordhaus, John Oneal, and Bruce Russett, "The Effects of the International Security Environment on National Military Expenditures: A Multicountry Study," *International Organization* 66, no. 3 (June 2012): 491–513.

38. This is based on Goldsmith's preferred specification (Model 5), adding a dummy variable for decline with outliers excluded. Our variable for decline was significant at the $p < 0.05$ level ($p=0.035$). Holding all other variables at their mean, decline reduced a state's predicted defense burden by 6.9 percent (from 1.51 percent to 1.40 percent of GDP). For the original model, see Goldsmith, "Bearing the Defense Burden," 563–64.

39. This difference is not statistically significant, $p=0.2114$, $t(-0.8034, 177.648df)$. The alliance comparison failed to achieve significance in any of our four comparisons. Somewhat surprisingly, it did achieve statistical significance when we examined seven- and ten-year windows around ordinal transitions. Perhaps declining powers initiate the search for allies close to their ordinal transition, but are only able to conclude formal agreements with new partners after longer stretches of time.

40. This difference is statistically significant at the 0.05 level, $p = 0.0412$, $t(-1.7701, 53.3096df)$.

41. See, for example, Alison Brysk, Craig Parsons, and Wayne Sandholtz, "After Empire: National Identity and Post-Colonial Families of Nations," *European Journal of International Relations* 8, no. 2 (June 2002): 269–71.

42. This difference is statistically significant at the 0.1 level, p = 0.0929, t(1.3352, 77.1935df).

43. This difference is significant at the p<0.01 level, p= 0.0049, t(2.6384, 88.9019df). This finding held in all four of our comparisons, and in all four time periods we considered.

44. Great Britain participated in seven and twelve militarized disputes in 1939 and 1940 respectively.

45. This difference does not achieve statistical significance, p=0.2456, t(0.6900, 174.375df). This finding regarding MID initiation is much more dependent on what comparison or time window one chooses. It achieves significance at the p<0.1 level in two of our comparison groups (outliers included, world wars excluded; outliers excluded, world wars included) as well as in one of our alternate time periods (three-year window).

46. Hostility ranges from 1 (no militarized action) to 5 (war). This difference does not achieve statistical significance, p=0.2565, t(0.6565, 101.048df). This null result was consistent across all four of our potential comparisons and alternative time windows.

47. We used the COW coding for dispute outcomes, which includes disputes that end in a win, lose, compromise, or stalemate. It is worth emphasizing that a plurality of disputes—43 percent—end in stalemate.

48. This difference is statistically significant at the p<0.001 level, p=0.0001, t(3.9791, 111.744df).

49. This difference is statistically significant at the p<0.001 level, p=0.0001, t(–4.0720, 243.845df).

50. The difference in participation in militarized disputes did not achieve statistical significance, p=0.1811, t(–0.9186, 56.964df). Difference in dispute initiation also failed to achieve significance, p=0.1331, t(–1.1238, 53.1903df).

51. We added a dummy variable with outliers included. Our variable was significant at the p < 0.001 level (p=0.000). Holding all other variables at their mean, decline reduced a state's predicted probability of dispute participation by 47 percent (from 3.19 percent to 1.68 percent). For original model, see Oneal and Russett, *Triangulating Peace*, pp. 171–74, 314.

52. We expand on this analysis using a wider sample of cases and robustness checks in Paul MacDonald and Joseph Parent, "Fast Falls and Fierce Fights: Relative Decline and Militarized Interstate Disputes in International Politics" (paper presented at the annual meeting of the International Studies Association, March 2013).

53. Snyder, *Myths of Empire,* chap. 2. See also Anthony D'Agostino, *The Rise of Global Powers: International Politics in the Era of the World Wars* (New York: Cambridge University Press, 2012), chap. 16.

54. G. John Ikenberry, *Liberal Leviathan* (Princeton: Princeton University Press, 2011), chap. 8. See also Charles Kupchan, *No One's World: The West, the Rising Rest, and the Coming Global Turn* (New York: Oxford University Press, 2013), chap. 7.

55. See Jonathan Kirshner, "The Tragedy of Offensive Realism: Classical Realism and the Rise of China," *European Journal of International Relations* 18, no. 1 (March 2012): 62–63.

56. This difference failed to achieve statistical significance, p=0.1632, t(–0.9846, 149.26df). We excluded the two world wars from all of the comparisons in this section.

57. This difference failed to achieve statistical significance, p=0.2800, t(–0.5843, 148.066df).

58. This difference achieved statistical significance at the p<0.1 level, p=0.0704, t(–1.4812, 141.087df).

59. This difference achieved statistical significance at the p<0.001 level, p=0.000, t(4.4949, 207.774df).

60. This difference achieved statistical significance at the p<0.001 level, p=0.0025, t(2.8392, 189.317df).

61. This is an argument emphasized by Nuno Monteiro, *Theory of Unipolar Politics* (New York: Cambridge University Press, 2014), chap. 6.

62. See, for example, Stephen Brooks and William Wohlforth, *America Abroad: The United States Global Role in the 21st Century* (New York: Oxford University Press, 2016), 4–5; Barry

Posen, *Restraint: A New Foundation for U.S. Grand Strategy* (Ithaca: Cornell University Press, 2014), chap. 2.

63. Most preventive war theorists focus on dyads but keep systemic consequences in frame. See Gilpin, *War and Change*, chap. 5; A. F. K. Organski and Jacek Kugler, *The War Ledger* (Chicago: University of Chicago Press, 1980), 49.

64. See Schweller, *Unanswered Threats*, 9–13; Charles Kupchan, *The Vulnerability of Empire* (Ithaca: Cornell University Press, 1994), 3–11.

65. See Graham Allison, "The Thucydides Trap: Are the U.S. and China Headed for War?" *Atlantic* (September 24, 2015); Gilpin, *War and Change*, chap. 5.

Studies in Revival

1. See, for example, Correlli Barnett, *The Collapse of British Power* (New York: Morrow, 1972); Keith Robbins, *The Eclipse of a Great Power: Modern Britain 1870–1975* (New York: Longman, 1983); and Aaron Friedberg, *The Weary Titan: Britain and the Experience of Relative Decline, 1895–1905* (Princeton: Princeton University Press, 1988).

2. See, for example, Jean-Marie Mayeur and Madeline Rebérioux, *The Third Republic from its Origins to the Great War, 1871–1914* (New York: Cambridge University Press, 1988); and William Fuller, *Strategy and Power in Russia, 1600–1914* (New York: The Free Press, 1992).

4. A Hegemon Temporizes

1. Palmerston had served as secretary of state for foreign affairs for all but five years between 1830 and 1851, and had been prime minister for all but sixteen months between 1852 and 1865.

2. See, for example, David Krein, *The Last Palmerston Government: Foreign Policy, Domestic Politics and the Genesis of "Splendid Isolation"* (Ames: Iowa State University Press, 1978); David Steele, "Palmerston's Foreign Policy and Foreign Secretaries 1855–1865," in *British Foreign Secretaries and Foreign Policy: From Crimean War to First World War*, ed. Keith Wilson (Wolfeboro: Croom Helm, 1987), 25–84; John Charmley, "Palmerston: 'Artful Old Dodger' or 'Babe of Grace'?" in *The Makers of British Foreign Policy: From Pitt to Thatcher*, ed. Thomas G. Otte (New York: Palgrave Macmillan, 2002), 75–97.

3. See, for example, Robert W. Seton-Watson, *Britain in Europe, 1789–1914: A Survey of Foreign Policy* (New York: Cambridge University Press, 1938), 465; Kenneth Bourne, *The Foreign Policy of Victorian England, 1830–1902* (New York: Oxford University Press, 1970), 110; Muriel Chamberlain, *'Pax Britannica'? British Foreign Policy, 1789–1914* (New York: Longman, 1988), 115, 124.

4. Bernard Porter, *Britain, Europe and the World 1850–1986: Delusions of Grandeur* (London: George Allen and Unwin, 1987), 36.

5. René Albrecht-Carrié, *A Diplomatic History of Europe Since the Congress of Vienna* (New York: Harper and Brothers, 1958), 139.

6. See, for example, Paul Kennedy, *Strategy and Diplomacy, 1870–1945* (London: Allen and Unwin, 1983), 15, 20; Paul Schroeder, "Munich and the British Tradition," *Historical Journal* 19, no. 1 (March 1976): 224; George Bernstein, "Special Relationship and Appeasement: Liberal Policy Towards America in the Age of Palmerston," *Historical Journal* 41, no. 3 (September 1998): 725–50.

7. For discussion of Britain's role, see Werner E. Mosse, "Queen Victoria and Her Ministers in the Schleswig-Holstein Crisis 1863–1864," *English Historical Review* 78, no. 307 (April 1963): 263–83; Keith Sandiford, *Great Britain and the Schleswig-Holstein Question, 1848–64: A Study in Diplomacy, Politics, and Public Opinion* (Toronto: University of Toronto Press, 1975).

8. *Hansard Parliamentary Debates*, 3rd series, 172 (1863), col. 1250.

9. *Hansard Parliamentary Debates*, 3rd series, 176 (1864), col. 745.

10. *Hansard Parliamentary Debates,* 3rd series, 143 (1864), col. 29.

11. *Hansard Parliamentary Debates,* 3rd series, 176 (1864), col. 841.

12. Gladstone diary entry (July 8, 1864), in *The Gladstone Diaries, Volume VI, 1861–1868,* ed. Henry Colin Grey Matthew (New York: Oxford University Press, 1978), 288.

13. The phrase was coined by Lord Derby. See Krein, *Last Palmerston Government,* 141; Sandiford, *Great Britain and the Schleswig-Holstein Question,* 122–23.

14. John Prest, *Lord John Russell* (Columbia: University of South Carolina Press, 1972), 398.

15. Thomas G. Otte, *The Foreign Office Mind: The Making of British Foreign Policy 1865–1914* (New York: Cambridge University Press, 2011), 23, 24.

16. Quoted in Steele, "Palmerston's Foreign Policy," 66.

17. Quoted in Otte, *Foreign Office Mind,* 29.

18. Russell to Lewis (July 26, 1862) quoted in *The Later Correspondence of Lord John Russell, 1840–1878,* ed. George Peabody Gooch (New York: Longmans, Green and Co, 1925), 2:299.

19. Quoted in Norman Rich, *Great Power Diplomacy, 1814–1914* (Boston: McGraw Hill, 1992), 218.

20. Disraeli speech at Free Trade Hall (April 4, 1872), quoted in Alexander Charles Ewald, *The Right Hon. Benjamin Disraeli, Earl of Beaconsfield, and His Times* (London: William Mackenzie, 1882), 2:231.

21. Lord Derby, "The Promotion of Scientific Industry (1874)", quoted in *Speeches and Addresses of Edward Henry XVth Earl of Derby,* ed. T. H. Sanderson and E. S. Roscoe (London: Longmans, 1894), 1:237, 1:239. The British were not alone; starting in the 1870s, German conservatives associated modernity with Americanization. See Fritz Stern, *The Politics of Cultural Despair: A Study in the Rise of the Germanic Ideology* (Berkeley: University of California Press, 1961), 131.

22. Quoted in Seton-Watson, *Britain in Europe,* 470.

23. For overviews, see Agatha Ramm, "Granville," in *British Foreign Secretaries and Foreign Policy: From Crimean War to First World War,* ed. Keith Wilson (Wolfeboro: Croom Helm, 1987), 86–100; Marvin Swartz, *The Politics of British Foreign Policy in the Era of Disraeli and Gladstone* (New York: St. Martin's Press, 1985), chap. 1.

24. Quoted in Charles R. M. F. Cruttwell, "Neutrality in Continental Affairs, 1866–1874," in *Cambridge History of British Foreign Policy 1783–1919,* ed. Adolphus W. Ward and George Peabody Gooch (New York: Macmillan, 1923), 3:21.

25. Granville to Gladstone (April 18, 1869), quoted in *The Political Correspondence of Mr. Gladstone and Lord Granville 1868–1876,* ed. Agatha Ramm (London: Offices of the Royal Historical Society, 1952), 1:20.

26. Disraeli speech at Free Trade Hall (April 4, 1872), quoted in Ewald, *Disraeli, Earl of Beaconsfield,* 2:231.

27. Edward Henry Stanley, the fifteenth Earl of Derby, previously Lord Stanley, not to be confused with his father Edward Smith-Stanley, the fourteenth Earl of Derby.

28. Lord Derby, "The Eastern Question (1876)," quoted in Sanderson and Roscoe, ed., *Speeches and Addresses,* 288.

29. As Brian Bond observes, "Not even Disraeli's romantic imperialism reversed the trend toward parsimony in military expenditure." Brian Bond, "Recruiting the Victorian Army, 1870–92," *Victorian Studies* 5, no. 4 (June 1962): 332.

30. *Hansard Parliamentary Debates,* 3rd series, 185 (1867), col. 1450. Both Stanley and Disraeli urged Peel to avoid large increases in the army estimates. See Richard Millman, *British Foreign Policy and the Coming of the Franco-Prussian War* (New York: Oxford University Press, 1965), 145–46.

31. As Hoppen argues, if "the Tory government of 1866–8 had been notably parsimonious in military matters, the new Secretary for War, Edward Cardwell . . . was determined to be more parsimonious still." K. Theodore Hoppen, *The Mid-Victorian Generation, 1846–1886* (New York: Oxford University Press, 1998), 602.

32. See *Hansard Parliamentary Debates,* 3rd series, 194 (1869), col. 1112–16. For a discussion, see Robert Biddulph, *Lord Cardwell at the War Office: A History of His Administration 1868–1874* (London: John Murray, 1904), 27–37.

33. *Hansard Parliamentary Debates,* 3rd series, 199 (1870), col. 1163.

34. See *Hansard Parliamentary Debates,* 3rd series, 185 (1867), col. 1463–69.

35. Edward Spiers, *The Late Victorian Army, 1868–1902* (New York: Manchester University Press, 1992), 9. See also Bond, "Recruiting the Victorian Army," 332–33; Albert Tucker, "Army and Society in England, 1870–1900: A Reassessment of the Cardwell Reforms," *Journal of British Studies* 2, no. 2 (May 1963), 130–31.

36. See Spiers, *Late Victorian Army,* 19–20.

37. *Hansard Parliamentary Debates,* 3rd series, 204 (1871), col. 358.

38. See Biddulph, *Cardwell at the War Office,* 50–55; Correlli Barnett, *Britain and Her Army, 1509–1970: A Military, Political and Social Survey* (New York: William Morrow and Company, 1970), 309; Spiers, *Late Victorian Army,* 303.

39. See Spiers, *Late Victorian Army,* 18.

40. Barnett, *Britain and Her Army,* 309.

41. See Tucker, "Army and Society in England," 110–11, 140–41; Spiers, *Late Victorian Army,* 2, 24.

42. As a result, by 1878, the first class and militia reserves totaled 37,000 men, far short of the 80,000 that Cardwell had viewed as sufficient. See *Hansard Parliamentary Debates,* 3rd series, 238 (1878), col. 673.

43. In 1879, for example, there were 82 battalions overseas compared to just 59 at home. Figure cited in Tucker, "Army and Society in England," 134.

44. See *Hansard Parliamentary Debates,* 3rd series, 204 (1871), col. 329–30.

45. See *Hansard Parliamentary Debates,* 3rd series, 209 (1872), col. 880.

46. *Hansard Parliamentary Debates,* 3rd series, 222 (1875), col. 1467.

47. See *Hansard Parliamentary Debates,* 3rd series, 227 (1876), col. 1237–1264.

48. See Sydney Buxton, *Finance and Politics: A Historical Study, 1783–1885* (London: John Murray, 1888), 2:44.

49. Figures cited in Buxton, *Finance and Politics,* 156, 158, 160.

50. The cumulative cost of wars in South Africa and Afghanistan alone totaled some £12.3 million, only £4.5 million of which was met with immediate taxation. Figures cited in Buxton, *Finance and Politics,* 258–29.

51. Figures come from Brian R. Mitchell, *British Historical Statistics* (New York: Cambridge University Press, 1988), passim.

52. *Hansard Parliamentary Debates,* 3rd series, 209 (1872), col. 1832.

53. *Hansard Parliamentary Debates,* 3rd series, 191 (1868), col. 96–97.

54. *Hansard Parliamentary Debates,* 3rd series, 224 (1873), col. 1150.

55. See Charles P. Stacey, *Canada and the British Army, 1846–1871: A Study in the Practice of Responsible Government* (Toronto: University of Toronto Press, 1963), 198, 201.

56. Peter Burroughs, "Defence and Imperial Disunity," in *Oxford History of the British Empire: The Nineteenth Century,* ed. Andrew Porter (New York: Oxford University Press, 1999), 332.

57. See Carl Adolf Bodelsen, *Studies in Mid-Victorian Imperialism* (Copenhagen: Gyldendal, 1924), 89–93; Henry Colin Gray Matthew, *Gladstone, 1809–1874* (New York: Oxford University Press, 1986), 188; Burroughs, "Defence and Imperial Disunity," 329–30.

58. Quoted in Spiers, *Late Victorian Army,* 4. See also Swartz, *Politics of British Foreign Policy,* 11.

59. See *Hansard Parliamentary Debates,* 3rd series, 199 (1870), col. 1162.

60. Figures cited in *Hansard Parliamentary Debates,* 3rd series, 204 (1871), col. 331.

61. Burroughs, "Defence and Imperial Disunity," 333.

62. Figures cited in Burroughs, "Defence and Imperial Disunity," 333.

63. See William P. Morrell, *British Colonial Policy in the Mid-Victorian Age: South Africa, New Zealand, the West Indies* (New York: Oxford University Press, 1969); John Cell, *British Colonial Administration in the Mid-nineteenth Century: The Policy-Making Process* (New Haven: Yale University Press, 1970), 95, 113–16

64. *Hansard Parliamentary Debates,* 3rd series, 191 (1868), col. 96–97.

65. See Peter B. Waite, "Edward Cardwell and the Confederation" *Canadian Historical Review* 43, no. 1 (March 1962): 23; James Gibson, "The Colonial Office View of Canadian Federation, 1856–1868" *Canadian Historical Review* 35, no. 4 (December 1954): 303–4.

66. See Kenneth Bourne, *Britain and the Balance of Power in North America,1815–1908* (Berkeley: University of California Press, 1967), 300; Barnett, *Britain and Her Army*, 318.

67. See Edmund George Petty-Fitzmaurice Fitzmaurice, *The Life of Granville George Leveson Gower, Second Earl of Granville, K.G., 1815–1891, Vol. 2* (Berkeley: University of California Press, 1905), 22.

68. Gladstone to Granville (May 29, 1869), quoted in Ramm, *Political Correspondence of Gladstone and Granville*, 24

69. Quoted in Otte, *Foreign Office Mind*, 75.

70. See William Harbutt Dawson, "Forward Policy and Reaction, 1874–1885," in *The Cambridge History of British Foreign Policy, 1783-1919*, ed. Adolphus William Ward and George Peabody Gooch (New York: Cambridge University Press, 2011), 147.

71. See Cruttwell, "Neutrality in Continental Affairs," 1; Millman, *British Policy and the Franco-Prussian War*, 6–37.

72. *Hansard Parliamentary Debates*, 3rd series, 183 (1866), col. 576. On the connection Russell drew between "peace" and "economy" abroad and "work to be done" at home, see J. Parry, "Past and Future in the Later Career of Lord John Russell," in *History and Biography: Essays in Honor of Derek Beales*, ed. Timothy C. W. Blanning and David Cannadine (New York: Cambridge University Press, 1996), 163, 166.

73. Quoted in Bourne, *Foreign Policy of Victorian England*, 387. Clarendon was even blunter: "The idea of our spending one shilling or one drop of blood in the banditti quarrel which is now going on in Germany is simply absurd." Clarendon to Russell (March 31, 1866), quoted in Gooch, *Later Correspondence of Lord John Russell*, 2:345.

74. Quoted in Seton-Watson, *Britain in Europe*, 470.

75. *Hansard Parliamentary Debates*, 3rd series, 184 (1866), col. 1253–56.

76. See Cruttwell, "Neutrality in Continental Affairs," 24; Seton-Watson, *Britain in Europe*, 491–92.

77. See Ramm, "Granville," 88; Steiner, "Fall of Great Britain," 49; Richard Shannon, *Gladstone: Volume II 1865–1898* (Chapel Hill: University of North Carolina Press, 1999), 87–89.

78. Quoted in Otte, *Foreign Office Mind*, 65.

79. Granville to Gladstone (October 7, 1870), quoted in Fitzmaurice, *Life of Granville*, 2, 63.

80. Quoted in Otte, *Foreign Office Mind*, 67.

81. See Cruttwell, "Neutrality in Continental Affairs," 52; Seton-Watson, *Britain in Europe*, 500.

82. Ramm, "Granville," 92.

83. See, in particular, Adrian Cook, *The Alabama Claims: American Politics and Anglo-American Relations, 1865–1872* (Ithaca: Cornell University Press, 1975).

84. One of the chief obstacles here was Charles Sumner, the chairman of the Senate Committee on Foreign Relations, who insisted that Britain withdraw "from this hemisphere, including provinces and islands" as part of a deal. Sumner to Fish (January 15, 1871), quoted in Robert Balmain Mowat, *The Diplomatic Relations of Great Britain and the United States* (Farmington Hills: Gale 2013), 212.

85. See Bourne, *Foreign Policy of Victorian England*, 96; Cook, *Alabama Claims*, 179–86; Matthew, *Gladstone*, 186. Matters appeared to be settled until December 1871, when the Americans laid before the arbitration panel a claim that included not only direct damages caused by the *Alabama*, but also indirect damages resulting from the prolongation of the war. The English press decried American perfidy, but behind the scenes, Granville convinced the Americans to abandon their more excessive demands. See Cook, *Alabama Claims*, 233–40.

86. Granville to Schenck (February 3, 1872), quoted in Fitzmaurice, *Life of Granville*, 2, 96.

87. Roy Jenkins, *Gladstone: A Biography* (New York: Random House, 2002), 356. For similar assessments, see Ramm, "Granville," 91; Cook, *Alabama Claims*, 244–46.

88. See Seton-Watson, *Britain in Europe*, 483; M. R. D. Foot, "Great Britain and Luxemburg 1867," *English Historical Review* 67, no. 264 (July 1952), 352–79; F. Roy Bridge and Roger Bullen, *The Great Powers and the European States System, 1814–1914* (New York: Longman, 2004), 107.

89. Disraeli to Stanley (April 22, 1867), quoted in Millman, *British Foreign Policy and the Franco-Prussian War*, 77.

90. For details of the Belgian railway dispute, see Gordon Craig, "Great Britain and the Belgian Railways Dispute of 1869," *American Historical Review* 50, no. 4 (July 1945): 738–61.

91. Quoted in Seton-Watson, *Britain in Europe,* 490. See also Craig, "Great Britain and the Belgian Railways Dispute," 754.

92. Clarendon to Lyons (April 21, 1869), quoted in Millman, *British Foreign Policy and the Franco-Prussian War,* 141.

93. Granville to Lyone (August 4, 1870), quoted in Millman, *British Foreign Policy and the Franco-Prussian War,* 205.

94. Otte, *Foreign Office Mind,* 52

95. Quoted in Cruttwell, "Neutrality in Continental Affairs," 20.

96. Gladstone praised "the signal prudence of Mr. Disraeli during the anxious period of the Controversy with the United States." Quoted in Jenkins, *Gladstone,* 358.

97. *Hansard Parliamentary Debates,* 3rd series, 199 (1870), col. 209.

98. W. David McIntyre, *The Imperial Frontier in the Tropics, 1865–75: A Study of British Colonial Policy in West Africa, Malaya and the South Pacific in the Age of Gladstone and Disraeli* (New York: Macmillan, 1967), 51.

99. Cardwell admitted he had "adversaries to contend with both on the right and the left . . . [and could not] give entire satisfaction to everybody." *Hansard Parliamentary Debates,* 3rd series, 214 (1873), col. 1143.

100. See Nini Rodgers, "The Abyssinian Expedition of 1867–1868: Disraeli's Imperialism or James Murray's War?" *Historical Journal* 27, no. 1 (March 1984): 146, cf. 142–44, 149. For an alternative interpretation, which views the expedition as an effort to distract from domestic unrest, see Freda Harcourt, "Disraeli's Imperialism, 1866–1868: A Question of Timing," *The Historical Journal* 23, no. 1 (March 1980), 104.

101. The parliamentary undersecretary was "against taking fresh territory" but "Basutoland must soon break up and become ours or the Boers." Adderley Minute (October 25, 1866), quoted in C. J. Uys, *In the Era of Shepstone: Being a Study of British Expansion in South Africa, 1842–1877* (Lovedale: Lovedale Press, 1933), 48.

102. Kimberly Minute (May 22, 1873), quoted in W. David McIntyre, "British Policy in West Africa: The Ashanti Expedition of 1873–4," *Historical Journal* 5, no. 1 (March 1962): 29.

103. Kimberly to Cardwell (July 26, 1873), quoted in McIntyre, *Imperial Frontier in the Tropics,* 143. See also Robert Edgerton, *The Fall of the Asante Empire* (New York: Free Press, 1995), 100–101.

104. See John Keegan, "The Ashanti Campaign, 1873–4," in *Victorian Military Campaigns,* ed. Brian Bond (New York: Praeger, 1967), 190–96; John Fynn, "Ghana-Asante," in *West African Resistance: the Military Responses to Colonial Occupation,* ed. Michael Crowder (London: Hutchinson, 1971), 49–50.

105. See Emily Sadka, *The Protected Malay States* (Kuala Lumpur: University of Malaya Press, 1968), 26–37; Nicholas Tarling, "The Establishment of Colonial Regimes," in *Cambridge History of Southeast Asia, Volume Two, The Nineteenth and Twentieth Centuries,* ed. Nicholas Tarling (New York: Cambridge University Press, 1992), 13–22, 28–34.

106. Kimberly to Gladstone (September 10, 1873), quoted in McIntyre, *Imperial Frontier in the Tropics,* 205.

107. See Sadka, *Protected Malay States,* 46–49; John M. Gullick, *Rulers and Residents: Influence and Power in the Malay States, 1870–1920* (New York: Oxford University Press, 1992), 13–21.

108. As with Basutoland, the move was designed in part to preempt Afrikaner claims. See Leonard Thompson, "The Subjection of the African Chiefdoms, 1870–1898," in *The Oxford History of South Africa, Volume Two,* ed. Monica Wilson and Leonard Thompson (New York: Oxford University Press, 1971), 255–56.

109. Disraeli complained the continental powers were "asking us to sanction them in their putting the knife to the throat of Turkey." Quoted in Matthew Smith Anderson, *The Eastern Question, 1774–1923* (New York: St. Martin's, 1966), 183. Derby held a much different view. "To the Premier, the main thing is to please and surprise the public by bold strokes . . . to me, the first object is to keep England out of trouble." Quoted in Swartz, *Politics of British Foreign Policy,* 47.

110. In December 1875, Britain accepted a note calling for reforms, but refused to endorse stronger memorandum five months later designed to pressure the Sultan. British efforts to reach a negotiated compromise during the 1876 Constantinople Conference were likewise undermined by divisions between the British plenipotentiary Lord Salisbury, who sought to work with his Russian counterpart, and the British consul Sir Henry Elliot, who encouraged Ottoman intransigence. See Dawson, "Forward Policy and Reaction," 96–97, 113; Seton-Watson, *Britain in Europe*, 517–18, 521–22.

111. Quoted in Seton-Watson, *Britain in Europe*, 523.

112. Reinforcements from India were dispatched to Malta, and the Cabinet eventually agreed to a vote of credit and to dispatch ships to the Dardanelles. The latter move prompted foreign secretary Derby to resign. See Seton-Watson, *Britain in Europe*, 535; P. J. V. Rolo, "Derby," in *British Foreign Secretaries and Foreign Policy*, ed. K. M. Wilson (London: Croom Helm, 1987), 117.

113. The powers bristled at the creation of a semi-autonomous Greater Bulgaria under Russian supervision. Lord Salisbury, having replaced Derby at the Foreign Office, seized the diplomatic opening. He worked with Austria-Hungary and Germany to reduce the size of a semi-autonomous Bulgaria, scale back Russian expansion in Asia Minor, and impose a modest slate of reforms on the Turks. See Seton-Watson, *Britain in Europe*, 533, 542–44; Bridge and Bullen, *Great Powers and European States System*, 123–25.

114. The Treaty of Berlin was a serious departure from the British government's initial defense of the integrity of the Ottoman Empire: three provinces had achieved their independence, and two more had been granted considerable autonomy. While the *Dreikaiserbund* had been riven apart, this outcome was transitory: the alliance was reconstituted in 1881 under Bismarck's more active, controlling supervision. For similarly skeptical takes, see Porter, *Britain, Europe and the World*, 38; Bridge and Bullen, *Great Powers and the European States System*, 125; Otte, *Foreign Office Mind*, 149.

115. Disraeli was a key figure leading this charge, although his enthusiasm for empire was both complicated and intermittent. See Stanley Stembridge, "Disraeli and the Millstones," *Journal of British Studies* 5, no. 1 (1965): 122–25; and Colin C. Eldridge, *England's Mission; the Imperial Idea in the Age of Gladstone and Disraeli, 1868–1880* (London: Macmillan, 1973), 176–80.

116. The term comes from Albrecht-Carrié, *Diplomatic History of Europe*, 169–70.

117. See Dawson, "Forward Policy and Reaction," 84.

118. See Clement Francis Goodfellow, *Great Britain and South African Confederation 1870–1881* (New York: Oxford University Press, 1966), 71; Bill Guest, "Colonists, Confederation, and Constitutional Change," in *Natal and Zululand from Earliest Times to 1910*, ed. Andrew Duminy and Bill Guest (Pietermaritzburg, South Africa: University of Natal Press, 1989), 146–69.

119. See Ronald Robinson, John Gallagher, and Alice Denny, *Africa and the Victorians: The Official Mind of Imperialism* (New York: Palgrave Macmillan, 1978), 122–60; Alexander Schölch, "The 'Men on the Spot' and the English Occupation of Egypt in 1882," *Historical Journal* 19, no. 3 (September 1976): 773–85; Antony G. Hopkins, "The Victorians and Africa: A Reconsideration of the Occupation of Egypt, 1882," *Journal of African History* 27, no. 2 (June 1986): 378–79.

120. Northbrook Cabinet Memo (December 24, 1883), quoted in Robinson and Gallagher, *Victorians and Africa*, 134.

5. A Hegemon Wakes Up

1. See, for example, George W. Monger, *The End of Isolation: British Foreign Policy 1900–1907* (New York: Thomas Nelson and Sons, 1963), chap. 1; Christopher Howard, *Splendid Isolation: A Study of Ideas Concerning Britain's International Position and Foreign Policy during the Later Years of the Third Marquis of Salisbury* (New York: St. Martin's Press, 1967), 14–15; and Cedric J. Lowe and Michael L. Dockrill, *The Mirage of Power: Volume One, British Foreign Policy 1902–1914* (Boston: Routledge, 1972), 1–3.

2. George W. Monger, "The End of Isolation: Britain, Germany, and Japan, 1900–1902," *Transactions of the Royal Historical Society* 13 (1963), 120.

3. Paul Kennedy, *The Realities Behind Diplomacy: Background Influences on British External Policy, 1865–1980* (Boston: Allen and Unwin, 1981), 21.

4. See Geoffrey R. Searle, *The Quest for National Efficiency: A Study in British Politics and Political Thought, 1899–1914* (Berkeley: University of California Press, 1971), 45–50.

5. Quoted in David Steele, "Salisbury and the Soldiers," in *The Boer War: Direction, Experience, and Image*, ed. John Gooch (Portland: Frank Cass, 2000), 3.

6. Monson to Salisbury (October 24, 1899), *British Documents on the Origins of the War, 1898–1914*, ed. George Peabody Gooch and Harold Temperley (London: Her Majesty's Stationery Office, 1926–1938), I, no. 286.

7. Rumbold to Salisbury (February 2, 1900), *British Documents* (hereafter *BD*), I, no. 310.

8. Thomas Pakenham, *Boer War* (New York: Abacus, 1991), 543. See also Shula Marks, "War and Union, 1899–1910," in *Cambridge History of South Africa, Volume Two, 1885–1994*, ed. Robert Ross, Anne Kelk Mager, and Bill Nasson (New York: Cambridge University Press, 2011), 158.

9. Figure cited in Geoffrey Russell Searle, *A New England: Peace and War 1866–1918* (New York: Clarendon Press, 2005), 298. See also Rhodri Williams, *Defending the Empire: The Conservative Party and British Defence Policy, 1899–1914* (New Haven: Yale University Press, 1991), 9.

10. Hamilton to Curzon,(March 15, 1901), quoted in Monger, "End of Isolation," 106.

11. Brodrick to Curzon (November 9, 1900), quoted in Lowell Satre, "St. John Brodrick and Army Reform, 1901–1903," *Journal of British Studies*, 15, no. 2 (Spring 1976): 119.

12. Opinion reported in Hamilton to Curzon (July 4, 1901), quoted in Monger, *End of Isolation*, 13.

13. Kerr to Selborne (September 2, 1901), quoted in Thomas G. Otte, *The China Question: Great Power Rivalry and British Isolation 1894–1905* (New York: Oxford University Press, 2007), 293.

14. Figure cited in Monger, *End of Isolation*, 10.

15. Second Report of Committee (December 30, 1902), quoted in Monger, *End of Isolation*, 4.

16. Salisbury to Northcote (June 8, 1900), quoted in John A. S. Grenville, *Lord Salisbury and Foreign Policy* (London: Athlone Press, 1970), 295.

17. Hamilton to Curzon (April 2, 1902), quoted in Grenville, *Lord Salisbury and Foreign Policy*, 322.

18. Grey to Lyttelton (April 15, 1906), quoted in Keith Robbins, *Sir Edward Grey: A Biography of Lord Grey of Fallodon* (London: Cassell, 1971), 136. See also Francois Crouzet, "Trade and Empire: The British Experience from the Establishment of Free Trade until the First World War," in *Great Britain and Her World, 1750–1914: Essays in Honour of W. O. Henderson*, ed. Barrie Ratcliffe (Manchester, U.K.: Manchester University Press, 1975), 209–36.

19. Figure cited in Bill Nasson, *South African War* (London: Bloomsbury, 1999), 285. In 1901 alone, spending on the army exceeded £94 million, almost half of Britain's total national expenditure. Figure cited in Hew Strachan, "The Boer War and Its Impact on the British Army, 1902–14," in *"Ashes and Blood": The British Army in South Africa 1795–1914*, ed. Peter Boyden, Alan Guy, and Marion Harding (London: National Army Museum, 1999), 85.

20. Figures cited in David Omissi and Andrew Thompson, "Investigating the Impact of the War," in *The Impact of the South African War*, ed. David Omissi and Andrew Thompson (New York: Palgrave, 2002), 9.

21. Quoted in Monger, *End of Isolation*, 168. Lord Cromer confided, "The two greatest dangers at present are backwardness in education and unsound finance—by which term I mean more specifically spending more money than we can afford." Cromer to Balfour (October 15, 1903), quoted in Lowe and Dockrill, *Mirage of Power*, 8

22. Geoffrey Searle, "'National Efficiency' and the 'Lessons' of the War," in Omissi and Thompson, eds., *Impact of the South African War*, 205.

23. Salisbury to Curzon (October 17, 1900), quoted in Monger, *End of Isolation*, 17.

24. Lansdowne to Lascelles (March 18, 1901), quoted in Grenville, *Lord Salisbury and Foreign Policy*, 341.

25. Balfour cabinet letter (December 14, 1903), quoted in Ruddock F. Mackay, *Balfour: Intellectual Statesman* (New York: Oxford University Press, 1985), 166–67.

26. See, in particular, Francis Harry Hinsley, ed., *British Foreign Policy Under Sir Edward Grey* (New York: Cambridge University Press, 1977), passim; Keith Wilson, "Grey," in *British Foreign Secretaries and Foreign Policy: From Crimean War to First World War*, ed. Keith Wilson (Wolfeboro, N.H.: Croom Helm, 1987), 172–97 Keith Neilson, "'Control the Whirlwind': Sir Edward Grey as Foreign Secretary, 1906–16," in *The Makers of British Foreign Policy: From Pitt to Thatcher*, ed. Thomas G. Otte (New York: Palgrave, 2002), 128–49.

27. *Hansard Parliamentary Debates*, 3rd series, 156 (1906), col. 1413.

28. Quoted in Muriel E. Chamberlain, *Pax Britannica? British Foreign Policy 1789-1914* (New York: Routledge, 1989), 166.

29. Quoted in Andrew Roberts, *Salisbury: Victorian Titan* (London: Phoenix Press, 2006), 807.

30. *Hansard Parliamentary Debates*, 3rd series, 90 (1901), col. 1653.

31. Quoted in Roberts, *Salisbury*, 768.

32. *Hansard Parliamentary Debates*, 4th series, 119 (1903), col. 302. Economy-minded members of the cabinet, prominent critics in the press, and a group of young Unionist backbenchers known as the Hughligans vigorously condemned the war secretary's plans as extravagant. See Searle, *A New England*, 316; and Williams, *Defending the Empire*, 22.

33. Arnold-Forster admitted that "the capacities of this country to spend money on its armaments are not infinite." Quoted in *Hansard Parliamentary Debates*, 4th series, 131 (1904), col. 337.

34. *Hansard Parliamentary Debates*, 4th series, 143 (1905), col. 1401. See Tucker "Army Reform in the Unionist Government," 94; Searle, *A New England*, 318–19.

35. Balfour to King (June 14, 1904), quoted in Edward Spiers, *Haldane: An Army Reformer* (Edinburgh: Edinburgh University Press, 1980), 52.

36. Figured cited in Williams, *Defending the Empire*, 59.

37. Fisher to Thursfield (July 5, 1903), quoted in Jon Tetsuro Sumida, *In Defence of Naval Supremacy: Finance, Technology, and British Naval Policy, 1889–1914* (Boston: Unwin Hyman, 1989), 27.

38. See Sumida, *Defence of Naval Supremacy*, 26–29.

39. *Hansard Parliamentary Debates*, 4th 144 (1905), col. 173.

40. *Hansard Parliamentary Debates*, 4th, 153 (1906), col. 664.

41. Figure cited in Sumida, *Defence of Naval Supremacy*, 185–86.

42. For details, see Satre, "St. John Brodrick and Army Reform," 121–22; Edward Spiers, *The Army and Society, 1815–1914* (New York: Longman, 1980), 245–46; Williams, *Defending the Empire*, 13.

43. See John Gooch, "Sir George Clarke's Career at the Committee of Imperial Defence, 1904–1907," *Historical Journal* 18, no. 3 (September 1975): 564–65; Albert Tucker, "The Issue of Army Reform in the Unionist Government, 1903–5," *Historical Journal* 9, no. 1 (March 1966): 97.

44. See Arthur J. Marder, *The Anatomy of British Sea Power: A History of British Naval Policy in the Pre-Dreadnought Era, 1880–1905* (London: Frank Cass, 1940), 418; Ruddock F. Mackay, *Fisher of Kilverstone* (New York: Oxford University Press, 1974), 274–84; Williams, *Defending the Empire*, 35–39.

45. See Marder, *Anatomy of British Sea Power*, 483–95; Arthur J. Marder, *From the Dreadnought to Scapa Flow*, Vol. 1: The Road to War, 1904–1914 (Annapolis: Naval Institute Press, 2013), 36–45; Samuel R. Williamson, Jr., *The Politics of Grand Strategy: Britain and France Prepare for War, 1904-1914* (Cambridge: Harvard University Press, 1969), 238.

46. Haldane Memorandum (January 1, 1906), quoted in Spiers, *Haldane*, 77.

47. See Williamson, *Politics of Grand Strategy*, 90–91; Spiers, *Haldane*, 81, 83, 86–87, 109–10; Spiers, *Army and Society* 276–78.

48. Haldane to Campbell-Bannerman (January 27, 1907), quoted in Spiers, *Haldane*, 107.

49. For criticisms, see Williamson, *Politics of Grand Strategy*, 100; John Gooch, *Plans of War: The General Staff and British Military Strategy c. 1900–1916* (New York: Routledge, 1974), 106; Robbins, *Sir Edward Grey*, 178–79; Edward Spiers, "Reform of the Regular Army: Scope for Revision," *British Journal of International Studies* 6, no. 1 (April 1980): 73–74.

50. See especially the conclusions in Spiers, *Haldane*, 199, 279–80. Haldane's reforms were also more ambitious than the 1881 Childers' reforms, which were essentially a second wave of the Cardwell reforms.

51. Quoted in Denis Judd, *Balfour and the British Empire: A Study in Imperial Evolution, 1874–1932* (London: Macmillan, 1968), 37. See also Max Egremont, *Balfour: A Life of Arthur James Balfour* (London: William Collins, 1980), 154.

52. See Franklyn A. Johnson, *Defence by Committee: The British Committee of Imperial Defence, 1885-1959* (New York: Oxford University Press), 49–58; John MacKintosh, "The Role of the Committee of Imperial Defence before 1914," *English Historical Review* 77, no. 304 (July 1962): 493.

53. See Spiers, *Haldane*, 124; Strachan, "Boer War and the British Army," 88.

54. See Zara S. Steiner, *Britain and the Origins of the First World War* (New York: Macmillan, 1974), 35; Williams, *Defending the Empire*, 25; Spiers, *Haldane*, 79–80.

55. Searle, *Quest for National Efficiency*, 233.

56. While Balfour used the committee on a regular basis, his successors did not. Asquith rarely used the institution, and the full committee met only three times in 1910. Figure cited in Nicholas D'Ombrain, *War Machinery and High Policy* (New York: Oxford University Press, 1973), 17.

57. See David W. Sweet, "Great Britain and Germany, 1905–1911," in Hinsley, ed., *British Foreign Policy Under Grey*, 228-32; Robbins, *Sir Edward Grey*, 202–3.

58. Figures cited in Sumida, *Defence of Naval Supremacy*, 189. See also George C. Peden, *Arms, Economics and British Strategy* (New York: Cambridge University Press, 2009), chap. 1.

59. Grey to Asquith (February 5, 1909), quoted in Lowe and Dockrill, *Mirage of Power*, 32

60. An unexpected deficit in 1909 reversed these efforts, leading to a small increase to the income tax and on tobacco duties. See Bernard Mallet, *British Budgets, 1887–88 to 1912–13* (London: Macmillan, 1913), 209, 230, 246, 289.

61. See Mallet, *British Budgets*, 262, 291, 319.

62. See Mallet, *British Budgets*, 274, 291. See also Bruce Murray, *The People's Budget: Lloyd George and Liberal Politics* (Oxford: Clarendon Press, 1980), chap. 1.

63. This category includes expenditure on education, old age pensions, labor exchanges, and insurance commissions. Figures cited in Mallet, *British Budgets*, 508–9.

64. Figures come from Brian R. Mitchell, *British Historical Statistics* (New York: Cambridge University Press, 1988), passim.

65. Quoted in d'Ombrain, *War Machinery and High Policy*, 5.

66. Hamilton to Curzon (April 25, 1901), quoted in Monger, *End of Isolation*, 36–37.

67. See Lowe and Dockrill, *Mirage of Power*, 97.

68. *Daily News* interview (December 5, 1907), quoted in Spiers, *Haldane*, 65.

69. Quoted in Arthur J. Marder, *Fear God and Dread Nought: The Correspondence of Admiral of the Fleet Lord Fisher of Kilverstone, Vol. 2* (London: Jonathan Cape, 1956), 469. See also Paul Kennedy, *The Rise and Fall of British Naval Mastery* (New York: Penguin, 1976), 217; and Charles Kupchan, *The Vulnerability of Empire* (Ithaca: Cornell University Press, 1994), 116–17.

70. Williamson, *Politics of Grand Strategy*, 18. See also Marder, *Anatomy of British Sea Power*, 479–92.

71. Williamson, *Politics of Grand Strategy*, 104. See also Marder, *Road to War*, 71–75.

72. Williamson, *Politics of Grand Strategy*, 239. That same year, Fisher fobbed off as many threats as possible to the Dominions, saying, "We manage the job in Europe, they'll manage it against the Yankees, Japs, and Chinese." Quoted in Christopher Bell, "Sentiment *vs* Strategy: British Naval Policy, Imperial Defence, and the Development of Dominion Navies, 1911–14," *International History Review* 37, no. 2 (June 2015): 264.

73. See Williamson, *Politics of Grand Strategy*, 254–55, 265–67.

74. Churchill to Haldane (May 6, 1912), quoted in Williamson, *Politics of Grand Strategy*, 267.

75. Officials in the Foreign Office feared denuding the Mediterranean might unnerve Turkey and embolden Italy. To assuage these fears, Churchill authorized the retention of two or three battle cruisers at Malta and accepted the need to reach more definitive naval arrangements with the French. See Keith A. Hamilton, "Great Britain and France, 1911–1914," in

Hinsley, ed., *British Foreign Policy Under Grey*, 331; Williamson, *Politics of Grand Strategy*, 274–83; Robbins, *Sir Edward Grey*, 262.

76. Figure cited in Kennedy, *Rise and Fall of British Naval Mastery*, 228.

77. See Ian Nish, *Anglo-Japanese Alliance: The Diplomacy of Two Island Empires, 1894–1907* (London: Athlone, 1966).

78. For persuasive arguments that the alliance was aimed primarily at Russia, see Steiner, *Britain and the Origins of the First World War*, 28; Paul J. V. Rolo, "Landsdowne," in *British Foreign Secretaries and Foreign Policy*, ed. Keith M. Wilson (London: Croom Helm, 1987), 162.

79. As Otte argues, the combination of "financial and naval factors . . . brought the Japanese option into sharper focus." Otte, *China Question*, 292.

80. Selborne Memorandum (September 4, 1901), quoted in Zara Steiner, "Great Britain and the Creation of the Anglo-Japanese Alliance," *Journal of Modern History* 31, no. 1 (March 1959), 30.

81. Otte, *China Question*, 306.

82. As Salisbury famously argued, "The liability of having to defend the German and Austrian frontiers against Russia is heavier than that of *having to defend the British Isles against France* . . . therefore, in its most naked aspect the bargain would be a bad one for this country." Salisbury Memorandum (May 29, 1901), *BD*, II, no. 86.

83. Salisbury and Balfour had the greatest doubts about a Japanese alliance, with both fearing being dragged into an unwanted war. Salisbury fretted, "There is no limit: and no escape. We are pledged to war." Salisbury Memo (January 7, 1907), quoted in Keith M. Wilson, *The Policy of the Entente: Essays on the Determinants of British Foreign Policy, 1904-1914* (New York: Cambridge University Press, 2010), 52.

84. Otte describes the alliance as "an arrangement with a peripheral power involving limited obligations and with the object of safeguarding Britain's regional interests." Thomas G. Otte, *The Foreign Office Mind: The Making of British Foreign Policy, 1865-1914* (New York: Cambridge University Press, 2013), 271. For similar interpretations, see Kennedy, *Realities Behind Diplomacy*, 117; Chamberlain, *Pax Britannica*, 163.

85. See, in particular, Christopher Andrew, *Théophile Delcassé and the Making of the Entente Cordiale: A Reappraisal of French Foreign Policy, 1898–1905* (New York: St. Martin's Press, 1968); and Paul J. V. Rolo, *Entente Cordiale: The Origins and Negotiation of the Anglo-French Agreements* (New York: St. Martin's Press, 1969).

86. For the claim that events in the Far East added urgency, see Nish, *Anglo-Japanese Alliance*, 287; Lowe and Dockrill, *Mirage of Power*, 8; Rolo, "Landsdowne," 165.

87. See Williamson, *Politics of Grand Strategy*, 12–15.

88. Porter concludes that entente was not a departure, but "followed . . . the pattern of the past: eliminating causes of conflict rather than preparing for conflict." Bernard Porter, *Britain, Europe and the World, 1850–1982* (London: Unwin Hyman, 1983), 74.

89. Lansdowne to Monson (April 8, 1904), *BD*, III, no. 416.

90. Spring-Rice to Mallet (April 13, 1904), quoted in Otte, *Foreign Office Mind*, 289.

91. For background, see Rogers Platt Churchill, *The Anglo-Russian Convention of 1907* (Cedar Rapids: Torch Press, 1939); Beryl Williams, "Great Britain and Russia, 1905 to the 1907 Convention," in Hinsley, ed., *British Foreign Policy Under Grey*, 133–48.

92. Quoted in Roberts, *Salisbury*, 770.

93. See John Gooch, "Sir George Clarke's Career at the Committee of Imperial Defence," 560–61; Williamson, *Politics of Grand Strategy*, 95.

94. General Staff Report (1907), quoted in Williams, "Great Britain and Russia," 135–36. See also Beryl J. Williams, "The Strategic Background to the Anglo-Russian Entente of August 1907," *The Historical Journal* 9, no. 3 (1966), 365, 372.

95. Mackay argues that as a result of these vulnerabilities, the Balfour government became "anxious to minimize the possibility of a conflict" through "an accommodation with Russia." Mackay, *Balfour*, 124.

96. Sanderson to Scott (April 12, 1901), quoted in Otte, *Foreign Office Mind*, 265. Sanderson likewise declared, "The process of working in constant antagonism [with Russia] is too expensive." Sanderson to Spring-Rice (August 6, 1907), quoted in Williams, "Great Britain and Russia," 137.

97. See Mackay, *Balfour*, 171; Rolo, "Lansdowne," 167; Otte, *Foreign Office Mind*, 296.

98. Grey Minute (July 16, 1907), quoted in Williams, "Great Britain and Russia," 137. The Indian secretary Lord Morely likewise admitted, "That is the fundamental argument for the Convention for we have not got the men to spare and that's the plain truth of it." Morely to Minto (September 19, 1907), quoted in Monger, *End of Isolation*, 285.

99. Hardinge to Nicolson (September 4, 1907) and Hardinge to Grey (April 26, 1906), quoted in Otte, *Foreign Office Mind*, 305.

100. See Williams, "Great Britain and Russia," 140–43.

101. Grey emphasized his desire to secure "a good understanding with Germany," although "it must be one which will not imperil those which we have with France and Russia." Grey to Goschen (September 1, 1909), *BD*, VI, no. 195.

102. See Lansdowne to Bertie (May 17, 1905), *BD*, III, no. 94. Rolo describes Lansdowne's approach as "a policy of bolstering France without giving any categorical guarantees." Rolo, "Lansdowne," 167–68.

103. Grey warned the German ambassador that if Berlin forced war on Paris, "public feeling would be so strong that it would be impossible to be neutral." Grey to Lascelles (January 9, 1906), *BD*, III, no. 229). Conversely, he told the French ambassador that he "did not think people in England would be prepared to fight in order to put France in possession of Morocco." Grey to Bertie (January 31, 1906), *BD*, III, no. 219.

104. He encouraged these compromises while simultaneously declaring "cordial co-operation with France in all parts of the world remains a cardinal point of British policy." Grey to Bertie (March 15, 1906), *BD*, III, no. 357.

105. As Grey explained, "The balance of power in Europe was preserved by the present grouping, and I should not think of wishing to disturb it." Grey to Cartwright (January 6, 1909), *BD*, V, no. 505.

106. Grey even promised to consider a future revision of the Straits question in Russia's favor. Through this concession, Grey "averted a collision between his Russian and Turkish policies." David W. Sweet, "The Bosnian Crisis," in *British Foreign Policy Under Sir Edward Grey*, ed. Hinsley, 181.

107. See Sweet, "Bosnian Crisis," 190.

108. Hardinge to Edward (March 26, 1909), quoted in Lowe and Dockrill, *Mirage of Power*, 84.

109. Grey told the French that British military support would only be forthcoming in a possible war if France had "no reasonable and honourable way of avoiding it." Grey to Goschen (March 9, 1912), *BD*, VI, no. 531.

110. Grey to Bertie (July 20, 1911), *BD*, VII, no. 405.

111. Grey emphasized "the impossibility of our standing aside, and disinteresting ourselves, if changes in the situation developed adversely to our interests." Grey to Goschen (July 21, 1911), *BD*, VII, no. 411.

112. See Keith M. Wilson, *Empire and Continent: Studies in British Foreign Policy from the 1880s to the First World War* (London: Mansell, 1987), 95; and Phillip M. H. Bell, *France and Britain, 1900–1940: Entente and Estrangement* (New York: Longman, 1996), 47.

113. See Zara Steiner, "The Foreign Office under Sir Edward Grey, 1905–1914" in Hinsley, ed., *British Foreign Policy Under Grey*, 51.

114. See Richard J. Crampton, "The Balkans, 1909–1914," in *British Foreign Policy Under Grey*, ed. Hinsley, 269.

115. Germany adopted amendments to its existing naval law in both 1905 and 1907 that accelerated capital ship construction. See Jonathan Steinberg, "The German Background to Anglo-German Relations, 1905–1914," in *British Foreign Policy Under Grey*, ed. Hinsley, 201–9.

116. Grey Memorandum (July 31, 1908), *BD*, VI, appendix III.

117. See Crowe Memorandum (January 1, 1907), *BD*, III, appendix A.

118. Efforts were made at the 1906 Hague Conference, in both 1909 and 1910 after a change of ministries in Berlin, and as part of the Haldane Mission in 1912. See David W. Sweet, "Great Britain and Germany, 1905–1911," in *British Foreign Policy Under Grey*, ed. Hinsley, 218; Robbins, *Sir Edward Grey*, 234; Steiner, *Britain and the Origins of the First World War*, 97.

119. Grey Minute on Goschen to Grey (April 11, 1910), *BD*, VI, no. 344.

120. Richard T. B. Langhorne, "Great Britain and Germany, 1911–1914," in Hinsley, ed., *British Foreign Policy Under Grey*, 300. The permanent undersecretary warned the Germans were seeking to "entangle us in some engagement which would absolutely prevent us from having full liberty of action." Nicolson to Goschen (April 1, 1912), *BD*, VI, no. 562.

121. See Langhorne, "Great Britain and Germany," 311; Marian Kent, "Constantinople and Asiatic Turkey," in *British Foreign Policy Under Sir Edward Grey*, ed. Francis Harry Hinsley (New York: Cambridge University Press, 2008), 152–54.

122. Nicolson to Goschen (February 28, 1911), quoted in Otte, *Foreign Office Mind*, 353.

123. See Robbins, *Sir Edward Grey*, 133; Chamberlain, *Pax Britannica*, 165; Steiner, *Britain and the Origins of the First World War*, 41.

124. Keith G. Robbins, "The Foreign Secretary, the Cabinet, Parliament and the Parties," in *British Foreign Policy Under Grey*, ed. Hinsley, 8.

125. Robbins, *Sir Edward Grey*, 252.

126. Chamberlain, *Pax Britannica*, 165. Otte likewise concludes, "Britain's diplomatic elite provided a strong element of continuity in the country's foreign policy." Otte, *Foreign Office Mind*, 407.

127. Hamilton argues that "Grey displayed a greater readiness than his immediate predecessor to accept the Anglo-French understanding as a fundamental and permanent element in Britain's relations with the continental powers." Keith A. Hamilton, "Great Britain and France, 1905–1911," in *British Foreign Policy Under Grey*, ed. Hinsley, 113.

128. Steiner, *Britain and the Origins of the First World War*, 39.

129. Although it is possible to overstate the differences between the liberal imperialists and the rest of the party, see George L. Bernstein, "Campbell-Bannerman and the Liberal Imperialists," *Journal of British Studies* 23, no. 1 (Autumn 1983), 118–19; Cameron Hazlehurst, "Asquith as Prime Minister, 1908–1916," *English Historical Review* 85, no. 336 (July 1970), 522.

130. Steiner, *Britain and the Origins of the First World War*, 154.

131. As Steiner concludes, "Sir Edward Grey was his own master." Steiner, "The Foreign Office under Sir Edward Grey," 69.

132. Balfour to Brodrick (October 28, 1903), quoted in Judd, *Balfour and the British Empire*, 240.

133. Quoted in David W. Sweet and Richard T. B. Langhorne, "Great Britain and Russia, 1907–1914," in *British Foreign Policy Under Grey*, ed. Hinsley, 236.

134. Grey to Scott (September 21, 1912), quoted in Neilson "'Control the Whirlwind': Sir Edward Grey as Foreign Secretary," 141.

135. Selborne Memorandum (January 17, 1901), quoted in Monger, *End of Isolation*, 11.

136. Grey Minute (February 10, 1909), quoted in Steiner, *Britain and the Origins of the First World War*, 48.

137. Lansdowne to Balfour (December 12, 1901), quoted in Monger "End of Isolation," 120.

138. Lord Morely, quoted in Ira Klein, "The Anglo-Russian Convention and the Problem of Central Asia," *Journal of British Studies* 11, no. 1 (November 1971), 134.

139. Grey to Hardinge (January 28, 1912), quoted in Sweet and Langhorne, "Great Britain and Russia," 251.

140. For the strong version of this argument, which portrays Grey as naïve and confused, see Luigi Albertini, *The Origins of the War of 1914*, trans. Isabella Massey (London: Oxford University Press, 1953), 2:197. A milder version of this argument, which sympathizes with Grey but views his diplomatic balancing act as impossible, see Michael Ekstein, "Some Notes on Sir Edward Grey's Policy in July 1914," *Historical Journal* 15, no. 2 (June 1972): 348; J. Paul Harris, "Great Britain," in Richard Hamilton and Holder Herwig, eds., *The Origins of World War I* (New York: Cambridge University Press, 2003), 294.

141. See, for example, Paul Schroeder, "World War I as Galloping Gertie: A Reply to Joachim Remak," *Journal of Modern History* 44, no. 3 (September 1972): 323–25; Wilson, "Grey," 188–89.

142. See Grey's candid conversation with the German ambassador described in Grey to Rumbold (July 6, 1914), *BD*, XI, no. 32 See also Robbins, *Sir Edward Grey*, 287; Keith Wilson, "Britain," in Keith Wilson, ed., *Decisions for War 1914* (New York: St. Martin's Press, 1995), 186.

143. As a ploy to extract British concessions, German policymakers deliberately promoted the misperception that there were distinct peace and war factions in Berlin. See Michael Ekstein, "Sir Edward Grey and Imperial Germany," *Journal of Contemporary History* 6, no. 3 (1971): 126, 128.

144. See Ekstein, "Some Notes on Sir Edward Grey's Policy in July 1914," 323–24.

145. Quoted in Steiner, *Britain and the Origins of the First World War*, 225.

146. This warning came two days after Grey had cautioned that in the event of war, "[England] would place herself unconditionally by the side of France and Russia." Quoted in Wilson "Britain," 187, 190.

147. Quoted in Holger H. Herwig "Germany," in Keith Wilson, ed., *Decisions for War 1914* (New York: St. Martin's Press, 1995), 181.

148. See Gerhard Ritter, *The Schlieffen Plan: A Critique of a Myth* (Westport: Praeger, 1958), 161–64.

149. Chamberlain, *Pax Britannica*, 175. Neilson reaches a similar conclusion: "The impetus for war came from Vienna and Berlin, not from London." Neilson, "Grey as Foreign Secretary," 141. Steiner concurs that "the British role was of secondary importance." Steiner, *Britain and the Origins of the First World War*, 126.

150. Barbara Tuchman, *The Guns of August* (New York: Random House, 2004), 145–46.

151. See Williamson, *Politics of Grand Strategy*, 48, 77–78, 90.

152. See Williamson, *Politics of Grand Strategy*, 172–73, 366.

153. Williamson, *Politics of Grand Strategy*, 244–47, 320–321.

154. This lack of influence was "inherent in Britain's situation at that time." See Porter, *Britain, Europe, and the World*, 76.

155. Joachim Remak, "The Third Balkan War: Origins Reconsidered," *Journal of Modern History* 43, no. 3 (Fall 1971), 366.

156. Quoted in Monger, *End of Isolation*, 13. His language may have been figurative, but strikingly Britain was becoming the third ranked power in the system when he said it.

157. See David Stevenson, *Armaments and the Coming of War: Europe 1904–1914* (New York: Oxford University Press, 1996), 2–8; David Herrmann, *The Arming of Europe and the Making of the First World War* (Princeton: Princeton University Press, 1996), 234.

6. A Descending Whirligig

1. Figure cited in Dietrich Geyer, *Russian Imperialism: The Interaction of Domestic and Foreign Policy, 1860–1914* (New Haven: Yale University Press, 1987), 5.

2. Quoted in Alexander Polunov, *Russia in the Nineteenth Century: Autocracy, Reform, and Social Change, 1814–1914* (New York: M.E. Sharpe, 2005), 165.

3. As Pintner notes, from 1725 to 1850, Russia was successful in nearly every major conflict; from 1850–1917, it almost never was. See Walter Pintner, "The Burden of Defense in Imperial Russia, 1725–1914," *Russian Review* 43, no. 3 (July 1984): 231.

4. See Alfred Rieber, "Persistent Factors in Russian Foreign Policy: An Interpretive Essay," in *Imperial Russian Foreign Policy*, ed. Hugh Ragsdale and Valerii Nikolaevich Ponomarev (New York: Cambridge University Press, 1993), 356.

5. A term derived from Gorchakov's famous quip—"La Russie ne boude pas, mais se recueille"—which serves as the epigraph to this chapter. Quoted in David Schimmelpenninck van der Oye, "Russian Foreign Policy, 1815–1917," in *The Cambridge History of Russia, Volume II: Imperial Russia, 1689–1917*, ed. Dominic Lieven (New York: Cambridge University Press, 2006), 561. See also Barbara Jelavich, *A Century of Russian Foreign Policy, 1814–1914* (New York: Lippincott, 1964), 134; and Andrei Tsygankov, *Russia and the West from Alexander to Putin: Honor in International Relations* (New York: Cambridge University Press, 2014), 149–50.

6. See Geoffrey Hoskin, *Russia and the Russians: A History*, 2nd ed. (Cambridge: Harvard University Press, 2011), 315.

7. For debt estimates, see Bruce Menning, *Bayonets Before Bullets: The Imperial Russian Army, 1861–1914* (Bloomington: Indiana University Press, 1992), 11; W. Bruce Lincoln, *The Great*

Reforms: Autocracy, Bureaucracy, and the Politics of Change in Imperial Russia (DeKalb: Northern Illinois University Press, 1990), 147.

8. See Menning, *Bayonets before Bullets*, 11.

9. As Miliutin observed, "The requirements of foreign policy dictate, in large measure, the lower limits below which it is impossible to permit the Empire's military strength to fall." Miliutin in 1862, quoted in Lincoln, *Great Reforms*, 150.

10. Quoted in Alfred Rieber, "Interest-Group Politics in the Era of the Great Reforms," in *Russia's Great Reforms, 1855–1881*, ed. Ben Eklof, John Bushnell, and Larissa Zakharova (Bloomington: Indiana University Press, 1994), 74.

11. German mobilization and technological gaps made Russian military officials profoundly alarmed about the Polish salient and Western front. See David Alan Rich, *The Tsar's Colonels: Professionalism, Strategy, and Subversion in Late Imperial Russia* (Cambridge: Harvard University Press, 1998), 4, 86–87, 90–94, 218–19; Alex Marshall, *The Russian General Staff and Asia, 1800–1917* (New York: Routledge, 2006), 68, 95.

12. See Firuz Kazemzadeh, *Russia and Britain in Persia, 1864–1914: A Study in Imperialism* (New Haven: Yale University Press, 1968), 40.

13. Quoted in Geyer, *Russian Imperialism*, 76.

14. Quoted in Hosking, *Russia and the Russians*, 287.

15. Figure cited in William Fuller, *Civil-Military Conflict in Imperial Russia, 1881–1914* (Princeton: Princeton University Press, 1985), 60.

16. Quoted in Jacob Kipp, "Strategic Railroads and the Dilemmas of Modernization," in *Reforming the Tsar's Army: Military Innovation in Imperial Russia from Peter the Great to the Revolution*, ed. David Schimmelpenninck van der Oye and Bruce Menning (New York: Cambridge University Press, 2004), 102.

17. Quoted in Richard Weeks, "Peter Shuvalov and the Congress of Berlin: A Reinterpretation," *Journal of Modern History* 51, no. 1 (March 1979): D1060.

18. See Martin Smith Anderson, *The Eastern Question, 1774–1923: A Study in International Relations* (New York: Macmillan Press, 1966), 201, 207; William Langer, *European Alliances and Alignments 1871–1890*, 2nd ed. (New York: Vintage Books, 1950), 172. There was a push to no avail by Prince Alexander Bariatinskii and others to expand the conflict to India for a more favorable outcome. Others also campaigned for expansion in vain. See Marshall, *Russian General Staff and Asia*, 36, 46.

19. Quoted in David MacKenzie, *The Serbs and Russian Panslavism, 1875–1878* (Ithaca: Cornell University Press, 1967), 327.

20. Geyer, *Russian Imperialism*, 117.

21. Quoted in William Fuller, *Strategy and Power in Russia, 1600–1914* (New York: The Free Press, 1992), 337–38, emphasis in original. See also George Kennan, *The Decline of Bismarck's European Order: Franco-Russian Relations 1875–1890* (Princeton: Princeton University Press, 1979), 362.

22. Pares describes the policy of Alexander III toward Bulgaria as "that of a bear with a sore head." Bernard Pares, *A History of Russia* (New York: Alfred Knopf, 1953), 432.

23. Morier to Rosebery (July 21, 1886), quoted in Barbara Jelavich, *Russia's Balkan Entanglements, 1806–1914* (New York: Cambridge University Press, 2004), 193.

24. Kennan, *Decline of Bismarck's European Order*, 202.

25. Quoted in Flemming Splidsboel-Hansen, "Past and Future Meet: Aleksandr Gorchakov and Russian Foreign Policy," *Europe-Asia Studies* 54, no. 3 (May 2002): 380.

26. Quoted in Astrid Tuminez, *Russian Nationalism Since 1856: Ideology and the Making of Foreign Policy* (Lanham, Md.: Rowman and Littlefield, 2000), 110.

27. Quoted in David Schimmelpenninck van der Oye, *Toward the Rising Sun: Russian Ideologies of Empire and the Path to War with Japan* (DeKalb: Northern Illinois University Press, 2001), 115.

28. Jomini to Giers (July 4, 1888), quoted in Jelavich, *Russia's Balkan Entanglements*, 195.

29. Quoted in George Kennan, *The Fateful Alliance: France, Russia, and the Coming of the First World War* (New York: Pantheon Books, 1984), 147. It is worth noting that there was minor Russian involvement in Ethiopia in the 1890s, but little came of Russian contact with Africa. See

Roger Kanet, "The Soviet Union and Sub-Saharan Africa: Communist Policy in Africa, 1917–1965" (PhD diss., Princeton University, 1966), 9–14.

30. Fuller, *Civil-Military Conflict*, 49.

31. Quoted in Menning, *Bayonets before Bullets*, 91.

32. See William N. Medlicott, *Bismarck, Gladstone, and the Concert of Europe* (London: Athlone Press University of London, 1956), 244; Geyer, *Russian Imperialism*, 112.

33. Fuller, *Strategy and Power*, 332.

34. Pintner, "Burden of Defense," 258.

35. See Fuller, *Civil-Military Conflict*, 49; John Bushnell, "Miliutin and the Balkan War: Military Reform vs. Military Performance," in *Russia's Great Reforms, 1855–1881*, ed. Ben Eklof, John Bushnell, and Larissa Zakharova (Bloomington: Indiana University Press, 1994), 139–58.

36. Quoted in Fuller, *Strategy and Power*, 338.

37. Fuller, *Civil-Military Conflict*, 61

38. Miliutin, quoted in Menning, *Bayonets before Bullets*, 11.

39. For figures on active versus reserve forces, see Menning, *Bayonets before Bullets*, 29, 100, 108–9.

40. The tsar announced the policy in 1870, but it took several years for it to be fully approved. See Robert Baumann, "Universal Service Reform: Conception to Implementation, 1873–1883," in *Reforming the Tsar's Army: Military Innovation in Imperial Russia from Peter the Great to the Revolution*, ed. David Schimmelpenninck van der Oye and Bruce Menning (New York: Cambridge University Press, 2004), 12; Bushnell, "Miliutin and the Balkan War," 151.

41. See Fuller, *Strategy and Power*, 283–84.

42. David MacKenzie, *Imperial Dreams, Harsh Realities: Tsarist Russian Foreign Policy, 1815–1917* (New York: Cengage, 1994), 57. See also David Stone, *A Military History of Russia: From Ivan the Terrible to the War in Chechnya* (Westport: Praeger, 2006), 136.

43. See Bushnell, "Miliutin and the Balkan War," 144–45.

44. See Fuller, *Strategy and Power*, 323–24.

45. See Menning, *Bayonets before Bullets*, 111–12.

46. See Menning, *Bayonets before Bullets*, 104–7; Chris Bellamy, *Red God of War: Soviet Artillery and Rocket Forces* (London: Brassey's Defence Publishers, 1986), 22–25.

47. See Fuller, *Strategy and Power*, 339–40; Menning, *Bayonets before Bullets*, 116–20; Geyer, *Russian Imperialism*, 33–42.

48. Obruchev to Giers (October 27, 1883), quoted in Fuller, *Strategy and Power*, 339.

49. See Fuller *Civil-Military Conflict*, 54; and Menning, *Bayonets before Bullets*, 114.

50. See Forrestt Miller, *Dmitrii Miliutin and the Reform Era in Russia* (Nashville: Vanderbilt University Press, 1968), 86; Lincoln, *Great Reforms*, 148, 152, 154; Rich, *Tsar's Colonels*, 68–71.

51. See Fuller, *Civil-Military Conflict*, 9–10; Menning, *Bayonets before Bullets*, 33–38.

52. Figure cited in Lincoln, *Great Reforms*, 154.

53. See Walter Pintner, "Reformability in the Age of Reform and Counterreform, 1855–1894," in *Reform in Russia and the U.S.S.R.: Past and Prospects*, ed. Robert Crummey (Chicago: University of Illinois Press, 1989), 96–97; John Steinberg, *All the Tsar's Men: Russia's General Staff and the Fate of the Empire, 1898–1914* (Baltimore: Johns Hopkins University Press, 2010), 38.

54. See Rich, *Tsar's Colonels*, 110–11, 168; Menning, *Bayonets before Bullets*, 98; and Matitiahu Mayzel, "The Formation of the Russian General Staff, 1880–1917: A Social Study," *Cahiers du Monde Russe et Soviétique* 16, nos. 3–4 (July-December 1975): 297–321.

55. See Rich, *Tsar's Colonels*, 179–81; Menning, *Bayonets before Bullets*, 99; Carl Van Dyke, *Russian Imperial Military Doctrine and Education, 1832–1914* (Westport: Praeger, 1990), 95–96.

56. See Menning *Bayonets before Bullets*, 103, Fuller *Civil Military Conflict*, 12; Hosking, *Russia and the Russians*, 195.

57. See Walter Pintner, "The Nobility and the Officer Corps in the Nineteenth Century," in *The Military and Society in Russia, 1450–1917*, ed. Eric Lohr and Marshall Poe (Boston: Brill, 2002), 241–52; Brian Taylor, *Politics and the Russian Army: Civil-Military Relations, 1689–2000* (New York: Cambridge University Press, 2003), 58.

58. See Fuller, *Civil-Military Conflict*, 60–62.

59. See Pintner, "The Burden of Defense in Imperial Russia," 249–50, 258; Fuller, *Civil-Military Conflict*, 67.

60. Witte pursued this policy ambivalently. See Olga Crisp, "Some Problems of French Investment in Russian Joint-Stock Companies, 1894–1914," *Slavonic and East European Review* 35, no. 84 (December 1956): 237–39; and Geyer, *Russian Imperialism*, 146.

61. See Olga Crisp, "Some Problems of French Investment in Russian Joint-Stock Companies," 199; Geyer, *Russian Imperialism*, 148.

62. Figures cited in Geyer, *Russian Imperialism*, 37. See also Malcolm E. Falkus, *The Industrialisation of Russia, 1700–1914* (London: MacMillan, 1972), 54.

63. On Russian railroads and conflicting economic and strategic imperatives, see Felix Patrikeeff and Harold Shukman, *Railways and the Russo-Japanese War: Transporting War* (New York: Routledge, 2007); Jacob Kipp, "Strategic Railroads and the Dilemmas of Modernization," in *Reforming the Tsar's Army: Military Innovation in Imperial Russia from Peter the Great to the Revolution*, ed. David Schimmelpenninck van der Oye and Bruce Menning (New York: Cambridge University Press, 2004), 82–103.

64. Figures cited in Schimmelpenninck van der Oye, *Toward the Rising Sun*, 76. There were of course many factors that caused the Russian growth spurt in the 1890s, and that spurt is sometimes exaggerated, but previous reforms made a significant, if secondary, contribution. See Peter Gatrell, "The Meaning of the Great Reforms in Russian Economic History," in *Russia's Great Reforms, 1855–1881*, ed. Ben Eklof, John Bushnell, Larissa Zakharova (Bloomington: Indiana University Press, 1994), 85, 99.

65. See Polunov, *Russia in the Nineteenth Century*, 196.

66. Figures cited in John M. Hobson, "The Military-Extraction Gap and the Wary Titan: The Fiscal Sociology of British Defence Policy, 1870–1913," *Journal of European Economic History*, 22, no. 3 (1993): 464–65.

67. Fuller, *Strategy and Power*, 329. See also Menning, *Bayonets before Bullets*, 94.

68. Rich, *Tsar's Colonels*, 209.

69. During an important strategic conference, Obruchev reported that "the armed forces of Russia in their present condition [were] insufficient for the defense of her security." Quoted in Fuller, *Strategy and Power*, 296. See also Rich, *Tsar's Colonels*, 97–99.

70. Quoted in Marshall, *Russian General Staff and Asia*, 68. Russia still spent major funds reinforcing Asia, but this money paled in comparison to that spent on the west. See ibid., 70–71, 76.

71. See Fuller, *Civil-Military Conflict*, 15; and Marshall, *Russian General Staff and Asia*, 68.

72. Quoted in Geyer, *Russian Imperialism*, 117.

73. Ivo Lederer, "Russia and the Balkans," in *Russian Foreign Policy: Essays in Historical Perspective*, ed. Ivo Lederer (New Haven: Yale University Press, 1962), 438.

74. Russian decision-makers had toyed with this idea idly for years. See Anderson, *Eastern Question*, 257, 259, 263; A. J. P. Taylor, *The Struggle for Mastery in Europe 1848–1918* (New York: Oxford University Press, 1977), 270, 359; William Langer, *The Diplomacy of Imperialism, 1890–1902*, 2nd ed. (New York: Alfred Knopf, 1951), 338–45.

75. Fuller, *Strategy and Power*, 371–72.

76. Germany was thrilled and the Austrians surprised by Russia's generous terms. See John White, *Transition to Global Rivalry: Alliance Diplomacy and the Quadruple Entente, 1895–1907* (New York: Cambridge University Press, 1995), 45; F. Roy Bridge, *From Sadowa to Sarajevo: The Foreign Policy of Austria-Hungary, 1866–1914* (New York: Routledge, 1972), 232–33. It was not easy to maintain calm. In 1903, the tsar and the Austrian emperor met at Mürzsteg to again deflate Balkan tension. See Ian Nish, *The Origins of the Russo-Japanese War* (New York: Longman, 1985), 187; Duncan Perry, "Death of a Russian Consul: Macedonia 1903," *Russian History* 7, nos. 1–2 (1980), 212.

77. Versions of this cynical diplomacy can be observed in Russia's annexation of Tashkent (1865), Bukhara (1866), Samarkand (1868), Khiva (1873), and Kokand (1875). See Firuz Kazemzadeh, "Russia and the Middle East," in *Russian Foreign Policy: Essays in Historical Perspective*, ed. Ivo Lederer (New Haven: Yale University Press, 1962), 497–98.

78. Russia also stayed on the sideline when Britain intervened in Persia that same year. Tsar Alexander II explained: "Our collision with that power [Britain] would be a signal for a general and stubborn war under circumstances and in a situation extremely unfavorable to us." Quoted in Kazemzadeh, *Russia and Britain in Persia*, 51; cf. Barbara Jelavich, "Great Britain and the Russian Acquisition of Batum, 1878–1886," *Slavonic and East European Review* 48, no. 110 (January 1970): 49.

79. Rose Louise Greaves, *Persia and the Defence of India 1884–1892: A Study in the Foreign Policy of the Third Marquis of Salisbury* (London: Athlone Press The University of London, 1959), 76.

80. See Greaves, *Persia and the Defence of India 1884–1892*, 130.

81. Quoted in Geyer, *Russian Imperialism*, 114. See also Taylor, *Struggle for Mastery in Europe*, 301.

82. See Fuller *Strategy and Power*, 364–66.

83. Lamsdorf report to Emperor, 1897, quoted in Fuller, *Strategy and Power in Russia*, 364.

84. Sarah C. Paine, *Imperial Rivals: China, Russia, and Their Disputed Frontiers* (New York: M. E. Sharpe, 1996), 135, also 141, and 157–59.

85. As the historian John LeDonne argues, "the Russians, recognizing that they had more to gain from a friendly policy toward China, retreated." John LeDonne, *The Russian Empire and the World, 1700–1917: The Geopolitics of Expansion and Containment* (New York: Oxford University Press, 1996), 191.

86. Quoted in Paine, *Imperial Rivals*, 163.

87. See Lawrence Battistini, "The Korean Problem in the Nineteenth Century," *Monumenta Nipponica* 8, no. 1/2 (1952): 58; and Alexander Lukin, "Russian Views of Korea, China, and the Regional Order in Northeast Asia," in *Korea at the Center: Dynamics of Regionalism in Northeast Asia*, ed. Charles Armstrong, Gilbert Rozman, Samuel Kim, and Stephen Kotkin (New York: M. E. Sharp, 2006), 24.

88. See Geyer, *Russian Imperialism*, 94–95; Anderson, *Eastern Question*, 216; Medlicott, *Bismarck, Gladstone, and the Concert of Europe*, 38, 257.

89. See Geyer, *Russian Imperialism*, 56–57; Taylor, *Struggle for Mastery in Europe*, 267; Glenn Snyder, *Alliance Politics* (Ithaca: Cornell University Press, 1997), 101.

90. See Snyder, *Alliance Politics*, 102, and 105.

91. Quoted in Medlicott, *Bismarck, Gladstone, and the Concert of Europe*, 334. In 1884, Giers triumphed over nationalist elements, including the Russian ambassador Peter Saburov, who wanted the alliance modified from a defensive agreement to an offensive tool that could help Russia seize the Turkish Straits. See MacKenzie, *Imperial Dreams*, 117.

92. Quoted in Kennan, *Fateful Alliance*, 147.

93. Quoted in Polunov, *Russia in the Nineteenth Century*, 170.

94. See Anderson, *Eastern Question*, 235; Kennan, *Decline of Bismarck's European Order*, 209–10.

95. See Melvin Wren, "Pobedonostsev and Russian Influence in the Balkans, 1881–1888," *Journal of Modern History* 19, no. 2 (June 1947), 141; William Langer, "The Franco-Russian Alliance (1890–1894)," *Slavonic Review* 3, no. 9 (March 1925), 569.

96. See M. P. Hornik, "The Mission of Sir Henry Drummond-Wolff to Constantinople, 1885–1887," *English Historical Review* 55, no. 220 (October 1940): 598–623; Taylor, *Struggle for Mastery in Europe*, 315; Anderson, *Eastern Question*, 250. There was some Russian retaliation: a secret agreement in 1887 with Persia not to build rail lines with another power "*before consulting with His Majesty the Emperor.*" Quoted in Greaves, *Persia and the Defence of India 1884–1892*, 149.

97. See Andreas Dorpalen, "Tsar Alexander III and the Boulanger Crisis in France," *Journal of Modern History* 23, no. 2 (June 1951): 131; Geyer, *Russian Imperialism*, 153; Kennan, *Decline of Bismarck's European Order*, 342. Not long after this, Russia forbade foreigners (read Germans) from buying Russian real estate. See William Langer, *The Franco-Russian Alliance 1890–1894* (Cambridge: Harvard University Press, 1929), 32.

98. See Fuller, *Strategy and Power*, 351.

99. See Kennan, *Fateful Alliance*, 76.

100. See Gordon Martel, "The Near East in the Balance of Power: The Repercussions of the Kaulla Incident in 1893," *Middle Eastern Studies* 16, no. 2 (May 1980): 25.

101. See E. Malcolm Carroll, *French Public Opinion and Foreign Affairs, 1870–1914* (New York: The Century Co., 1931), 153; Snyder, *Alliance Politics*, 111; Kennan, *Decline of Bismarck's European Order*, 393–95, 406.

102. See Langer, *Franco-Russian Alliance*, 104.

103. See Langer, "Franco-Russian Alliance," 563–64, 559.

104. See Kennan, *Fateful Alliance*, 175; and Langer, *Franco-Russian Alliance*, 393. By 1899, both the Balkans and Alsace-Lorraine would be under the treaty's umbrella. See Charles Porter, *The Career of Théophile Delcassé* (Philadelphia: University of Pennsylvania Press, 1936), 144. It was a secret because Russia did not want to endanger negotiations for a commercial agreement with Germany or to tempt a German preventive attack. See Snyder, *Alliance Politics*, 120–21; and Langer, *Franco-Russian Alliance*, 263–326.

105. See Kennan, *Fateful Alliance*, 181.

106. On the commercial treaty, see Kennan, *Fateful Alliance*, 245; and Langer, *Franco-Russian Alliance*, 334.

107. See Langer, *Franco-Russian Alliance*, 355.

108. See Polunov, *Russia in the Nineteenth Century*, 173.

109. Menning, *Bayonets before Bullets*, 119, see also 111, 117, 120.

110. Fuller, *Strategy and Power*, 362.

111. Rich, *Tsar's Colonels*, 84, see also 93–96.

112. Fuller, *Strategy and Power*, 332.

113. Geyer, *Russian Imperialism*, 113.

114. See Fuller, *Civil-Military Conflict*, 11; Pintner, "Reformability in the Age of Reform and Counterreform," 96–97; Steinberg, *All the Tsar's Men*, 38.

115. Quoted in MacKenzie, *Imperial Dreams*, 97. Giers likewise claimed that that the Turkoman territories were conquered "by necessity to ensure a defensive position against English hostility." Geyer, *Russian Imperialism*, 114. Our translation.

116. Quoted in Fuller, *Strategy and Power*, 301–2.

117. MacKenzie, *Imperial Dreams*, 140.

118. On this incident, see also Nish, *Origins of the Russo-Japanese War*, 39; Langer, *Diplomacy of Imperialism*, 476.

119. White, *Transition to Global Rivalry*, 86.

120. See Geyer, *Russian Imperialism*, 199; Lukin, "Russian Views of Korea, China, and the Regional Order in Northeast Asia," 26; Nish, *Origins of the Russo-Japanese War*, 47–48. The Russians put little stock in the deal—the foreign minister, Baron Roman Romanovich Rosen, referred to it as "a rather lame and pointless convention." Quoted in Ernest Batson Price, *The Russo-Japanese Treaties of 1907–1916 Concerning Manchuria and Mongolia* (Baltimore: Johns Hopkins Press, 1933), 19.

121. See White, *Transition to Global Rivalry*, 75.

122. The Russian Far East was economically a big loss. See Patrikeeff and Shukman, *Railways and the Russo-Japanese War*, 2; Fuller, *Strategy and Power*, 374.

123. Quoted in Schimmelpenninck van der Oye, *Toward the Rising Sun*, 192. The diplomatic cost was significant, China, Japan, the United Kingdom, and the United States condemned the move. See John Albert White, *The Diplomacy of the Russo-Japanese War* (Princeton: Princeton University Press, 1964), 54–58.

124. Quoted in Anatolii V. Ignatev, "The Foreign Policy of Russia in the Far East at the Turn of the Nineteenth and Twentieth Centuries," in *Imperial Russian Foreign Policy*, ed. Hugh Ragsdale (New York: Cambridge University Press, 1993), 257.

125. Bezobrazov was joined by such luminaries as the minister of the interior Vyacheslav Plehve, Admiral Yevgeni Alekseyev, Rear-Admiral Aleksei Abaza, Grand Duke Alexander Mikhailovich, and General Nnikolay Ivanov, but opposed by the most powerful ministers: Witte, Kuropatkin, and Lamsdorf. See Langer, *Diplomacy of Imperialism*, 748, 764–65; Marc Ferro, *Nicholas II: Last of the Tsars*, trans. Brian Pierce (New York: Oxford University Press, 1993), 65.

126. See Lukin, "Russian Views of Korea, China, and the Regional Order in Northeast Asia," 29.

127. Quoted in David MacLaren McDonald, *United Government and Foreign Policy in Russia 1900–1914* (Cambridge: Harvard University Press, 1992), 55–56. For an alternative interpretation, see Dale Copeland, *Economic Interdependence and War* (Princeton: Princeton University Press, 2015), 109–22.

128. See Nish, *Origins of the Russo-Japanese War*, 242.

129. See Wren, "Pobedonostsev and Russian Influence in the Balkans," 141; Taylor, *Struggle for Mastery in Europe*, 323.

130. High-level warnings of strategic overextension and straitened economic circumstances were unanimous and continuous. See Kazemzadeh, *Russia and Britain in Persia, 1864–1914*, 465; Fuller, *Strategy and Power*, 395; Nish, *Origins of the Russo-Japanese War*, 164; Andrew Malozemoff, *Russian Far Eastern Policy 1881–1904, with Special Emphasis on the Causes of the Russo-Japanese War* (Berkeley: University of California Press, 1958), 248–49.

131. Figure cited in Schimmelpenninck van der Oye, "Russian Foreign Policy" 567.

132. Quoted in Fuller, *Strategy and Power*, 373.

133. Quoted in Fuller, *Strategy and Power in Russia*, 370. See also Schimmelpenninck van der Oye, *Toward the Rising Sun*, 155–56.

134. Quoted in Schimmelpenninck van der Oye, *Toward the Rising Sun*, 192.

135. Quoted in MacKenzie, *Imperial Dreams*, 144.

136. MacKenzie, *Imperial Dreams, Harsh Realities*, 135.

137. LeDonne, *Russian Empire and the World*, 211.

138. Menning, *Bayonets Before Bullets*, 92.

7. "Les Jeux Sont Faits"

1. See, for example, Bertrand Taithe, *Defeated Flesh: Medicine, Welfare, and Warfare in the Making of Modern France* (Lanham: Rowman and Littlefield, 1999), 4–17; Karine Varley, *Under the Shadow of Defeat: The War of 1870–71 in French Memory* (New York: Palgrave Macmillan, 2008), chap. 1; Rachel Chrastil, *Organizing for War: France, 1870–1914* (Baton Rouge: Louisiana State University Press, 2010), 38–49.

2. Quoted in E. Malcolm Carroll, *French Public Opinion and Foreign Affairs, 1870–1914* (New York: The Century Co., 1931), 93. See also William Langer, *European Alliances and Alignments 1871–1890*, 2nd ed. (New York: Vintage Books, 1950), 284; David Watson, "France, Europe, and the World: International Politics since 1880," in *Modern France: 1880–2002*, ed. James McMillan (New York: Oxford University Press, 2003), 104.

3. Quoted in Henri Brunschwig, *French Colonialism 1871–1914: Myths and Realities* (London: Pall Mall, 1966), 177.

4. The historian Jonathan House documents how "French soldiers remembered the first campaigns of the Franco-Prussian War, in which a colonially oriented French army failed to exploit its defensive success." Jonathan House, "The Decisive Attack: A New Look at French Infantry Tactics on the Eve of World War I," *Military Affairs* 40, no. 4 (December 1976): 164.

5. Lyons to Derby (October 31, 1876), quoted in John P. T. Bury, *Gambetta and the Third Republic* (New York: Longman, 1973), 329.

6. Quoted in Carroll, *French Public Opinion*, 74.

7. Varley, *Under the Shadow of Defeat*, 46.

8. Quoted in Jean-Marie Mayeur and Madeleine Rebérioux, *The Third Republic from its Origins to the Great War, 1871–1914*, trans. J. R. Foster (New York: Cambridge University Press, 1988), 126.

9. General Cosseron de Villenoisy, quoted in Alan Mitchell, *Victors and Vanquished: The German Influence on Army and Church in France after 1870* (Chapel Hill: University of North Carolina Press, 2011), 101.

10. Quoted in Christopher Andrew, *Théophile Delcassé and the Making of the Entente Cordiale: A Reappraisal of French Foreign Policy 1898–1905* (New York: Macmillan, 1968), 15–16.

11. Quoted in John P. T. Bury and Robert P. Tombs, *Thiers, 1797–1877: A Political Life* (Boston: Allen and Unwin, 1986), 217. Thiers similarly argued, "The true *revanche* of which we are thinking is the reconstitution of France." Quoted in Bury, *Gambetta and the Third Republic*, 328

12. Gambetta speech (September 1875), quoted in Bury, *Gambetta and the Third Republic*, 335.

13. Robert D. Anderson, *France 1870–1914: Politics and Society* (New York: Routledge, 1984), 144.

14. Quoted in Bury, *Gambetta and the Third Republic*, 332. An 1876 Republican campaign pamphlet likewise stated, "After the war and the invasion, the legacy of the last reign, France seeks repose." Quoted in Chrastil, *Organizing for War*, 38.

15. Quoted in Thomas Power, *Jules Ferry and the Renaissance of French Imperialism* (New York: King's Crown, 1944), 163

16. The Chamber of Deputies was so skeptical of intervention that Ferry referred to it as "simply a police operation." Brunschwig, *French Colonialism*, 55, cf. 570. See also Graham Stuart, *French Foreign Policy: From Fashoda to Sarajevo* (New York: Century Co., 1921), 13; Frederick Quinn, *The French Overseas Empire* (Westport: Praeger, 2000), 128.

17. See Quinn, *French Overseas Empire*, 128; and John F. V. Keiger, *France and the Origins of the First World War* (New York: St. Martin's Press, 1988), 10.

18. See Carroll, *French Public Opinion*, 101; Mayeur and Reberioux, *Third Republic from its Origins to the Great War*, 96–97; Frederick Schuman, *War and Diplomacy in the French Republic: An Inquiry into Political Motivations and the Control of Foreign Policy* (New York: AMS Press, 1970 [1931]), 88, 101.

19. See Ferry in *France: Empire and Republic, 1850–1940*, ed. David Thomson (New York: Harper Torch Books, 1968), 307–9; cf. Charles Porter, *The Career of Théophile Delcassé* (Philadelphia: University of Pennsylvania Press, 1936), 95; Brunschwig, *French Colonialism*, 89, 96, 103.

20. Quoted in John Dreifort, *Myopic Grandeur: The Ambivalence of French Foreign Policy toward the Far East, 1919–1945* (Kent, Ohio: Kent State University Press, 1991), 3.

21. Quoted in Power, *Jules Ferry*, 192.

22. A Paris mob smeared Ferry as "le Tonkinois" and nearly tossed him in the Seine. See Carroll, *French Public Opinion*, 103; Mayeur and Rebérioux, *Third Republic from its Origins to the Great War*, 97, cf. 99.

23. Quinn, *French Overseas Empire*, 113. The historian Charles Sowerwine likewise observes that "Ferry's colonialism was deeply unpopular . . . because Ferry continually misled the Chamber with over-optimistic reports." Sowerwine, *France since 1870: Culture, Society, and the Making of the Republic* (New York: Palgrave Macmillan, 2009), 38. Even Ferry recognized that the public had been "sickened" by "adventures" abroad. Quoted in Christopher M. Andrew and A. Sydney Kanya-Forstner, *The Climax of French Imperial Expansion, 1914–1924* (Stanford: Stanford University Press, 1981), 10.

24. As one newspaper put it, "For a couple of dubious mines in Indochina, Ferry is pawning off to Germany our security, our dignity, and our hopes." Quoted in Brendan Simms, *Europe: The Struggle for Supremacy, from 1453 to the Present* (New York: Basic Books, 2013), 259.

25. Quoted in Keiger, *France and the Origins of the First World War*, 10.

26. See Carroll, *French Public Opinion*, 101.

27. Quoted in Porter, *Career of Théophile Delcassé*, 44. For a similar quote from politician Georges Clemenceau, see Gabriel Hanotaux, *Contemporary France*, vol. 4, *1877–1882* (New York: Putnam, 1909), 635.

28. Figures cited in Chrastil, *Organizing for War*, 6.

29. Quoted in David Ralston, *The Army of the Republic: The Place of the Military in the Political Evolution of France, 1871–1914* (Cambridge: MIT Press, 1967), 121.

30. Figure cited in Ralston, *The Army of the Republic*, 134.

31. Figure cited in Ralston, *The Army of the Republic*, 122.

32. Quoted in Arne Røksund, *The Jeune École: The Strategy of the Weak* (Boston: Brill, 2007), ix–x. Pothuau similarly admitted, "All our efforts must be concentrated on land. Indeed, what good will a navy do us now?" Quoted in Theodore Ropp, *The Development of a Modern Navy: French Naval Policy 1871–1904* (Annapolis: Naval Institute Press, 1987), 31.

33. Quoted in Ropp, *Development of a Modern Navy*, 140.

34. See Peter Flora, *State, Economy, and Society in Western Europe 1815–1975: Volume 1: The Growth of Mass Democracies and Welfare States* (London: Macmillan, 1983), 378–82. This was all while government expenditures as a percentage of GDP held steady around 11 percent. See Brian R. Mitchell, *International Historical Statistics: Europe 1750–2000*, 5th ed. (New York: Palgrave Macmillan, 2003), 817–19; Richard Bonney, "The Apogee and Fall of the French Rentier Regime, 1801–1914," in *Paying for the Liberal State: The Rise of Public Finance in Nineteenth Century Europe*, ed. José Luis Cardoso and Pedro Lains (New York: Cambridge University Press, 2013), 81–102.

35. Quoted in Ralston, *Army of the Republic*, 132.

36. Figure cited in Allan Mitchell, "'A Situation of Inferiority': French Military Reorganization after the Defeat of 1870," *American Historical Review* 86, no. 1 (February 1981): 22–23. Comparative budget analysis likewise shows that in 1892 Germans were spending 730 million francs while the French were at 560 million, a gap that would widen in the coming years. See Allan Mitchell, "The Freycinet Reforms and the French Army, 1883–1893," *Journal of Strategic Studies* 4, no. 1 (1981): 52.

37. Quoted in Jack Snyder, *The Ideology of the Offensive: Military Decision Making and the Disasters of 1914* (Ithaca: Cornell University Press, 1984), 55. The chief of the General Staff concurred: "We ought to have forces equivalent to those of the Germans." Quoted in Mitchell, "Freycinet Reforms," 21.

38. See Richard Challener, *French Theory of Nation in Arms, 1866–1939* (New York: Russell & Russell, 1965), 60. On the 1889 conscription law, see Eugen Weber, *Peasants into Frenchmen: The Modernization of Rural France, 1870–1914* (Stanford: Stanford University Press, 1976), 293, 294, 298; George Peabody Gooch, *Franco-German Relations 1871–1914* (New York: Longmans, Green and Co., 1923), 27.

39. See *The Statesman's Yearbook* (London: Macmillan, 1870), 74; Challener, *French Theory of Nation in Arms*, 38, 44, 46–47; and *The Statesman's Yearbook* (London: Macmillan, 1885), 75. Joseph Monteilhet puts the number of total military manpower at 1914 at 4 million. See Joseph Monteilhet, *Les Institutions Militaires de la France, 1814–1932* (Paris: Alcan, 1932), 219. See also André Corvisier, Claude Carlier, Henry Dutailly, Jean-Charles Jauffret, Philippe Masson, Jules Maurin, and Francine Roussane, *Histoire Militaire de la France: Tome 3, de 1871 à 1940* (Paris: Presses Universitaires de France, 1992), 19.

40. See Meredith Perry Gilpatrick, "Military Strategy on the Western Front from 1871 to 1914" (PhD diss., University of Chicago, 1957), 334; Ralston, *Army of the Republic*, 105; Adolph Rosengarten Jr., "The Evolution of French Military Manpower Policy from 1872–1914," *Military Affairs* 45, no. 4 (December 1981): 181.

41. In 1883, top army officials gloomily acknowledged that French reserves were too low in quality and quantity. See Challener, *French Theory of Nation in Arms*, 34, 43–44; also Rosengarten, "Evolution of French Military Manpower Policy," 182; Raoul Girardet, *La Société Militaire dans la France Contemporaine, 1815–1939* (Paris: Librairie Plon, 1953), 169.

42. See Challener, *French Theory of Nation in Arms*, 51; Mitchell, "Freycinet Reforms," 23. French military officials were ambivalent about reserves and their dependence on and deployment of them vacillated. See Snyder, *The Ideology of the Offensive*, 68–69; Gilpatrick, "Military Strategy on the Western Front," 491–92; and Monteilhet, *Les Institutions Militaires de la France*, chap. 5.

43. See Ropp, *Development of a Modern Navy*, 191, 226.

44. See Ralston, *Army of the Republic*, 87.

45. See Mayeur and Rebérioux, *Third Republic from Origins to Great War*, 127; Langer, *European Alliances and Alignments*, 491.

46. The Commission for Reorganization of the Army, quoted in Ralston, *Army of the Republic*, 50.

47. For a similar periodization, see Mitchell, "Freycinet Reforms," 19; Jean Doise and Maurice Vaïsse, *Diplomatie et Outil Militaire, 1871–1991* (Paris: Imprimerie Nationale, 1987), 29. The arc of events followed a course of increasing inclusion of military conscription but shorter training periods: in 1868 military service was seven years by law, in 1869 it fell to five years, in 1889 it dropped to three, and in 1905 it hit two years before going back up to three in 1913.

NOTES TO PAGES 135-138

48. See Mayeur and Rebérioux, *Third Republic from its Origins to the Great War*, 15; Monteil-het, *Les Institutions Militaires de la France*, chap. 6. On the conservatism of these reforms, see Arpad Kovacs, "French Military Legislation in the Third Republic, 1871–1940," *Military Affairs* 13, no. 1 (Spring 1949): 3–4.

49. See Stefan Possony and Etienne Mantoux, "Du Picq and Foch: The French School," in Edward Mead Earle, *Makers of Modern Strategy: Military Thought from Machiavelli to Hitler* (New York: Atheneum, 1967), 218; Gilpatrick, "Military Strategy on the Western Front," 166.

50. See Ralston, *Army of the Republic*, 150.

51. Quoted in Ralston, *The Army of the Republic*, 183. Freycinet hoped the General Staff would become "analogous to the one which had permitted Marshal von Moltke to achieve such great results." Quoted in Mitchell, "Freycinet Reforms," 20.

52. The CSG was founded in 1872, but it did not meet from 1874 to 1881. See Allan Mitchell, "Thiers, MacMahon, and the Conseil supèrieur de la Guerre," *French Historical Studies* 6, no. 2 (Autumn 1969): 232–52; Gilpatrick, "Military Strategy on the Western Front," 316–17.

53. Douglas Porch, *The March to the Marne: The French Army, 1871–1914* (New York: Cambridge University Press, 1981), 52–53.

54. See Porch, *The March to the Marne*, 42.

55. See Mitchell, "'Situation of Inferiority,'" 56; Porch, *March to the Marne*, 43; and Ropp, *Development of a Modern Navy*, 177.

56. On the paltry steps through the mid-1880s, see Ropp, *Development of a Modern Navy*, 42, 57–59, 92, 106, 109, 118–19, 122, 125.

57. See Ropp, *The Development of a Modern Navy*, 48, 126, 177, 227, 293.

58. See Mitchell, *German Influence in France*, 186; A. J. P. Taylor, *The Struggle for Mastery in Europe 1848–1918* (New York: Oxford University Press, 1977), 225.

59. See Flora, *State, Economy, and Society*, 382.

60. See Flora, *State, Economy, and Society*, 382.

61. Porch, *March to the Marne*, 54.

62. Mitchell, "Freycinet Reforms," 26.

63. Quoted in Porch, *March to the Marne*, 43.

64. Figures cited in John M. Hobson, "The Military-Extraction Gap and the Wary Titan: The Fiscal Sociology of British Defence Policy, 1870–1913," *Journal of European Economic History* 22, no. 3 (1993): 464–65.

65. In 1881, the minister of marine Auguste Gougeard was thinking in terms of coastal defenses and nearby naval strong points, but in 1886 the minister of marine Aube thought in terms of multiplying bases and colonies. See Ropp, *Development of a Modern Navy*, 34, 157–58, 167, 178, 180, 198.

66. Ropp, *Development of a Modern Navy*, 263, 267, see also 198, 235.

67. Ropp, *The Development of a Modern Navy*, 318, 352, 357.

68. The Jeune École's popularity depended on the minister of marine and came in waves (1886–87, 1895, 1902) followed by counter-movements. But the rise of dreadnought technology finally demoted *Jeune École* notions in France. See Lawrence Sondhaus, "Strategy, Tactics, and the Politics of Penury: The Austro-Hungarian Navy and the *Jeune École*," *Journal of Military History* 56, no. 4 (October 1992): 589; Røksund, *Jeune École*, 106, 162, 226–29; Corvisier et al., *Histoire Militaire de la France*, 124–34.

69. Anthony Clayton, *France, Soldiers and Africa* (London: Brassey's, 1988), 212–13, 219, 246–48.

70. Calculations based on Frederick Martin, ed., *The Statesman's Yearbook* (London: MacMillan, 1880), 69; and J. Scott Keltie, ed., *The Statesman's Yearbook* (London, MacMillan, 1900), 530.

71. Clayton, *France, Soldiers and Africa*, 312–13, 315, 336.

72. Figure cited in Porch, *March to the Marne*, 139–40.

73. Clayton, *France, Soldiers and Africa*, 248.

74. See Taylor, *Struggle for Mastery*, 225–27; Norman Rich, *Great Power Diplomacy, 1814–1914* (New York: McGraw Hill, 1992), 220–21; Hajo Holborn, *A History of Modern Germany, 1840–1945* (Princeton: Princeton University Press, 1982), 237–38.

75. Quoted in Bury, *Gambetta and the Third Republic*, 328. Policymakers came to accept that France would not be able to retake the lost provinces at any foreseeable point, and in the early

1880s, there was a noticeable thaw in Franco-German relations. See Langer, *Franco-Russian Alliance*, 405; Robert Aldrich, *Greater France: A History of French Overseas Expansion* (New York: St. Martin's Press, 1996), 29.

76. See Mitchell, *German Influence in France*, 184–85.

77. Quoted in Carroll, *French Public Opinion*, 133.

78. See Mayeur and Rebérioux, *Third Republic from its Origins to the Great War*, 171.

79. See Robert Aldrich and John Connell, *France's Overseas Frontier: Departements et Territoires D'Outre Mer* (New York: Cambridge University Press, 1992), 39; Quinn, *French Overseas Empire*, 115.

80. Power, *Jules Ferry*, 92.

81. See Power, *Jules Ferry*, 128–29; Dennis W. Brogan, *France under the Republic: The Development of Modern France (1870–1939)* (New York: Harper, 1940), 243.

82. Quoted in James Cooke, *New French Imperialism, 1880–1910: The Third Republic and Colonial Expansion* (Hamden: Archon, 1973), 30.

83. Delcassé to Grodet (December 4, 1893), quoted in Robinson and Gallagher, "The Partition of Africa," in *The Decline, Revival, and Fall of the British Empire*, ed. Anil Seal (New York: Cambridge, 1982), 50. See also Porter, *Career of Théophile Delcassé*, 78. In 1887, France stopped its subsidies to Gabon and warned its administrator in the Congo that "we cannot stay indefinitely in a period of costly exploration." Freycinet to Brazza (April 12, 1886), quoted in Robinson and Gallagher, "The Partition of Africa," 35.

84. Delcassé to Dodds (February 22, 1893), quoted in Porter, *Career of Théophile Delcassé*, 81; also ibid., 40.

85. See Brunschwig, *French Colonialism*, 102.

86. Langer, *Franco-Russian Alliance*, 140.

87. See Andrew, *Théophile Delcassé and the Entente Cordiale*, 33–34.

88. See Langer, *Franco-Russian Alliance*, 331.

89. See George F. Kennan, *The Decline of Bismarck's European Order: Franco-Russian Relations, 1875–1890* (Princeton: Princeton University Press, 1981), 22–23; Langer, *Franco-Russian Alliance*, 13.

90. See Kennan, *Decline of Bismarck's European Order*, 286; also Andreas Dorpalen, "Tsar Alexander III and the Boulanger Crisis in France," *Journal of Modern History* 23, no. 2 (June 1951), 133.

91. See Langer, "Franco-Russian Alliance," 567.

92. See David N. Collins, "The Franco-Russian Alliance and Russian Railways, 1891–1914," *Historical Journal* 16, no. 4 (December 1973): 777; Langer, *Franco-Russian Alliance*, 119.

93. See Kennan, *Decline of Bismarck's European Order*, 68.

94. See Langer, *Diplomacy of Imperialism*, 130.

95. On French overtures to Italy around this time, see Langer, *Franco-Russian Alliance*, 116; Langer, *European Alliances and Alignments*, 471–72; Langer, *Diplomacy of Imperialism*, 10. On French overtures to Britain at this time, see Carroll, *French Public Opinion*, 153; Kennan, *Decline of Bismarck's European Order*, 108; Taylor, *Struggle for Mastery*, 352–354.

96. See Langer, "Franco-Russian Alliance," 570.

97. See Langer, "The Franco-Russian Alliance (1890–1894)," 569.

98. Georges Michon, *The Franco-Russian Alliance 1891–1917*, Norman Thomas, trans. (London: Allen and Unwin, 1929), 20.

99. See Langer, *Franco-Russian Alliance*, 218.

100. See John F. V. Keiger, *France and the World Since 1870* (London: Arnold, 2001), 52. The original defensive scheme was Sèrè's de Rivières notion of "corridors" channeling German advance. That faded after 1877. By 1880, the CSG moved to putting defensive forts wherever possible, small, cheap, and numerous, and soon transitioned to a few, immense fortifications, which were seldom completed. See Mitchell, "Situation of Inferiority," 52–53, 61–62.

101. See Gilpatrick, "Military Strategy on the Western Front," 507, 713.

102. These statistics can be found in David Stevenson, "War by Timetable? The Railway Race before 1914," *Past & Present*, no. 162 (February 1999): 168–69, 175–76; see also Allan Mitchell, "Private Enterprise or Public Service: The Eastern Railway Company and the French State in the Nineteenth Century," *Journal of Modern History* 69, no. 1 (March 1997): 18–41.

103. Anderson, *France 1870–1914*, 140.
104. Quoted in Quinn, *French Overseas Empire*, 114.
105. Figure cited in James McMillan, "Consolidating the Republic: Politics 1880–1914," in *Modern France 1880–2002*, ed. James McMillan (New York: Oxford University Press, 2003), 14.
106. Keiger, *France and the Origins of the First World War*, 7.
107. Quoted in Porch, *March to the Marne*, 47.
108. See Quinn, *French Overseas Empire*, 111, 159.
109. There is a lively debate about whether business interests had a significant influence on French colonial policy in these conditions. See Mark B. Hayne, *The French Foreign Office and the Origins of the First World War, 1898–1914* (New York: Oxford University Press, 1993), 42–43, see also 37, 50, 56; L. Abrams and D. J. Miller, "Who Were the French Colonialists? A Reassessment of the *Parti Colonial*, 1890–1914," *Historical Journal* 19, no. 3 (September 1976): 718; and Christopher M. Andrew and A. Sydney Kanya-Forstner, "French Business and the French Colonialists," *Historical Journal* 19, no. 4 (December 1976): 987.
110. See Brunschwig, *French Colonialism*, 106, see also 105.
111. Christopher M. Andrew, "The French Colonialist Movement During the Third Republic: The Unofficial Mind of Imperialism," *Transactions of the Royal Historical Society* 26 (1976): 145.
112. The *parti*'s victories tended to be when French foreign policy was indifferent or pushing in the same direction. When the two were at odds, the foreign ministry did as it pleased with little penalty. See Abrams and Miller, "Who Were the French Colonialists?" 718; Andrew, "French Colonialist Movement," 144.
113. See Quinn, *French Overseas Empire*, 116; Ropp, *Development of a Modern* Navy, 142; Andrew and Kanya-Forstner, *Climax of French Imperial Expansion*, 19.
114. Moreover, French cabinets from 1885 on were habitually indifferent to colonial affairs, and that reflected public opinion. See Andrew and Kanya-Forstner, *Climax of French Imperial Expansion*, 7, also 10–11; Langer, *European Alliances and Alignments*, 284.
115. This in part reflected Delcassé and Hanotaux's differing levels of enthusiasm. See Alf Andrew Heggoy, *The African Policies of Gabriel Hanotaux* (Athens: University of Georgia Press, 1972), 5–7.
116. Andrew, *Théophile Delcassé and the Entente Cordiale*, 45.
117. Eugen Weber, *The Nationalist Revival in France, 1905–1914* (Berkeley: University of California Press, 1959), 26. See also Carroll, *French Public Opinion*, 172.
118. Delcassé to wife (October 22, 1898), quoted in Andrew, *Théophile Delcassé and the Entente Cordiale*, 92. See also Porter, *Career of Théophile Delcassé*, 205–6, 212.
119. Quoted in Quinn, *French Overseas Empire*, 1.
120. Quoted in Cooke, *New French Imperialism*, 96.
121. Negotiations with Spain on Morocco fell through for domestic political reasons in Spain, but they would pay off with better terms for France in 1904. See Porter, *Career of Théophile Delcassé*, 154–56, 164, 184; Stuart, *French Foreign Policy*, 154; Hayne, *The French Foreign Office and the Origins of the First World War*, 98–99, 113–14.
122. On the heels of these agreements were consolidating deals in 1903 and 1904. See Stuart, *French Foreign Policy*, 82; Hayne, *The French Foreign Office and the Origins of the First World War*, 112.
123. See Stuart, *French Foreign Policy*, 8, 82; Keiger, *France and the Origins of the First World War*, 18; Porter, *Career of Théophile Delcassé*, 150–51.
124. Quoted in Phillip M. H. Bell, *France and Britain 1900–1940: Entente and Estrangement* (New York: Longman, 1996), 32.
125. Bell, *France and Britain 1900–1940*, 30.
126. The crisis was caused by the wrongful conviction of French officer Alfred Dreyfus for espionage in 1894. Dreyfus would be fully exonerated in 1906, but the scandal peaked in 1898–19 during his retrial.
127. Freycinet's 1888–90 revival of the CSG was probably in violation of an 1873 law, for example, but no one objected. Similarly, the naval program of 1890 was never approved of by parliament "except vaguely in its first year." Ralston, *Army of the Republic*, 95, 186–87, 198; Ropp, *Development of a Modern Navy*, 198.

128. In 1905, mandatory service fell from three to two years and what few exemptions remained were erased. A conscription law would pass in 1913 restoring the service term to three years. In general, these reforms had important social implications, though they did not significantly alter France's fighting ability. See Kovacs, "French Military Legislation," 5; Rosengarten, "Evolution of French Military Manpower Policy," 182; Doise and Vaïsse, *Diplomatie et Outil Militaire*, 165.

129. This led to spying and intrigue, the so-called *affaire des fiches*. See Kovacs, "French Military Legislation," 6.

130. See Challener, *French Theory of Nation in Arms*, 89; Ralston, *Army of the Republic*, 252.

131. See Kovacs, "French Military Legislation," 7.

132. See Porch, *March to the Marne*, 77, 80, 83–84, 89–90, 92–93, 102, 105, 107, 109, 193, 200, 204; Snyder, *The Ideology of the Offensive*, 73, 77; Joel Setzen, "Background to the French Failure of August 1914: Civilian and Military Dimensions," *Military Affairs* 42, no. 2 (April 1978): 87.

133. See Robert Doughty, "French Strategy in 1914: Joffre's Own," *Journal of Military History* 67, no. 2 (April 2003): 427–54; House, "The Decisive Attack," 165.

134. See Joseph Arnold, "French Tactical Doctrine, 1870–1914," *Military Affairs* 42, no. 2 (April 1978): 66; Setzen, "Background to the French Failure," 88; Michael Howard, "Men Against Fire: Expectations of War in 1914," *International Security* 9, no. 1 (Summer 1984): 51–52, 56.

135. See William C. Fuller, *Strategy and Power in Russia, 1600–1914* (New York: Free Press, 1992), 337–38; Kennan, *Decline of Bismarck's European Order*, 362; Brunschwig, *French Colonialism*, 177; Power, *Jules Ferry*, 192.

136. See David MacKenzie, *Imperial Dreams, Harsh Realities: Tsarist Russian Foreign Policy, 1815–1917* (New York: Harcourt Brace, 1994), 97; Fuller, *Strategy and Power*, 301–2.

8. Tsar Power

1. See Dominic Lieven, *Empire: The Russian Empire and Its Rivals* (New Haven: Yale University Press, 2001), 286–87; William Fuller, "The Imperial Army," in *The Cambridge History of Russia: Volume II, Imperial Russia, 1689–1917*, ed. Dominic Lieven (New York: Cambridge University Press, 2006), 553.

2. Russia was especially vulnerable to German coercion. In 1902 Germany accounted for 41 percent of Russian exports and 35 percent of Russian imports. See Dietrich Geyer, *Russian Imperialism: The Interaction of Domestic and Foreign Policy, 1860–1914* (New Haven: Yale University Press, 1987), 163.

3. See John White, *Transition to Global Rivalry: Alliance Diplomacy and the Quadruple Entente, 1895–1907* (New York: Cambridge University Press, 1995), 31; David Schimmelpenninck van der Oye, *Toward the Rising Sun: Russian Ideologies of Empire and the Path to War with Japan* (DeKalb: Northern Illinois University Press, 2001), 77.

4. See William Fuller, *Strategy and Power in Russia, 1600–1914* (New York: Free Press, 1992), 377–78; John Albert White, *The Diplomacy of the Russo-Japanese War* (Princeton: Princeton University Press, 1964), 47.

5. See White, *Transition to Global Rivalry*, 30; William Langer, *The Diplomacy of Imperialism, 1890–1902*, 2nd ed. (New York: Alfred Knopf, 1951), 748–49, 764–65. Before his death in 1900, the foreign minister Muraviev came around to Witte's view, too. See Andrew Malozemoff, *Russian Far Eastern Policy 1881–1904, with Special Emphasis on the Causes of the Russo-Japanese War* (Berkeley: University of California Press, 1958), 121–22. See also Theodore von Laue, *Sergei Witte and the Industrialization of Russia* (New York: Columbia University Press, 1963), 307.

6. See Bruce Menning and John Steinberg, "Lessons Learned: The Near-Term Military Legacy of 1904–5 in Imperial Russia," in *The Treaty of Portsmouth and Its Legacies*, ed. Steven Ericson and Allen Hockley (Hanover: Dartmouth College Press, 2008), 77; Raymond Esthus, *Double Eagle and Rising Sun: The Russians and Japanese at Portsmouth in 1905* (Durham, N.C.: Duke University Press, 1988), 35–36.

7. Quoted in Esthus, *Double Eagle and Rising Sun*, 65.

8. Quoted in Geyer, *Russian Imperialism*, 253. Security, Kokovtsov said, depended on economic stability first. He insisted that diplomacy be the primary solution to Russia's problems by "appropriate orientation of our foreign policy." Quoted in Geyer, *Russian Imperialism*, 256.

9. Quoted in Fuller, *Strategy and Power*, 412.

10. See Peter Gatrell, *Government, Industry and Rearmament in Russia, 1900–1914: The Last Argument of Tsarism* (New York: Cambridge University Press, 1994), 317.

11. Quoted in Gatrell, *Government, Industry and Rearmament*, 317.

12. Quoted in Jennifer Siegel, *Endgame: Britain, Russia and the Final Struggle for Central Asia* (New York: Tauris, 2002), 71.

13. Quoted in David Herrmann, *The Arming of Europe and the Making of the First World War* (Princeton: Princeton University Press, 1996), 153.

14. Quoted in Fuller, *Strategy and Power*, 415.

15. Quoted in Fuller, *Strategy and Power*, 395. For policymakers concurring, see White, *Transition to Global Rivalry*, 205; David MacLaren McDonald, *United Government and Foreign Policy in Russia 1900–1914* (Cambridge: Harvard University Press, 1992), 159, 190.

16. Quoted in Fuller, *Strategy and Power*, 421, see also 422. All the ministries consulted agreed. See Langer, *Diplomacy of Imperialism*, 667.

17. See Gatrell, *Government, Industry and Rearmament*, 66.

18. Statistics are given in constant pounds. See David Stevenson, *Armaments and the Coming of War: Europe, 1904–1914* (New York: Oxford University Press, 1996), 4. See also Gatrell, *Government, Industry and Rearmament*, 22.

19. It is important to note that military spending trends do not closely follow the performance of the overall economy, which grew at 1.5 percent from 1900 to 1906, and 6.3 percent from 1907 to 1913. See John McKay, *Pioneers for Profit: Foreign Entrepreneurship and Russian Industrialization* (Chicago: University of Chicago Press, 1970), 3–4; Peter Gatrell, *The Tsarist Economy 1850–1917* (New York: St. Martin's Press, 1986), 219; Alexander Polunov, *Russia in the Nineteenth Century: Autocracy, Reform, and Social Change, 1814–1914* (New York: M. E. Sharpe, 2005), 200.

20. See Fuller, *Strategy and Power*, 436; and Gatrell, *Government, Industry and Rearmament*, 126, 138.

21. See Stevenson, *Armaments and the Coming of War*, 145; also William Fuller, *Civil-Military Conflict in Imperial Russia, 1881–1914* (Princeton: Princeton University Press, 1985), 227; also W. Thomas Wilfong, "Rebuilding the Russian Army, 1905–14: The Question of a Comprehensive Plan for National Defense," (PhD diss., Indiana University, 1977), 130.

22. See *The Statesman's Yearbook* (London: Palgrave Macmillan, 1900), 957–58.

23. See *The Statesman's Yearbook* (London: Palgrave Macmillan, 1905), 1076–1077; Herrmann, *Arming of Europe*, 234.

24. See John Bushnell, "Peasants in Uniform: The Tsarist Army as a Peasant Society," *Journal of Social History* 13, no. 4 (Summer 1980): 565; Bruce Menning, *Bayonets Before Bullets: The Imperial Russian Army, 1861–1914* (Bloomington: Indiana University Press, 1992), 226; Norman Stone, *The Eastern Front 1914–1917* (New York: Penguin, 1998), 214.

25. Herrmann, *Arming of Europe*, 132.

26. See Stone, *Eastern Front*, 265.

27. See Wilfong, "Rebuilding the Russian Army," 69–71, 73, 76–77.

28. See Herrmann, *Arming of Europe*, 69, 134–35, 205; Stevenson, *Armaments and the Coming of War*, 78.

29. See Fuller, *Civil-Military Conflict*, 220–22; Gatrell, *Government, Industry and Rearmament*, 130–31; Wilfong, "Rebuilding the Russian Army," 86–87, 151–53, 159, 65.

30. Herrmann, *Arming of Europe*, 134; see also Menning, *Bayonets before Bullets*, 227–28; Stevenson, *Armaments and the Coming of War*, 153.

31. See Stevenson, *Armaments and the Coming of War*, 78.

32. Scholars argue the problem was less material insufficiency than poor decision making. See Gatrell, *Government, Industry and Rearmament*, 63–64; Stone, *Eastern Front*, 58, 131.

33. See Bushnell, "Peasants in Uniform," 567; Gatrell, *Government, Industry and Rearmament*, 22–23.

34. As much as one-third of the Russian army was used for internal security between 1906 and 1908, angering the war minister. See Jack Snyder, *The Ideology of the Offensive: Military Decision Making and the Disasters of 1914* (Ithaca: Cornell University Press, 1984), 166; Allan Wildman, *The End of the Russian Imperial Army: The Old Army and the Soldiers' Revolt* (Princeton: Princeton University Press, 1980), 64.

35. On the fortress controversy, see Bruce Menning, "Mukden to Tannenberg: Defeat to Defeat, 1905–1914," in *The Military History of Tsarist Russia*, ed. Frederick Kagan and Robin Higham (New York: Palgrave Macmillan, 2002), 215–17; Wilfong "Rebuilding the Russian Army," 79, 134–38; Gatrell, *Government, Industry and Rearmament*, 130–31.

36. See Wilfong, "Rebuilding the Russian Army," 138; Stevenson, *Armaments and the Coming of War*, 151, 155–56.

37. See Menning, *Bayonets before Bullets*, 219; Evgenii Podsoblyaev, "The Russian Naval General Staff and the Evolution of Naval Policy, 1905–1914," trans. Francis King and John Biggart, *Journal of Military History* 66, no. 1 (January 2002): 54.

38. See Donald Mitchell, *A History of Russian and Soviet Sea Power* (New York: MacMillan Publishing, 1974), 280, also 184, 272, 281.

39. See Stone, *Eastern Front*, 29; Mitchell, *History of Russian and Soviet Sea Power*, 274, 282; Niall Ferguson, *The Pity of War* (New York: Basic Books, 1999), 85.

40. On their contrasting styles, see William Fuller, *The Foe Within: Fantasies of Treason and the End of Imperial Russia* (Ithaca: Cornell University Press, 2006), 256; Roberta Thompson Manning, *The Crisis of the Old Order in Russia: Gentry and Government* (Princeton: Princeton University Press, 1982), 37.

41. Menning and Steinberg, "Lessons Learned," 78, see also 80.

42. Essentially, three posts were combined. See Wilfong, "Rebuilding the Russian Army," 92; and Christopher Clark, *The Sleepwalkers: How Europe Went to War in 1914* (New York: Harper Perennial, 2014), 215.

43. See Fuller, *Strategy and Power*, 410; Walter Pintner, "Russian Military Thought: The Western Model and the Shadow of Suvorov," in *Makers of Modern Strategy: From Machiavelli to the Nuclear Age*, ed. Peter Paret (Princeton: Princeton University Press, 1986), 364; Wilfong, "Rebuilding the Russian Army," 69, 71, 73, 76–77, 85.

44. See Herrmann, *Arming of Europe*, 93.

45. See Fuller, *Civil-Military Conflict*, 195.

46. See Fuller, *Civil-Military Conflict*, 220–22; Wilfong, "Rebuilding the Russian Army," 86–87. Reform sparked harsh reaction. See Steinberg, *All the Tsar's Men*, 155, 187; Peter von Wahlde, "A Pioneer in Russian Strategic Thought: G. A. Leer, 1829–1904," *Military Affairs* 35, no. 4 (December 1971): 151–52.

47. On Russian aviation, see Clark, *Sleepwalkers*, 479; Pertti Luntinen, *French Information on the Russian War Plans, 1880–1914* (Helsinki: Societas Historica Finlandiae, 1984), 165; Fuller, "Imperial Army," 550.

48. Quoted in David Schimmelpenninck van der Oye, "Reforming Military Intelligence," in *Reforming the Tsar's Army: Military Innovation in Imperial Russia from Peter the Great to the Revolution*, ed. David Schimmelpenninck van der Oye and Bruce Menning (New York: Cambridge University Press, 2004), 150.

49. See Raymond Garthoff, "The Military as a Social Force," in *The Transformation of Russian Society: Aspects of Social Change since 1861*, ed. Cyril Black (Cambridge: Harvard University Press, 1967), 326; see also Matitiahu Mayzel, "The Formation of the Russian General Staff, 1880–1917: A Social Study," *Cahiers du Monde Russe et Soviétique* 16, nos. 3–4 (July–December 1975): 302; Walter Pintner, "The Burden of Defense in Imperial Russia, 1725–1914," *Russian Review* 43, no. 3 (July 1984): 258–59.

50. See Menning, *Bayonets before Bullets*, 277, see also 236, 246, 248, 271, 275. See also Fuller, *Strategy and Power*, 457; Wildman, *End of the Russian Imperial Army*, 70.

51. See Fuller, *Strategy and Power*, 426–427, 450; Menning, *Bayonets before Bullets*, 220, 227–28; Wildman, *End of the Russian Imperial Army*, 69–70.

52. His personnel policies would have ruinous results for himself and the country. Among the marginalized were Witte, Rödiger, and Stolypin. Among the tsar's darlings were Bezobrazov,

Rasputin, and Sukhomlinov, the persistent support of whom estranged the military and society from the tsar and widened the cracks that led to revolution. See John David Walz, "State Defense and Russian Politics under the Last Tsar" (PhD diss., Syracuse University, 1967), 155.

53. See McDonald, *United Government*, 2–7; Stone, *Eastern Front*, 22.

54. Quoted in Fuller, *Civil-Military Conflict*, 233.

55. Fuller, *Strategy and Power*, 411.

56. Mark von Hagen, "Autocracy Defeats Military Reform on Eve of First World War," *Russian History* 38, no. 1 (January 2011): 152.

57. Fuller, *Civil-Military Conflict*, 262, see also 259; Menning and Steinberg, "Lessons Learned," 80–81; John Steinberg, *All the Tsar's Men: Russia's General Staff and the Fate of the Empire, 1898–1914* (Baltimore: Johns Hopkins University Press, 2010), 156–57, 189–90.

58. See Wilfong, "Rebuilding the Russian Army," 170–71; Herrmann, *Arming of Europe*, 231.

59. Quoted in Schimmelpenninck van der Oye, *Toward the Rising Sun*, 72, 75.

60. Figures from Gatrell, *Tsarist Economy*, 221.

61. Figures from Gatrell, *The Tsarist Economy*, 221.

62. See Paul Gregory, *Russian National Income, 1885–1913* (New York: Cambridge University Press, 1982), 77; Gatrell, *Tsarist Economy*, 41, 45, 192; cf. Raymond Goldsmith, "The Economic Growth of Tsarist Russia 1860–1913," *Economic Development and Cultural Change* 9, no. 3 (April 1961): 441–43.

63. See McKay, *Pioneers for Profit*, 3–4, 6; David Landes, *The Wealth and Poverty of Nations: Why Some are So Rich and Some So Poor* (New York: Norton, 1999), 268; also Arcadius Kahan, "Capital Formation during the Period of Early Industrialization in Russia, 1890–1913," in *The Cambridge Economic History of Europe: Volume III, Part 2: The Industrial Economies Capital, Labour, and Enterprise*, ed. Peter Mathias and Michael Moissey Postan (New York: Cambridge University Press, 1978), 290.

64. See Paul Gregory, *Russian National Income, 1885–1913* (New York: Cambridge University Press, 1982), 442.

65. See Landes, *Wealth and Poverty of Nations*, 268; Hugh Seton-Watson, *The Decline of Imperial Russia: 1855–1914* (New York: Praeger, 1961), 285.

66. See Gatrell, *Tsarist Economy*, 50.

67. Ferguson, *Pity of War*, 263. Others agree, see Stone *Eastern Front*, 35–36, 159, 208–11.

68. Alexander Gerschenkron, *Europe in the Russian Mirror: Four Lectures in Economic History* (New York: Cambridge University Press, 1970), 113; Alexander Gerschenkron, *Economic Backwardness in Historical Perspective: A Book of Essays* (Cambridge: Harvard University Press, 1962), 22.

69. See Gatrell, *Tsarist Economy*, xii, 232; McKay, *Pioneers for Profit*, 7, 10; Arcadius Kahan, "Government Policies and the Industrialization of Russia," *Journal of Economic History* 27, no. 4 (December 1967): 460, 477.

70. Olga Crisp, *Studies in the Russian Economy before 1914* (New York: Barnes and Noble Books, 1976), 26. See also McKay, *Pioneers for Profit*, 37; Gatrell, *Tsarist Economy*, 228.

71. Figures cited in John M. Hobson, "The Military-Extraction Gap and the Wary Titan: The Fiscal Sociology of British Defence Policy, 1870–1913," *Journal of European Economic History*, 22, no. 3 (1993): 464–65.

72. See Luntinen, *French Information*, 35–36, 61, 207, 214, 220–21; Fuller, *Strategy and Power*, 384, 396, 425; Rich, *Tsar's Colonels*, 220. On defense in the East, see Alex Marshall, *The Russian General Staff and Asia, 1800–1917* (New York: Routledge, 2006), 186; Fuller, "Imperial Army," 186–89.

73. See Pintner, "Russian Military Thought," 371; Herrmann, *Arming of Europe*, 133, 135.

74. Stevenson, *Armaments and the Coming of War*, 154, 318, 324–25.

75. See Wilfong, "Rebuilding the Russian Army," 141.

76. Walz, "State Defense," 125–26; also Luntinen, *French Information*, 226–28, 231–32; Wilfong, "Rebuilding the Russian Army," 138–39, 141.

77. Snyder, *Ideology of the Offensive*, 166. General Danilov devoted fifty-three divisions to Germany and nineteen to Austria.

78. See Podsoblyaev, "Russian Naval General Staff," 53, also 63, 67.

79. Quoted in David MacLaren McDonald, "A Lever without a Fulcrum: Domestic Factors and Russian Foreign Policy, 1905–1914," in Hugh Ragsdale, ed., *Imperial Russian Foreign Policy* (New York: Cambridge University Press, 1993), 283. See also Menning and Steinberg, "Lessons Learned," 90; Patricia Weitsman, *Dangerous Alliances: Proponents of Peace, Weapons of War* (Stanford: Stanford University Press, 2004), 129.

80. Quoted in McDonald, "Lever without a Fulcrum," 291.

81. See White, *Transition to Global Rivalry*, 285–88. A possible exception to that was when Russia sought land in Azerbaijan in 1909, which led to slightly greater involvement in Northern Persia. See Siegel, *Endgame*, 51. Izvolsky's misadventures over the Bosnian annexation crisis also caused Russia to rein in its ambitions in the Middle East. See Firuz Kazemzadeh, *Russia and Britain in Persia, 1864–1914: A Study in Imperialism* (New Haven: Yale University Press, 1968), 528.

82. See Kazemzadeh, *Russia and Britain in Persia*, 319–20, 384; Rogers Platt Churchill, *The Anglo-Russian Convention of 1907* (Cedar Rapids, Iowa: Torch Press, 1939), 142, also 229. Sazonov complained he got more help from the Central Powers than his entente partners. See Ira Klein, "The Anglo-Russian Convention and the Problem of Central Asia, 1907–1914," *Journal of British Studies* 11, no. 1 (November 1971): 139.

83. On Russian passivity in the region after 1905, see Kazemzadeh, *Russia and Britain in Persia*, 468, 474; White, *Transition to Global Rivalry*, 272.

84. Quoted in Churchill, *Anglo-Russian Convention*, 155.

85. See White, *Transition to Global Rivalry*, 8, 240, 275; Menning, *Bayonets before Bullets*, 90.

86. See Matthew Smith Anderson, *The Eastern Question, 1774–1923: A Study in International Relations* (New York: Macmillan Press, 1966), 264; Siegel, *Endgame*, 10; Geyer, *Russian Imperialism*, 252.

87. See Raymond Esthus, "Nicholas II and the Russo-Japanese War," *Russian Review* 40, no. 4 (October 1981), 410–11; Geyer, *Russian Imperialism*, 214; White, *Diplomacy of the Russo-Japanese War*, 171.

88. See Fuller, *Strategy and Power*, 423; White, *Transition to Global Rivalry*, 251.

89. See Esthus, *Double Eagle and Rising Sun*, 197.

90. Masato Matsui, "The Russo-Japanese Agreement of 1907: Its Causes and the Progress of Negotiations," *Modern Asian Studies* 6, no. 1 (January 1972), 33; also White, *Transition to Global Rivalry*, 226, 269; Lukin, "Russian Views of Korea, China, and the Regional Order in Northeast Asia," 29.

91. See Snyder, *Alliance Politics*, 275. The Russians informed the French that help could not be forthcoming for at least three years and the Polish frontier had been denuded of troops and supplies. See Stevenson, *Armaments and the Coming of War*, 71; also Siegel, *Endgame*, 105.

92. See Glenn Snyder, *Alliance Politics* (Ithaca: Cornell University Press, 1997), 278–79; Weitsman, *Dangerous Alliances*, 129–30; cp. Geyer, *Russian Imperialism*, 250–51.

93. Kazemzadeh, *Russia and Britain in Persia*, 595.

94. See Fuller, *Strategy and Power*, 417; Seton-Watson, *Decline of Imperial Russia*, 331; Siegel, *Endgame*, 66.

95. See Anderson, *Eastern Question*, 283–85; Fuller, *Strategy and Power*, 421.

96. Quoted in Herrmann, *Arming of Europe*, 118; see also 113, 115, 127.

97. Quoted in Herrmann, *Arming of Europe*, 127.

98. See Stevenson, *Armaments and the Coming of War*, chap. 3; Herrmann, *Arming of Europe*, 132; Snyder, *Alliance Politics*, 281.

99. See Seton-Watson, *Decline of Imperial Russia*, 332–33; Snyder, *Alliance Politics*, 283. Russia ingratiated itself with Germany so successfully that Britain was suspicious. See Kazemzadeh, *Russia and Britain in Persia*, 561.

100. See Snyder, *Alliance Politics*, 284–85.

101. See Snyder, *Alliance Politics*, 288–89.

102. Geyer, *Russian Imperialism*, 275; also Clark, *Sleepwalkers*, 353.

103. See Clark, *Sleepwalkers*, 124–31.

104. On French diplomatic cables, see Snyder, *Ideology of the Offensive*, 182; also Snyder, *Alliance Politics*, 290.

105. For repeated examples, see Snyder, *Alliance Politics*, 284–85, 288–90, 293–96; Snyder, *Ideology of the Offensive*, 169, 181–82, 185–87, 196; cf. Scott Sagan, "1914 Revisited: Allies, Offense, and Instability," *International Security* 11, no. 2 (Fall 1986): 153, 163.

106. On Russian rail lines, see Pintner, "The Burden of Defense in Imperial Russia, 1725–1914," 249–50, 258; Fuller, *Civil-Military Conflict*, 67, 439; Geyer, *Russian Imperialism*, 259.

107. The French had little faith in the Russian navy. See Arthur Marder, *The Anatomy of British Sea Power: A History of British Naval Policy in the Pre-Dreadnought Era, 1880–1905* (New York, Knopf, 1940), 399, 436; Fuller, *Strategy and Power*, 196; Walz, "State Defense" 232–33.

108. See Menning and Steinberg, "Lessons Learned," 92.

109. See Pintner, "Russian Military Thought," 371; Fuller, *Strategy and Power*, 388, 428–30, 442–44; also Stone, *Eastern Front*, 33.

110. See Snyder, *Alliance Politics*, 295. For the military agreement, see Charléty Sébastien, ed., *Documents Diplomatiques Français, 1871–1914*, 3ième Série, 1911–1914, VIII (Paris: Imprimerie Nationale, 1935), no. 79.

111. General Danilov thought French offensive tactics suicidal, but still ordered Russian offensives out of strategic desperation to relieve the French. See Snyder, *Ideology of the Offensive*, 157, 165, 170, 181–82, 184, 188, 196; Sagan "1914 Revisited," 163.

112. Whether this deal would have held is unclear; the terms were growing ragged around 1914. See Klein, "Anglo-Russian Convention," 144–45; Siegel, *Endgame*, xviii, 186, 189.

113. See Esthus, *Double Eagle and Rising Sun*, 203; Sarah C. Paine, *Imperial Rivals: China, Russia, and Their Disputed Frontiers* (New York: M. E. Sharpe, 1996), 275, 290, 292, 298; Ernest Batson Price, *The Russo-Japanese Treaties of 1907–1916 Concerning Manchuria and Mongolia* (Baltimore: The Johns Hopkins University Press, 1933), 44.

114. See Klein, "Anglo-Russian Convention," 139; Paine, *Imperial Rivals*, 275, 290, 292, 298.

115. See Fuller, *Strategy and Power*, 439.

116. See Stone, *Eastern Front*, 54; Stevenson, *Armaments and the Coming of War*, 323.

117. Debatably the most salient cleavage was between those fighting for an autocracy with rule of law (e.g. Witte, Stolypin, the Duma), and those clutching the core features of tsarist absolutism. The latter won. See Mark Steinberg, "Russia's *fin-de-siècle*, 1900–1914," in *The Cambridge History of Russia: Volume III, the Twentieth Century*, ed. Ronald Grigor Suny (New York: Cambridge University Press, 2006), 71; Andrew Verner, *The Crisis of Russian Autocracy: Nicholas II and the 1905 Revolution* (Princeton: Princeton University Press, 1990), 350; Dominic Lieven, *Russia's Rulers Under the Old Regime* (New Haven: Yale University Press, 1989), 153.

118. On the weakness of the business lobby, see Gatrell, *Government, Industry and Rearmament*, 163–66; McKay, *Pioneers for Profit*, 385; Dominic Lieven, *The Aristocracy in Europe, 1815–1914* (New York: Columbia University Press, 1992), 223.

119. See Polunov, *Russia in the Nineteenth Century*, 221–28.

120. There was a purge of reformers in late 1908 early 1909, yet the tsar reluctantly permitted many of the liberal reforms he had previously objected to. See Wilfong, "Rebuilding the Russian Army," 92–94; Mark von Hagen, "Autocracy Defeats Military Reform," 152, 156.

121. See Fuller, *Strategy and Power*, 437; Gatrell, *Government, Industry and Rearmament*, 133.

122. See Fuller "Imperial Army," 545; Luntinen, *French Information*, 197.

123. On Plan 20, see Wilfong, "Rebuilding the Russian Army," 144; Menning, *Bayonets before Bullets*, 239.

124. See Luntinen, *French Information*, 126, 129; Snyder, *Ideology of the Offensive*, 179; Walz, "State Defense," 152.

125. On the galling lack of oversight, see Snyder, *Ideology of the Offensive*, 186–87, 196.

126. Russia meddled in Korea, China, and Persia, and turned Mongolia into a buffer state. See Paine, *Imperial Rivals*, 275, 290, 292, 298; Anderson, *Eastern Question*, 289–90; Siegel, *Endgame*, xviii.

127. See Clark, *Sleepwalkers*, 220, 266–72.

128. See Seton-Watson, *Decline of Imperial Russia*, 323–24.

129. Moltke verged on despair in February 1914: "Russia's preparedness for war has made gigantic progress since the Russo-Japanese war, and it is now much greater than ever in the

past." Quoted in Stone, *Eastern Front*, 37. See also Lieven, *Aristocracy in Europe*, 226–27; Gatrell, *Government, Industry and Rearmament*, 320.

130. Marshall, *Russian General Staff and Asia*, 188.

131. See Fuller, *Strategy and Power*, 459.

132. See Stevenson, *Armaments and the Coming of War*, 157.

133. Witte likened the tsar to a child. See Esthus, "Nicholas II and the Russo-Japanese War," 396–97. Many senior voices warned the tsar Russia was in no shape to go to war before World War I, including Durnovo, Witte, Kokovtsev, Rosen, and Rasputin. See Fuller, *Foe Within*, 259.

134. See Fuller, *Strategy and Power*, 462.

135. There was high turnover under Nicholas, though not all of it his doing. See Paine, *Imperial Rivals*, 249; Dominic Lieven, *Nicholas II: Twilight of the Empire* (New York: St. Martin's Press, 1993), 70.

136. See Dominic Lieven, *Russia's Rulers Under the Old Regime* (New Haven: Yale University Press, 1989), 284–85.

137. See Walz, "State Defense," 155; Seton-Watson, *Decline of Imperial Russia*, 270–71; Stone, *Eastern Front*, 225–26, 261, 263.

138. Stevenson, *Armaments and the Coming of War*, 77. See also Gatrell, *Government, Industry and Rearmament*, 127–29, 321; Stone, *Eastern Front*, 51, 58–59; Lieven, *Aristocracy in Europe*, 223.

139. See Marc Ferro, *Nicholas II: Last of the Tsars*, trans. Brian Pierce (New York: Oxford University Press, 1993), 4, 70; Herrmann, *Arming of Europe*, 195.

140. See Lieven, *Russia's Rulers Under the Old Regime*, 286–87.

141. See Ian Nish, *Origins of the Russo-Japanese War* (New York: Longman, 1985), 253.

142. See McDonald, *United Government*, 106.

143. Historians generally consider Russian military progress in this period as enormous. See Wilfong, "Rebuilding the Russian Army," 170; Gatrell, *Government, Industry and Rearmament*, 328; Herrmann, *Arming of Europe*, 231; cf. Menning, *Bayonets before Bullets*, 237.

9. The Utopian Background

1. See Steven Ward, "Explaining Accommodation Failure" (paper presented at the annual meeting of the International Studies Association, New Orleans, 2015), 2.

2. Randall Schweller, *Unanswered Threats: Political Constraints on the Balance of Power* (Princeton: Princeton University Press, 2006), 76. See also Elizabeth Kier, *Imagining War: French and British Military Doctrine between the Wars* (Princeton: Princeton University Press, 1999), 55; Mark Brawley, "Neoclassical Realism and Strategic Calculations: Explaining Divergent British, French, and Soviet Strategies toward Germany between the World Wars (1919–1939)," in *Neoclassical Realism, the State, and Foreign Policy*, ed. Steven Lobell, Norrin Ripsman, and Jeffrey Taliaferro (New York: Cambridge University Press, 2009), 96.

3. While the causes of French defeat in 1940 remain controversial, the decadence hypothesis has come under heavy criticism. See Peter Jackson, "Recent Journeys Along the Road Back to France, 1940," *Historical Journal* 39, no. 2 (June 1996): 497–510; Robert Young, *France and the Origins of the Second World War* (New York: St. Martin's Press, 1996), 19–42.

4. By way of comparison, Germany had mobilized 154 and lost 30. Figures cited in Roger Price, *A Concise History of France* (New York: Cambridge University Press, 1993), 219.

5. See Frederick Schuman, *War and Diplomacy in the French Republic: An Inquiry into Political Motivations and the Control of Foreign Policy* (New York: AMS Press, 1970 [1931]), 255.

6. Quoted in Jacques Bariéty, "France and the Politics of Steel, from the Treaty of Versailles to the International Steel Entente, 1919–1926," in *French Foreign and Defence Policy, 1918–1940: The Decline and Fall of a Great Power*, ed. Robert Boyce (New York: Routledge, 1998), 45.

7. Quoted in Benjamin Martin, *France and the Après Guerre, 1918–1924: Illusions and Disillusionment* (Baton Rouge: Louisiana State University Press, 1999), 90–91.

8. Quoted in Judith Hughes, *To the Maginot Line: The Politics of French Military Preparation in the 1920s* (Cambridge: Harvard University Press, 1971), 185–86.

9. Quoted in Arnold Wolfers, *Britain and France between Two Wars: Conflicting Strategies of Peace since Versailles* (Hamden: Archon Books, 1963), 33. Our translation.

10. Quoted in Walter McDougall, *France's Rhineland Policy, 1914–1924: The Last Bid for a Balance of Power in Europe* (Princeton: Princeton University Press, 1978), 151. Our translation.

11. Quoted in Nicole Jordan, *The Popular Front and Central Europe: The Dilemmas of French Impotence, 1918–1940* (New York: Cambridge University Press, 1992), 5.

12. See Hughes, *To the Maginot Line*, 119.

13. See Peter Jackson, *Beyond the Balance of Power: France and the Politics of National Security in the Era of the First World War* (New York: Cambridge University Press, 2013), 416.

14. See Wolfers, *Britain and France*, 84–86; cf. Patrick Cohrs, *The Unfinished Peace after World War I: America, Britain and the Stabilisation of Europe, 1919–1932* (New York: Cambridge University Press, 2006), 580; Zara Steiner, *The Lights that Failed: European International History, 1919–1933* (New York: Oxford University Press, 2005), 678.

15. Quoted in McDougall, *France's Rhineland Policy*, 136.

16. See McDougall, *France's Rhineland Policy*, 178, 233.

17. See McDougall, *France's Rhineland Policy*, 239; Schuman, *War and Diplomacy*, 285; Jackson, *Beyond the Balance of Power*, 396–97. French industrialists opposed the occupation but went along with it anyway. See Schuman, *War and Diplomacy*, 279.

18. See Schuman, *War and Diplomacy*, 296.

19. See Jordan, *Popular Front and Central Europe*, 7; also Gerald Feldman, *The Great Disorder: Politics, Economics, and Society in the German Inflation, 1914–1924* (New York: Oxford University Press, 1997); Charles Maier, *Recasting Bourgeois Europe: Stabilization in France, Germany, and Italy in the Decade after World War I* (Princeton: Princeton University Press, 1975), 579, 594.

20. See Anthony Adamthwaite, *Grandeur and Misery: France's Bid for Power in Europe, 1914–1940* (New York: Arnold, 1995), 73.

21. Jon Jacobson, "Is There a New International History of the 1920s?" *The American Historical Review* 88, no. 3 (June 1983): 623; Stephen Schuker, *The End of French Predominance in Europe: The Financial Crisis of 1924 and the Adoption of the Dawes Plan* (Chapel Hill: University of North Carolina Press, 1976), 3, 392; Jackson, *Beyond the Balance of Power*, 479.

22. Richard Challener, "The French Foreign Office: The Era of Philippe Berthelot," in *The Diplomats, 1919–1939*, ed. Felix Gilbert and Gordon Craig (Princeton: Princeton University Press, 1953), 54.

23. See Hughes, *To the Maginot Line*, 145; Adamthwaite, *Grandeur and Misery*, 13. According to historian Peter Jackson, there was no equivalent reshuffling of military brass because of how marginalized they had become. See Jackson, *Beyond the Balance of Power*, 465, 470–71.

24. Quoted in Edward David Keeton, *Briand's Locarno Policy: French Economics, Politics, and Diplomacy, 1925–1929* (New York: Garland, 1987), 94–95.

25. Keeton, *Briand's Locarno Policy*, 94; cf. Jackson, *Beyond the Balance of Power*, 353, 360.

26. See Jon Jacobson and John Walker, "The Impulse for a Franco-German Entente: The Origins of the Thoiry Conference, 1926," *Journal of Contemporary History* 10, no. 1 (January 1975): 165–66; Carolyn Webber and Aaron Wildavsky, *A History of Taxation and Expenditure in the Western World* (New York: Simon and Schuster, 1986), 447; Brian R. Mitchell, *International Historical Statistics: Europe 1750–2000*, 5th ed. (New York: Palgrave Macmillan, 2003), 819, 838; Thelma Liesner, *One Hundred Years of Economic Statistics: United Kingdom, United States of America, Australia, Canada, France, Germany, Italy, Japan, Sweden* (New York: Facts on File, 1989), 194.

27. See Jari Eloranta, "The Demand for External Security by Domestic Choices: Military Spending as an Impure Public Good among Eleven European States, 1920–1938" (PhD diss., European University Institute, 2002), 85. For slightly different figures, see Webber and Wildavsky, *History of Taxation*, 451; Peter Flora, *State, Economy, and Society in Western Europe 1815–1975: Volume 1: The Growth of Mass Democracies and Welfare States* (London: Macmillan, 1983), 376.

28. Quoted in Hughes, *To the Maginot Line*, 111.

29. Spending began to flutter at higher levels after, however, bouncing from 5.1 billion francs in 1926 to 6.2 billion in 1928 to 10.1 billion in 1930 to 5.1 billion in 1932. See Liesner, *One Hundred Years*, 194.

30. See Eloranta, "Demand for External Security," 112, 116–17, 123. See also Price, *Concise History of France*, 235; *Statesman's Yearbook* (London: Macmillan, 1919–29), 836–68; Niall Ferguson, *The Cash Nexus: Money and Power in the Modern World, 1700–2000* (New York: Basic Books, 2002), 44.

31. See Flora, *State, Economy, and Society*, 380.

32. On the French Navy, see Barry Posen, *The Sources of Military Doctrine: France, Britain, and German between the World Wars* (Ithaca: Cornell University Press, 1984), 105; on the French Air Force, see Flora, *State, Economy, and Society*, 131–35.

33. Quoted in Valentine Thomson, *Briand: Man of Peace* (New York: Covici-Friede, 1930), 255. See also Hughes, *To the Maginot Line*, 134; Steiner, *Lights that Failed*, 374.

34. See Steiner, *Lights that Failed*, 378; Martin, *France and the Après Guerre*, 92; Peter Jackson, "French Security and a British 'Continental Commitment' after the First World War: Reassessment," *English Historical Review* 136, no. 519 (April 2011): 356–59.

35. Fragmentary data and different methods of accounting make precise numbers problematic, but the *Statesman's Yearbook* puts the total number of French Metropolitan and Colonial forces at 698,000 in 1922, and 735,000 in 1926. These figures would come down only after 1929. See *Statesman's Yearbook* (London: Macmillan, 1919–31), 853–908.

36. Irving Gibson, "Maginot and Liddell Hart: The Doctrine of Defense," in *Markers of Modern Strategy: Military Thought from Machiavelli to Hitler*, ed. Edward Mead Earle (New York: Atheneum, 1967), 366.

37. See Richard Challener, *The French Theory of the Nation in Arms, 1866–1939* (New York: Russell & Russell, 1965), 172–73.

38. Hughes, *To the Maginot Line*, 173–78.

39. See Posen. *Sources of Military Doctrine*, 108; Robert Doughty, *The Seeds of Disaster: The Development of French Army Doctrine, 1919–1939* (Hamden: Archon Books, 1985), 18–19.

40. Gibson, "Maginot and Liddell Hart," 370.

41. See Hughes, *To the Maginot Line*, 116, 159–63; Challener, *Nation in Arms*, 175–76.

42. Challener, *Nation in Arms*, 215.

43. See Doughty, *Seeds of Disaster*, 21. Because of poor pay and conditions, France's professional cadre of 100,000 soldiers seldom amounted to more than 70,000 at first. See Hughes, *To the Maginot Line*, 171.

44. See Challener, *Nation in Arms*, 191.

45. Hughes, *To the Maginot Line*, 172–73.

46. See John F. V. Keiger, *France and the World Since 1870* (London: Arnold, 2001), 58.

47. From 1927 to 1930, Generals Pétain and Debeney suppressed tactical initiative, but experiments with mobility would revive after 1930 when Gamelin and Weygand rose to power. See Brian Bond and Martin Alexander, "Liddell Hart and De Gaulle: The Doctrines of Limited Liability and Mobile Defense," in *Makers of Modern Strategy: from Machiavelli to the Nuclear Age*, ed. Peter Paret (Princeton: Princeton University Press, 1986), 603–4, 606–8.

48. Bond and Alexander, "Liddell Hart and De Gaulle," 604.

49. Quoted in Bond and Alexander, "Liddell Hart and De Gaulle," 608.

50. Posen, *Sources of Military Doctrine*, 139; see also Bond and Alexander, "Liddell Hart and De Gaulle," 600, 621.

51. See Posen, *Sources of Military Doctrine*, 106, 130, 135, 138; Bond and Alexander, "Liddell Hart and De Gaulle," 623.

52. See Ernest May, *Strange Victory: Hitler's Conquest of France* (New York: Hill and Wang, 2000), 10; Posen, *Sources of Military Doctrine*, 118; Adamthwaite, *Grandeur and Misery*, 159–60.

53. Of course, foreign lending remained essential to the French economy. See Philippe Bernard and Henri Dubief, *The Decline of the Third Republic, 1914–1938* (New York: Cambridge University Press, 1985), 129.

54. For total expenditures and expenditures by category, see Flora, *State, Economy, and Society*, 381.

55. See John F. V. Keiger, *Raymond Poincaré* (New York: Cambridge University Press, 1997), 334; also Bernard and Dubief, *Decline of the Third Republic*, 173, 179; Jacques Néré, *The Foreign Policy of France from 1914 to 1945* (Boston: Routledge and Kegan Paul, 1975), 100; Anthony

Adamthwaite, *The Lost Peace: International Relations in Europe, 1918–1939* (New York: St. Martin's, 1981), 113–15.

56. See Mitchell, *International Historical Statistics*, 838; Liesner, *One Hundred Years*, 194.

57. Of twenty-seven European countries and the United States, only Latvia, Bulgaria, and Poland grew appreciably faster. See Joan Roses and Nikolaus Wolf, "Aggregate Growth, 1913–1950," in *The Cambridge Economic History of Modern Europe, Volume 2: 1870 to the Present*, ed. Stephen Broadberry and Kevin H. O'Rourke (New York: Cambridge University Press, 2010), 188–90.

58. See David Landes, *The Unbound Prometheus: Technological Change and Industrial Development in Western Europe from 1750 to the Present*, 2nd ed. (New York: Cambridge University Press, 2003), 364; Schuker, *End of French Predominance*, 13; cf. Adamthwaite, *Grandeur and Misery*, 131.

59. Landes, *Unbound Prometheus*, 382, see also 386; Adamthwaite, *Grandeur and Misery*, 130.

60. Figures calculated using data in Jari Eloranta, "The Demand for External Security by Domestic Choices: Military Spending as an Impure Public Good Among Eleven European States, 1920–1938" (PhD diss., European University Institute, 2002), 112, 116–17, 123.

61. Posen, *Sources of Military Doctrine*, 105. A 1930 memorandum to the French prime minister explicitly discusses that geography forced France to consider its armaments as interdependent. See Adamthwaite, *Lost Peace*, 111–12.

62. See *Statesman's Yearbook* (1922–30), 837–910.

63. Quoted in Néré, *Foreign Policy of France*, 66, see also Adamthwaite, *Lost Peace*, 67.

64. See Patrick Manning, *Francophone Sub-Saharan Africa, 1880–1995* (New York: Cambridge University Press, 1998), 66; Christopher M. Andrew and A. Sydney Kanya-Forstner, *The Climax of French Imperial Expansion, 1914–1924* (Stanford: Stanford University Press, 1981).

65. Steiner, *Lights that Failed*, 44.

66. Andrew and Kanya-Forstner, *Climax of French Imperial Expansion*, 214. Many of France's claims were sanctioned by the British. See Bernard and Dubief, *Decline of the Third Republic*, 103.

67. Andrew and Kanya-Forstner, *Climax of French Imperial Expansion*, 223.

68. See Adamthwaite, *Grandeur and Misery*, 95; Néré, *Foreign Policy of France*, 60–61.

69. See Keiger, *France and the World Since 1870*, 56.

70. See Néré, *Foreign Policy of France*, 45.

71. Quoted in Andrew and Kanya-Forstner, *Climax of French Imperial Expansion*, 230.

72. Quoted in Andrew and Kanya-Forstner, *Climax of French Imperial Expansion*, 229.

73. Dennis W. Brogan, *France Under the Republic: The Development of Modern France (1870–1939)* (New York: Harper and Brothers, 1940), 577.

74. See Andrew and Kanya-Forstner, *Climax of French Imperial Expansion*, 235.

75. See Bernard and Dubief, *Decline of the Third Republic*, 104; Cohrs, *Unfinished Peace*, 61.

76. For the British and French postwar positions, see Robert Boyce, *The Great Interwar Crisis and the Collapse of Globalization* (New York: Palgrave Macmillan, 2009), 95; Néré, *Foreign Policy of France*, 50; Bruce Kent, *The Spoils of War: The Politics, Economics, and Diplomacy of Reparations, 1918–1932* (New York: Oxford University Press, 1989), 10.

77. See Andrew and Kanya-Forstner, *Climax of French Imperial Expansion*, 218.

78. McDougall, *France's Rhineland Policy*, 112.

79. Steiner, *Lights that Failed*, 200–201. See also Adamthwaite, *Grandeur and Misery*, 105.

80. Walter McDougall describes the fallout: "Germany had dealt the Allies an unforgivable 'slap in the face,' while Britain responded by demanding more concessions of France." McDougall, *France's Rhineland Policy*, 202.

81. See Cohrs, *Unfinished Peace*, 107; Steiner, *Lights that Failed*, 237; Schuker, *End of French Predominance*, 19.

82. Quoted in McDougall, *France's Rhineland Policy*, 368. See also Sally Marks, "Smoke and Mirrors: In Smoke-Filled Rooms and the Galerie des Glaces," in *The Treaty of Versailles: A Reassessment after 75 Years*, ed. Manfred Boemeke, Gerald Feldman, and Elisabeth Glaser (New York: Cambridge University Press, 1998), 366–67; Cohrs, *Unfinished Peace*, 9, 167; Schuker, *End of French Predominance*, 383, 386.

83. See Jackson, "French Security," 374; Steiner, *Lights that Failed*, 399, see also McDougall, *France's Rhineland Policy*, 246–47.

84. See Jordan, *Popular Front and Central Europe*, 50–51.

85. Here, too, policy was very continuous between leaders in large part because it was in line with French public opinion. See Jon Jacobson, *Locarno Diplomacy: Germany and the West, 1925–1929* (Princeton: Princeton University Press, 1972), 370–71, 374, 382; Keiger, *Raymond Poincaré*, 311, 321; Piotr Wandycz, *The Twilight of French Eastern Alliances, 1926–1936: French-Czechoslovak-Polish Relations from Locarno to the Remilitarization of the Rhineland* (Princeton: Princeton University Press, 1988), 60.

86. See Néré, *Foreign Policy of France*, 73; Jackson, *Beyond the Balance of Power*, 491, 493; Steiner, *Lights that Failed*, 401; Peter Jackson, "Deterrence, Coercion, and Enmeshment—French Grand Strategy and the German Problem after World War I," in *The Challenge of Grand Strategy: The Great Powers and the Broken Balance between the World Wars*, ed. Steven Lobell, Jeffrey Taliaferro, and Norrin Ripsman (New York: Cambridge University Press, 2013), 59; Wandycz, *Twilight of French Eastern Alliances*, 35.

87. Quoted in Jackson, "French Security," 377; and quoted in Jackson, "Deterrence, Coercion, and Enmeshment," 59.

88. See Cohrs, *Unfinished Peace*, 274–75, see also Néré, *Foreign Policy of France*, 98.

89. Wandycz, *Twilight of French Eastern Alliances*, 157.

90. Bariéty, "France and the Politics of Steel," 44; Keiger, *France and the World Since 1870*, 127.

91. See Eric Bussiére, "Economics and Franco-Belgian Relations in the Inter-War Period," in *French Foreign and Defence Policy, 1918–1940: The Decline and Fall of a Great Power*, ed. Robert Boyce (New York: Routledge, 1998), 79–80.

92. See Martin, *France and the Après Guerre*, 256; cf. Wandycz, *Twilight of French Eastern Alliances*, 23.

93. Bernard and Dubief, *Decline of the Third Republic*, 122.

94. Wandycz, *Twilight of French Eastern Alliances*, 148–49. See also Martin, *France and the Après Guerre*, 256.

95. See Bernard and Dubief, *Decline of the Third Republic*, 220; Néré, *Foreign Policy of France*, 106.

96. McDougall, *France's Rhineland Policy*, 60, see also 68, 86–87.

97. Jackson, "French Security," 352; see also Jordan, *Popular Front and Central Europe*, 49; Peter Jackson, "Politics, Culture, and the Security of France: A Reinterpretation of French Foreign and Security Policy after the First World War," *French Historical Studies* 34, no. 4 (Fall 2011): 577–81.

98. Quoted in John Keiger, "Raymond Poincaré and the Ruhr Crisis," in *French Foreign and Defence Policy, 1918–1940: The Decline and Fall of a Great Power*, ed. Robert Boyce (New York: Routledge, 1998), 50.

99. See Wolfers, *Britain and France*, 76; Millerand quoted in Jackson, *Beyond the Balance of Power*, 337–38; Seydoux quoted in McDougall, *France's Rhineland Policy*, 175.

100. Quoted in Jackson, "French Security," 351.

101. Boyce, *Great Interwar Crisis*, 58, see also 68. Coordinated defense planning between Britain and France would have to wait a very long time. See George Peden, "Chamberlain, the British Army, and the 'Continental Commitment,'" in *Shaping British Foreign and Defence Policy in the Twentieth Century: A Tough Task in Turbulent Times*, ed. Malcolm Murfett (New York: Palgrave Macmillan, 2014), 86–110; Young, *In Command of France*, 221–29.

102. Wolfers, *Britain and France*, 72, see also Jackson, "Deterrence, Coercion, and Enmeshment," 48–50; Jackson, *Beyond the Balance of Power*, 503; Néré, *Foreign Policy of France*, 122.

103. Quoted in Jackson, "French Security," 364.

104. Quoted in Boyce, *Great Interwar Crisis*, 113.

105. Quoted in Boyce, *Great Interwar Crisis*, 336, see also 57; cf. Wandycz, *Twilight of French Eastern Alliances*, 217; Anthony Adamthwaite, *France and the Coming of the Second World War 1936–1939* (New York: Routledge, 1977), 15.

106. See Bernard and Dubief, *Decline of the Third Republic*, 105; Jonathan Helmreich, "The Negotiation of the Franco-Belgian Military Accord of 1920," *French Historical Studies* 3, no. 3 (Spring 1964): 361–62, 365, 370; Sally Marks, "Ménages à Trois: The Negotiations for an

Anglo-French-Belgian Alliance in 1922," *International History Review* 4, no. 4 (November 1982): 543, 551–52.

107. On France and Rhenish autonomy, see Jackson, *Beyond the Balance of Power*, 342, 391; McDougall, *France's Rhineland Policy*, 48, 280; Steiner, *Lights that Failed*, 23.

108. Steiner, *Lights that Failed*, 225, see also McDougall, *France's Rhineland Policy*, 280; Cohrs, *Unfinished Peace*, 118–19.

109. Quoted in Steiner, *Lights that Failed*, 225.

110. See Steiner, *The Lights that Failed*, 295.

111. Jackson, *Beyond the Balance of Power*, 366.

112. See Steiner, *Lights that Failed*, 151.

113. Wandycz, *Twilight of French Eastern Alliances*, 5.

114. See Steiner, *Lights that Failed*, 287–88.

115. Wolfers, *Britain and France*, 115. Our translation.

116. See Posen, *Sources of Military Doctrine*, 124, 127, 130, 138–39.

117. Jackson, *Beyond the Balance of Power*, 370, see also 366; Posen, *Sources of Military Doctrine*, 106, 115, 130.

118. Keeton, *Briand's Locarno Policy*, 360; see also Wandycz, *Twilight of French Eastern Alliances*, 23, 55, 60.

119. The Czechoslovakian army was the most powerful of the group. By 1938 it was nearly half as large as Germany's and nearly as well equipped. See Posen, *Sources of Military Doctrine*, 110.

120. Wandycz, *Twilight of French Eastern Alliances*, 15–16, 153; see also Young, *France and the Origins of the Second World War*, 17–18; Jackson, *Beyond the Balance of Power*, 485.

121. The policy to channel the German flood east was only made explicit in the 1930s. See Jordan, *Popular Front and Central Europe*, 49, 91.

122. Hughes, *To the Maginot Line*, 192–93; see also Keeton, *Briand's Locarno Policy*, 98; Doughty, *Seeds of Disaster*, 33.

123. Jordan, *Popular Front and Central Europe*, 16–17; Keeton, *Briand's Locarno Policy*, 98. Contrary to the prevailing view, Generals Weygand and Gamelin remained interested in retaining offensive capability and mobility in the 1930s. See Bond and Alexander, "Liddell Hart and De Gaulle," 607, 609, 620–21; Posen, *Sources of Military Doctrine*, 117, 140.

124. Wandycz, *Twilight of French Eastern Alliances*, 108.

125. See Keiger, *France and the World Since 1870*, 56. See also Martin Alexander, "In Defence of the Maginot Line: Security Policy, Domestic Politics and the Economic Depression in France," in *French Foreign and Defence Policy, 1918–1940: The Decline and Fall of a Great Power*, ed. Robert Boyce (New York: Routledge, 1998).

126. See J. E. Kaufmann and H. W. Kaufmann, *The Maginot Line: None Shall Pass* (Westport: Praeger, 1997), 12–13; Young, *France and the Origins of the Second World War*, 20; Anthony Kemp, *The Maginot Line: Myth and Reality* (New York: Military Heritage Press), 46. Incidentally, though it was not much tested, the Maginot Line fared well in actual fighting. See Doughty, *Seeds of Disaster*, 69–70.

127. See Jacobson, *Locarno Diplomacy*, 361.

128. See Doughty, *Seeds of Disaster*, 21, 57; Posen, *Sources of Military Doctrine*, 112–15.

129. When Hitler came to power, there were discussions in France about forcibly removing him. Contrary to the predictions of preventive war theorists, however, these notions never became a viable policy option.

130. Adamthwaite, *Grandeur and Misery*, viii.

131. Challener, *Nation in Arms*, 138; see also Adamthwaite, *Grandeur and Misery*, 156–57, 166, 168. One could object that the national organization bill, which planned to ready France for total war and passed the Chamber in 1924 by 500 to 31 in a meager four days, was shelved, unreconciled with the Senate until 1938. Yet an outside expert found that "many of its objectives had been achieved through decrees and instructions" from the CSDN, and delayed ratification had not delayed the major parts of French mobilization plans. See Adamthwaite, *Grandeur and Misery*, 193–95, 234.

132. See Keiger, *Raymond Poincaré*, 272.

133. See Keiger, "Poincaré and the Ruhr Crisis," 53–55.

134. See Jackson, "French Security," 360; Andrew and Kanya-Forstner, *Climax of French Imperial Expansion*, 231; Bernard and Dubief, *Decline of the Third Republic*, 110.

135. See Schuman, *War and Diplomacy*, 272–73; Keiger, "Poincaré and the Ruhr Crisis," 49, 53; Robert Young, *Power and Pleasure: Louis Barthou and the Third French Republic* (Montreal: McGill-Queen's University Press, 1991), 168.

136. Quoted in Martin, *France and the Après Guerre*, 134.

137. McDougall, *France's Rhineland Policy*, 190.

138. See Keiger, "Poincaré and the Ruhr Crisis," 54–55; Jackson, "French Security," 362–63; Gordon Wright, *Raymond Poincaré and the French Presidency* (Stanford: Stanford University Press, 1942), 248.

139. See Wandycz, *Twilight of French Eastern Alliances*, 458.

140. See Eloranta, "Demand for External Security," 83.

141. Challener, "French Foreign Office," 52.

142. See Doughty, *Seeds of Disaster*, 112, 118.

143. See Cohrs, *Unfinished Peace*, 183–84, 520; Keiger, "Poincaré and the Ruhr Crisis," 49; Schuman, *War and Diplomacy*, 272–73; Jackson, "French Security," 368–69, 371, 376, 380; Néré, *Foreign Policy of France*, 70; McDougall, *France's Rhineland Policy*, 164; Young, *France and the Origins of the Second World War*, 12; and Challener, *Nation in Arms*, 140. For a historiographical overview, see Peter Jackson, *France and the Nazi Menace: Intelligence and Policy Making, 1933–1939* (New York: Oxford University Press, 2000), 1–2.

144. Challener, "French Foreign Office," 83.

145. See Phillip M. H. Bell, *France and Britain, 1900–1940: Entente and Estrangement* (New York: Longman, 1996), 182; Donald Cameron Watt, *Too Serious a Business: European Armed Forces and the Approach of the Second World War* (Berkeley: University of California Press, 1975), 37. This agreement was very popular in France; only one cabinet member opposed it. See Bernard and Dubief, *Decline of the Third Republic*, 286; and Wandycz, *Twilight of French Eastern Alliances*, 358.

146. See Wolfers, *Britain and France*, 81, 101.

147. See Néré, *Foreign Policy of France*, 152.

148. Néré, *Foreign Policy of France*, 153; also Posen, *Sources of Military Doctrine*, 126.

149. See Néré, *Foreign Policy of France*, 154.

150. Néré, *Foreign Policy of France*, 183–84.

151. A point made by Bond and Alexander, "Liddell Hart and De Gaulle," 598.

152. An argument made by Young, *In Command of France*, 2.

153. See Fuller, *Strategy and Power*, 459; Néré, *Foreign Policy of France*, 66; Adamthwaite, *Lost Peace*, 67.

154. See David G. Herrmann, *The Arming of Europe and the Making of the First World War* (Princeton: Princeton University Press, 1997), 81.

Conclusion

1. Allison's cases suggest a 75 percent probability. See Graham Allison, "The Thucydides Trap: Are the U.S. and China Headed for War?" *Atlantic* (September 24, 2015); also T. V. Paul, "The Accommodation of Rising Powers," in *Accommodating Rising Powers: Past, Present, Future*, ed. T. V. Paul (New York: Cambridge University Press, 2016), 7.

2. Walter Russell Mead, "The Return of Geopolitics: The Revenge of the Revisionist Powers," *Foreign Affairs* 93, no. 3 (May/June 2014): 77.

3. Robert Kaplan, "Eurasia's Coming Anarchy: The Risks of Chinese and Russian Weakness," *Foreign Affairs* 95, no. 2 (March/April 2016): 33.

4. Michael Cohen, "It's Coming from Inside the House," in *A Dangerous World? Threat Perception and U.S. National Security*, ed. Christopher Preble and John Mueller (Washington: Cato Institute, 2014), 167.

5. Thucydides, *The Landmark Thucydides: A Comprehensive Guide to the Peloponnesian War*, trans. Richard Crawley (New York: Free Press, 1996), 16 [I.23.6].

6. See Robert Gilpin, *War and Change in World Politics* (Princeton: Princeton University Press, 1981), 10–11; Immanuel Wallerstein, *World Systems Analysis* (Durham: Duke University Press, 2004), 58–59; Ronald Tammen et al., *Power Transitions: Strategies for the 21st Century* (New York: Chatham House, 2000), 49.

7. See John Vazquez, "Was the First World War a Preventive War? Concepts, Criteria, and Evidence," in *The Outbreak of the First World War: Structure, Politics, and Decision-Making*, ed. Jack Levy and John Vazquez (New York: Cambridge University Press, 2014), 199–223.

8. See Dale Copeland, *Economic Interdependence and War* (Princeton: Princeton University Press, 2015), chap. 3.

9. See Jack Snyder, *Myths of Empire: Domestic Politics and International Ambition* (Ithaca: Cornell University Press, 1991), chap. 3.

10. See Paul Kennedy, *The Rise and Fall of the Great Powers: Economic Change and Military Conflict from 1500 to 2000* (New York: Lexington Books, 1987), xxii; Aaron Friedberg, *The Weary Titan: Britain and the Experience of Relative Decline, 1895–1905* (Princeton: Princeton University Press, 1988), 286; Randall Schweller, *Unanswered Threats: Political Constraints on the Balance of Power* (Princeton: Princeton University Press, 2006), 46–47.

11. See E. Malcolm Carroll, *French Public Opinion and Foreign Affairs, 1870–1914* (New York: Century, 1931), 103.

12. The French war minister Louis Barthou, quoted in Judith Hughes, *To the Maginot Line: The Politics of French Military Preparation in the 1920s* (Cambridge: Harvard University Press, 1971), 111.

13. See William Fuller, *Strategy and Power in Russia, 1600–1914* (New York: Free Press, 1992), 377–78, 423.

14. John Mearsheimer, "The Gathering Storm: China's Challenge to U.S. Power in Asia," *Chinese Journal of International Relations* 3, no. 4 (2010): 382.

15. G. John Ikenberry, "The Rise of China and the Future of the West: Can the Liberal System Survive?" *Foreign Affairs* 87, no. 1 (January/February 2008): 24.

16. Robert Blackwill and Ashley Tellis, *Revising U.S. Grand Strategy Toward China* (New York: Council on Foreign Relations, 2015), 4.

17. Michael Swaine, "The Real Challenge in the Pacific," *Foreign Affairs online* (April 20, 2015).

18. Martin Jacques, *When China Rules the World: The End of the Western World and the Birth of the New Global Order*, 2nd ed. (New York: Penguin, 2012), 11, 16.

19. Arvind Subramanian, *Eclipse: Living in the Shadow of China's Economic Dominance* (Washington: Petersen Institute for International Economics, 2011), 4.

20. Michael Beckley, "China's Century? Why America's Edge Will Endure," *International Security* 36, no. 3 (Winter 2011/2012): 44, 78.

21. Quoted in David Shambaugh, *China Goes Global: The Partial Power* (New York: Oxford University Press, 2013), 311.

22. Barack Obama, "Commencement Address at the United States Military Academy at West Point," (May 28, 2014), https://obamawhitehouse.archives.gov/the-press-office/2014/05/28/remarks-president-united-states-military-academy-commencement-ceremony.

23. A decade ago, Angus Maddison, on whose data our analysis is based, put the transition point at 2018. See his, *Contours of the World Economy, 1–2030: Essays in Macro-Economic History* (New York: Oxford University Press, 2007), 340.

24. All figures in this section are from the World Bank "Databank" http://databank.worldbank.org, accessed March 30, 2017.

25. Robert Lieber, *Power and Willpower in the American Future: Why the U.S. Is Not Destined to Decline* (New York: Cambridge University Press, 2012), 41. See also Beckley, "China's Century?," 58–59.

26. Thomas Christensen, *The China Challenge: Shaping the Choices of a Rising Power* (New York: Norton, 2015), chaps. 1, 3; Jonathan Kirschner, *American Power after the Financial Crisis* (Ithaca: Cornell University Press, 2014), 17, 140–41, 149–51.

27. Obama, "Commencement Address."

28. Hillary Clinton, "America's Pacific Century," *Foreign Policy* (November 2011).

29. White House, "President Barack Obama's Inaugural Address" (January 21, 2009), https://obamawhitehouse.archives.gov/blog/2009/01/21/president-barack-obamas-inaugural-address.

30. White House, *National Security Strategy* (May 2010), p. ii, http://nssarchive.us/NSSR/2010.pdf.

31. Colin Dueck, *The Obama Doctrine: American Grand Strategy Today* (New York: Oxford University Press, 2015), 14.

32. Robert M. Gates, "A Balanced Strategy: Reprogramming the Pentagon for a New Age," *Foreign Affairs*, 88, no. 1 (January/February 2009): 28–40.

33. Figures cited in Paul K. MacDonald and Joseph M. Parent, "The Banality of Retrenchment," *Foreign Affairs* online (March 9, 2014), https://www.foreignaffairs.com/articles/united-states/2014-03-09/banality-retrenchment.

34. Figures cited in Office of the Undersecretary for Defense (Comptroller), "National Defense Budget Estimates for FY 2016 (Green Book)" (March 2015), Table 7–5.

35. Figures cited in "Green Book," Table 2–1.

36. Figure cited in Andrew Fickert and Lawrence Kapp, "Army Active Component/Reserve Component Mix: Considerations and Options for Congress," *Congressional Research Service* (December 5, 2014), 2.

37. General Accounting Office, "Special Operations Forces: Opportunities Exist to Improve Transparency of Funding and Assess Potential to Lessen Some Deployments," (July 15, 2015), 2, 16, 22. Figures combine supplemental and base spending.

38. Department of Defense, "Major Budget Decisions Briefing from the Pentagon" (26 January 2012). See also Robert M. Gates, *Duty: Memoirs of a Secretary at War* (New York: Vintage, 2015), 460, 590.

39. Figure cited in Leo Shane, "Pentagon: Another BRAC Round Would Save Money," *Military Times* (March 3, 2015), https://www.militarytimes.com/news/pentagon-congress/2015/03/03/pentagon-another-brac-will-save-money/.

40. Leo Shane, "The Pentagon's 'Force of the Future' Plan Just Got Trashed in Congress," *Military Times* (February 25, 2016), https://www.militarytimes.com/news/pentagon-congress/2016/02/25/the-pentagon-s-force-of-the-future-plan-just-got-trashed-in-congress/.

41. Before drawing down, of course, Obama raised troops as part of his Afghan "surge." Figures taken from Michael O'Hanlon and Ian Livingston, "Iraq Index" (Washington: Brookings Institution, November 2011), 13; Ian Livingston and Michael O'Hanlon, "Afghan Index" (Washington: Brookings Institution, November 2015), 4.

42. See Andrew Feickert, "Army Drawdown and Restructuring: Background and Issues for Congress," *Congressional Research Service* (February 28, 2014): 7–9.

43. See Janine Davidson and Lauren Dickey, "America's Pivot to Asia has Some Serious Military Muscle," *National Interest* (April 16, 2015), http://nationalinterest.org/blog/the-buzz/fact-americas-rebalance-asia-has-some-serious-military-12652.

44. North Atlantic Treaty Organization "Financial and Economic Data Relating to NATO Defence" (2012), 6.

45. Calculations based on Stockholm International Peace Research Institute "Military Expenditure Database," http://www.sipri.org/databases/milex, accessed March 30, 2017.

46. Quoted in Ryan Lizza, "The Consequentialist: How the Arab Spring Remade Obama's Foreign Policy," *New Yorker* (May 2, 2011), 55.

47. Quoted in Jeffrey Goldberg, "The Obama Doctrine: The President Explains His Hardest Decisions about America's Role in the World," *Atlantic* (April 2016): 76.

48. See Paul K. MacDonald and Joseph M. Parent, "The Retrenchment War: Why the War Against ISIS Will Be Fought on the Cheap," *Foreign Affairs* online (September 24, 2014), https://www.foreignaffairs.com/articles/united-states/2014-09-24/retrenchment-war.

49. See Lisa Ferdinando, "Carter Reiterates Call for Peaceful Resolution in South China Sea," *DoD News* (November 4, 2015).

50. For Trump's views on foreign policy, see "A Transcript of Donald Trump's Meeting with The Washington Post Editorial Board," *Washington Post* (March 21, 2016); "Transcript: Donald Trump Expounds on His Foreign Policy Views," *New York Times* (March 26, 2016);

"Transcript: Donald Trump's Foreign Policy Speech," *New York Times* (April 27, 2016); "Transcript of Donald Trump's Speech on National Security in Philadelphia," *Hill* (September 7, 2016).

51. See Max Fisher, "Uncertainty over Donald Trump's Foreign Policy Risks Global Instability," *New York Times* (November 9, 2016); Robert Gebelhoff, "Donald Trump's Foreign Policy Inexperience is a True Liability," *Washington Post* (November 11, 2016).

52. See "Transcript: Donald Trump on NATO, Turkey's Coup Attempt, and the World," *New York Times* (July 21, 2016).

53. Joe Gould, "White House 'Skinny Budget' Faces Congressional Headwinds," *Defense News* (March 15, 2017).

54. Stephen Brooks, G. John Ikenberry, and William Wohlforth, "Don't Come Home, America: The Case Against Retrenchment," *International Security* 37, no. 3 (Winter 2012/2013): 10. They have since clarified that their definition of retrenchment focuses largely on alliance commitments. See Stephen Brooks and William Wohlforth, *America Abroad: The United States Global Role in the 21st Century* (New York: Oxford University Press, 2016), 4–5.

55. Beckley, "China's Century?," 78.

56. Barry Posen, "Pull Back: The Case for a Less Activist Foreign Policy," *Foreign Affairs* 92, no. 1 (January/February 2013): 127.

57. John Mearsheimer, "Imperial by Design," *National Interest* 111 (January/February 2011): 34.

58. Brooks, Ikenberry and Wohlforth, "Don't Come Home, America," 7; Beckley "China's Century?," 78, respectively.

59. For a fuller articulation of our views, see Joseph M. Parent and Paul K. MacDonald, "The Wisdom of Retrenchment: America Must Cut Back to Move Forward," *Foreign Affairs* (November/December, 2011): 32–47.

60. Barry R. Posen, *Restraint: A New Foundation for U.S. Grand Strategy* (Ithaca: Cornell University Press, 201), 21–22, 75–76.

61. Quoted in James Mann, *The Obamians: The Struggle Inside the White House to Redefine American Power* (New York: Penguin, 2013), 60

Index

CPSIA information can be obtained
at www.ICGtesting.com
Printed in the USA
LVHW110056030221
678154LV00007B/676